ROBERT BIERSTEDT

Department of Sociology
New York University

ADVISORY EDITOR TO DODD, MEAD & COMPANY

PROFESSION OF MEDICINE

A Study of the Sociology of Applied Knowledge

"The end for which we live is a certain kind of activity, not a quality. Character gives us qualities, but it is in our actions—what we do—that we are happy or the reverse."

ARISTOTLE

PROFESSION OF MEDICINE

A Study of the Sociology of Applied Knowledge

ELIOT FREIDSON

New York University

DODD, MEAD & COMPANY

NEW YORK 1970

LIBRARY OF CONGRESS CATALOG CARD NUMBER: 72–108049

PRINTED IN THE UNITED STATES OF AMERICA

FOR
JANE,
OLIVER,
&
MATTHEW

EDITOR'S INTRODUCTION

THE first paragraph of Eliot Freidson's book invites our attention to the fact that the word "profession" has a dual meaning. It is, in the first place, a species of a generic concept, namely, "occupation," and, in the second, an avowal or promise. In the first sense we have a semantic problem, the problem of articulating, in the Aristotelian manner, the *species differentia* which distinguishes a profession from other activities and endeavors which belong to the *genus* occupation. This, of course, is a serious sociological problem, and many efforts have been directed to its solution. We are all inclined to think that there is a difference, let us say, between those who practice surgery and those who fill prescriptions at the corner pharmacy, those who argue a case at law and those who serve as notaries, those who lecture on the history of philosophy and those who teach the multiplication table. Is there a continuum here, or can genuine discontinuities be discerned? The answer belongs to logic and to language, and is of considerable interest to sociologists.

The second meaning of "profession," however, is of concern to everyone. It concerns everyone who has ever consulted a physician, engaged the services of a lawyer, solicited the advice of a minister, or sat in a college classroom. These people—and it is a group to which we all belong—can always ask whether the avowal or promise has been fulfilled. Does the profession do what it promises to do? Does it accomplish what it professes? These are the kinds of questions to which the author is especially sensitive as he writes on the profession of medicine. It may be a profession which, like other professions as well, contains endemic defects, defects that can be attributed not to its practitioners but to its organization and structure. One may, in conforming to the norms of his profession, perform at the same time a disservice to the public whose interests the profession supposedly supports and satisfies.

The self-regulatory process, for example, often used as one criterion of a profession, is intended to guarantee the competence of its members and to protect its clients from those, in the medical profession, who have less than complete respect for the Hippocratic Oath to which they have all subscribed. The self-regulatory process, however, may not be working in a satisfactory manner. Expected standards of performance may not be met. The sanctions applied by the profession to errant and negligent members may not suffice because of errant and negligent utilization. Furthermore, the process of professionalization itself may introduce a narrow and parochial view of the community the profession is designed to serve. The doctor may indulge in a misplaced—or possibly exaggerated—emphasis upon therapy, the lawyer upon property, the professor upon learning, the cleric upon sanctity. Thus, a certain "ethnocentrism" may arise, a tendency to view and to evaluate the community of clients in terms of a professional rather than a more universal criterion. A professional is a specialist by definition, but the more he specializes in the pursuit of his profession the more he may be induced to sacrifice the larger point of view and retreat, in turn, from the highest of ethical standards. In every profession, as Freidson wisely observes, there is an ineradicable moral element. And he would doubtless agree with George Bernard Shaw that "Every profession is a conspiracy against the laity."

The problem of promise and avowal is only one of a number of questions to which Eliot Freidson addresses himself in this book—a book that is remarkable both for its cogency and for its penetration. Another is the character of illness, the degree to which it is susceptible to social rather than physiological definition, the degree, in short, to which it is an artifact of a doctor-patient relationship rather than a fact of a patient's organic condition. There is a difficult and complex problem here, one that would elude those who are sociologically unsophisticated and those—to say the same thing—who are unaware of the Baconian idols of the tribe, cave, marketplace, and theater. The author of this book is neither unsophisticated nor unaware. He offers us a close and comprehensive discussion of this problem, a discussion that will almost certainly provoke the medical profession into disagreement and response.

The profession of sociology, in short, has something to say to the profession of medicine. In this book it is the doctor, so to speak, who is the patient or, more precisely, it is the entire organization of medical care that receives a diagnostic treatment by an eminent sociologist. If not all physicians and surgeons will agree with it, neither will all sociologists. But no one will doubt that we have in these pages a careful and diligent examination of a profession, a profession that enjoys a prestigious position not only in modern societies but in primitive societies as well. Those who are privileged to read this book will regard it not only as a contribution to the sociology of medicine, and not only as a contribution to the sociology of the professions in general, but as a contribution, in addition, to the sociology of knowledge.

Robert Bierstedt

PREFACE

NO book can fail to reflect the time in which it is written, and this book is no exception to the rule. In our day we seem to be turning away from an uncritical optimism about the role of specialized knowledge in ordering human affairs. We have not yet arrived at a satisfactory new position, however, and in the meantime we are treated to despairing violence and self-defeating anti-intellectualism on the part of laymen and their champions, self-interested elitism on the part of the intellectual classes, and downright authoritarianism on the part of even those political leaders with humanitarian intentions. Markedly absent from those reactions is an attempt to deal with the issue empirically and analytically. Knowledge and expertise, whether accepted or rejected, tend to be seen as things existing in and of themselves rather than as abstractions which are realized by the activities of men organized into occupational careers and groups.

In this book I try to show that the occupational organization of the work of one learned profession constitutes a dimension quite as distinct and fully as important as its knowledge, and that the social value of its work is as much a function of its organization as it is of the knowledge and skill it is said to possess. Sociological analysis of occupational organization can, I believe, aid greatly in the formulation of an intelligent policy toward the role of the professional expert in public affairs. But in order to be sound, such analysis must attend as closely to empirical detail as to conceptual clarity. Unfortunately, most of the copious literature on the problem is very general. Here I try to provide just such needed detail in assessing the social role of one of the major professions. That detail, however, should be viewed in the light of two important issues of freedom in our time.

One is raised by the fact that professions characteristically seek the freedom to manage their knowledge and work in their own way, protected from lay interference. Indeed, they celebrate the ideal of men who may be trusted to control their own affairs responsibly and in the public interest. In this book I shall comment on both the nature of professional freedom and the manner in which it is exercised. The second issue lies in the problem of the proper role of the knowledgeable man, or expert, in governing the affairs of laymen. Insofar as the influence of the expert is strong, and his jurisdiction far-ranging, the layman's freedom to govern his own affairs however he chooses is restricted. Part of the analysis in this book attempts to assess the justification for increasing the influence of the man of applied knowledge at the expense of the freedom of others.

In writing this book the opportunity to obtain critical reactions to early drafts has been very valuable to me. I have been fortunate to have had aid from a number of people. I am especially indebted to Judith Lorber for her detailed criticism of several drafts of the entire book, and to Howard S. Becker, Robert Bierstedt, and Paul J. Sanazaro for their many comments on most draft chapters. Others have commented on specific chapters closely related to their own interests: they are Peter L. Berger, Vern L. and Bonnie Bullough, Joel R. Davitz, Mark G. Field, Blanche Geer, Irwin Goffman, Herbert Klarman, Donald Mainland, David Mechanic, Derek L. Phillips, Richard Quinney, Thomas J. Scheff, George A. Silver, Erwin O. Smigel, Merwyn Susser, Kerr L. White, and Irving K. Zola. These friends and colleagues have been far more helpful to me than they know, and I thank them all.

ELIOT FREIDSON

CONTENTS

PROFESSION OF MEDICINE

A Study of the Sociology of Applied Knowledge

INTRODUCTION

THIS book presents an extended analysis of a profession. As its title implies, emphasis is on both sides of the meaning of the word —"profession" as a special kind of occupation, and "profession" as an avowal or promise. As I shall try to show in the chapters that follow, it is useful to think of a profession as an occupation which has assumed a dominant position in a division of labor, so that it gains control over the determination of the substance of its own work. Unlike most occupations, it is autonomous or self-directing. The occupation sustains this special status by its persuasive profession of the extraordinary trustworthiness of its members. The trustworthiness it professes naturally includes ethicality and also knowledgeable skill. In fact, the profession claims to be the most reliable authority on the nature of the reality it deals with. When its characteristic work lies in the attempt to deal with the problems people bring to it, the profession develops its own independent conception of those problems and tries to manage both clients and problems in its own way. In developing its own "professional" approach, the profession changes the definition and shape of problems as experienced and interpreted by the layman. The layman's problem is re-created as it is managed—a new social reality is created by the profession. It is the autonomous position of the profession in society which permits it to re-create the layman's world.

From these observations it is possible to identify two major problems for analysis presented to the sociologist by the profession. First, one must understand how the profession's self-direction or autonomy is developed, organized, and maintained. Second, one must understand the relation of the profession's knowledge and procedures to professional organization as such and to the lay world. The first is a problem of social organization; the second a problem of the sociology of knowledge.[1] These are the problems I shall attempt to deal with in my analysis of one of the major professions of modern society—medicine.

Medicine, however, is not merely one of the major professions of our time. Among the traditional professions established in the European universities of the Middle Ages, it alone has developed a systematic connection with science and technology. Unlike law and the ministry, which have no important connection with modern science and technology, medicine has developed into a very complex division of labor, organizing an increasingly large number of technical and service workers around its central task of diagnosing and managing the ills of mankind. Too, it has surpassed the others in prominence. Since the production of goods and other forms of real property are far less of a problem to postindustrial societies than is the welfare of their citizens, since welfare has come to be defined in wholly secular terms, and since the notion of illness has itself been expanded to include many more facets of human welfare than it did in earlier times, medicine has displaced the law and the ministry from their once dominant positions. Indeed, in one way or another, the profession of medicine, not that of law or the ministry or any other, has come to be the prototype upon which occupations seeking a privileged status today are modeling their aspirations. The better we understand medicine, then, the better we will be able to understand the problems that may be posed by the professionalization of the key service workers of the welfare state.

My intent in this book is to contribute to our understanding of professions by making a close analysis of the profession of medicine. Obviously, this is a treacherous undertaking, for as Rueschemeyer has pointed out,[2] there are such important differences between

[1] Peter L. Berger and Thomas Luckmann, *The Social Construction of Reality* (Garden City, New York: Doubleday and Co., 1966), and particularly Burkart Holzner, *Reality Construction in Society* (Cambridge: Schenkman Publishing Co., 1968).

[2] Dietrich Rueschemeyer, "Doctors and Lawyers: A Comment on the Theory of the Professions," *The Canadian Review of Sociology and Anthropology,* I (1965), 17–30.

merely the two professions of law and medicine that accurate generalization from one to the other, let alone from one to all others, is very difficult. But since no man can gain command over much of the relevant data on more than one of the established professions, the choice is between comparison of several professions by a few oversimple variables, and close examination of one in all its complexity with an eye toward the many. I have chosen to do the latter.

In order to illuminate all professions by the close examination of one, however, it is necessary to remain at a level of abstraction that prevents confusing the unique with the general. This means that one's guiding concepts may not stem from the peculiarities of the concrete profession one is studying. It means that one must in some sense stand apart from and outside of the specific profession one is studying. In the case of medicine or law or the ministry, one must use analytical concepts that allow comparisons of one with the others. Such concepts cannot come from any single profession, for each profession has its special preoccupation, its view of the world, and its "science." Thus, in order to study medicine in such a way as to clarify and extend our understanding of professions in general, one must not adopt medicine's own concepts of its mission, its skill, and its "science." Since professions are collective human enterprises as well as vehicles for special knowledge, belief, and skill, sociology can focus on their common organization as groups quite apart from their different concepts, providing the general concepts by which they may be made individually comparable. It is to this task that I hope to contribute. By detailed analysis of medicine I hope to demonstrate the usefulness of seeing the profession as a kind of occupational organization in which a certain state of mind thrives and which, by virtue of its authoritative position in society, comes to transform if not actually create the substance of its own work.

I shall begin the book with a discussion of how a profession differs from an ordinary occupation by contrasting the position of healing in society at different times in history and by arguing that, while the end or aim of healing has not changed, the position in society of the occupations devoted to healing has changed. I shall point out how medicine has attained its rather special status, how it has become dominant in an elaborate division of labor, and how, even in circumstances where it is not wholly free of state control, it is at the very least formally free to control the content if not the terms of its own work. I shall argue that this special type of occupation is characteristically autonomous and self-regulating.

Turning to more detailed analysis of American medical institutions, I shall discuss the varied settings in which medical work is performed, and I shall look at the manner in which, under the condition of professional autonomy, medical work is guided or controlled from within. This will lead to a characterization of the informal organization of the profession, which orders what is known about variation in work performance, and which shows how individuals in local communities are linked in with the profession's formal organization.

Finally, the last major section of the book will deal with the object of the work of medicine—illness. Consonant with my concern to develop concepts general enough to permit systematic comparison across individual professions, I shall not make extensive use of the medical notion of illness. Rather, I shall treat illness as a social concept which, like "crime" and "sin," refers to deviation from social and moral expectations which are embedded in an official order which the professions come to represent. I shall try to show how the professional frame of mind as well as the organization of professional work both influence the nature of its concepts, and I shall try to show how the layman also contributes to the process of constructing the social reality of illness.

Throughout the book my exposition will attempt to present a suggestive model for the analysis of professions in general and consulting professions in particular. Some exposition must therefore be addressed to the problem of definition and classification. More importantly, some must include comments on substantive areas which are necessary for a logically coherent analysis but about which little reliable or systematic information is available. For the sake of the completeness of the logic, I shall have to discuss such areas anyway, relying more on my own research experience and sense of plausibility than I would like. Those who may disagree with me about the facts in such obscure areas of professional behavior should bear in mind the logical demands of the analysis which require me to speculate, for here the analysis is most important. While I am hardly uninterested in the profession of medicine as such, which I have been studying for some years, my interest has been sustained by the degree to which the study of medicine can be a proving ground for the development of more adequate ways of analyzing occupations and professions than exist in sociology today. It is about medicine that I write, but I write of it as a species of occupation first and as medicine itself only second.

PART I.

THE FORMAL ORGANIZATION OF A PROFESSION

"The system exhibits two principal features, the spontaneous coming together of the practitioners in associations, and the regulative intervention of the State. ... It is the purpose of the professional associations to achieve, and of the state, where it intervenes, to grant, some degree of monopoly of function to the practitioners."

—A. M. Carr-Saunders *and* P. A. Wilson

1.

THE EMERGENCE OF MEDICINE AS A CONSULTING PROFESSION

In all societies people diagnose sickness and adopt various methods for managing it. In most societies some individuals are thought to be specially knowledgeable about sickness and its management and are sought out for help by the sick or their families. In many cases such healers are compensated for their help: some merely supplement their daily living by healing; others develop sufficient trade to gain their living primarily by the practice of healing and so develop a vocation, becoming members of a true occupation. But all healers are not called doctors or physicians, nor are they usually considered to be professionals in any other sense than that of making a living from their work (the opposite of amatèurs). Those occupations which are distinguished from others by being called professions are considerably more special.

The Problem of "Profession"

Beyond being full-time pursuits of some significance or social prominence, it is difficult to find very much agreement on a definition of the word "profession." This is so for a number of reasons. First, the word is evaluative as well as descriptive.[1] Virtually all self-conscious occupational groups apply it to themselves at one

[1] See the review of a number of definitions in Morris L. Cogan, "Toward a Definition of Profession," *Harvard Educational Review,* XXIII (1953), 33–50.

time or another either to flatter themselves or to try to persuade others of their importance. Occupations to which the word has been applied are thus so varied as to have nothing in common save a hunger for prestige. This state of affairs has led Becker, for one, to claim that it is hopeless to expect the word to refer to more than a social symbol which people attach to some occupations but not to others.[2] A second reason for the disagreement surrounding the meaning of the word lies in the strategies commonly underlying the process of definition. People frequently draw up definitions first by deciding that certain occupations "are" professions and then by attempting to determine the characteristics these occupations have in common. Since people do not agree on which occupations "are" professions—librarians? [3] social workers? [4] nurses? [5]—their definitions vary with the occupations they include (and exclude) or else are alike on such an abstract level as to be virtually inapplicable to the task of distinguishing real occupations. Finally, there is the matter of purpose or intent underlying definition. As I have already suggested, some definitions have an intent that is primarily invidious and only secondarily analytical. Where the intent is analytical, analytical interest may vary: some focus on cultural values or knowledge; others focusing on individual commitment and identification. The outcome of such varied interest is substantive variation in definitions.

For these reasons, it should be clear that it would be folly to be dogmatic about any definition of "profession" or to assume that its definition is so well known that it warrants no discussion. For myself, it seems necessary to state my essential assumptions. First, I assume that if anything "is" a profession, it is contemporary medicine. By examining it carefully, we can learn more about what the class "profession" includes than we can from examining less clear-cut occupational cases. Second, I assume that the analytical variables

[2] Howard S. Becker, "The Nature of a Profession," in National Society for the Study of Education, *Education for the Professions* (Chicago: National Society for the Study of Education, 1962), pp. 27–46.

[3] William J. Goode, "The Librarian: From Occupation to Profession?" *The Library Quarterly,* XXI (1961), 306–318.

[4] Abraham Flexner, "Is Social Work a Profession?" *School and Society,* I (1915), 901–911.

[5] See Chapter 3 of this book.

of social organization are more useful discriminants than those of norms, attitudes, or ethics and that, in fact, the former has a closer relationship to behavior than the latter. My definitions and analysis shall therefore emphasize more the social organization than the social psychology of the medical profession.

The Profession Today and Yesterday

Most writers on medicine seem to have in their minds some very general notion of medicine as being any activity related to diagnosing and treating illness. Such a usage is so inclusive as to cover everything from individual practices of self-diagnosis and self-treatment in simple societies ("folk medicine") to the most esoteric researches in biochemistry. Essentially, such usage refers to the knowledge of a particular occupation. Consonant with my purpose, I am concerned with medicine as an occupation whose members engage in diagnosing and treating the illnesses of those who consult them for such help. Men at work is my interest first, and only secondarily their knowledge. Medicine, then, in this sociological usage, is an organized consulting occupation which may serve as the discoverer, carrier, and practitioner of certain kinds of knowledge, but which is not a body of knowledge as such. Furthermore, it is an occupation first, and only on occasion a profession.

If we consider the profession of medicine today, it is clear that its major characteristic is preeminence. Such preeminence is not merely that of prestige but also that of expert authority. This is to say, medicine's knowledge about illness and its treatment is considered to be authoritative and definitive. While there are interesting exceptions like chiropractic and homeopathy, there are no representatives of occupations in direct competition with medicine who hold official policy-making positions related to health affairs. Medicine's position today is akin to that of state religions yesterday—it has an officially approved monopoly of the right to define health and illness and to treat illness. Furthermore, as its great prestige reflects, it is highly esteemed in the public mind. Its position is not a long-established one; in fact, it is less than a hundred years old. If medicine was a "profession" in the past, it was a profession of quite different characteristics than today's. During most of recorded time there was not a single occupation identifiable as "medicine," for there were many kinds of healer. After the rise of the university in Europe, medicine became primarily a "learned profession." Only recently has it become a true, consulting profession, and only recently has it attained the strength and stability which now characterize its preeminence.

The Case of Zande Medicine

The clearest way to see some of the essential elements involved in the development of a profession having the characteristics of present-day medicine is to look closely at an instance where practitioners who diagnosed and treated illness did not constitute a stable occupation, let alone a profession. Such a negative case is provided by E. E. Evans-Pritchard's classic study of the Azande of East Africa published in 1937.[6] He described the position of an insecure and unstable occupation lacking the prerequisites to become a profession. Let us look at that occupation.

The Zande witch doctor did two kinds of work. First, he held public seances at which he divined the cause of the misfortunes, including illnesses, that sufferers brought him. Public seances were rather festive events in which more than one witch doctor usually performed. The performers wore special hats and ornaments and used such special tools as whistles and medicines. Within a magic circle, which established their social distance from the lay spectators, they danced and sang to the accompaniment of lay drums and gongs until they worked themselves into a state of exhaustion. At this point, spectators who wished to determine or divine the source of some problems gave gifts ("fees") to the performers. A witch doctor took a long time to answer these questions, first asking the "patient" a number of questions, such as the names of his wives. When answering in public, he rarely named the individual who was the source of the witchcraft that caused the misfortune, but rather only hinted at the identity.

Second, the witch doctor had a "private practice," which Evans-Pritchard called "leechcraft," consisting of the administration of special drugs to a client and the removal, by sucking, of magical

[6] I rely wholly on E. E. Evans-Pritchard, *Witchcraft, Oracles and Magic Among the Azande* (Oxford: Clarendon Press, 1937), for the following exposition.

pellets supposedly embedded in the sufferer's body. Although the witch doctor possessed no monopoly over divination as such or over the use of drugs, he did possess a monopoly over the removal of magical pellets. This service had to be paid for because the medicine was believed not to become "hot" and therefore really operative unless payment was made. And like most patients the world over, the layman was reluctant to pay unless his suffering was believed serious and had not succumbed to prior self-treatment or treatment advised by elder, more experienced kinsmen.

In neither case was trade so large or important that the Zande witch doctor was a prestigious figure in his society. In some other societies, medicine men and witch doctors have had a considerably more important position.[7] The unimportant position of the Zande witch doctor is not the result of differences in knowledge and practice, however, because his practices were very much like those found in other African cultures. The poor position of the Zande witch doctor is explained by the generally held Zande theory of the cause of misfortune and the proper method of determining solution or cure. Essentially, the Zande conception of witchcraft was so mechanical and impersonal that schooled human knowledge and intervention were considered irrelevant to coping with it: no specially *trained occupation* could be of much importance in dealing with misfortune caused by witchcraft.

Among the Azande when Evans-Pritchard studied them, witchcraft was not believed to be an immaterial force but a malevolent material substance present in the bodies of witches. The substance was believed to be genetically transmitted, sons inheriting it from fathers and daughters from mothers, and it was believed to grow in potency as the body carrying it grew and matured. As a material substance, it was believed to be always present in the bodies of witches, though it could be inactive or cool. Furthermore, as befits a material substance, its influence could operate only locally, not over great distances: witches from the local community, not elsewhere, were blamed for the blighting of crops, the disappearance of game, death, disease, and other evils.

[7] See, for example, the survey in W. T. Corbett, *The Medicine-Man of the American Indian and His Cultural Background* (Springfield, Illinois: Charles C Thomas, 1935).

Witchcraft was blamed only when misfortune occurred even though sensible and reasonable precautions had been taken against their natural occurrence. The man who was not looking at what he was doing when he cut himself and then did not take care of the wound was likely to blame only himself, not witchcraft, when he fell ill. However, if a man suffered some misfortune that he could not explain by reference to his own or another's human failings, witchcraft would be imputed and the question of whose witchcraft was involved would be raised. The individual witch was not necessarily held personally responsible because it was believed that witchcraft could be "hot" without the carrier's knowledge or intent. Confronted by evidence that his witchcraft was to blame, the carrier could apologize, swear lack of intent, and beg his witchcraft substance to cool.

One critical problem of treatment, analogous to diagnosis, was divination, which was used to discover the individual who was the carrier of the causal substance of misfortune. One method of divination was the rubbing-board oracle, consisting of a board with a groove in it within which a plug was rubbed. Oracles were read in whether or not the plug stuck as it was rubbed. Second, there was the termite oracle: a stick or two was pushed into one of the runways of a termite hill, whether or not one was eaten by the termites constituting the oracle. Third was the poison oracle, in which a chicken was administered a poisonous fluid; the oracle constituting whether or not it died. All three oracles could be administered by any layman who had the proper equipment—these oracles were forms of self-diagnosis using mechanical or nonhuman aids. Only in the public ceremony was the service of a "professional," or witch doctor always required—a form of consultation and diagnosis using a "professional" occupational skill.

In Zande culture, assumptions about witchcraft favored the lay methods of diagnosis because in them the human element is least intrusive. Witchcraft was conceived of as a physical and natural force, independent of human wish. In divination one is likely to come closest to the truth when wishful human bias is least likely to influence the results. Therefore, those types of divination in which the human element intruded least were most valued. The Azande recognized that it was very easy to make the plug stick in the rubbing board, deliberately or unconsciously; and they recognized that it was quite easy for witch doctors to deceive. Thus neither the rubbing board nor the witch doctor was valued as a definitive or conclusive method of divination. The termite oracle was believed to be less dependent on the person administering it and was valued more. The poison oracle was even less likely to be biased and was most respected. It had, in fact, been assigned some legal value.

Clearly, the witch doctor was in an insecure position. He was granted occasional individual "art," but no special occupational "craft." Laymen believed that some witch doctors were reliable consultants, but their reliability was ascribed to their *hereditary* possession of the potent substance of witchcraft in their bodies, not to any special *occupational* skill or knowledge. Laymen persisted in believing that whatever paraphernalia the witch doctor had and whatever acts he performed were quite irrelevant to his performance save as entertainment—the value of his work did not stem from *learned* skills.

Conditions for a Profession of Witchcraft

The witch doctors attempted to cope with this situation in two ways. First, they tried to support their occupational value by maintaining that the efficacy of their work was a function of the knowledge they *gained* while apprenticed to a master. They claimed that before they did their work they ate special substances which allowed them to divine witchcraft; these special, secret substances allowed them to acquire the power of witchcraft without having inherited it: getting a proper technical education in magical drugs and other substances was all that was necessary to make a good witch doctor.

Second, they assumed special "professional" mannerisms to mark themselves off from laymen—peculiar ways of dress and speech and the use of a special professional name when they worked, and, in the case of removing magic pellets, deliberate fakery to impress the client. The latter was rationalized in an especially interesting way. When confronted by a disillusioned apprentice whom Evans-Pritchard helped to discover the fraud involved in removing magic pellets, a master claimed that the public had to be induced to continue in treatment by such fakery, because while it was impressed by pellets, it was not impressed by the medicines that really did the curing. The fakery was justified as a placebo—a harmless therapy deliberately given by the consultant to please the patient—which kept the patient in treatment so he could gain the benefits of the practitioner's *real* craft. None of these devices, however, was sufficient foundation for a strong occupation, let alone a profession. While it may not be possible to specify all of the necessary conditions for such a foundation, the case of the Zande witch doctor is suggestive of several of some importance.

To be secure, it might seem that the witch doctor must first gain nearly exclusive control over all the bona fide methods of divining witchcraft, including access to strategic elements of the necessary technology so that no layman can use them without his aid. It may not be necessary that he control all the technology, but merely some necessary part of the whole—plugs, but not rubbing boards, for example. Alternatively, it is not even necessary that he control the technology as such so long as he manages to control the conditions of its use or administration—when it can be used, for example. Not even control over administration is necessary so long as the occupation gains the exclusive competence to interpret the outcome. No matter which of these strategies is adopted, clearly one minimum condition of control is that *the occupation has gained command of the exclusive competence to determine the proper content and effective method of performing some task.*

Second, to be secure, the occupation must establish its success on knowledge and skill which can be obtained only by becoming a member of the occupational group. If preeminent knowledge and skill stems from an accident of heredity, whether inheriting witchcraft or a bone-setter's "touch," or from a supernatural "calling" or "gift," then it is always possible that people outside the occupation can claim equal or superior skill. *The occupational group, then, must be the prime source of the criteria that qualify a man to work in an acceptable fashion.*

But how can these two conditions come about? We must remember that whereas the Zande witch doctor claimed competence based upon training, he did not gain any important degree of control over the tasks of divination. Even if we postulate a situation in which the witch doctor is made the "official" diviner, we could easily imagine the results—that laymen would continue to use their own inexpensive methods anyway and avoid the witch doctor except when all else had failed. Like the physician, the witch doctor is a consultant who must be consulted before he can work. People cannot be forced to use him. Without some faith or respect for his capacities, they may choose to consult no one rather than to consult him. Mere formal or official control over the performance or interpretation of a task is therefore not sufficient for the survival of a consulting, personal-service occupation. What is also needed is *general public belief in the consulting occupation's competence, in the value of its professed knowledge and skill.* Without such belief, there will be little consultation.

Clearly, such belief can have a variety of grounds. One such ground is the congruence of an occupation's work with general beliefs about that work. In the case of the Azande, the substance of general belief was such as to preclude the possibility that an occupational group could divine effectively. But the Zande witch doctors were on the right track: if they had succeeded in persuading their clientele that their schooled use of herbs could temporarily create potent witchcraft in them, they would at least have established themselves as one highly reliable source for consultation. In this case, the grounds for public belief would be the compatibility of the witch doctors' practices with the general cultural system of belief. That ground, however, could not be established.

Since any method which is merely compatible with the general cultural beliefs of his society is likely to have the same results or effect, however, such compatibility is insufficient for acceptance. It gives no competitive advantage over any other method which is also compatible. One competitive advantage is the efficacy of the witch doctor's methods. If his divinations and his retrieval of magical pellets led to alleviation of illness and other misfortunes more often than other methods, faith in him might have grown markedly; presumably, the Zande witchdoctor failed on this ground as well.

Medicine and the Witch Doctor

Historically, I believe it can be said that medicine, too, failed to achieve the basic conditions for development into a consulting occupation of true professional status until recently, so that while it has not been an occupation whose knowledge and skill (or "science") was of the same content, it has in the past been an occupation whose position in society and whose organization have been quite similar to that of the Zande witch doctor. Indeed, medicine was not even a single recognized and organized occupational group until, at the very earliest, the Middle Ages. At that time, as Bullough has demonstrated,[8] medicine did obtain *official* recognition of its own university training as the prime source of the criteria qualifying a man to practice healing. The physician was granted the exclusive competence to determine the proper content and effective method of treating the sick. *Official* medicine, however, had only a loose, variable connection with the general cultural beliefs of the population and was more a learned than a practicing profession. The bulk of everyday consultation of healers by the general population was not controlled by the organized medical occupation. It became a true consulting profession in the late nineteenth century after having developed a sufficiently scientific foundation that its work seemed superior to that of irregular healers. It consolidated its position in the twentieth century as it improved the education of its average practitioner and as the education of the population rose to meet and receive its ministrations.

The Development of Medical Technology

I believe that the empirically demonstrable outcome of medical work is important to its development as a consulting profession. Analytically, this is a question of the cultural acceptability of the practices of a special occupational group to a receiving public. While we need not believe that men are thoroughly rational pragmatists, uninfluenced by wishful thinking or by a priori assumptions about the nature of the commonsensical world, or, in the case of medicine, immune to the influence of faith and hope on bodily processes, there is nonetheless a massive collection of evidence that rational and pragmatic material advantage plays an important even if not exclusive role in public acceptance.[9] Experientially, the work

[8] Vern L. Bullough, *The Development of Medicine as a Profession* (New York: Hafner Publishing Co., 1966).

[9] See the reviews of the literature in the following: Homer G. Barnett, *Innovation: The Basis of Cultural Change* (New York: McGraw-Hill Book Co., 1953); H. F. Lionberger, *Adoption of New Ideas and Practices* (Ames, Iowa: Iowa State University Press, 1960); E. Rogers, *Diffusion of Innovations* (New York: The Free Press of Glencoe, 1962).

of the doctor is first of all concretely directed to the solution of a practical problem, just like the work of the witch doctor. Until it had a scientific foundation, the doctor's work could offer its users little advantage over that of a host of other healers.

Unfortunately, most historians of medicine have been concerned solely with documenting discoveries of those isolated bits of information that we now consider to be scientifically true. Looking back from our present-day perspective of "modern science," the historian is inclined to pass through the centuries picking out the "valid" elements of medical knowledge and assembling a chronology of truths that add up to become present-day scientific medicine. In such histories, particularly when they are inflamed by undetached conceptions of the dignity and glory of medicine, it is difficult to perceive that in the past (as in the present), the individually discovered truths were often embedded in and undiscriminated from a mass of ineffectual or even harmful procedures, some of which were merely empirical usages and some of which were systematically derived from theories no less peculiar than those of the Azande. The net benefit to the patient of being served by a physician who made or used one valid discovery but who in his practice embedded that discovery in a mass of false medical conventions was no doubt small. Furthermore, there was no evidence that all healers of a time, even in a particular "school," used such truths in their actual practice. Since histories of medicine are usually histories of medical discovery and discoverers rather than histories of everyday medical work, they fail to communicate how inadequate and how radically different from today the everyday work of the practitioner was. This must never be forgotten.

Recognizing that a developed body of medical knowledge existed in earlier cultures than that of Greece and that Greek medicine was influenced by those earlier civilizations,[10] it is conventional to begin with the Greeks because of the distinctly natural rather than supernatural approach to disease on the part of some of its healers.[11] Most particularly, the Hippocratic physicians emphasized careful

[10] For those earlier times, see Henry E. Sigerist, *A History of Medicine*, Vols. I and II (New York: Oxford University Press, 1951).

[11] In this section I rely on a number of standard histories of medical knowledge, particularly that of E. W. Ackerknecht, *Short History of Medicine* (New York: The Ronald Press Co., 1955).

observation and description of disease and its course, with a view to accurate prognosis. Treatment was fairly conservative, relying mostly on diet and little on drugs or surgery. The assumption was that nature was in itself healing and that the physician should merely assist rather than tamper with nature. The Hippocratic conception of health rested on the idea of a harmonious blend of the humors (blood, phlegm, black bile, and yellow bile, originating in the heart, brain, liver, and spleen, respectively), disease being a defective mixture of the four. Also involved in their conception of health and illness were the state of the pneuma, social and climatic influences, and the patient's constitution.

But the Hippocratics were not the only physicians in Greek and Hellenistic times. Many schools participated in describing and classifying diseases, organs, and biological processes. During the seven hundred years of medicine beginning with the Hippocratics and ending with Galen, there were such specifically named schools as the Dogmatists, the Empiricists, and Aesclepiades, the Methodists, and the Pneumatists, many of whom did not subscribe to the humoral conception of disease. A number of observations were recorded during this period that now are considered correct—including careful anatomical descriptions of such things as the eye, the trachea, the duodenum, and the genitalia, and clinical descriptions of diabetes, leprosy, and tetanus.

The Greek period is generally said to culminate in the synthesis of Galen of Pergamon (A.D. 130–201), whose influence was felt in medicine for considerably more than a thousand years after. Galen's work was dominated by an Aristotelian teleology—every organ having a special purpose and therefore serving a special function—and, like Aristotle and some of the physicians preceding him, subscribed to a humoral conception of illness. Galen's own anatomical and physiological work was extraordinary, but his most important influence on later times stemmed from his systematic speculation. So authoritative had his work become by the late Middle Ages that doctors supervising dissections of human cadavers would see no more than what Galen described, even though Galen had apparently never dissected a human and postulated such patently peculiar features of anatomy as the horned uterus and the five-lobed liver.

With the Renaissance, however, the pace of new discoveries

quickened and the weight of old theories lightened. The new voyages of discovery brought contact with new botanicals and therefore new drugs for treatment. In the sixteenth century, Vesalius' work in anatomy corrected many Galenic errors and added new precision of its own. Paracelsus' introduction of specific remedies from such minerals as lead, arsenic, and sulfur, along with his chemical theory of disease, shook the old humoral theory. And Ambroise Paré made important contributions to surgery.

During the seventeenth and eighteenth centuries there was a continually accelerating increment of careful observation, and there were specialized discoveries of technique as well. One of the most important advances is often thought to be Harvey's proof of the circulation of the blood by the use of experimental as well as morphological arguments. However, notwithstanding his great accomplishment and those of others, the most important developments of the time for medicine do not seem to have been medical as such, but rather scientific and technological, such as the invention of the microscope and the work in physics of Newton and Galileo. The development of physics and chemistry made possible for the first time a systematically scientific foundation for medicine.

Without a systematic foundation medical practice could not fail to be more than a variety of traditional conceptions supplemented by quite variable individual clinical judgment. Of course, the humoral theory was a systematic foundation of sorts, and there is, of course, always some inconsistency and ignorance in such a task of applied knowledge as is medicine, but until a truly scientific foundation could be established no adequate way of sorting and analyzing the total range of clinical experience could exist. Operating on a purely pragmatic or clinical level, what is to us bizarre could coexist peacefully beside what is to us accurate and true.[12] Without a systematic notion of the causes of the pathologies that have been carefully described and classified in the past, or the causes for the success of a new drug or procedure, progress could not be other than halting and confused, and the work of individuals could not

[12] For a compendium of the worthless or dangerous practices of such luminaries as the Hippocratic writers, Galen, Paracelsus, Paré, and Osler, see Arthur K. Shapiro, "A Contribution to a History of the Placebo Effect," *Behavioral Science,* V (1960), 109–135.

be other than highly variable according to individual opinion and experience.

No single event stands by itself, and none is by itself of signal importance. However, the discovery in 1860 that a bacillus causes anthrax was of critical importance in the history of medicine, for at one stroke the conflict among various theories was resolved. In the hands of Pasteur, Koch, and others, the idea of specific causative agents of disease was established, and disease after disease fell to the investigations that followed. As one historian put it, "for the first time in history, *causes* of numerous diseases became known. The way was opened for a replacement of symptomatic or empirical treatment by causal treatment and prevention."[13] Furthermore, the technological development of anesthesia and asepsis allowed successes in surgery that were never possible before, even though surgeons had earlier developed fairly refined skills and knowledge. Those accomplishments created a *qualitative* break with the past, making possible for the first time the predictable and reliable control of a wide spectrum of human ills by virtually any well-trained practitioner of the occupation, not solely by a great clinician. For the first time, as L. J. Henderson put it, an average patient treated by an average practitioner could expect a better than fifty-fifty chance of improvement. Distinction between physician and so-called quack needed no longer to rest on the academic certification of the superiority of one superstition over another.

The clergy could attain some limited occupational stability by capturing the state's subscription to the dogma of which it was custodian. The lawyer needed merely to gain control over access to the courts, where lay the direction of political power. But the physician depended for his strength upon individual, personal decisions to seek him out, and so needed to attract to him the public at large. The quality of his work did not equip him to do so until the late nineteenth century.

The Development of Occupational Organization

Parallel to the development of a technically or scientifically adequate foundation of medical work was the development of a socio-

[13] Ackerknecht, *op. cit.,* p. 171.

logical foundation to create an occupation so well established in its society as to become a true consulting profession—in command of the criteria that qualify men to work at healing, of exclusive competence to determine the proper content and effective method of performing medical work, and freely consulted by those thought to need its help.

Before the Middle Ages there was probably no clear identity attached to physicians except in the most general way, for no practitioner with a special title of "doctor" existed, and in some times and places there was no single occupational name for healers.[14] Throughout the centuries, healers varied markedly both in the schools and practicing groups to which they subscribed and in their training and skill. In the ears of virtually every patient group there was a confusing din of claims, some sounding learned and some sounding comfortably homely and simple. Those healers who considered themselves especially learned and rational—that is, many of those who could read and write, leave records, and thus become candidates for the privilege of being claimed as lineal ancestors by us—were surrounded by a motley collection of other practitioners, some with no pretense at having more than a knack at setting bones or a store of special knowledge of simple herbal remedies transmitted by family lore and others with a great deal of pretense at science and theory.

If one is to be fully aware of the meaning of the physician's past (if we can even speak of "the" physician at all realistically), one must keep in mind the fact that at no time in history did he have anything like a complete monopoly over healing services, informal or formal. It is still virtually impossible to prevent a patient from treating himself or from seeking help from friends or relatives. And for whatever the reason, a complete formal monopoly has never been granted medicine by the state. In modern times legal exceptions to the monopoly are few but exist nonetheless, as in the case of the chiropractor in the United States, for example. In past times, exceptions to monopoly were the rule. Why was this so, and what were the implications of this for occupational organizations? Let us review briefly the social circumstances of work of those

[14] See, for example, Vern L. Bullough, "The Term 'Doctor,'" *Journal of the History of Medicine and Allied Sciences,* XVIII (1963), 284–287.

healers whom our historians have chosen as the "legitimate" rather than quack physicians of the past, again beginning with the Greeks, but bearing in mind that our knowledge of the past is almost completely dependent on the special prejudices of the political and literary elite who handed down their documents to us.[15]

In the case of Greek healers, we find unstable, defensive occupations, hopefully drawn together into a series of clusters of apprentices and former apprentices around the masters who taught them, each cluster preserving from each other cluster the secrets it learned from its master and each rather aggressively competing with the other for trade. Indeed, some of the intellectual and technical characteristics of each school or cluster seem to have been brought into being by the practical problem of succeeding in a competitive situation as well as by the problem of gaining a clientele under conditions of itinerant practice. The Hippocratic healer's interest in prognosis (that is, forecasting the course of an illness), for example, has been discussed by Sigerist as a device cultivated by workers without local reputations but needing some method of impressing a critical patient, of establishing a reputation, and of attracting a clientele quickly in a town where one does not stay long. The Hippocratics themselves (or at least some writers of the Hippocratic corpus) deplored the use of devices used by their competitors to attract a clientele—the prescription of exotic remedies, for example, and the cultivation of strange ways of talking and dressing.[16]

Before the Middle Ages, the healers about whom we have been informed most by history are those who treated or worked for the

[15] Among the more useful works bearing on the history of medical practice are Lester S. King, *The Medical World of the Eighteenth Century* (Chicago: University of Chicago Press, 1958); George Rosen, *A History of Public Health* (New York: MD publications, 1958); Richard H. Shryock, *The Development of Modern Medicine, An Interpretation of the Social and Scientific Factors Involved* (New York: Alfred A. Knopf, 1947); Henry E. Sigerist, *On the Sociology of Medicine,* ed. M. I. Roemer (New York: MD Publications, 1960); Ernest S. Turner, *Call the Doctor* (New York: St. Martin's Press, 1959); Bullough, *The Development of Medicine, op. cit.*

[16] See Henry L. Sigerist, "On Hippocrates," *Bulletin of the History of Medicine,* II (1934), 190–214; Louis Cohn-Haft, *The Public Physician of Ancient Greece* (Northampton, Massachusetts: Smith College, 1956); *Hippocrates,* tr. and ed. W. H. S. Jones, Vols. I and II, "Loeb Classical Library" (London: William Heinemann, 1923 and 1943).

elite. We are more in the dark about those who cared for the craftsman, the peasant, and the slave. In some cases, the elite contracted with reputable healers to care for certain segments of the general population: such was the case with physicians of Greece; Galen was apparently hired to care for gladiators in Rome; and physicians were hired to treat ghetto populations in the Middle Ages.[17] We may be sure, however, that in Greek as in succeeding times, the folk had its own humble practitioners who, although historically inconspicuous, nonetheless gave the most care to the most people. These "folk practitioners" began to show up in historical documents as a special class once they could be clearly distinguished from "respectable" healers. The university-conferred title of "doctor" constituted the first stable source of distinction; the medieval university thus, for the first time in history, created definite and distinct administrative criteria for establishing a single occupational identity within the vague collection of healers who were in practice at the time. The development of the university and of medical schools within it facilitated the attempt by the state and its chosen group of healers to formally regulate occupations related to health. Such legislation as that of Roger II of Sicily in 1140 and Frederik II in 1224 represented early, if not first, attempts at the regulation of healing practices on such a set of credentials.[18]

Also facilitating formal regulation was the development of guilds as clearly secular associations, composed of men drawn together by common work and to some degree held responsible for the public welfare. Both the medieval university and the guild gave specific public identity to the physician and set up the mechanisms by which his standing relative to other occupations could be fairly clearly established. Technically, he was preeminent among related workers like grocers and apothecaries and supervised their work. However, neither university nor guild could by themselves establish the physician's monopoly over the work of healing because they could not create widespread public confidence and thus encourage widespread public utilization of physician services. Guild

[17] See Jacob R. Marcus, *Communal Sick-Care in the German Ghetto* (Cincinnati: The Hebrew Union College Press, 1947).

[18] An earlier examining and licensing board was established in Baghdad in A.D. 931.

and university physicians formed an elite, and a small one at that. Clients were restricted largely to the nobility and the wealthy, and there was little evidence that even the elite was wholly faithful to the university-trained physician, so common was the cultivation and support of irregular practitioners.[19] The urban poor and the peasant got along with slight medical attention, using instead the lay practitioners willing to serve them. While physicians were respected as educated members of the elite, they did not seem to have great authority as healers. The establishment of national professional associations for medicine in England, Germany, and other countries provided, in the nineteenth century, yet another aid to professional monopoly, but public confidence was still lacking. For this to be gained, more attainments than a university degree seemed to be necessary.

In the United States, mass distaste for the remedies of bleeding and purging, offered by the physician as his educated scientific treatment of choice in the eighteenth and nineteenth centuries, led to the support of a variety of more palatable healing movements and, in the nineteenth century, to a thriving alcohol- and opium-laden patent-medicine trade.[20] Thus, guild and licensing laws notwithstanding, no single group of healers, physicians included, had obtained a real rather than merely formally sponsored monopoly of healing services by the nineteenth century. In the United States, it was especially difficult to create a distinct occupation merely by distinct credentials. Egalitarianism led to feelings that no man's freedom to heal others should be hampered by medical licensing laws, and the expansion of the frontier precluded the enforcement of any elaborate set of rules about who may heal. On the frontier virtually anyone could practice healing, and many called themselves "doctor."[21] Those who wished a degree could obtain one rather easily by attending a proprietary medical school.[22] There

[19] See the discussion of "quacks" in King, *op. cit.*, in W. S. C. Copeman, *Doctors and Disease in Tudor Times* (London: Dawson's, 1960), and especially in Turner, *op. cit.*

[20] See James H. Young, *The Toadstool Millionaires* (Princeton: Princeton University Press, 1961).

[21] See M. E. Pickard and R. C. Puley, *The Midwest Pioneer, His Ills, Cures and Doctors* (Crawfordville, Indiana: R. E. Banta, 1945).

[22] See, for example, Thomas Neville Bonner, *Medicine in Chicago, 1850–1950* (Madison: The American History Research Center, 1957).

was thus not only an enormous number of "doctors" in the United States by the end of the nineteenth century but also an enormous confusion ill calculated to assimilate and convey to the public the scientific advances of the century or gain its wholehearted confidence.

Only in the twentieth century was licensing widely established in the United States, and based on uniform standards for medical education.[23] With uniform training, every licensed physician could be expected to have a basic technical education more or less equivalent to every other's and distinct from that of any other kind of healer. With the political consolidation of the nation could come also the possibility of enforcing licensing laws. With a sound technical basis to his training, the physician could win confidence and establish the justice of his claim of privilege. And finally, with mass education the public developed knowledge and belief that became more like that of the physician himself and therefore it became more receptive to his work. The outcome was control over the practice of healing that has never before been enjoyed by medicine.

Technology and Consulting Professions

In my discussion of the development of medicine to its present form of organization I have been arguing that an essential feature of a useful concept of profession is the possession of something of a monopoly over the exercise of its work. I have argued further, specifically in the case of medicine, that a significant monopoly could not occur until a secure and practical technology of work was developed. It is necessary, though not sufficient, for medicine because the survival of medical practice depends upon the choice of laymen to consult it. Choice to consult cannot be forced; it must be attracted. The "good results" of medical practice with a sound foundation of knowledge, I believe, is one important source of attraction.

Obviously, "good results" are not necessary for the monopolies of other occupations that have been called professions—for the

[23] See the discussion of various national types of medical schools in the early twentieth century in Abraham Flexner, *Medical Education* (New York: The Macmillan Co., 1925). The earlier "Flexner Report," of course, damned American medical schools in detail.

scholar, or the clergyman, for example. The expertness of the physician is of a different character than that of the scholar. Like the lawyer, the physician's job is to solve the practical problems that people bring to him. He is not the custodian of a revealed dogma whose job it is to distinguish the genuinely revealed from the spurious, nor is he the repository and elaborator of the theory and imputed knowledge accumulated by a society. The request is, "Doctor, do something," not, "Doctor, tell me if this is true or not." In this sense there is a profound difference between what might be called the consulting professions and the scholarly or learned scientific professions. The former survive by providing to a varied lay clientele services that are expected to solve practical problems. They must attract the confidence of the lay clientele, the most effective way of doing so being to provide adequate solutions to their problems. The latter, however, can survive solely by gaining the interest and patronage of a special, powerful sponsor without having to gain general lay confidence. Scholarly or learned scientific professions can gain their monopoly over work solely by the conjunction of professional association and state support. Consulting professions have to take the test of practical problem solving applied by their lay clientele. These two types of occupation may be members of one very general class, "profession," but the conditions for their establishment and maintenance are so distinct that one risks great confusion by considering them together.[24] Failure to distinguish between the two leads to failure to recognize the profound change in the character of medicine as a profession that has occurred only recently. At least since the Middle Ages, medicine did maintain the status of a scholarly or learned profession. But the position of medicine as a consulting profession resembled that of the Zande witch doctor until recently.

[24] It should be clear that here, as elsewhere in this book, I follow the analytical distinction in Everett C. Hughes, "Psychology: Science and/or Profession," in Everett C. Hughes, *Men and Their Work* (New York: The Free Press of Glencoe, 1958), pp. 139–144.

2.

POLITICAL ORGANIZATION AND PROFESSIONAL AUTONOMY

IN the first chapter I attempted to show that the development of medicine into a full-fledged profession involved the interaction of a number of distinct variables. The university medical school of the Middle Ages laid the foundation for the development of clear criteria by which a specific group of workers could be identified. It also aided in creating a self-conscious occupational group sharing a common background of training. Given the importance of the higher learning to the elite of that age, those new university-trained doctors gained the support of the state in becoming the arbiters of medical work. So it was that medicine developed official control over its work, control that became fully operative once the work itself became desirable and attractive to the population at large.

The foundation of medicine's control over its work is thus clearly political in character, involving the aid of the state in establishing and maintaining the profession's preeminence. The occupation itself has formal representatives, organizational or individual, which attempt to direct the efforts of the state toward policies desired by the occupational group. Thus, it is by the interaction between formal agents or agencies of the occupation and officials of the state that the occupation's control over its work is established and shaped. The most strategic and treasured characteristic of the profession—its autonomy—is therefore owed to its relationship to the sovereign state from which it is not ultimately autonomous. And the autonomy of the individual practitioner exists within social and political space cleared and maintained for his benefit by political and formal occupational mechanisms. Clearly, professional autonomy is not absolute: the state has ultimate sovereignty over all and grants conditional autonomy to some. To understand such autonomy one must understand the character of formal occupational organization and its relation to the political policies of the state. Can an occupation be truly "autonomous," a profession "free," when it must submit to the protective custody of the state? In the specific case of medicine, it might be thought that, to the extent that medicine is dependent on the state for its position of preeminence, it is vulnerable to nonprofessional or lay controls which are anathema.

Obviously, this is a very important question for our understanding of medicine in particular and professions in general, important both to a theory of professions and to social policy. In this chapter I wish to explore the degree to which the profession's autonomy may be diminished by its ultimate dependence on the state. I shall review the relations between the formal institutions of medicine and those of the state in three national instances representing important variations in relationships. I will emphasize the degree to which national professional associations are privately controlled and possess formal legal authority delegated by the state. Critical to the analysis will be consideration of the various dimensions of professional autonomy—dimensions that we can distinguish roughly by pointing to the knowledgeable judgment and technique of the work as pure technology, on the one hand, and on the other hand to what V. O. Key, Jr., called "the mores, customs and habits that develop around work—jobways, so to speak." [1]

Essentially, in this chapter I shall argue that in widely diverse political contexts the state uniformly leaves in the hands of the profession control over the technological side of its work. What varies as relations with the state vary is control over the social and economic organization of work. I shall suggest that loss of control

[1] V. O. Key, Jr., *Politics, Parties and Pressure Groups*, 5th ed. rev. (New York: Thomas Y. Crowell Co., 1964), p. 125.

over such organization does not reduce the most critical and important element of professional autonomy and that loss of control over them has no necessary relationship to diminished professional status. Emphasis will be placed on what seems to have prime analytical importance in the relations between professions and the state: so long as a profession is free of the technical evaluation and control of other occupations in the division of labor, its lack of ultimate freedom from the state, and even its lack of control over the socio-economic terms of work do not significantly change its essential character as a profession. A profession need not be entrepreneur in a free market to be free.

Finally in preface, it is necessary to raise a caution. All three nations I shall discuss are large, complex, and changing. The United States seems to be going through particularly rapid change. In the case of each nation I shall discuss, some of the facts I cited in the first draft of this book had to be changed in the second and yet again in the final version. Furthermore, the facts presented stem from monographs which themselves are outdated by the time they are published. There is no way to publish an analytical work that is as up to date as a newspaper. Therefore, all I can claim here is that, to the best of my knowledge, the facts cited were correct and the best available at the time they are cited. More important, however, is my intent, which is to discuss three national situations as examples of a logical range of variation of state power over professional work. Because the United States usefully illustrates one extreme, I deliberately avoid complicating the analysis with the fairly revolutionary economic and social changes that the next decade or two seems to hold for medicine there. My purpose is more analytical than reportorial, emphasizing the logical distinctiveness of each national example in the light of my central question about professional autonomy.

Medicine in the United States

Medicine in the contemporary United States provides us with a fairly good example of a profession with considerable socio-economic as well as technical autonomy. Its formal organizational representative—or professional association—has been delegated many of the powers that the state elsewhere has reserved for itself, and its practitioners have otherwise been quite free of lay interference.[2] While, as we shall see, the national, state and local professional societies are by no means the sole source of rule making and rule enforcement for practitioners, they do constitute the basic, formal, quasi-legal organizational framework within which the profession works.

It seems accurate to say that at the time of writing this book there is no organized national system of health services in the United States, though a national system of financing medical care has begun in the form of Medicare.[3] Instead, there is a congeries of varied community, county, and state organizations and programs, some overlapping and some in conflict with others, few being coordinated in function; some being financed and managed by private agencies, some public, and some financed by public and managed by private agencies.[4] Federal agencies provide ambulatory and hospital care for military personnel and dependents, as well as for veterans, Indians, and others.[5] State and community public agencies provide ambulatory and hospital care for the medically indigent, the poor, and sufferers of special illnesses like tuberculosis, and provide special services for schoolchildren. State or more often locally constituted public agencies are responsible for the sanitation of public places and resources. By far the bulk of all hospital and nursing-home services is provided under privately organized auspices, increasingly with the aid of public tax funds and quasi-public insurance funds, but still resting on the foundation of private philan-

[2] Much useful information about the relations between professions and government in the United States is to be found in Corinne Lathrop Gilb, *Hidden Hierarchies: The Professions and Government* (New York: Harper & Row, 1966).

[3] For the development of Medicare, see Eugene Feingold, *Medicare: Policy and Politics* (San Francisco: Chandler Publishing Co., 1966). For general discussions of financing medical care, see Seymour E. Harris, *The Economics of American Medicine* (New York: The Macmillan Co., 1964); and Herbert E. Klarman, "Financing Health and Medical Care," in D. W. Clark and B. MacMahon, eds., *Preventive Medicine* (Boston: Little, Brown and Co., 1967), pp. 741ff.

[4] See R. H. Hamlin, *Voluntary Health and Welfare Agencies in the United States* (New York: Schoolmaster's Press, 1961).

[5] See Duncan W. Clark, "Social Welfare," in Clark and MacMahon, *op. cit.*, pp. 781–812; and Duncan W. Clark, "Governmental Health Programs and Services," in Clark and MacMahon, *op. cit.*, pp. 813–847.

thropic donations and of charges to those who use the services. Some hospitals are organized under religious auspices, some are operated as secular, nonprofit, "community" institutions that are nominally private.[6] Most of the ambulatory services are provided by physicians and others practicing on an individual, fee-for-service basis.

This is not the place to discuss in detail how all services bearing on health are organized, or disorganized, in the United States. What is to the point is the great amount of autonomy granted to practitioners in such a system and the fact that the central, formal sources of leverage in preserving or qualifying the autonomy offered by such a loose, localized system is a private, national organization that has firm, well-organized roots in the local community and that, through those local roots, has the greatest single influence on the organization of medical care in the United States. I refer to the American Medical Association.[7]

The AMA is a national association composed of state and territorial (or constituent) societies and county (or component) societies. However, an individual cannot belong to the national AMA without membership in a county or district society, which makes the local society of practitioners critical to representation. Each county society sets its own qualifications for membership. By and large, policy is that all "reputable and ethical" licensed M.D.'s are eligible for admission to membership, but there is such ambiguity in the meaning of those terms that plausible complaints of arbitrariness have been raised on occasion in criticism of county society admission practice. Recent attempts have been made in the AMA to prevent race from being a criterion of admission to county societies.

County society members vote directly for their officials and their representatives to the state "assembly," or House of Delegates. These delegates select the state officers and elect state representa-

[6] See Walter J. McNerney *et al.*, *Hospital and Medical Economics,* 2 vols. (Chicago: Hospital Research and Educational Trust, 1962).

[7] See D. R. Hyde *et al.*, "The American Medical Association: Power, Purpose and Politics in Organized Medicine," *Yale Law Journal,* LXIII (1954), 938–1022, which, while out of date in some particulars, is virtually the only source of its kind. See also James G. Burrow, *AMA, Voice of American Medicine* (Baltimore: Johns Hopkins University Press, 1963), for a history.

tives to the national House of Delegates. The latter elects the president and other AMA officers, including the Board of Trustees. The Board of Trustees, and particularly its smaller Executive Committee, must act like corporate directors in exercising continuous daily control of the association, for the House of Delegates meets only semiannually. The board approves all expenditures and appoints the executive vice-president, who is the manager of the association. Standing committees or councils are elected by the House of Delegates or appointed by the Board of Trustees: a full-time staff assists the councils' direction of the AMA's activities in various fields.

This structure is apparently dominated by a comparatively small group of men who maintain power by virtue of the nominating procedures characteristic of the organization. At the time of writing this book, on the county level the president appoints the nominating committee which puts up a slate to be voted on. The state president does the same. Since state and national associations forbid electioneering, organized opposition to the official slate has rarely succeeded and the official slate is almost always elected. The reelection of incumbent delegates is common, and "new blood" is uncommon. These electoral practices are of course not very unusual for occupational associations in general, being by no means peculiar to the AMA.[8] Their consequences are also common: in the face of the characteristic general apathy of the membership, the dead-hand method of selecting officers and representatives, and the usual policy of the *Journal* of the AMA not to print opinions in disagreement with the positions of the House of Delegates or Board of Trustees, a fairly united front is presented to the outside world by the association when it acts as the official spokesman for medicine.

The organization of the American Medical Association, then, is monolithic, facilitating the exercise of what power it has over health affairs. But what is the actual power it has to exercise, and how is it exercised? A major source of the power of the AMA over individual physicians lies in the fact that no other professional association of any significance in the United States provides the doctor with an alternative to membership in his local medical society and that his membership can be critical to his career. On occasion,

[8] See the general discussion of this problem in S. M. Lipset *et al., Union Democracy* (Garden City, New York: Anchor Books, 1962).

membership in the AMA has been used as a criterion of professional competence by employing groups like the U.S. Navy. In the past a nonmember was ineligible for specialty board examinations and ratings and is today sometimes ineligible for appointment to a hospital staff. Nonmembership is likely to lead to higher malpractice insurance premiums and, on occasion, even to denial of such insurance. Membership in the AMA, we must remember, is contingent on membership in the local society, and admission to the county society is entirely at the society's arbitrary discretion; there exists no real right to a hearing and no appeal from the county society's verdict. In the past, the threat of denial or expulsion of members has been used to punish physicians who undertook to work on an economic basis repugnant to local members of county medical societies—physicians in the Elk City Cooperative, the Puget Sound Group Health Cooperative, and the Health Insurance Plan of Greater New York have all been denied membership in county societies and so in the national association.

Apart from having great influence over the careers of individuals by being able to deny them membership which is virtually required for many medical activities, the AMA has had a distinguished history of advancing the minimum technical standards of health services. For many decades it has been engaged in promoting high standards in drug manufacture, dietary foods, and therapeutic and diagnostic devices, having sponsored the Pure Food and Drug Act of 1906 and having inserted into its code of ethics an item forbidding the prescription of secret remedies. It has given research awards, and it aids the communication of scientific knowledge and procedures through its journals, lecture programs, and conventions. It has been active in combating practice by nonmedical men and in shaping standards for the training of paramedical practitioners. Its Bureau of Investigation has kept a file of known "quacks" and has aided in their apprehension and prosecution. It has also attempted to eliminate or limit the practice of competitors in the division of labor. In the case of chiropractic, which can be practiced legally in many states, AMA pressure is to limit practice to "manual adjustment of the spinal column." Osteopathic practice has also been limited, though like the homeopaths of the nineteenth century, osteopaths seem to be becoming absorbed into the medical profession, since osteopathic schools now mostly accept and conform to AMA standards. In the case of psychology, medical societies have on occasion attempted to prevent licensure, attempting to make only a person bearing the M.D. degree legally competent to treat nervous and mental disorders. Finally, mention might be made of the role of the AMA in setting standards for the training, registration, licensing, or certification of a number of paramedical specialties—a direct formal collaborative role in the case of medical record librarians, medical technologists, and occupational therapists, and an indirect but powerful role in the case of many others, especially those trained in hospitals, such as inhalation therapists and X-ray technicians.

Aside from controlling other occupations, the AMA also controls both the quality and to a degree the quantity of physicians available to the nation. All states require graduation from an acceptable medical school as a prerequisite for a medical license. State medical examining boards define "acceptable" schools as those approved by the joint committee of the AMA and the Association of American Medical Colleges. They rely on these private professional associations for accreditation, as is a joint committee (with the American Hospital Association) relied on for approving hospitals for postgraduate specialized training of physicians. Standards for approval and accreditation, coupled with visiting inspection procedures, have certainly raised and maintained minimal standards of medical education.

The AMA's influence on the quality of health services has been limited largely to the influence that may be expected from enforcing minimal standards of training for licensing and from making advanced and new technical information available to practitioners through professional journals and postgraduate "refresher" courses of instruction. The general unstated presumption seems to be that every physician equipped with a minimal education should be free to practice according to his best judgment no matter how many years it has been since he obtained his education. Voluntary activity by county medical societies is presumed to assure the maintenance of ethical and technical standards appropriate to practice, while civil malpractice suits by aggrieved patients are deplored. The activities of local medical societies vary widely throughout the country, however, so that we may say that the only uniform set of minimal standards imposed on medical practice, as opposed to medical education and licensing, is to be found in hospitals approved for graduate specialty training, in which the conditions of instruction influence practitioners as well as students.

Aside from the limitation of competing practice, the setting of minimum educational and licensing standards, and the circulation of up-to-date scientific information bearing on the technology of medical practice, the AMA has been most prominent in its concern with controlling the socioeconomic organization of medical practice. In spite of its official acceptance of the general principle of group practice and of the use of the insurance principle in financing medical care, its "Principles of Medical Ethics" are predicated on a model of individual rather than cooperative forms of practice, financed on a fee-for-service rather than an insured, prepaid basis. The past twenty years have seen tremendous pressures, economic, political, and technological, on the traditional form of entrepreneurial medical practice, but AMA policy has been to prevent as much change as possible, a policy rationalized more on "ethical" than on technical grounds.

In the case of salaried practice, the AMA has objected primarily to employment by an organization of a physician for whose services individuals pay the organization rather than the practitioner. There has been little objection to salaried research work, public health, teaching, and military work, nor has there been very much objection to one physician employing another on salary. There has been a great deal of objection (primarily by specialty societies, but not without AMA support) to the employment by hospitals of radiologists, anesthesiologists, and pathologists even though there is no really critical doctor-patient relationship to be protected from incursions by a "third party." The argument is that the dignity of the profession is lowered, that it leaves an opening to pressure on the part of the hospital administration which could lower the standards of practice, and that in general it makes exploitation of the physician possible. Indeed, the logic here demonstrates the curious asymmetry of AMA arguments about conditions of practice in general: apart from the issue of "dignity," it claims that the quality of the physician's work is vulnerable and responsive to circumstances in which the physician is the employee of an organization giving services to individuals who contract with and pay that "third party" rather than the physician. However, it does not concede that if the quality of physician's work varies (and can be compromised) in response to such social and economic circumstances of practice, then it is also in danger of compromise in circumstances of solo fee-for-service practice, where the physician depends on individual fees and satisfying individual lay tastes. Nonetheless, the argument has been that critical elements of professional autonomy influencing the quality of practice are in danger in all circumstances in which the solo, fee-for-service model is not used.

The method of organizing payment for medical services has been an active interest of the AMA for some time. Originally, it did nothing but hamper private health insurance plans, but upon the real threat of government health insurance in the 1940's, it has come to support private over public plans, particularly those in which no laymen exercise control over the economic terms of practice. It has had little against indemnity plans, which simply reimburse the patient a set amount for his treatment and leave him with the duty of paying the fee asked by the physician. Thus, it settled for "direct billing" in the case of Medicare and is not unhappy about it now. But it has been quite careful about medical service plans which, in return for a set premium, allow the patient the opportunity of medical consultation at no significant additional out-of-pocket cost, for in such a case it is the insurance plan that pays the doctor, not the patient. So long as such plans are under medical society auspices, however, like "Blue Shield," they have come to be acceptable.

The major controversy has been with lay or government-sponsored service plans, and here the AMA has emphasized the issue of professional control over the plan. The issue has essentially been that of control over the *terms* of physician participation in such plans—the social organization of practice, and the type and level of physician compensation for such practice. To meet AMA approval the terms of practice in such plans have in the past had to be set by a committee representing all the doctors in the community, including those who do not wish to participate in the plan. This requirement, of course, makes it difficult to create an approved plan that is of financial advantage to the consumer. Local medical societies have fought such plans by expulsion or by threatening expulsion. They have circulated lists of approved plans to encourage their members to boycott or refuse to consult physicians in undesired plans and enlisting the medical staff in hospitals to deny staff privileges to physicians in such plans. These bitter forms of resistance to prepaid consumer-oriented service plans are usually justified by reference to the word "ethics"—by which is meant the unfairness of certain types of competition among doctors and the undesirability (as well as competitive unfairness) of restricting the freedom of choice of doctor by patients. The charge that the men who work in such plans are technically incompetent or that working in such plans involves technical incompetence has rarely been made persuasively. The basic point is the preservation of the free entrepreneurial status of the physician.

By and large, it should be clear that in the United States, the medical professional association has represented a position of fairly important control over the quality and the terms of medical practice. While obviously here, as elsewhere, the state has ultimate authority in matters of licensing and prosecution of practitioners, much of its authority has either been given to the AMA or been based on the advice of the AMA. In the case of licensing, state officials are usually nominated by representatives of medical societies. The AMA has used its power to raise and maintain scientific standards and to raise and maintain the economic position of the profession. In a general way, and in spite of recent national insurance legislation for the elderly and the medically indigent, it has flourished in a situation in which physicians are free to practice with few formal constraints not of their own making. Indeed, the physician's freedom in the United States has been taken to be prototypical of professional freedom as such. But in other countries physicians do not have autonomy in as many areas of work as in the United States. The question is how this bears on the character of the profession there.

Medicine in England and Wales[9]

The British system has become considerably more organized than the American. Shortly after World War II, the British Medical Association came to recognize the strength of public need and political pressure for an extended national health plan and negotiated with the government a National Health Service. Direct control over the technical side of medical care was left in the hands of the BMA and other professional bodies, but control over the terms of practice was negotiated with the government and embodied into law to create a national system of organizing and paying for health services for all citizens.

On July 5, 1948, the Ministry of Health took over the administrative and fiscal structure of health services. Every resident was given free access to a full range of existing health services at no direct out-of-pocket cost to him. The services were supported mostly by general tax revenues, a small proportion from a special payroll deduction. A three-part organizational and administrative structure was created that paralleled the structure that had already existed: (1) the hospital and specialist services; (2) the general practitioners, dentists, pharmacists, and other community health services; (3) public health services, including maternal and child care, school health services, immunization programs, and the like. Only the first two are especially important for our present purposes.

In England and Wales there are fifteen regional hospital groups, each with a governing board appointed by and reporting to the Ministry of Health. Teaching hospitals are organized separately into

[9] In this section I rely on a number of works, including Almont Lindsey, *Socialized Medicine in England and Wales* (Chapel Hill: University of North Carolina Press, 1962); "Health Services in Britain," London: British Information Services, 1965; Richard Titmuss, *Essays on the 'Welfare State,'* (London: George Allen and Unwin, 1958); P. Gemmill, *Britain's Search for Health* (Philadelphia: University of Pennsylvania Press, 1960); Harry Eckstein, *The English Health Services* (Cambridge: Harvard University Press, 1959), and *Pressure Group Politics: The Case of the British Medical Association* (Stanford, California: Stanford University Press, 1960); M. Susser and T. Watson, *Sociology in Medicine* (London: Oxford University Press, 1962); Rosemary Stevens, *Medical Practice in Modern England* (New Haven: Yale University Press, 1966); and Gordon Forsyth, *Doctors and State Medicine* (Philadelphia: J. B. Lippincott Co., 1967).

their own unit, reporting directly to the ministry through their own body. The fifteen hospital regional boards in England and Wales cover 350 hospital management committees, which supervise over 2,600 hospitals. Regional hospital boards, however, rather than the hospital management committees, hire the senior staff members of the hospitals; hospital management committees hire the rest. Salaries are negotiated nationally by representatives of the occupations involved directly with the ministry. The distribution of specialists, the classification of hospitals, and the determination of hospital resources are ultimately determined nationally but are based on recommendations by regional hospital boards and management committees. These latter are run by unpaid citizens, including a minority of representatives of medicine, and some paid clerical assistance. They have policy-making, administrative, and planning responsibility, but no fiscal authority.

The hospitals themselves are staffed by consultants (called "specialists" in the United States), general practitioners having little if any access to the hospital. The staff of consultants is paid by salary according to grade and the proportion of time put into hospital work (if part-time). The consultant comes to have tenure and himself controls a certain number of beds. It is the consultant rather than the GP who determines whether or not a patient is to be hospitalized. A committee headed by a prominent physician, its decisions secret, may give "merit awards" to about a third of the specialists annually, but aside from these, progress through the grades is fairly regular and, to some physicians' eyes, rather slow. Consultant positions being formal bureaucratic positions connected with a finite number of available hospital beds, it would follow that there is a de facto ceiling on mobility operating and that many aspirants to consultantships are disappointed. These latter seem to constitute the system's loudest critics—and emigrants.

The general practitioner is paid on a capitation basis—that is, not by the number of times he sees a patient, but by the number of patients for whose care he is responsible during the course of the year no matter how many services each needs. He can have a set maximum number of patients on his list, though if he has a paid physican assistant or is a member of a partnership, he can add a given number of patients to his list. Unlike general practitioners, dentists are paid on a fee-for-service basis, the fee negotiated with the Ministry of Health. Pharmacists are paid on a prescription basis, the prices negotiated with the ministry.

The ministry attempts to use differential financial rewards to encourage what are considered desirable practices. For the general practitioner a special "loading" of capitation fees was introduced in 1952 so as to pay the doctor more per patient when the total number of his patients falls within a given optimal range, the size of the capitation payment dropping off as the number of patients goes beyond that range. GP's can also receive special fees for giving maternity services, treating temporary residents, training assistants, supplying drugs and appliances, and conducting local clinic sessions and the like. To encourage rural practice, doctors in such areas get substantial mileage payments and extra new-practice allowances. There are, furthermore, special hardship payments for elderly doctors with small lists, a pension scheme for all participating doctors, and a privileged tax position.

By and large, the National Health Service is quite concerned with placating organized medicine—at least the more powerful segments of such. The health program is so popular generally that neither of the major political parties is inclined to attack it. The service itself is organized in a way that attempts to protect the physician from lay influence and leave the physician free to practice as he will. Above and beyond his NHS patients, the physican can have as many private patients as he wishes. Furthermore, by demand of the BMA in 1950, restrictions have been placed on the ease with which patients could change their NHS doctors—a waiting period was introduced, and in many cases the written consent of the original doctor required. Nonetheless, there is a fairly complete freedom of choice for both physician and patient. The patient may choose any practitioner and may see him on a private-fee basis if he wishes. The physician need not take NHS patients if he so chooses, limiting himself solely to private patients, whether he be consultant or GP. If he takes NHS patients, he may still take as many private patients as he wishes. And hospitals often reserve "pay beds" or "amenity beds" for private patients and those who wish to avoid waiting for a regular bed or wish to pay for more privacy or comfort than standard facilities provide. Patients themselves may choose to use some private form of health insurance rather than use National Health services.

One final point is that, in contrast to the purely voluntary system of the United States, a mechanism for receiving and investigating patient complaints is built into the National Health Service. This means that the patient may more easily harass a physician who has displeased him than is possible in the United States. There are 134 Executive Councils in England and Wales that are responsible for the management of GP, dental, pharmacist, and optician services in their locality. They are heavily professional in composition and are assisted by local committees representing the various professions. They are required to set up service committees to investigate patient complaints and may recommend to the Minister of Health that money be withheld from practitioners failing to comply with their terms of service. A special tribunal decides those cases in which it is proposed that a practitioner be disqualified from NHS. However, a number of safeguards surround the position of the practitioner. The deliberations of the NHS tribunal are secret. The complainants are not allowed counsel, but the defendant physician is allowed BMA representation which is at least quasi-legal in competence. There is right of appeal to the minister of health, but while the ministry can overrule the tribunal, it may do so only in favor of the accused practitioner.

While there is apparently no persistent, severe dissatisfaction with the NHS among patients [10] or practitioners [11] (though as we shall see, it is a very mixed response difficult to characterize simply), there are operational problems that flare up periodically. One major problem is the question of incentives to better technical practice. Payment per head has no necessary relation to the quality of care, and in some cases—as in the standard tax deduction of overhead by which the physician saves money if his actual overhead is kept low—there is positive discouragement to improving the physical facilities of practice. Furthermore, the GP is even more isolated from the consultant and the hospital than he was before the NHS

[10] For a good picture of patient and GP responses to the NHS, see Ann Cartwright, *Patients and Their Doctors* (London: Routledge and Kegan Paul, 1967).

[11] For a recent survey of GP's, see David Mechanic, "General Practice in England and Wales," *Medical Care*, VI (1968), 245–260.

came into being. He is thus cut off from sources of new medical knowledge and is prone to feel like a mere disposal agent for the consultant.[12] And he is tempted to be reluctant to refer maternity cases to consultants because of the danger of losing them (and the special compensation he gets for them). The segregation of the GP from the hospital and the consultant was apparently the result of the pressure of the stronger and more prestigious consultants during the negotiation of the terms of the NHS.[13] Indeed, the consultant system, which was established in deference to the wishes of the spokesmen for the consultants themselves, seems to be so narrow and rigid that young men aspiring to consultantships seem more prone to leave the country than to practice as GP's or eke out a precarious living while waiting for an NHS appointment.

There is also controversy in the British system surrounding the level of compensation of physicians and other practitioners in the system, the regulations designed to distribute practices geographically by public needs that prevent the physician from setting up his practice wherever he wishes, and the paperwork required of NHS physicians. The first of these problems has led on occasion to threats of mass withdrawal of physicians from participation in the NHS. These problems, however, are insignificant by comparison with those of mechanisms conducive to improving the quality of care, with the isolation of the GP, and with the limited mobility within the structure of consultant services, all of which seem to have been created by segments of the profession rather than by lay officials or by the bureaucratization attendant on any insurance scheme, public or private. Indeed, many of the peculiarities of the National Health Service seem to stem directly from the fact that it was set up and is run with the cooperation and consultation of the private and independent associations representing the health professions. Much as in the American system, professional associations dominate such prime institutions as the Central Health Services Council and such crucial "grass-roots" units as the Local Medical Committee. Where official administrative units with duties bearing on professionals exist, professional representation is high. Indeed,

[12] Stevens, *op. cit.*, analyzes at great length the problem of the consultant and the GP in England.

[13] See Eckstein, *Pressure Group Politics, op. cit.*

the influence of physician members on laymen in such groups as regional hospital boards and hospital management committees has been so great that the Guillebaud Committee once recommended that medical representation be reduced to 25 per cent or less.[14]

By and large, the English system is one in which the state finances and organizes the administration of health services. Unlike the United States, the British state has in essence set up administrative rules controlling where the doctor may work, what terms he will work for if he chooses to work within the system, and how the system will be financed—rules determined only partly by the private professional associations of the nation. Nonetheless, the private associations are recognized as the legitimate representatives of the profession, and they do negotiate with the state the terms of work. The British Medical Association does not, therefore, completely control many of the social and economic aspects of practice, but in its role in the General Medical Council it still controls the licensing of practitioners, and by its place on the Central Health Services Council as well as on official regional and local committees, it strongly influences the formulation of practice usages. Furthermore, it still controls the determination of the technical standards of medical work and seems to have the strongest voice in determining what is "ethical" and "unethical."

Medicine in the Soviet Union [15]

In the Soviet Union there is no private, independent association like the AMA or the BMA to serve as a spokesman for the profession. The very concept of professional autonomy seems to be rather weak; it is limited to the freedom of expert technical judgment and apparently excludes any say in how work is organized. Since 1918, Soviet health services have been organized into a single health

14 A recommendation cited in Susser and Watson, *op. cit.*, p. 160.

15 In this section I rely most heavily on the extremely useful recent work, Mark G. Field, *Soviet Socialized Medicine: An Introduction* (New York: The Free Press of Glencoe, 1967). See also "Report of the U.S. Public Health Mission to the U.S.S.R., August 13–September 14, 1957," U.S. Public Health Service Publication No. 649 (Washington, D.C.: Government Printing Office, 1958), and "Hospital Services in the U.S.S.R.," Report of the U.S. Delegation on Hospital Systems Planning, U.S. Public Health Service Publication No. 930–F–10 (Washington, D.C.: Government Printing Office, 1966).

system by a commissariat of health protection. At present, this national health system is planned, financed, and supervised by what is now called the Ministry of Health; the minister is a member of the Council of Ministers, which is the major executive unit of the Soviet Union. There is, in fact, a whole variety of stratified counterparts, each with responsibility for units of descending geographic size and political importance, from ministries of autonomous republics to municipal or rural districts, and, at the lowest administrative level, rural hospital, microdistrict (*uchastok*), and factory health unit chief physicians. Each health unit is responsible both to a superior health unit and to a superior governmental unit, the latter providing it with logistic and financial support.

Apart from several special exceptions like the medical care of the armed forces, the Ministry of Health attempts to control virtually all resources and services closely related to health. The "All-Union" Ministry of Health has advisory relations with the Academy of Medical Sciences and direct administrative relations with the state trust for pharmaceutical raw materials. The ministry includes departments devoted to planning for capital construction, to producing pharmaceuticals and other medical supplies, to medical education, to public health organization, and to administering special medical services such as radiology. Republican health ministries are more complex, with a scientific medical council and with "administrations" for sanitation, maternal and child care, medical schools, medical personnel, specialized sanitoria, scientific research institutes, and the like. In the regional or provincial health department there is a similar, though simpler departmentalization, to which are attached surgeons, gynecologists, obstetricians, pediatricians, communicable disease specialists and others serving as "chief specialists," responsible for the standards of practice, staffing, and postgraduate education in the health services in their administrative specialty units. Locally operative municipal or rural health departments finance and administer local medical facilities and appoint staff. They are responsible for the health of the local population and for maintaining liaison with such voluntary community organizations as Red Cross or Red Crescent societies. In rural districts, the chief physician of the rural district hospital has come to serve as the manager of local health services.

Within this general framework, most health services are provided to the population by physicians working in polyclinics attached to district hospitals. There is also a variety of other health units for industrial and farm workers, students, and other distinct segments of the population, and there are special facilities for tubercular, venereal disease, cancer, and mental[16] patients, as well as emergency-care units.

What is the place of the medical profession in this system? It is without ambiguity in the position of a civil service. Physicians hold positions created and sustained by the state, with little (but by no means no) opportunity for private practice. Furthermore, their positions are salaried; the salaries are set by decree. Their working hours are determined bureaucratically (generally at 6½ hours per day), and bureaucratic norms are established to set the tempo of their work (in 1960, for example, pediatricians were expected to see an *average* of five patients per outpatient clinic hour). What is perhaps most important for our national comparisons, however, is that the physician may appear to be almost wholly a creature of the state in that he has no sociopolitically independent position from which to stand outside the state. While "private" professional associations in the form of the Pirogov Society and the post-revolutionary All-Russian Union of Professional Associations did exist, they were dissolved by decree in the early 1920's and arrangements were made for joining physicians with the state-created All-Russian Federated Union of Medical Workers. Physicians thus belong to merely one technically outvoted section or unit of medical workers of all kinds, a union which is an arm of the state.

I have seen no information about the activities of the union to which physicians belong and may, therefore, be wrong in guessing that it is likely to be a weaker representative of the profession than a private union or association; it is unlikely to be able to mount so drastic a thing as a strike, as was done recently by medical groups in Belgium, Chile, and Canada; and it is unlikely to threaten mass withdrawal from the state health system, as did the British Medical

[16] For psychiatry in the U.S.S.R., see Mark G. Field and Jason Aronson, "The Institutional Framework of Soviet Psychiatry," *The Journal of Nervous and Mental Disease,* CXXXVIII (1964), 305–322; and Mark G. Field, "Soviet and American Approaches to Mental Illness: A Comparative Perspective," *Review of Soviet Medical Sciences,* I (1964), 1–36.

Association recently over the issue of compensation. At best, it may request or strongly urge better working conditions for physicians. Hence, it may be said that it has little control over the socio-economic usages of medical practice. And since there is not much opportunity, let alone encouragement, for private practice in the Soviet Union, the physician has no place to go if he is dissatisfied with his working conditions.

In the Soviet Union, then, the physician has no secure economic position independent of the state. But does this mean that he is not a true "professional"? Surely one does not have to be an entrepreneur in a free market or a monopoly holder in a "free" market of scarce services in order to be a professional. What is generic to the professional is control over his technique or skill, monopoly over its practice. While there is evidence of some occasional ambiguity to such control in Communist countries, where ideology has at times led to state emphasis on such practices as acupuncture (in China), or to such orientations as that of Lysenko or Pavlov (in the Soviet Union), what evidence there is seems to point to the freedom of the "professional" practitioner to determine technique, given the limitation that financing imposes. As bureaucratic as the state system of services may be, the lay heads of large-scale and general administrative units all seem to rely on medical advisory units, whereas the heads of practicing units like hospitals and polyclinics all seem to be physicians. And while a physician who is a member of the Communist party is likely to rise higher in the medical hierarchy than one who is not, he is still a physician, not a layman. Furthermore, as in the case of the medically condemned "cancer cure," Krebiozen, in the United States, laymen in the Soviet Union can make a political issue of medical judgment, but even the all-powerful Central Committee of the Communist party refused to intervene when, in 1962, contrary to some strong lay opinions, the Academy of Medical Sciences and the Ministry of Health declared a cancer cure worthless. The Central Committee disqualified itself as an expert, leaving determination of the medically valuable to physicians.[17]

Thus, in the Soviet Union, physicians do not directly control the

[17] Referred to in Field, *Soviet Socialized Medicine, op. cit.*

economic and administrative arrangements of their work, for they are employees of the state and have no representation by bargaining agents outside the state. Nonetheless, they do seem to control directly the techniques they use as well as the evaluation of such techniques. It has been implied by Field [18] that, insofar as the physician is a state employee, his very judgment about the disposition of his cases is subject to the influence of state policy, not to speak of the "production norms" imposed on him. In this sense he is no longer supposed to be able to adopt a "professional" stance of being concerned with the patient's own good. Nonetheless, I would argue that the pressure of state policy on the physician to, for example, minimize sick leave in order to maximize factory production, does not undermine the autonomy of technical judgment so much as establish the social or moral premises upon which the judgment of illness is based—premises that exist everywhere, varying in content and in self-consciousness.[19] That the profession's autonomy should extend to self-determination of such premises—a task for which the physician has no special qualification, moral or technical—is a dubious advantage to anyone. Indeed, in every country, including the United States, the physician is on occasion required by law to place the public health ahead of the privacy and convenience of the highly infectious or otherwise socially dangerous patient.[20] What seems most relevant for our purposes in examining the status of medicine in the Soviet health system is not that the physician does not possess the right to decide for himself what is in the public interest and what weight to give private interest, but that he does maintain the right to diagnose and prescribe according to criteria that are rooted in medical knowledge and to have his work evaluated by colleagues, not by laymen. This is certainly the very heart of professional autonomy, and it seems to exist as strongly in the Soviet Union as in the United States and Great Britain. Expertise seems to have its own leverage.

[18] Mark G. Field, *Doctor and Patient in Soviet Russia* (Cambridge: Harvard University Press, 1957), *passim.*

[19] In Part III of this book I shall discuss at some length the social and moral assumptions underlying the diagnosis of illness.

[20] Relevant here are the comments on responsibility in T. H. Marshall, *Class, Citizenship and Social Development* (Garden City, New York: Anchor Books, 1964), pp. 158–179.

The State and Zones of Professional Autonomy

The three examples discussed were chosen to demonstrate a range of variation in the political organization of the profession and its relation to the state. It is the range of gross variation that is important here, not the slight empirical details which may change tomorrow. The empirical examples were chosen because they suggest, even if they do not fully constitute, a logical range of variation in the organization of modern professional services. At one extreme, *partially* represented by the contemporary United States, the state uses the profession as its source of guidance, exercising its power in such a way as to support the profession's standards and create a sociopolitical environment in which the profession is free from serious competition from rival practitioners and firmly in control of auxiliary workers. Within that state-protected environment, the profession has sufficient power of its own to control virtually all facets of its work without serious interference from any lay group. This is professional autonomy of rather comprehensive scope, including autonomy in selecting the economic terms of work, the location and social organization of work, and the technical content of the work. In contrast to earlier times, when anyone was legally free to practice, this comprehensive autonomy is protected by a state-supported monopoly. At the other logical extreme, *partially* represented by the contemporary Soviet Union, the state-supported monopoly grants professional autonomy solely to determination of the technical content of work. Administrators and policy-makers representing the state control the economic terms of work, its location, and its social organization, leaving the profession no option but to accept their terms.

In assessing these extremes we must ask how useful it is to consider both of them, and what lies in between, to represent professions. There is of course no doubt that the extreme of comprehensive autonomy in all zones of work is compatible with the idea of a profession—indeed, it constitutes the kind of entrepreneurial position that nineteenth-century Western liberal notions of "freedom" readily embrace. But how about the other extreme? There surely we can say that it represents the barest minimum of autonomy for a profession. Some may argue that an occupation that does not control the exercise of the skills over which it claims exclusive knowledge could not be called a profession. Nonetheless I would argue that autonomy of technique is at the core of what is unique about the profession, and that, in fact, when this core autonomy is gained, at least segments of autonomy in the other zones follow after.[21]

The profession bases its claim for its position on the possession of a skill so esoteric or complex that nonmembers of the profession cannot perform the work safely or satisfactorily and cannot even evaluate the work properly. On this basis, nonmembers are excluded from practice and evaluation. Given the exclusion and its implied basic concession of autonomy, I would argue that in spite of any formal administrative framework imposed by the profession, autonomy in controlling its technique allows it to temper many elements of that framework beyond both the intent and even recognition of its planners and chief executives. This is particularly the case for medicine, where dangerous consequences can follow upon improper work, and where the *claim* of emergency and of possible dangerous consequences is a potent protective device.

Granted autonomy in his technique, the professional has a number of advantages which give him a sturdy wedge into other zones of practice. There is, first of all, the authority granted and deference obtained by his conceded expertise. Even in Soviet courts, where lay intervention in the legal process is institutionalized and encouraged, professionals seem to have more of an upper hand than the formal design would lead us to expect.[22] Second, there is influence on nontechnical zones of work that is contingent on assessments of the work itself: the professional can argue that he cannot perform his work adequately unless he is near a given group of colleagues or a given set of technical resources; he can argue that he cannot perform his work adequately if he must work alone or

[21] See William A. Glaser, "Socialized Medicine in Practice," *The Public Interest,* I (1966), 90–106.

[22] See G. Feifer, *Justice in Moscow* (New York: Dell Publishing Co., 1965). And see also the spirit in G. S. Pondoev, *Notes of a Soviet Doctor* (New York: Consultants Bureau, Inc., 1959), particularly Chapter 14, "Medical Ethics and Medical Secrecy," where the author argues from the "complex and varied" character of medical work to deny that formally constituted law can guide the doctor's activity. Even though Soviet law apparently recognizes no medical or other professional secrecy, Pondoev suggests that it is of functional advantage and should be observed by the practitioner.

if he is subject to structured interference; or he can claim that his cases are too complex to handle safely or well on an average of five an hour. Arguing from his conceded expertise in diagnosis and treatment, he is well equipped to influence if not control many other areas of his work. Only a fellow professional may say no, for counterargument can be justified only be reference to knowledge of the special characteristics of the work. Autonomy over the technical character of his work, then, gives him the wherewithal by which to be a "free" profession, even though he is dependent upon the state for estabishing and sustaining his autonomy.

3.

THE MEDICAL DIVISION OF LABOR

THUS far I have devoted myself almost wholly to medicine itself—to the emergence of an identifiable occupation which has gained the exclusive right to practice medicine by virtue of the support of the state and its own occupational organization. In my discussion of the process by which the occupation emerged, it was not possible to deal with medicine alone, however, for what we today call medicine was only one of many occupations devoted to healing. Medicine, after all, sought the *exclusive* right to practice in face of the fact that many kinds of healers were practicing.

Apart from occupations which were driven out of practice or were driven underground into the urban slums, the countryside, and the cultist drawing room, there have been many occupations—pharmacy being a good example—which provided services related to healing and which, if unregulated, could in fact become healing consultantships competitive with physicians' practices. The services of many such occupations are useful to the physician and necessary to his practice, even if dangerous to his monopoly. As I pointed out earlier, the solution of the physician's problem was not, as it was in the case of direct competitors, to be found by driving such occupations out of practice, but rather by gaining from the state control over those occupations' activities so as to limit what they could do and to supervise or direct their activities. Thus, the state has both made it illegal for other workers to compete with physicians and given physicians the right to direct the activities of related occupations. "In a way unparalleled in any other industry, the physician controls and influences his field and all who venture near it."[1] Whereas the division of labor in nonprofessionalized fields is ordered by historical accident, economic and political power, competition, and purely functional interdependence, the division of labor surrounding the highly professionalized activity of healing is ordered by the politically supported dominant profession. Formally, it is a hierarchy. In this chapter, I wish to discuss the hierarchical character of the medical division of labor and most particularly the status of the paramedical occupations to be found within it. The essential question I wish to address is the analytical difference between medicine as a profession and the other occupations in the medical division of labor.

Paramedical Occupations[2]

There are few traditional tasks of healing performed by physicians which are not also performed by nonphysician health personnel. In fact, many of the tasks now performed by nonphysician health personnel were once considered the everyday prerogatives of physicians themselves and so cannot in purely technical terms be considered something distinct from what the doctor does. What the physician does is a part of a larger technical division of labor and sometimes not a very distinct or generic part. It is the physician's *control* of the division of labor that is distinct. Those occupations falling under his control are called "paramedical." To understand both the technology and sociology of the medical, therefore, one must understand the character of the paramedical.

The term "paramedical" refers to occupations organized around the work of healing which are ultimately controlled by physicians. Physician control is manifested in a number of ways. First, much of the technical knowledge learned by paramedical workers during

[1] Dale L. Hiestand, "Research into Manpower for Health Services," *Milbank Memorial Fund Quarterly*, XLIV (1966), Part II, p. 148.

[2] Portions of this section are from "Paramedical Personnel" by Eliot Freidson. Reprinted with permission of the publisher from *International Encyclopedia of the Social Sciences*, David L. Sills, ed. Vol. 10, pp. 114–120.

their training and used in their work tends to be discovered or enlarged upon or at the very least approved of by physicians. Second, the tasks performed by paramedical workers tend to assist rather than replace the focal tasks of diagnosis and treatment. Third, paramedical workers tend to be subordinate, in that their work tends to be performed at the request or "order" of, and is often supervised by, physicians. Finally, the prestige assigned to paramedical occupations by the general public tends to be less than that to physicians.

These characteristics are such that the paramedical occupations may be distinguished from established professions by their relative lack of autonomy, responsibility, authority, and prestige. However, the fact that they are by definition organized around an established profession and, in varying degrees, partake of some but not all of the elements of professionalism, allows us to distinguish them from many other occupations, and, indeed, to argue that they represent a sociologically distinct form of occupational organization.

Nonetheless, it may be noted that paramedical occupations are not adequately distinguished by reference to their health-related tasks. Occupations usually called "paramedical" are those that have fallen or have been pulled into the professionally ordered division of labor. Other occupations which may actually perform some of the same technical tasks but which stand in a different relationship to the dominant profession (as, for example, an herbalist compared to a pharmacist) are not called "paramedical" but rather "quack" or "irregular." Therefore, the differences between the "paramedical" and the "quack" do not necessarily arise from what each does or how he does it but from the relations each has to the dominant profession. The paramedical worker, being under "discipline," is more easily distinguished sociologically than technologically. The paramedical occupations are not merely part of a technologically differentiated division of labor but, more important, part of a division of labor organized around and controlled by a central, dominant profession.

Distinct as it is, this "paraprofessional" pattern is not common. For example, while there is a fairly elaborate division of labor revolving around law in the United States, it would not be appropriate to use the term "paralegal" for bailiffs, accountants, notaries, real estate brokers, and bankers in the same way we use "paramedical" for nurses and laboratory technicians. Nor does the prefix seem properly employed to designate the division of labor connected with any other established profession, though it has recently been used to distinguish teachers' aides in public schools. In the United States, only medicine seems to have imposed such definite order on the occupations surrounding it.

Development of the Division of Labor

A division of labor around the tasks of diagnosing and treating human ills has always existed in one form or another in most human societies. There have always been diagnosticians, herbalists, midwives, and nurses, even if only on a part-time, amateur basis. The distinctive division of labor labeled "paramedical," however, is relatively new and is complex only in the highly industrialized societies of the world where modern medicine is established. Even where it is found, it varies a great deal in the completeness of its integration around and control by the medical profession. Unfortunately, no adequate cross-national comparisons of the organization of health workers exist to provide even the basic descriptive information necessary for analysis, so much of the indication of the types and sources of variation must be based on scattered bits of information.

In Europe, the beginnings of a distinctly paramedical division of labor began to emerge at least by the time of the development in cities of the corporate guild [3] and the university. The city provided the population density necessary for the support of a variety of full-time specialists. The guild provided health-related occupations with viable organization by which it became possible to hammer out a distinct identity in both the official and the public eye and to press for exclusive rights to that identity and the work it involves. The right to have something of a monopoly of title and function and to control in a fairly strict way access into and progress through the occupational career, however, was obtained from the

[3] See the descriptions of various English occupations' development in E. M. Carr-Saunders and P. A. Wilson, *The Professions* (Oxford: Clarendon Press, 1933), and in G. Millerson, *The Qualifying Associations* (London: Routledge and Kegan Paul, 1964).

state. In exchange for that right the occupations gained organization, but they also became subject to assignment into a relatively well-defined *official* position in a larger division of labor, a position that often involved enforced subordination to members of quite another guild. Occupations trained in the university had a stronger claim, by virtue of their aura of learning and "science," to a superordinate position. University training gave physicians and surgeons a stronger political position for persuading the state to subordinate to them such competitors as apothecaries, grocers, and barbers, not to speak of allowing them to prosecute the irregular practitioners. This could be so even when it was doubtful that the actual knowledge and skill of the university-trained practitioner in those days equipped him to practice any more effectively than his self-taught or apprenticed competitor.

With the development of the university and the guild in European cities, then, rose a rudimentary organization of full-time health workers, organized at least in part under the supervision of physicians and surgeons. As I have already noted, for centuries this organization was highly unstable, from within rife with undisciplined competition and from without weakened by the persistence of a great variety of irregular practitioners. Similar to the position of health services in the nonindustrial countries of today, the medical division of labor was fairly stable only in the areas of the city where a well-to-do gentry was prone to patronize it. In the urban slums and in the countryside the poor and the peasantry persisted in relying on folk remedies, largely part-time practitioners, and on occasion itinerant irregulars, the first two being part of their own culture, the third playing on their culture. There were in essence two health systems, the largest rooted in the culture of the peasant, the most prominent in the learned traditions of Western civilization. Before the latter could become at once stable and universal, the former had to be destroyed or at least severely restricted. Not until the twentieth century in Europe and North America did anything resembling a stable and extensive division of labor dominated by physicians emerge. In the nonindustrial countries of the world today, such a division of labor does not yet exist to any great degree.

By the twentieth century the medical profession was at last able to establish a secure mandate to provide the central health service.

In England, the country GP had been drawn into regular medical ranks. In Russia, the feldsher had been in part replaced by and in part subordinated to the physician. In the United States, the many different kinds and qualities of practitioners all democratically calling themselves "doctor" were reduced to some uniformity. Control over the focal tasks of diagnosis and prescription was thereby secured, though some specialties that evolved separately, such as dentistry and veterinary medicine, were able by virtue of their easily segregated functions and their capacity to practice as entrepreneurs to maintain themselves separately. Finally, by virtue of its major role as arbiter in the application of new scientific discoveries, the profession could order around itself the proliferating new technical personnel.

It is in this context that the development of the contemporary paramedical division of labor can be understood as something much more complex than merely rationally functional or technical differentiation. Because of the importance of social, political, and economic factors, there is great variation in the origin and present position of occupations related to health. Some historic specialties like dentistry survived fairly independently of the paramedical division of labor. Others, like pharmacy and more particularly optometry, were not fully integrated into the paramedical division of labor, being at least partially independent of it. Still others, like the bone-setter and, in the United States, the midwife, were taken over by the physician himself, laymen and amateurs being driven out of practice. Others, the most prominent of which is nursing, maintained an ancient function while being brought firmly under medical control. And finally, with some few exceptions, such new specialists as laboratory technicians, rising with the new medical science and technology inside the walls of the hospital and medical school, developed unequivocally as part of an established paramedical division of labor. In this process, historical accident and national differences seem to play no small part.

Hierarchy in the Division of Labor

The paramedical division of labor is a stratified system, the occupations of which are in varying degrees integrated around the work of the physician. All occupations in the system are given less prestige than the physician by society at large.[4] Consonant with this differential prestige, the backgrounds of those recruited into all paramedical occupations are likely to be lower than those recruited into medicine itself. Furthermore, there is a hierarchy of prestige and authority *among* paramedical workers, with nurses, for example, being higher than attendants and technicians. This hierarchy, too, is likely to be reflected in the social origins of the workers. In the grossest comparison between physicians and paramedical workers, the latter are to a disproportionate degree women and of the less valued ethnic, racial, and religious groups in the United States. With the special exception of sex, those differences in background and personal characteristics are also likely to be ranged in an orderly way through the paramedical ranks.

The order of the hierarchy of the paramedical division of labor can be exaggerated, however. The interrelations of paramedical workers can be seen clearly only as part of a broader process that embraces physicians, health workers who are not part of the paramedical division of labor, and the institutions in which medical and nonmedical health services are provided. One of the major variables mediating interoccupational relations in the health services seems to be functional autonomy—the degree to which work can be carried on independently of organizational or medical supervision, and the degree to which it can be sustained by attracting its own clientele independently of organizational referral or referral by other occupations, including physicians. On the whole, the more autonomous the occupation and the greater the overlap of its work with that of physicians, the greater is the potential for conflict, legal or otherwise. Such conflict is seen between chiropractor and physician in the United States, homeopath and physician in the Soviet Union, and "native" practitioner and physician in virtually all nonindustrial countries of the world.

The most interesting conflicts, however, occur within the paramedical division of labor during the course of the growth of new occupations capable of attaining functional autonomy. In the United States, where the movement toward professional trappings is strong and extensive, and physicians are not able by virtue of their num-

[4] See Albert J. Reiss, Jr., *Occupations and Social Status* (New York: The Free Press of Glencoe, 1962).

bers to perform cheaply all the traditional functions demanded of them, such conflict is common, focusing around the question of whether or not nonphysicians are to be allowed to offer health services independently of medical supervision. The outcome has been, in such increasingly successful cases as the clinical psychologist, virtual independence in practice, limited by legal inability to prescribe drugs. But clinical psychology is only one example; the growth of new techniques and of new occupations to practice them, impelled by the force of professionalization, seems to be giving new shape to the paramedical division of labor. Some years ago it could be visualized more or less as a pyramid, with the physician at the apex. In present-day United States, the pyramid seems to be changing into a less clearcut structure, at the top of which is a plateau along which are arranged physicians as well as other autonomous but consulting and loosely cooperating new professionals.

Recruitment and Training

Training also follows a pattern whose order roughly parallels the prestige, independence, and imputed responsibility of the work. Training ranges from professional schools associated with universities requiring a full higher education before several years of training, at one extreme, to short, informal, on-the-job training at the other. Between those extremes are those in which are varied the length, formality, and abstractness of the training, carried out in such institutions as the hospital training school, the proprietary technical school, apprenticeships, and the like.[5] In the United States, where the university is a considerably less clearly defined institution than elsewhere, more paramedical education is to be found with professional trappings. In Europe, technical training schools separate from the university are more likely to exist for the education of even the higher prestige paramedical occupations, but the trend seems to be to imitate the American model.

The paramedical ranks are also inclined to be ordered by the

[5] See the table of occupational training periods in Walter I. Wardwell, "Limited, Marginal and Quasi-Practitioners," in Howard E. Freeman, Sol Levine and Leo G. Reeder, *Handbook of Medical Sociology* (Englewood Cliffs, N.J.: Prentice-Hall, 1963), pp. 216–217.

length and type of training required by the occupation—the longer, the more formal, and the closer training is to the university, the higher the position in the division of labor. It follows from this that the higher the position, the greater must be the investment of time and energy in training, the less casual can be the recruitment and so the greater must be the commitment to the occupation. Recruitment to the many low-skill positions in the paramedical division of labor seems to be a simple function of the labor market and the demand for unskilled service workers willing to do unpleasant work. Recruitment to the higher skill positions, however, is considerably more problematic, the difficulties compounded in those occupations traditionally filled by women.

Nursing is a fairly well-documented example of the problems of recruitment and training in the paramedical occupations. The difficulty in nursing is not attracting people to undergo training as such, for quite a few people begin training. The problem lies in recruiting women who will stay in training and subsequently pursue a lifetime career. Women are likely to be torn between commitment to work and to marriage and family—such conflict, observed often among nursing students, is closely related to school dropouts or subsequent job turnover.

Leaders of nursing in the United States have attempted to contend with the problem by emphasizing the professional qualities of the occupation, presumably hoping to create a stronger "professional" commitment to work. However, the problem seems to be inherent in the position of women in the labor force and does not seem soluble by professionalization. Even in the case of that most professional of professions, medicine, only a modest proportion of women in the United States qualified to practice actually do so.[6] One might therefore suspect that the most likely solution for a social system like that of the United States would be found in changing the organization of the job so as to accommodate to the demands of marriage and family.

In European countries the position of women in the medical and paramedical labor force is somewhat different, owing, apparently,

[6] See R. A. Dykman and J. M. Stalnaker, "Survey of Women Physicians Graduating from Medical Schools, 1925–1940," *Journal of Medical Education*, XXXII (1957), Part II, pp. 1–38.

to national differences in the occupational roles of women, small though significant differences in the class system, and finally, to the level of industrialization and the general standard of living.[7] The latter consideration brings up another aspect of recruitment and training in the paramedical division of labor. Clear evidence is lacking, but general opinion seems to be that it is becoming more and more difficult to recruit people into the medical jobs that require considerable investment of time and money in technical training. If this is so, it might be understood as a symptom of a larger process of advanced industrialization.

In the early stages of industrialization, the health services constituted a major and conspicuous source of social and economic mobility to which those willing and able to invest in specialized training could aspire. At present, the demand for skilled technical services has developed markedly in *other* segments of the economy, thereby providing a considerably wider universe of opportunity than existed earlier. As an older, fairly closely organized system, requiring relatively extensive investment in training but offering relatively inflexible and frequently subordinate career lines, the health services seem handicapped in competing for a limited pool of potential workers, medical as well as paramedical. Part of the pervasive emphasis on professionalism within the paramedical division of labor in the United States seems to be an attempt to increase the attractiveness of the work and thereby aid in recruiting the best possible workers.

However, the emphasis on professionalism is most often strong only during the course of training, which is where the leaders of the occupation are most likely to be influential. But insofar as professionalism is likely to emphasize intellectual and technical skill, there is the danger of dissatisfying students whose motives for entering the occupation are not so much intellectual as humanitarian—a danger that has been observed in nursing schools.[8] More

[7] For a French view, see Jean Bui-Dang-Ha Doan and D. R. Lévy, "Les Femmes dans la médecine et les professions libérales," *Cahiers de sociologie et de démographie médicales,* IV (1964), 123–136; and Jean Bui-Dang-Ha Doan, "Quelques aspects de la féminisation dans les professions libérales et médicales," *Le concours medical,* LXXXVII (1965), 1480–1486.

[8] Cf. R. G. Corwin, "The Professional Employee: A Study of Conflict in Nursing Roles," *American Journal of Sociology,* LXVI (1961), 604–615.

important for present concerns is the likelihood that when paramedical students are imbued with a professional ideology emphasizing their dignity and autonomy, but begin work in settings where they are distinctly subordinate, they are in for what has been called "reality shock." And if the student's indoctrination has been thorough, his relations with other occupations in the paramedical hierarchy are likely to be somewhat difficult.

Professionalism and the Case of the Nurse [9]

It has been implied that the greatest opportunity for developing functional autonomy seems to exist for those occupations that can operate outside the walls of organizations, particularly such medically organized institutions as clinics and hospitals. The nurse, whose leaders in the United States and abroad have with great energy sought to establish unique skills and full professional status, seems fated to remain subject to the doctor's orders in part because of the fact that her work is largely carried on in the hospital. Interestingly enough, it appears that *in order to* attain semiprofessional status, the nurse had to become part of the subordinate paramedical division of labor, and so handicap her chance for subsequent professional status. Let us examine her case in more detail, since she is not only an important member of the paramedical division of labor but also represents a critical problem for the delineation of a useful concept of "profession."

Nursing functions have always been performed in every society, perhaps even more frequently than healing functions as such. In the recorded past it has always been something of an occupation too. There has always been an awareness of the need for the bedside care of the sick and characteristic techniques of practice that involve at least cooling a fevered body and feeding a sick person. From the physician's point of view, the need has been for someone

[9] In this section I rely on such histories as Brian Abel-Smith, *A History of the Nursing Profession* (London: William Heinemann, 1960); Richard H. Shryock, *The History of Nursing, An Interpretation of the Social and Medical Factors Involved* (Philadelphia: W. B. Saunders Co., 1959); and Bonnie Bullough and Vern L. Bullough, *The Emergence of Modern Nursing* (New York: The Macmillan Co., 1964). Fred Davis, ed., *The Nursing Profession* (New York: John Wiley & Sons, 1966), also contains useful historical and social comments by some of the contributors.

who could be relied on to carry out his orders in caring for a patient when he was not present. Indeed, in the Hippocratic corpus it was suggested that the physician's apprentice be left behind at the bedside to carry out the doctor's orders in a more reliable way than could be expected of the patient or his family.[10] Apart from military operations and urban areas, care of the sick in ancient times seems to have been carried out mostly in the patient's home, a place where the patient's family, if not the patient himself, could exercise fairly strong controls over what was done for him. Perhaps because of this, little seems to be known about the nurses practicing in that context except that they do appear to have existed, if only as nursemaids.

The rise of Christianity changed the definition of illness from a generally naturalistic one to a religious and supernatural one. Important to the definition was the motive underlying care of the sick—the idea of charity, which led to the founding of hospitals as well as to the giving of care to the sick for religious rather than functional purposes, for one's own salvation if not more for the patient's.[11] Here was bedside care on a full-time basis, but practiced more as a spiritual exercise than as an occupation, and granted to a special, degraded segment of the population for moral rather than therapeutic reasons. An example of the religious nursing of earlier times is to be found in the case of the Hôtel-Dieu of Paris. The attendants were Augustinian nuns, qualified for nursing only by their piety and inclination toward good works. The nuns naturally accumulated extensive clinical experience as individuals, but this never became much of a part of the lore of the occupation as such because it was not passed down or used in instructing novices. Indicative of the kind of care provided is the report that there were complaints for a thousand years that the sisters were more

[10] "Let one of your pupils be left in charge, to carry out instructions without unpleasantness, and to administer the treatment. . . . Never put a layman in charge of anything, otherwise, if a mischance occur, the blame will fall on you." *Hippocrates,* tr. W. H. S. Jones, Vol. 2 (London: William Heinemann, 1943), p. 299.

[11] See the discussion of Christianity in George Rosen, "The Hospital—Historical Sociology of a Community Institution," in Eliot Freidson, ed., *The Hospital in Modern Society* (New York: The Free Press of Glencoe, 1963), pp. 1–36.

interested in prayer and the confessional than in giving medicines, enemas, or the like, or in washing the patients and cutting their hair. Furthermore, the nursing nuns acknowledged no authority except that of their ecclesiastical superior, having been reported as often flouting the instructions of doctors—even tearing up the doctor's prescriptions if they didn't like them. Because of their attitude, it was difficult to perform postmortems in the hospital, sometimes difficult to do a venesection, give emetics, and even mineral waters. The nuns were reported to have covered their eyes during delivery so as not to see the anus of a newborn child, to have resisted treatment of venereal disease, and to have avoided attending unmarried mothers. They were sent away from Hôtel-Dieu in 1908 only to return later with state diplomas and secular licenses.

In the monastic orders we find full-time nurses who visit the home to give bedside care and, more important, stay in hospitals to give bedside care to patients. The problem lay in the content of their care, which was not schooled in some set of paramedical techniques, and which was motivated by spiritual rather than natural therapeutic intent. In addition, the authority for their care was not medical, so that even when medical knowledge advanced bedside care stood still. In these nurses, then, we find a full-time occupation fundamentally outside of the medical division of labor even though working in physical proximity with physicians and surgeons, an occupation that is "nursing" but that is not paramedical.

Historically, the bedside ministrations of nuns were at least respectable. Their charitable, religious impulses dignified what was in fact very dirty work—until recently, hospitals were for the extremely poor, and any respectable person stayed at home when he was ill. Religious impulses could dignify the job of caring for such a pariah, though such care even today comes close to being body-servant work performed by chambermaid, valet, barber, and waiter. Such tasks are especially difficult to dignify when they are performed for the lowest strata of society, for while some may consider it to be a privilege to remove the garters of a king, no one feels privileged by changing the sheets of an illiterate tubercular. Services to such people could be dignified as a special form of self-abasement, but not as merely a job.

The secular nurse, like the monastic nurse, was not especially schooled in techniques of bedside care and had no clear technical relationship to the practice of hospital medical care. Furthermore, unlike the monastic nurse, she lacked any basis for public respect. By the nineteenth century in England, at least, hospital nursing was dominated by the stereotype of drunken and degraded Sairey Gamp, quite outside the respectable medical division of labor. But during that century, both in England and elsewhere, marked changes occurred in the occupation that made it an integral part of the paramedical division of labor. Analysis of those changes and their significance might be aided by examining in detail the special case of England, which was graced by Florence Nightingale.[12]

Florence Nightingale noted that "on February 7, 1837, God spoke to me and called me to His service." Since she was a Protestant, she had no spiritual director who could channel her energy into a monastic order, and since she did not initially know what God called her for, she spent some time trying to find her mission. Five years after her call, she heard of the work of a German pastor who was undertaking the unusual task of giving technical nursing training. Two years after that, she realized that her call was to help the sick in hospitals. She also came to believe, quite contrary to the prevailing notions of her time, that a good nurse must undergo special training in a number of skills, that being merely a tender woman is not enough to be a good nurse. She therefore wanted to go to Germany to learn nursing from Pastor Fliedner, but her family was so horrified at the idea that not until nine years after she heard of the pastor was she able to take training from him.

In 1853 she was again in England as superintendent of the Institution for the Care of Sick Gentlewomen in Distressed Circumstances. At that institution, neither improper patients nor surgery students were allowed entrance. As a gentlewoman administering an institution in which other gentlewomen gave nursing care, she was confronted by the problem of being a lady as opposed to being a nurse: Can a lady take orders from a physician? Should a lady nurse a nonlady? Should a lady be present at physical examina-

[12] For my discussion of Nightingale I rely mainly on Cecil Woodham-Smith, *Florence Nightingale* (New York: McGraw-Hill Co., 1951). Abel-Smith, *op. cit.*, was also useful.

tions? These questions, though based on questions of social status rather than religious obedience, were generically the same as those asked by nuns in earlier time, for they point to the primacy of being a lady or a nun over being a nurse. Nursing was not itself a self-sufficient occupational role or identity, independent of other roles.

The Crimean War gave Nightingale the opportunity to leave her post as superintendent and to organize a contingent of nurses to care for the wounded near the battleground. She was given absolute control of a contingent of nuns, bawdy women, and Anglican sisters. Her first efforts were to strip them of any femininity they had and place them above moral reproach. She gave them ugly uniforms, refused to allow them to wear any ornaments, forbade them to go out except in the company of another member of the contingent, and rationed alcohol.

Armed with her nurses and with money raised by public subscription, she entered Scutari and was confronted by the appalling suffering of the wounded troops. But the military physicians refused to use either the nurses or the money from the public subscription. Nightingale in turn refused to allow any of her nurses to undertake to give any service at all on their own initiative. Her nurses' services were to be granted only when specifically requested by the doctors. No nurse could give food to any patient without the doctor's written order. No nurse could soothe or clean a patient without the doctor's order. Nuns were forbidden to engage in religious visiting. Nightingale thus required that what the nurse did for the patient was a function of what the doctor felt was required for the care of the patient. Even such unskilled tasks as feeding a patient were thus defined as part of the medical regimen. All nursing work flowed from the doctor's orders, and thus nursing became a formal part of the doctor's work, a technical trade rather than a "natural" practice of femininity or a part of the exercise of charitable impulses. *Nursing thus was defined as a subordinate part of the technical division of labor surrounding medicine.*

When her nursing services were finally used at Scutari they were a great success, and on her return to England in 1860 Florence Nightingale found herself a public heroine. A subscription established the Nightingale Fund, to be used to establish a training school for this new type of nurse. Physicians were not very enthusiastic about the training school, and one eminent one, South, wrote, "As regards the nurses or Ward-maids, these are in much the same position as housemaids, and require little teaching beyond that of poultice-making." [13] But in spite of this lack of enthusiasm on the part of some, the training school was founded, and a new kind of nurse emerged from it. Nightingale's trainees were placed as supervisors or matrons in hospitals so that they would then be able to train those already working in hospitals. Her special trainees were carefully selected for their social class and their morals and were deliberately trained as technical personnel.

Florence Nightingale believed that the issue of ladies being nurses, or nurses ladies, was theoretically irrelevant, as was the matter of being a dedicated servant of humanity. What was critical was character, ability, and training. Given able recruits, she devoted herself to training nurses and developing their character. Her emphasis on *both* character and substantive training led her to oppose the 1886 proposal that a body of examiners of nurses be created independently of the training schools to approve nurses and establish the basis for an official register of nurses. While technical knowledge could be tested by examination, character could not; only the personal recommendation of the training-school matron, which takes character into consideration equally with education, is to be relied upon.

Nightingale's position on examination and registry had the effect of supporting a very personal sponsorship structure in nursing careers. Any number of nurses could get a diploma, but only those close to highly regarded and powerful nursing-school matrons could get the good jobs. The others entered private-duty nursing. The problem was then, as it still is today in a number of fields, that while nursing diplomas from different schools could mean quite different things, the uninformed prospective employers could not perceive the difference, since each is a diploma. Without some general system of examination, furthermore, there is no set of minimum standards serving as the common denominator of diplomas from varied schools. In the United States, for example, diploma mills

[13] Quoted in Woodham-Smith, *op. cit.*, p. 233.

arose for nursing as they did for medicine, and hospital schools were prone to exploit the cheap labor of nursing students rather than to instruct them.[14] Employers outside the personal sponsorship system had no guarantee that a nurse with a diploma met basic standards. Pressures mounted for registration and certification so that registration began to occur in the United States by 1903. But Nightingale's continued resistance to the idea in Great Britain was so powerful that registration did not occur until 1919. However, neither legally nor sociologically did these events create a secure occupation.

The Dilemmas of Nursing

By the turn of the century nursing had become a full-fledged occupation, rather than a sideline of gentility or charity, and a fairly dignified occupation with a status independent of the clientele it served. As first established, its "code" stressed skillful and intelligent execution of the doctor's orders, but in time the question began to be raised: "Are we subservient, or do we make intelligent responses to instructions?" The leaders of nursing came to be concerned that nursing be neither a dilution of medicine nor an accretion of the functions medicine has sloughed off. While nursing originally established itself as a full-fledged occupation of some dignity by tying itself to the coattails of medicine, it has come to be greatly concerned with finding a new, independent position in the division of labor.

One of its dilemmas, however, lies in the fact that its work can no longer be controlled by the occupation itself. Most nursing takes place inside the hospital, where nursing has not achieved autonomy. Outside the hospital the position of the private-duty nurse is entrepreneurial but is dependent nonetheless on the physician's standing orders and on the orders of the patient and his family. In the United States, few states require that all who nurse for hire must meet specific standards. Indeed, the requirement of specific standards is in any case unenforceable because of the very vague line between domestic work and nursing in the absence of a physician's instruc-

[14] See Mary Roberts, *American Nursing: History and Interpretation* (New York: The Macmillan Co., 1954), for this and other material bearing on the nursing problems perceived by the leadership of the occupation.

tions defining the latter. The only real way in which nursing standards can be maintained in private homes is by the line drawn by attending physicians: they can tolerate a domestic nursemaid to help their patient in one home and demand a registered nurse in another, depending on the medical needs they perceive. The nursing occupation cannot set such standards, let alone enforce them.

In any case, the old private-duty nurse who attended people at home is becoming rare now, and most private duty nursing is carried out in hospital. Some of the old home nurse's functions are being taken over by the visiting and the public health nurse. Unlike the former, however, public health nurses operate as agents of an organization which assumes responsibility for nursing practices. It is no longer necessary to get on a doctor's list of private-duty nurses, but it is now necessary to get a job in an organization that administers nursing services. The hospital nurse, of course, is even more obviously dependent on an organization. In or out of the hospital, the nurse today is typically required to become part of an organization in order to get work and depends upon the doctor's orders and requirements to delineate which tasks belong to nursing and which not. And the demanding patient can still make her feel like a servant. This is symptomatic of the secondary or assistant role she plays in the medical division of labor.

But nursing is moving toward new tasks. Prior to 1900, one could hardly point to the nurse as anything more than a willing and obedient servant. But as anesthetist and surgical assistant first, then as implementer of an increasingly precise and complex internal medicine—keeping precise charts, drawing and giving blood, dispensing drugs, and the like—the nurse had to become a surrogate doctor on occasion, familiar with part of the general theory and procedures of modern medicine in order to carry out the doctor's orders. As the sheer quantity of tasks around the patient's bed increased, however, the nurse tended to drop her traditional bedside tasks and moved toward supervision.[15] Specialties developed, a hierarchy grew up among them, and entirely new kinds of nurses emerged, some of whom, as "subprofessionals," took over traditional

[15] For an extended review of research studies, and a pointed expression of sociological changes in nursing, see Everett C. Hughes *et al.*, *Twenty Thousand Nurses Tell Their Story* (Philadelphia: J. B. Lippincott Co., 1958).

nursing tasks. The licensed practical nurse in the United States, equipped with one year of technical training, is among the latter.

The development of new occupations around nursing has naturally raised the question of their relationship to nursing. Understandably, the attempt by nursing is more to define a subordinate and restricted role than to create a full-fledged colleague, creating a paranursing hierarchy within the paramedical hierarchy. Graphic expression of this effort is to be found in the 1951 statement of the Joint Committee on Practical Nurse and Auxiliary Workers in Nursing Services:

> The practical nurse is a person trained to care for selected, subacutely and chronically ill patients, and to assist the professional nurse in a team relationship, especially in the care of those more acutely ill. She provides nursing service in institutions and in private homes where she is prepared to give household assistance where necessary. . . . A practical nurse works only under the direct orders of a licensed physician or the supervision of a registered professional nurse.[16]

In spite of the wishful clarification of relationships by such statements, studies reviewed by Hughes[17] indicate that even nursing aides with no formal training to speak of sometimes prepare and give medications and even start intravenous fluids. And in small, rural, proprietary or religious hospitals, Habenstein and Christ found registered nurses mowing the lawn and keeping financial records.[18] Without clear control over access to work or over the work to be performed, no occupation can expect much more, even though in a time of high demand and low nurse supply, workers can avoid the really unpleasant jobs and even practice the job-jumping which has been called "touristry."[19]

16 Quoted in Roberts, *op. cit.*, p. 459.

17 Hughes *et al.*, *op. cit.*

18 See R. W. Habenstein and E. A. Christ, *Professionalizer, Traditionalizer, Utilizer: An Interpretive Study of the Work of the General Duty Nurse in Non-Metropolitan Central Missouri General Hospitals* (Columbia, Missouri: University of Missouri, 1955).

19 Ruth H. Pape, "Touristry: A Type of Occupational Mobility," *Social Problems*, XI (1964), 336–344.

In all, we see nursing as an incompletely closed occupation in a state of change. Its roots in the doctor's work and authority led it to the sickbed and the paramedical division of labor, but its shucking of bedside care and its search for supervisory responsibility as a symbol of professionalism is now leading it away from the patient. In the United States the nurse may be aligning herself with hospital administration and uprooting her relation to medicine as such. This may be seen in part as a response to blocked mobility, for while as a bedside nurse she cannot avoid subordination to physicians, as an administrator she can. Administration is predicated on fairly general skills over which no occupation has as yet any monopoly: by forsaking the particularistic skills of nursing and moving into administrative positions the nurse may move up the hierarchy and attain equality with if not superordination to those in the medical hierarchy. We can therefore understand why it is that nurses who are preoccupied with attaining a fully independent status attempt to deprecate the Nightingale skills of bedside care—what was once called "nursing"—pass them on to lesser workers, and specialize in administrative work. The practice of traditional nursing skills is ultimately contingent on the judgment of a superordinate profession and so cannot constitute the basis for autonomy.[20]

Paraprofessional Professionalism

The curious dilemma of nursing is that it may be seen to be forsaking the tasks distinctive to it in order to change its position in the paramedical division of labor, a position carefully legitimated by its relation to medicine. To escape subordination to medical authority, it must find some area of work over which it can claim and maintain a monopoly, but it must do so in a setting in which the central task *is* healing and controlled by medicine. That is the problem of all paraprofessions in the medical division of labor.

Even if nursing is not representative of the whole range of occupations that fall into the paramedical division of labor, it does present a case typical of the problem of paramedical work in

20 See the interesting case of Israel, briefly noted by Ben-David, where nurses were initially very strong but then sank down into "the same struggle for status as . . . elsewhere," having been "deprofessionalized." Joseph Ben-David, "Professionals and Unions in Israel," *Industrial Relations*, V (1965), 54a.

general and indicative of some of the strategic elements of the paramedical division of labor. The major occupational problem of paramedical workers stems from their paramedical status, which obliges them to work under the direction of the physician because their work is given legitimacy by its relationship to the physician's work. They must either learn to find satisfaction in such subordination or find some independent source of legitimacy. In the former case they remain part of the medically dominated hierarchy that composes the major part of the present paramedical division of labor; in the latter, if successful, they assume a position outside though parallel to the medical hierarchy. Given the historical development of the formal organization of the division of labor, whereby the physician has prime and sometimes sole license to perform or order therapeutic procedures, tests, and drugs—a license reinforced by the authoritative identity of the physician in the public eye—the structure is quite conservative. But given the proliferation of paramedical technologies and tasks, the aspirations of old and new occupations, and the increasing complexity of the system grown up to administer those services, the structure, while more conservative than many others, is nonetheless embattled and vulnerable to challenge.

However, it seems that no small part of the stability of the structure is provided by *professionalism*, whereby subordinate occupations claim to the public and to themselves that they have worthy tasks of service and evidence the personal qualities of professionals. Indeed, the claim is to be a profession as such, if only by identification with the real profession of medicine. Subordination to the core profession is dignified by the task of therapy in which all occupations of the paramedical division of labor play some part, however small. Consider the following manifestation of that claim:

> I am a Medical Technologist, a thinking individual, able to work with my mind as well as with my hands. There is compensation in my work. In being a part of that profession whose end is the mental and physical well-being of mankind, my share lies in the performance of those technics whose results the physician will follow through and correlate with his clinical findings.

> Whether I plan to practice the profession of medical technology for one year or for the remainder of the time I am physically and mentally able, I shall use the same meticulous care in the performance of the tests as I would if upon the results depended the well-being of a member of my own family.
>
> As a medical technologist it is not my purpose or function to render a diagnosis, but to foster cooperation with the physician to whom laboratory data is indispensable.
>
> As a medical technologist, I am proud, with a pride that is tinctured with a true humility, with a pride in being one of the trio in the medical profession, the physician, the nurse, and the medical technologist, each of whom functions in his distinct way.
>
> As a medical technologist, I am independent, with a cooperative spirit in working with my fellows in the medical profession. I do not want to encroach upon anyone else's premises.[21]

Obviously, such a statement is intended to give dignity and pride to a subordinate worker. It includes careful identification of the occupation as, if not a profession, then at least *part* of a profession. It presumes to impute to itself the skill and ethicality of a profession. But clearly, the occupation is not in the same position in the division of labor as is medicine, a fact which is not changed by its members performing their work in the spirit of service and ethicality said to characterize members of professions. The occupation lacks the autonomy to control its own work, being instead subject to the orders and evaluation of other, superior occupations in the medical division of labor. Empirical measures of such subordination need not hinge solely on the interoccupational relations in various medical organizations, that is, on whether the worker "takes orders." Other measures can be determined by examining the character of their occupational associations[22] and by

[21] Reprinted from the *American Journal of Medical Technologists,* in *Hospital Management,* LXXXV (1958), 122.

[22] See the recent interesting paper, Ronald L. Akers and Richard Quinney, "Differential Organization of Health Professions: A Comparative Analysis," *American Sociological Review,* XXXIII (1968), 104–121, where medicine, dentistry, optometry, pharmacy, and chiropractic are compared.

examining the character of licensing procedures, including the occupational composition of licensing boards.[23]

Professions and Professionalism

My discussion in this chapter has led from consideration of the division of labor surrounding healing to evaluation of the analytical characteristics of the occupations fixed in the organization of the division of labor. While it is dangerous to assume too much fixity in organization since, in the United States in particular, many occupations are aggressively seeking to improve their prestige and position, nonetheless the comprehensiveness of its scope and the strategic importance of its focus virtually guarantees medicine's superiority over others. An aggressive occupation like nursing can have its own schools for training, can control licensing boards in many instances, and can have its own "service" in hospital, in this way giving the appearance of formal, state-supported, and departmental autonomy, but the work which its members perform remains subject to the order of another occupation. Legally and otherwise the physician's right to diagnose, cut and prescribe is the center around which the work of many other occupations swings, and the physician's authority and responsibility in that constellation of work are primary. As the case of nursing shows, those paramedical occupations which are ranged round the physician cannot fail to be subordinate in authority and responsibility and, so long as their work remains medical in character, cannot gain occupational autonomy no matter how intelligent and aggressive its leadership. To attain the autonomy of a profession, the paramedical occupation must control a fairly discrete area of work that can be separated from the main body of medicine and that can be practiced without routine contact with or dependence on medicine. Few if any of the present paramedical occupations deal with such potentially autonomous areas.

Consideration of the medical division of labor, then, yields yet another structural or organizational distinction to be made among occupations, a distinction which should, to my mind, be reflected

[23] A recent (and revealing) compendium is "State Licensing of Health Occupations," U.S. Public Health Service Publication No. 1758 (Washington, D.C.: U.S. Government Printing Office, 1968).

in the usage of the word "profession." Just as the contingencies of work of a consulting "profession" are objectively different from those of a scholarly "profession," in that the survival of the former but not the latter depends upon the free choice of individual, lay clients, so the position of the medical "profession" in the division of labor is objectively different from that of the nursing "profession." One is autonomous, and the other is not; one gives orders to all and takes orders from none, while the other gives orders to some and takes orders from others. Surely such a difference is of sufficient analytic significance to warrant separating the two kinds of occupation.

Finally may be mentioned a variable that is frequently connected with professions and that is apparently *not* differentiated by the structural distinctions I have pointed to. I refer to "professionalism," which may be defined as a set of attributes said to be characteristic of professionals. It is said to include such attitudes as commitment to one's work as a career so that one's work becomes part of one's identity and an emphasis on public service rather than private profit. As a collection of personal values or attitudes, it is analytically distinct from the structural attributes that I have been dealing with. Furthermore, it does not seem to be able to distinguish occupations in the medical division of labor so clearly as the structural variables, since there is little doubt that many members of such subordinate occupations as nursing manifest the same attitudes of professionalism as do members of the medical profession. While it may be that *more* physicians than nurses, aides, or medical technologists manifest professionalism—a fact that has not been empirically established—the difference is one of degree, while the structural differences among them are more definite and absolute. Indeed, professionalism seems to be able to exist independently of professional status. Thus, paramedical occupations hold a distinctly subordinate position in a complex division of labor dominated by a profession, a position whose character is at once obscured and made palatable by the claim of professionalism.

4.

THE FORMAL CHARACTERISTICS OF A PROFESSION

WHAT are the formal characteristics of the profession of medicine? In the most elementary sense, the profession is a group of people who perform a set of activities which provide them with the major source of their subsistence—activities which are called "work" rather than "leisure" and "vocation" rather than "avocation." Such activities are performed for compensation, not for their own sake. They are considered to be useful or productive, which is why those who perform them are compensated by others. When a number of people perform the same activity and develop common methods, which are passed on to new recruits and come to be conventional, we may say that workers have been organized into an occupational group, or an occupation. In the most general classification, a profession is an occupation.

However, a profession is usually taken to be a special kind of occupation, so that it is necessary to develop analytically useful distinctions between the profession and other occupations. I have argued that the most strategic distinction lies in legitimate, organized autonomy—that a profession is distinct from other occupations in that it has been given the right to control its own work. Some occupations, like circus jugglers and magicians, possess a de facto autonomy by virtue of the esoteric or isolated character of their work, but their autonomy is more accidental than not and is subject to change should public interest be aroused in it. Unlike other occupations, professions are *deliberately* granted autonomy, including the exclusive right to determine who can legitimately do its work and how the work should be done. Virtually all occupations struggle to obtain both rights, and some manage to seize them, but only the profession is *granted* the right to exercise them legitimately. And while no occupation can prevent employers, customers, clients, and other workers from evaluating its work, only the profession has the recognized right to declare such "outside" evaluation illegitimate and intolerable.

The Source of Professional Status

Obviously, an occupation does not "naturally" come by so unusual a condition as professional autonomy. The work of one group commonly overlaps, even competes, with that of other occupations. Given the ambiguity of much of reality, and given the role of taste and values in assessing it, it is unlikely that one occupation would be chosen spontaneously over others and granted the singular status of a profession by some kind of a popular vote. Medicine was certainly not so chosen. A profession attains and maintains its position by virtue of the protection and patronage of some elite segment of society which has been persuaded that there is some special value in its work. Its position is thus secured by the political and economic influence of the elite which sponsors it—an influence that drives competing occupations out of the same area of work, that discourages others by virtue of the competitive advantages conferred on the chosen occupation, and that requires still others to be subordinated to the profession. As I have shown, the position of medicine was so established, from the rise of the university to our day.

If the source of the special position of the profession is granted, then it follows that professions are occupations unique to high civilizations, for there it is common to find not only full-time specialists but also elites with organized control over large populations.[1] Further, the work of the chosen occupation is unlikely to

[1] For an important attempt to conceptualize "the patterned distribution and control of knowledge in a society," see Burkart Holzner, *Reality Construction in Society* (Cambridge: Schenkman Publishing Co., 1968).

have been singled out if it did not represent or express some of the important beliefs or values of that elite—some of the established values and knowledge of the civilization. In the case of medieval medicine, it was its connection with the ancient learning that singled it out. Furthermore, since it is chosen by the elite, the work of the profession need have no necessary relationship to the beliefs or values of the average citizen. But once a profession is established in its protected position of autonomy, it is likely to have a dynamic of its own, developing new ideas or activities which may only vaguely reflect and which may even contradict those of the dominant elite. The work of the profession may thus eventually diverge from that expected by the elite. If a profession's work comes to have little relationship to the knowledge and values of its society, it may have difficulty surviving. The profession's privileged position is given by, not seized from, society, and it may be allowed to lapse or may even be taken away.[2] It is essential for survival that the dominant elite remain persuaded of the positive value, or at least the harmlessness, of the profession's work, so that it continues to protect it from encroachment.

Consulting and Scholarly Professions

Some kinds of work require for their performance the cooperation of laymen and require for their survival some degree of popularity with laymen: they are practicing or consulting occupations which must sustain a direct, continuous relationship with a lay clientele. Work involving a clientele has consequences for occupational organization which are markedly different from work which does not. In the former case the worker must contend with clients who are from *outside* the occupational community and who therefore may not be familiar or sympathetic with his occupation's ideas and practices. In the latter case the worker must contend on a daily

[2] It can be argued that *as an occupation* the ministry has lost its professional position, particularly in countries where there is no state religion. In the United States the occupation controls ordination in individual churches but neither entrance into the occupation as such nor access to the legal privileges of the occupation (e.g., to perform a marriage ceremony). It is as if doctors could control entrance into and work in particular hospitals but not the development of competing hospitals or entrance into the occupation by those working at such hospitals.

basis only with his colleagues and other workers from *within* the occupational community. In the former case the survival of the occupation depends upon bridging the gap between worker and layman. Bridging the gap between worker and lay client is much more of a problem than bridging the gap between workers.

It is in the case of applied work, particularly work involving a broadly based lay clientele, that formal, legal controls are most likely to be imposed.[3] Only applied work is likely to have immediate consequences in human affairs, and some can be serious. When the public is considered too inexpert to be able to evaluate such work, those dominating society may feel that the public needs protection from unqualified or unscrupulous workers. Having been persuaded that one occupation is most qualified by virtue of its formal training and the moral fiber of its members, the state may exclude all others and give the chosen occupation a legal monopoly that may help bridge the gap between it and laymen, if only by restricting the layman's choice. The outcome is support of the profession by licensure or some other formal device of protecting some workers and excluding others. Licensing is much less likely to occur on behalf of the scholar or the scientist, for they are devoted to exploring intellectual systems primarily for the eyes of their colleagues. Nonetheless, in the case of the consulting or practicing professions such a legally exclusive right to work will not assure survival because the work cannot be performed, license or not, without being in some way positively attractive to a lay clientele.

Unlike science and scholarship, which create and elaborate the formal knowledge of a civilization, practicing professions have the task of applying that knowledge to everyday life. Practicing professions are the links between a civilization and its daily life and as such must, unlike science and scholarship, be in some sense joined to everyday life and the average man. Some of this linkage can be politically sustained—as when the legal order permits only one occupation to provide a given service to those seeking it—but some seems to depend upon the attractiveness of the work itself to the average man, upon the direct connection of the work with what the layman considers desirable and appropriate. In the case of medicine

[3] See Holzner, *op. cit.*, for the distinction between specialized knowledge and ideological knowledge.

I have argued that improvement in the pragmatic results of practice, as well as mass education which brought the average man's ideas, knowledge, and norms closer to that of the profession, led to it becoming a successful consulting profession where before it was primarily an officially supported scholarly or scientific profession with a small practice among the elite.

But even if my interpretation of the historical development of the status of medicine is open to question, I hope that my taxonomic point is at once clear and persuasive. The structural differences between scholarly, learned, or scientific "professions" and practicing or consulting "professions" are of much greater consequence to the way each is established and maintained, and to the daily problems of work on the part of their members, than are their similarities. While, in common usage, research scientists and physicians share the name "profession" and some common knowledge, these similarities have few consequences of significance. Indeed, as I shall point out in Chapter 5, even within the single profession of medicine, the differences between "client-dependent" and "colleague-dependent" practices are of critical importance for the way work is performed, and the differences between the practicing and the scientific worker's work experience are of critical importance for the way each looks at himself and his work. That the name "doctor" is shared by all, scientist and physician, practitioner and researcher, should not lead us to assume that they are all the same.

Profession and Paraprofession

Just as the analysis of the development of medicine led to the observation of analytical differences between consulting and scholarly professions, so the analysis of the division of labor surrounding the formal organization of healing tasks led to the observation of structural differences in the position of various occupations in that division of labor. In the case of medicine, the division of labor is not simply a functional arrangement of specialists. Some occupations—dentistry, for example—are autonomous professions in their own right, even if they are not as prestigious as medicine.[4] Others,

[4] Cf. Basil J. Sherlock, "The Second Profession: Parallel Mobilities of the Dental Profession and its Recruits," *Journal of Health and Social Behavior,* X (1969), 41–51.

usually called "paramedical," are part of a division of labor organized into a hierarchy of authority, established and enforced by law, and swinging around the dominant authority and responsibility of the medical profession. Some of the occupations which are subordinate members of the medical division of labor, however, call themselves and are frequently called by others, "professions."

These paramedical occupations, of which nursing is perhaps the most prominent example, are clearly in a markedly different position than is medicine, for while it is legitimate for them to take orders from and be evaluated by physicians, it is not legitimate for them to give orders to and to evaluate physicians. Without such reciprocity we can hardly consider them the equals of physicians. And without the autonomy of physicians we can hardly believe it to be useful for them to be classified as the same type of occupation as the physician. They are specifically and generically occupations organized around a profession—paraprofessional occupations. This in itself makes a distinct species of occupation, particularly when people in such an occupation, given their proximity to a profession, are encouraged to take on professional attributes and to claim to be a profession. But whatever the claim, they do not stand in the same structural position as the profession on which they model themselves.

It might be noted that paraprofessional occupations usually seek professional status by creating many of the same institutions as those which possess professional status. They develop a formal standard curriculum of training, hopefully at a university. They create or find abstract theory to teach recruits. They write codes of ethics. They are prone to seek support for licensing or registration so as to be able to exercise some control over who is allowed to do their work. But what they persistently fail to attain is full autonomy in formulating their training and licensing standards and in actually performing their work. Their autonomy is only partial, being secondhand and limited by a dominant profession. This is the irreducible criterion which keeps such occupations paraprofessions in spite of their success at attaining many of the institutional attributes of professions. And the discriminatory power of full autonomy belies the value of using instead such institutional arrangements as training and licensing. That such arrangements are useful conditions for the development of an autonomous occupation is certain; that they are necessary conditions is moot; that they are sufficient conditions is plainly false.

The Formal Criteria of Profession

In analyzing the position of medicine and its associated occupations I have deliberately avoided adopting most of the criteria of profession used by many writers. Indeed, I have just explicitly denied the importance of training and licensing. This is not the place for a detailed examination and analysis of the many definitions which have been published before and after Cogan's review.[5] It does seem necessary, however, to address the issue, even if briefly. Brevity is facilitated by the fact that no new criteria seem to have been added since Cogan's review, though various commentators, like me, emphasize one rather than another of the old. Furthermore, the parsimonious arrangement of those criteria by the most sophisticated and careful of recent analysts, William J. Goode, allows concentration on essentially two "core characteristics" of professions, from which ten other frequently cited characteristics are said to be derived.[6] These two core characteristics are "a prolonged specialized training in a body of abstract knowledge, and a collectivity or service orientation." [7] Among the "derived characteristics," which are presumably "caused" by the core characteristics, are five which refer to autonomy: "(1) The profession determines its own standards of education and training. . . . (3) Professional practice is often legally recognized by some form of licensure. (4) Licensing and admission boards are manned by members of the profession. (5) Most legislation concerned with the profession is shaped by that profession. . . . (7) The practitioner is relatively free of lay evaluation and control." [8] Obviously, in Goode's analysis, the core characteristics are critical criteria for professions insofar as they are said

[5] Morris I. Cogan, "Toward a Definition of Profession," *Harvard Educational Review*, XXIII (1953), 33–50.

[6] William J. Goode, "Encroachment, Charlatanism, and the Emerging Profession: Psychology, Medicine, and Sociology," *American Sociological Review*, XXV (1960), 902–914.

[7] *Ibid.*, p. 903.

[8] *Ibid.*, p. 903.

to be causal in producing professional autonomy as I have defined it, and many of the attributes others have specified. Let us look at them closely to see if this is so.

What precisely are the empirical referents of those core characteristics? In the first, training, are concealed at least three problems of specification—"prolonged," "specialized," "abstract." Since all training takes some time, how prolonged must training be to qualify? Since all training is somewhat specialized, how does one determine whether it is specialized enough to qualify? Since "abstract" is a relative rather than absolute term, how does one determine whether training is abstract or theoretical enough? It is difficult if not impossible to answer these questions with any reasonable degree of precision. Furthermore, I suggest that any answer one makes will fail to include all occupations clearly agreed to be professions or exclude all occupations clearly agreed not to be professions. Taking the three traditional professions of medicine, law, and the ministry, the range of variation in length of training (particularly in the ministry), the degree of specialization, and the amount and type of theory and abstract knowledge (particularly in the case of law) is in each case sufficiently wide that many other occupations not recognized as professions would fall within it. Nursing, for example, which is specifically excluded from the professions by Goode on the basis of training, falls within the range manifested by the three established professions.

Significantly, however, Goode excludes nursing because he feels its training is no more than "a lower-level medical education,"[9] which implies more the lack of autonomy it is supposed to produce than the specific attributes of nurse training. That is, it is not what nurses learn or how long it takes, but the fact that the bulk of what they learn is ultimately specified by physicians which is important. The objective content and duration of training is considerably less critical than occupational *control* over training. Indeed, in his analysis of the training of the librarian in another paper, Goode's comments rely most heavily on the issue of control—specifying that the occupation must help create the knowledge, "must be the final arbiter in any dispute about what is or is not valid knowledge," and

[9] *Ibid.*, p. 903.

must "largely [control] access to it through control over school admissions, school curriculums, and examinations." [10]

Thus, not training as such, but only the issue of autonomy and control over training granted the occupation by an elite or public persuaded of its importance seems to be able to distinguish clearly among occupations. Pharmacy and optometry, for example, have the same minimum period of training and probably the same degree of specialization and abstract knowledge (so far as one can specify proportion and quantity for such terms). However, in most states the trained optometrist may legally diagnose (e.g., do refractions) and prescribe (order, make, and fit corrective lenses), while the trained pharmacist may not; the optometrist is clearly moving much closer to professional autonomy while the pharmacist is firmly subordinated to medicine.[11] It does not seem to be the actual content of training that explains or produces the differences. As I suggested in my analysis of the medical division of labor, the possibilities for functional autonomy and the relation of the work of an occupation to that of dominant professions seem critical. And the process determining the outcome is essentially political and social rather than technical in character—a process in which power and persuasive rhetoric are of greater importance than the objective character of knowledge, training, and work.

Consonant with the political character of the process, I might point out that the leaders of all aspiring occupations, including nursing, pharmacy, and optometry, insist that their occupations do provide prolonged training in a set of special skills, including training in theory or abstract knowledge which is generic to their field. And they can point to required courses in theory to buttress their assertions. These are institutional facts whose truth cannot be denied, but their meaning is suspect because the content and length of training of an occupation, including abstract knowledge or theory, is frequently a product of the deliberate action of those who are trying to show that their occupation is a profession and should

[10] William J. Goode, "The Librarian: From Occupation to Profession?" in Howard M. Vollmer and Donald L. Mills, eds., *Professionalization* (Englewood Cliffs, New Jersey: Prentice-Hall, Inc., 1966), p. 36.

[11] Cf. Norman R. Denzin and C. J. Mettlin, "Incomplete Professionalization: The Case of Pharmacy," *Social Forces*, XLVI (1968), 375–82.

therefore be given autonomy.[12] If there is no systematic body of theory, it is created for the purpose of being able to say there is. The nature of an occupation's training, therefore, can constitute part of an ideology, a deliberate rhetoric in a political process of lobbying, public relations, and other forms of persuasion to attain a desirable end—full control over its work.

It does not seem to be the objective character of the training that leads to success in some cases and failure in others. A neutral observer like Goode cannot determine whether training is "really" abstract, prolonged, and specialized enough to push the occupation to professional status. It is rather the evaluation of such involved observers as legislators, the public, and representatives of other occupations that is critical to success, and the criteria used by each of these may differ from the other's. The legislator may calculate votes; the public, fears; and other occupations, jobs. While the characteristics of training frequently serve as criteria for licensing and otherwise identifying the members of an occupation, professional and otherwise, then, there seem to be no really definite and objective attributes of content and length of training which inevitably or even mostly precede professional status or distinguish professions from all other occupations.

Problematic as training is as a criterion, it has the virtue of empirical substance. The characteristics of an occupation's training refer to the formal rules and regulations embodied in the laws, regulations, and resolutions connected with political institutions, occupational associations, and educational organizations. The second "core characteristic" specified by Goode, however, and very commonly cited in other definitions, is much more problematic. The "collectivity or service orientation" usually refers to the orientation of the *individual* members of an occupation rather than to organi-

[12] A number of attempts have been made to outline the natural history of occupations aspiring to professional status. See, for example, Everett C. Hughes, *Men and Their Work* (New York: The Free Press of Glencoe, 1958); Theodore Caplow, *The Sociology of Work* (Minneapolis: University of Minnesota Press, 1954); Harold L. Wilensky, "The Professionalization of Everyone?" *American Journal of Sociology*, LXX (1964), 137–158. See also Corinne Lathrop Gilb, *Hidden Hierarchies, The Professions and Government* (New York: Harper & Row, 1966) for a number of comments on the way political status is developed by professions.

zations. But clearly, the attitudes of individuals constitute an entirely different kind of criterion than the attributes of occupational institutions. Unlike the latter, which can be determined empirically by the examination of legislation, administrative regulations, and other formal documents including prescribed curricula, the attitudes of individuals must be determined by the direct study of individuals.

The actual existence of professional training institutions, the number of years and the nature of the courses required for a degree, and the nature of examinations required for a license are certainly established as facts. But curiously enough, there appears to be no reliable information which actually demonstrates that a service orientation is in fact strong and widespread among professionals. The three kinds of data needed for such demonstration are missing: we do not know what proportion of professionals manifests a service orientation and with what intensity; we do not have information on the degree to which a service orientation is more intense and more widely distributed among professionals than other orientations; and we do not know whether the distribution and intensity of a service orientation among professionals is greater than that among other types of workers. Even when one is quite willing to stretch the points of the scanty and inelastic data available, the blunt fact is that discussions of professions assume or assert *by definition* and without supporting empirical evidence that "service orientation" is especially common among professionals. As I shall indicate in a later chapter, I do not deny the reality of a service orientation as such (though it would be good to demonstrate it empirically) so much as I deny its distinct, exclusive, or predominant possession by professional occupations. I have already pointed out that, as part of "professionalism," it can be fairly widespread among occupations which are not autonomous and which are not likely to be so in the future. Goode, in fact, agrees that while nursing has not become a profession, it does have nevertheless a service orientation. As a criterion of "profession," it is therefore of little value.

But a service orientation need not be considered to be an attribute of individual workers. On a different level of abstraction it can be considered to be an *institutional* attribute of an occupation. As a formal characteristic of an occupation, it is a claim about the membership as a body. The claim, of course, is also made by paraprofessions and by many other kinds of occupational organizations including trade unions and trade associations. As a property of occupational institutions, it too, like training, can be deliberately created so as to attempt to persuade politically important figures of the virtues of the occupation. Perhaps even more than curriculum, it can be created out of whole cloth, to improve the public image of the occupation. Like training, all that may be distinct to professions about a service orientation is *general acceptance of their claim*, acceptance that is fruit of their earlier success at persuasion. As Goode put it, "Only to the extent that the society believes the profession is regulated by this collectivity orientation will it grant the profession much autonomy or freedom from lay supervision and control."[13] Other occupations may actually have as great a proportion of members with such an orientation—that is not the issue. They may have codes of ethics, oaths, and other institutional attributes reflecting such an orientation—that, too, is not the issue. *The profession's service orientation is a public imputation it has successfully won in a process by which its leaders have persuaded society to grant and support its autonomy*. Such imputation does not mean that its members more commonly or more intensely subscribe to a service orientation than members of other occupations.

Formal Institutions and Professional Performance

In this chapter I have been arguing that the only truly important and uniform criterion for distinguishing professions from other occupations is the fact of autonomy—a position of legitimate control over work. That autonomy is not absolute, depending for its existence upon the toleration and even protection by the state and not necessarily including all zones of occupational activity. As I have shown in my comparison of the profession in three different nations, the single zone of activity in which autonomy *must* exist in order for professional status to exist is in the content of the work itself. Autonomy is the critical outcome of the interaction between political and economic power and occupational representation, interaction sometimes facilitated by educational institutions and other

[13] Goode, "The Librarian," *op. cit.*, p. 37.

devices which successfully persuade the state that the occupation's work is reliable and valuable.

Furthermore, I have argued that there is no stable institutional attribute which inevitably leads to such a position of autonomy. In one way or another, through a process of political negotiation and persuasion, society is led to believe that it is desirable to grant an occupation the professional status of self-regulative autonomy. The occupation's training institutions, code of ethics, and work are attributes which frequently figure prominently in the process of persuasion but are not individually or in concert, invariably, or even mostly, persuasive as *objectively determinable attributes.* It may be true that the public and/or a strategic elite always come to believe that the training, ethics, and work of the occupation they favor have some exclusive qualities, but this is a consequence of the process of persuasion rather than of the attributes themselves, and the attributes may not be said to be either "causes" of professional status or objectively unique to professions.[14]

With few exceptions, my discussion in this chapter has restricted itself almost entirely to the institutional, or formal, level of analysis, dealing with the profession as an organization, part of the larger organization of the state and of the social division of labor. If any individual men figured in the discussion, it was as spokesmen for the profession, leaders in negotiation and persuasion and in the creation and administration of professional associations, training institutions, and work organizations, not as men doing the characteristic everyday work of the profession. This level of analysis is perfectly appropriate for understanding the development of an occupation and its present-day organization, for it specifies the political, legal, and interoccupational structure which sets the general limits within which practitioners may work.

Formal criteria of profession thus establish the framework within which the behavior of all professional individuals takes place. But they are not able to specify whether or not individuals differ in their work performance, whether or not there are systematic differ-

[14] It may be noted that this argument is similar to, and in any case indebted to, that in Howard S. Becker, "The Nature of a Profession," National Society for the Study of Education, *Education for the Professions* (Chicago: National Society for the Study of Education, 1962), pp. 24–46.

ences, and, if so, what is the nature and source of systematic difference. On the formal level, all individuals are the same in that they have all met minimal standards in being recruited and trained, and so in being allowed to practice protected from some kinds of competition, and from the direction and evaluation of others. By such formal criteria, only variation in the ability, character, or other personal characteristics of individuals explains variation in performance. Essentially, such formal criteria do not really carry us over to performance or behavior as such. Such a connection, I believe, is provided only by the concrete and organized settings in which work and performance takes place. The broad limits to those work settings are dictated by the formal characteristics of the profession and its position in the polity and the economy, but their concrete structure is something to be analyzed in and of itself. Once the structure of work settings can be specified, I suggest, it becomes possible to understand and predict systematic variation in the work performance of professionals.

In the next part of this book I shall devote myself to a detailed examination of the professional work settings of medicine, with an eye to their relationship to professional performance. Since some variation is likely to be technically or ethically inappropriate—there being no reason to believe that the normal curve of the distribution of a trait through a population does not apply to professional populations—my analysis shall emphasize the way professional work settings may control or fail to control deviant performance. The question of control, after all, is the obverse of the question of autonomy, for autonomy is granted the profession with the understanding that it will itself, without outside interference, regulate or control the performance of its members. Just as autonomy is the test of professional status, so is self-regulation the test of professional autonomy.

PART II.

THE ORGANIZATION OF PROFESSIONAL PERFORMANCE

> "Both motives and actions very often originate not from within but from the situation in which individuals find themselves."
>
> —KARL MANNHEIM

5.

EVERYDAY WORK SETTINGS OF THE PROFESSIONAL

IN the interpretation of human affairs there seem to be two distinct and persistent perspectives. There is the view generically characteristic of religionists, educationists, and psychologists—that the kind of person a man is determines how he will behave quite independently of his environment. In moral terms this view holds that the world can be changed only by first directly changing the individual—whether by a gift of grace, by instruction, or by psychotherapy. There is also the view that a man's behavior is a function of the pressures of his environment, that his environment determines his consciousness and how he will behave independently of the kind of person he is. This view holds that the world can be changed by changing people's environment. In the former case the strategy of analysis is to determine what kind of individual is involved in a situation—his personality, his norms or beliefs, his education—and how these attributes influence his behavior. In the latter case the tendency is to examine how variation in environment is associated with variation in individual behavior.

Both orientations, stated so simply, are of course caricatures of what must be a much more complex truth which includes them together. Each, however, does represent a particular strategy of formulation and investigation, a selective emphasis that guides one's attention in the inevitable circumstance of not being able to study everything at once. Of the two orientations, I believe that far too much attention has been paid to the personal characteristics and attitudes of individual members of occupations and far too little to the work-settings. This is particularly the case for the professions. On the whole, students of the professions in general and medicine in particular have adopted the same individualistic value position of the men they study. They have been inclined to postulate and search for personal qualities that are distinctly "professional," qualities manifested in views of work, of self, and of clients which are supposed to be inculcated or at least intensified and stabilized in the course of professional education. Deficient behavior on the part of a professional tends to be explained as the result of being a deficient kind of person, or at least of having been inadequately or improperly "socialized" or educated in professional school. The most commonly suggested remedy for such behavior is reformation of the professional curriculum rather than of the circumstances of professional work: attempts are made to make practicing physicians more interested in dealing with problem patients by teaching them sociology in medical school and to make them interested in a comprehensive approach to the treatment of illness by assigning them to care for whole families in medical school.

Now there is no question at all that the education in attitude and skill that the physician obtains in medical school and in the hospital where he is an intern and resident is an *absolute* source of much of his performance as a practitioner. By that I mean that the difference between physicians and laymen is precisely such special training. Education, therefore, is certainly of great significance, not only for establishing formal criteria for licensing but also for establishing within individual members of the profession a core of knowledge and attitude.[1] Variations among medical institutions and among the students and faculty they recruit [2] are also plausibly connected with some of the variation in the performance of graduates.

[1] For an excellent discussion from this point of view, see Robert K. Merton, "Some Preliminaries to a Sociology of Medical Education," in Robert K. Merton *et al.*, eds., *The Student Physician: Introductory Studies in the Sociology of Medical Education* (Cambridge: Harvard University Press, 1957), pp. 3–79.

[2] For recent examples of studies of variation in schools, see Paul J. Sanazaro, "Research in Medical Education: Exploratory Analysis of a Blackbox,"

Nonetheless I argue that education is a less important variable than work environment. There is some very persuasive evidence that "socialization" does not explain some important elements of professional performance half so well as does the organization of the immediate work environment. Seeman and Evans found that the same individual physicians in a hospital behaved differently when the quality of supervision varied.[3] Peterson and his associates could find little relation between variations in professional education and the technical performance of general practitioners some years after graduation,[4] nor could Clute in a Canadian study of similar character.[5] A quite different study by Price found no relationship between grade-point average in medical school and performance in practice.[6] Piven's study of correctional caseworkers found no significant relation between professionally desirable "therapeutic" orientations to clients and the presence or absence of a professional caseworker education.[7] Carlin found no significant connection between the ethicality of lawyers and the law school they attended.[8] And in a rather unusual longitudinal study, Gray and his associates found that a group of equally "cynical" medical school graduates differed in their later "cynicism" according to the type of practice in which they engaged.[9] Such studies as these provide evidence that quite critical elements of professional behavior—the level of technical per-

---

Annals of the New York Academy of Sciences, CXXVIII (1965), 519–531, including his references to the work of Stern, Schumacher, and Hutchins.

[3] M. E. Seeman and J. W. Evans, "Stratification and Hospital Care," *American Sociological Review,* XXVI (1961), 67–80, 193–204.

[4] Osler L. Peterson *et al., An Analytical Study of North Carolina General Practice, 1953–1954* (Evanston, Illinois: Association of American Medical Colleges, 1956).

[5] Kenneth F. Clute, *The General Practitioner, A Study of Medical Education and Practice in Ontario and Nova Scotia* (Toronto: University of Toronto Press, 1963).

[6] P. B. Price *et al., Performance Measures of Physicians* (Salt Lake City: University of Utah Press, 1963).

[7] Herman Piven, "Professionalism and Organizational Structure," Unpublished D.S.W. dissertation, Columbia University, 1961.

[8] Jerome Carlin, *Lawyers' Ethics, A Survey of the New York City Bar* (New York: Russell Sage Foundation, 1966).

[9] Robert M. Gray *et al.,* "The Effect of Medical Specialization on Physicians' Attitudes," *Journal of Health and Human Behavior,* VII (1966), 128–132.

formance, the approach to the client, "cynicism" and ethicality—do not vary so much with the individual's formal professional training as with the social setting in which he works after his education. They reinforce my belief that it is at once attractively parsimonious and adequately true to assume that a significant amount of behavior is situational in character—that people are constantly responding to the organized pressures of the situations they are in at any particular time, that what they are is not completely but *more* their present than their past, and that what they do is *more* an outcome of the pressures of the situation they are in than of what they have earlier "internalized." [10]

In this chapter, then, I shall begin my analysis of the settings in which members of the profession work with the aim of understanding the major sources of variation in professional performance. Here, I shall concentrate on the everyday office-practice settings in which the bulk of medical care is given. Unfortunately, with a few important exceptions, not very much systematically gathered empirical information about office settings is available, nor has much sustained and systematic attention been paid to conceptualizing the implications of the settings for professional performance.[11] Perhaps part of the problem of conceptualization lies in the enormous variation in settings, from solo, consultative practice to specialized positions in bureaucratic organizations. Complicating the matter further is the existence of a variety of important kinds of interpersonal relations among professions that range from formal professional associations to informal colleague networks—interpersonal relations which cut through any single work setting, joining it to others. Nonetheless, in this chapter I shall attempt to indicate that range and to make some sense out of the variation.

[10] This position has been put more abstractly by Howard S. Becker, "Personal Change in Adult Life," *Sociometry*, XXVII (1964), 40–53.

[11] For some recent reviews, see E. Richard Weinerman, "Patients' Perceptions of Group Medical Care. A Review and Analysis of Studies of Choice and Utilization of Prepaid Group Practice Plans," *American Journal of Public Health*, LIV (1964), 880–889; E. Richard Weinerman, "Research into the Organization of Medical Practice," *Milbank Memorial Fund Quarterly*, LXVI (1966), Part II, 104–145; Kerr L. White, "General Practice in the U.S.," *Journal of Medical Education*, XXXIX (1964), 333–345; Kerr L. White, "Patterns of Medical Practice," in D. W. Clark and B. MacMahon, eds., *Preventive Medicine* (Boston: Little, Brown and Co., 1967), pp. 849–970.

Empirical Types of Practice Organization [12]

Everyday medicine is practiced in privacy. In the other established professions, work goes on in the publicity of the court, the church, and the lecture hall as often as in the office. The work of the doctor is characteristically conducted in the closed consulting room or the bedroom. Furthermore, the physician usually renders personal services to individuals rather than to congregations or classes. Perhaps because of these characteristics medicine is more likely than other established professions to be seen as a simple practitioner-client relationship than as an organization. But it is much more than merely a relationship: medicine is practiced in an organized framework which influences the behavior of both doctors and patients. Indeed, at present in the United States, the framework of practice seems to be moving toward more elaborate forms which may be expected to change the nature of the doctor-patient relationship.

The typical mode of medical practice in the United States is "solo practice." This involves a man working by himself in an office which he secures and equips with his own capital, with patients who have freely chosen him as their personal physician and for whom he assumes responsibility. Stereotypically he lacks any formal connection with colleagues.

But the phrase "solo practice" is as often used in an ideological as in a descriptive mode. It is, as Evang noted, a sacred cow in the medical profession of more than one country.[13] The ideological connotation has interesting analytical implications. One of the central themes is independence—the notion of "professional autonomy" —in which a man can do as he pleases. In order for autonomy to exist, the practitioner must work alone and must have no long-term obligation to his clients; he must be able to sever the relationship to his client at any time, and vice versa; a fee-for-service rather

12 Much of what follows is reprinted from my article, "The Organization of Medical Practice," in *Handbook of Medical Sociology* edited by Howard E. Freeman, Sol Levine, and Leo G. Reeder © 1963. By permission of Prentice-Hall, Inc., Englewood Cliffs, New Jersey.

13 Karl Evang, *Health Service, Society and Medicine* (London: Oxford University Press, 1960).

than a contractual financial arrangment is likely to encourage autonomous practice.

A truly autonomous fee-for-service solo arrangement is inherently unstable, however: it is eventually bound to fall under the control of either patients or colleagues. In a system of free competition the physician may neither count on the loyalty of his patient (with whom he has no contract) nor on that of his colleagues (with whom he has no ties and who are competing with him). Since his colleagues are competitors, he is not likely to solicit their advice or trade information, and he certainly will not refer his patients to them. Under these circumstances, he is quite isolated from his colleagues and relatively free of their control but at the same time he is very vulnerable to control by his clients. To keep them, he must give them what they want—whether tranquilizers, antibiotics or hysterectomies—or someone else will. Obviously, conscientious practice under these conditions is difficult and frustrating. It is hardly accurate to describe it as "autonomy."

Simple restriction of competition by banding together against the tyranny of client choice leads to the alternative tyranny of colleague choice. Realistically, "total autonomy" can result only under very special circumstances. It is plausible to think that when the supply of physicians is sufficiently restricted to fail to meet demand, control by the client may be avoided. If, in addition to a scarcity of physicians and other potential competitors, no large capital is required for initiating a practice, no consultations and no extra-consulting-room institutions like hospitals are necessary for its pursuit, control by colleagues can be avoided and "total autonomy" approached.

In the United States today, the supply of physicians in many areas is such that client control can be avoided; but increasingly, colleague control cannot. Dependence on colleagues in one way or another is the rule today in the United States because consultations, hospitals, and capital equipment are essential to modern practice. In short, present practice is not solo: it embraces a large variety of organized relationships, most of which currently emphasize colleague rather than client controls.

How do cooperative arrangements develop? Let us start with an ostensibly "solo" fee-for-service practice in a situation like that of the United States, where the supply of physicians is at least moderately restricted. Under such circumstances practice is only partially secure because the continual entrance of younger men into a system which does not include predictable retirement of the older practitioner always presents some threat of competition. In answer to the threat, one keeps his patients to himself, but to do this involves a deadly grind of perpetual availability for service. In order to take an evening or weekend off, or a vacation, or in order to be sick, one's practice must be "covered" by colleagues who can be relied on to avoid "stealing" patients. A cooperative arrangement is necessary.

The need for such organization becomes even more pressing when specialization is involved. Patients who must see more than one physician in the normal course of obtaining medical care might become attracted to any one of them and not go back to the man who made the referral. The danger of losing patients by referring them to a young internist seems to have led at least some general practitioners to avoid referring patients at all. In one study of Negro doctors, it was found that some refer patients to white rather than Negro consultants operating under the assumption that whites do not want to keep Negro patients and so will refer them back.[14] Effort to prevent referrals is patently unsatisfactory, however, since the conscientious practitioner on one occasion or another knows that his patient needs help he cannot give himself. He can send some, but not all, patients to a clinic or an out-patient department whose staffs presumably will not "steal" them. A rather natural and conventional solution is to work out a fairly definite reciprocal arrangement: the general practitioner habitually refers his patients to a limited number of specialists who may be trusted to act "ethically" by eventually returning his patients to him, and who, in turn, will refer patients needing general services to him.

The time has passed in the United States when the general practitioner was in a strong enough position to be the key "feeder" to a network of specialists. As the patient has developed more sophistication and the number of accessible specialists has increased, the patient circumvents the general practitioner and seeks out his own specialists. Indeed, the general practitioner's place is being taken by the internist and the pediatrician, and nonprofessional referrals

[14] Cf. Dietrich Reitzes, *Negroes and Medicine* (Cambridge: Harvard University Press, 1958).

are the major source of patients in urban settings for the average ophthalmologist, otorhinolaryngologist and orthopedist, if not also for the obstetrician-gynecologist, allergist, and dermatologist. Since there has ceased to be a single key "feeder" in the division of labor, there is danger of considerable confusion and irregularity in the disposition of the patient. Fairly well-integrated arrangements among physicians become important not only as a way of gaining and regulating access to patients but also as a way of of establishing among physicians regular channels of communication for information about the patient and his illness. The "colleague network" described by Hall may be used as the prototype of such an informal but well-integrated arrangement in American solo practice.[15] Indeed, one may suspect that this network is a strategic mode of regulating recruitment and access to work in all occupations in which objective criteria are not readily available to assess performance. Certainly the colleague network is very important in the academic and legal worlds.

Hall provides a lucid description of the colleague network:

> In so far as the doctors of a given community are established and possess relatively loyal clientele, they form a system. This system can effectively exclude the intruding newcomer. On the one hand they have control of the hospital system through occupying the dominant posts therein. On the other they tend to develop, in the course of time, through association, a sort of informal organization. Rights to position, status, power become recognized and upheld; mechanisms of legitimate succession and patterns of recruitment become established.
>
> The provision of medical facilities in a given community, in so far as a system or an order has been established, depends heavily on such an organization. As a matter of fact, the two matters discussed above, i.e., institutions and clienteles, are intimately related to the working of the informal organization. The allocation of positions in the institutions, the pace at which one receives promotions, the extent to which one has

[15] Oswald Hall, "The Informal Organization of the Medical Profession," *Canadian Journal of Economics and Political Science,* XII (1946), 30–41.

patients referred to him, all hinge on the workings of the informal organization. . . .

Sponsorship is not necessarily a one-sided process. It permits the newcomer to share in the established system of practicing medicine, but it also imposes responsibilities upon him. It obligates him to fulfill the minor positions in the institutional system. Where he needs expert advice or assistance it obligates him to turn to his sponsor. And if he is designated as successor to an established member of the profession he necessarily takes over the duties and obligations involved there. Hence the protege is essential to the continued functioning of the established inner fraternity of the profession.[16]

The kind of network Hall describes is more likely to exist in localities where there is a variety of hospitals and other medical institutions ordered hierarchically, with limited access by physicians. It is much less likely to be so definite and articulated in small cities where hospitals are virtually open community institutions. And even in large cities, the municipal and proprietary institutions at the bottom of the prestige hierarchy provide fairly free access to physicians irrespective of their location in colleague networks.[17] For this reason we can assume that the sociometric studies of Coleman, Katz, and Menzel portray the looser, more common form of colleague network in the United States.[18]

Because it is entirely informal, the colleague network represents the most elementary type of cooperative practice. But it has sufficient weakness to make it uncomfortably vulnerable to collapse. Under the solo system of practice, patients and hospitals are not always completely monopolized. Often the colleague network cannot completely control the treatment environment and so may lack the reliable patronage necessary to gain the cooperation of hungry young men. Furthermore, the good faith among peers upon which an informal system depends may break down in petty jealousies

[16] *Ibid.*, pp. 31–33.

[17] Cf. David Solomon, "Ethnic and Class Differences Among Hospitals as Contingencies in Medical Careers," *The American Journal of Sociology*, LXVI (1961), 463–471.

[18] James Coleman, Elihu Katz, and Herbert Menzel, *Medical Innovation, A Diffusion Study* (Indianapolis: The Bobbs-Merrill Co., 1966).

and antipathies. The large solo practice in the United States has developed some formal techniques of protecting itself. The successful physician may, as Hall suggested, send his overflow to a young physician in whom he takes an interest,[19] but he may and often does avoid sending out any cases at all by hiring the younger man to handle the routine cases and the grueling house and emergency calls. This lightens his burden while it reduces the danger of permanently losing patients. The employer-physician's position is particularly strong when the man he hires is not fully qualified to practice on his own (as is the case with some English medical assistants) or when it is very expensive or otherwise difficult to set up a practice (as is the case where practices must be bought or where competition is severe).

When the junior is in a position to break away and be a competitor, however, the hiring physician is very vulnerable, for each young man he introduces to his patients may take some of those patients with him when he leaves. One way to prevent that is by means of a legal document whereby the younger man agrees not to set up an independent practice in the same community when he does leave. Another way, which by no means rules out the first, is to take the young man into partnership.

The most common type of formal cooperative arrangement among peers is not the partnership, however, but what might be called the *association*—an arrangement whereby physicians share the expense of maintaining such common facilities as offices, equipment, assisting personnel, and the like, while they have their own patients. In addition, it is possible for physicians to "cover" each other by seeing each other's patients during vacations and other absences. In one form or another, this rudimentary type of formal cooperation is very widespread in the United States, particularly in city "professional buildings" with elaborate suites and in "medical arts centers" owned by the resident physicians.

From the association it is a short though by no means simple step to the *small legal partnership* in which profits from fees as well as overhead expenses are shared. The division of pooled fees is likely to be a constant bone of contention, however, since the prac-

[19] Oswald Hall, "Types of Medical Careers," *American Journal of Sociology*, LV (1949), 243–253.

tices of the partners, though overlapping, are not identical. This is particularly the case when specialties are involved, for one specialist may feel he brings in more money than the other and that he accordingly deserves a larger proportion of the profits. Nonetheless, if those problems can be overcome, the partnership is more reliable and more calculable than simpler forms of cooperation. In the colleague network doctors can arrange trustworthy coverage for each other so as to be able to enjoy leisure hours in spite of unpredictable patient demand. In the simple association this virtue is carried over, but the sharing of overhead costs reduces the ordinary expenses of practice per person and makes it possible to have more laboratory and diagnostic equipment. The partnership adds to these virtues its increased long-term financial security. Where practitioners of different ages are involved, the younger man may treat more patients at a time in his career when he could not expect many. In turn, the older man may have a higher income at a time in his career when patients would be retiring him or when he himself would be forced by his decreasing energy to relinquish patients. Moreover, where more than one specialty is involved, each can function as a referring agent to the other, with mutual advantage: the dubious ethics of fee-splitting, often functional in informal cooperative forms, becomes regularized in the partnership without raising an ethical problem. It constitutes some protection against the competition of practitioners outside the cooperative arrangement and also creates a situation where communication among practitioners about the patient is facilitated.

One requirement common to all forms of cooperation is access to a fairly large number of patients. Cooperative practice is comparatively large-scale in character and involves the ordering of expenses, referrals, consultations, and—in the case of partnerships—profits, into a system which meets the demands of a larger number of people than one man alone can handle. The more formal the arrangement, the more systematized and rational it becomes. At a certain point in the expansion of scale, however, a qualitative change in the form of cooperative practice occurs. "*Group practice*" is very often used to designate a form of association that goes beyond the scope connoted by the two-man partnership, but definitions have not been very helpful in delineating such difference. The value of the term, like the value of the term "solo practice," is limited by its ideological overtones. Rather than emphasizing autonomy and independence, the term emphasizes "groupness" and interdependence. But if "medical group practice is a formal association of three or more physicians providing services in more than one medical field or specialty, with income from medical practice pooled and redistributed to the members according to some prearranged plan," as one definition would have it,[20] it is hard to see how it need differ from the partnership except as such partnership does not involve more than one specialty. The difference between a two- and a three-man partnership does not seem sociologically significant, nor does the difference between a two-man partnership and a three-man "group." Since 57 per cent of the medical groups surveyed by Pomrinse and Goldstein had only three to five full-time physicians, obviously a large proportion of what are called "medical groups" are on the surface insignificantly different from partnerships.[21]

If numbers are to be used to define group practice, Jordan's [22] suggestion of the minimum number of five full-time physicians seems reasonable. Five full-time physicians, not all of them giving day-to-day routine medical care, can serve an ordinary population of anywhere from five to twenty thousand, depending on the proportion of general practitioners, internists, and pediatricians, the financial arrangements with patients, and the general style of practice. As the number of patients and doctors increases further, it seems likely that, modified somewhat by the strength of the doctor's bargaining position, some of the technical characteristics of bureaucracy will emerge: hierarchical organization, extensive division of labor, systematic rules and procedures, and the like. In a logically ideal sense, this may be seen as a bureaucratic practice.

Medical Performance in Office Practice

Thus far I have sketched a number of forms of medical practice and some of their functional characteristics. The variety may be

[20] This is the definition in S. David Pomrinse and Marcus S. Goldstein, "Group Practice in the U.S.," *Group Practice,* IX (1960), 845–859.

[21] *Ibid.*

[22] Edwin P. Jordan, ed., *The Physician and Group Practice* (Chicago: Year Book Publishers, Inc., 1958).

seen to distribute itself between two logically but not numerically important extremes. At one end there is a rarity, true solo practice. Empirically, it is unstable, merging into more common, loose forms of informal cooperation with colleagues. The colleague network represents a tighter but still informal type of cooperative practice. The "association" represents a simple variety of formal cooperation, while the small partnership and then the group practice are tighter and more complex forms. Finally, there is the tightest and most formal variety of practice, which may be called organizational or bureaucratic. But in order to make use of *empirical* materials dealing with practice, we must divide all these work-settings into two types to be able to parallel the common sense distinction between solo and group practice. The former category includes true solo and all types of informally cooperative practice. The latter includes, from the "association" on, all types of formally cooperative practice. By means of this distinction, we can ask how the form of work setting is related to professional performance.

Since the foremost claim of a profession is to special expertise, it follows that the first question to ask about various forms of professional practice concerns technical performance, or the quality of service provided. It is, unfortunately, the question about which there is least information. The opinion is fairly widespread that a physician cannot practice the best possible medicine without easy access to modern diagnostic and therapeutic facilities. Thus, it is reasonable to assume that the solo practitioner who lacks access to such facilities is least likely to do the best for his patient. Formal cooperative arrangements, whether simple or complex, are more likely to provide the capital to buy an extensive amount of equipment.

Furthermore, the isolation of the practicing physician from his colleagues is believed to be a significant element in the quality of care. It is presently believed that a physician must continually keep abreast of advances in scientific knowledge, relying less on the questionable but ubiquitous "education" of drug manufacturers and their representatives, and more upon the "education" provided by colleagues and scientific publications. As we have seen, solo practice as such cannot readily be classified as more or less isolated, for a considerable degree of informal but nonetheless real and important interaction can take place among loose networks of practitioners. Much of it, as Peterson observed, is bound to be about fishing, bridge, and golf,[23] but some is certainly about medicine.[24] Nonetheless, the fact that isolation in solo practice is *possible* marks it off from "group practice," whether a small partnership or a large-scale medical group. In this sense, group more than solo practice seems to encourage a higher quality of care. Indeed, Peterson reported a slight tendency for those in group practice to give a higher quality of care than those working alone,[25] though Clute apparently did not find such a tendency.[26]

In addition, care by a variety of specialists is held to be necessary these days. While solo practice does not preclude the use of specialists, group practice facilitates frequent consultation and exchange of professional information. Where a number of physicians of varied specialties work together within the same organization, it is not only easier to refer patients, but also to communicate and coordinate information about them. Coleman, Katz, and Menzel have demonstrated the importance of colleague relations to one facet of care—prescribing drugs.[27] Thus, it is to be expected that in group practice the fragmentation of care following upon specialization can be compensated for and that so-called comprehensive care is more likely to ensue.

Finally, there is the element of supervision, the quality of which Seeman and Evans have shown to influence medical performance.[28] The most reputable medical institutions—for example, medical school clinics and teaching hospitals—are characterized by doctors working in close association with each other and with some systematic supervision of work by chiefs of services, staff committees reviewing the treatment of patients who died, the tissue removed by surgery, and the like. Except in a purely educational context, where it is ideologically acceptable, the nature of supervision in such medical bureaucracies has received little attention, but it is indubitable

[23] Peterson, *op. cit.*, p. 83.

[24] Coleman, *op. cit.*, p. 110, found that when one shared his office, he adopted a new drug more quickly than one who works alone.

[25] Peterson, *op. cit.*

[26] Clute, *op. cit.*, p. 318.

[27] Coleman, *op. cit.*

[28] Seeman and Evans, *op. cit.*

that at least some formal administrative supervision almost always exists. Furthermore, the cultivation of a medical records system and the continuous accumulation of information in records is in itself supervisory, for while the records may not be subject to routine inspection, they may always be examined if some doubt arises about a physician's work. If, as Peterson assumes, systematic and complete records are an important element of competent medical care, bureaucratic practices, which are far more likely to encourage record keeping, can to this extent provide a higher quality of care.

In theory, then, formal and cooperative rather than informal and individual practice arrangements are more likely to provide good medical care. However, there are only scattered bits of evidence to support this theory. A negative reflection on the system of solo practice predominant in the United States might be noted in the finding that somewhat less than half of all surgical in-hospital procedures performed in the nation during 1957–58 were by men formally certified to practice surgery,[29] but this is not direct evidence that the quality of care in group practice is higher. Comparative studies are necessary.

One of the rare comparative studies in this area was made by the Health Insurance Plan of Greater New York, in which the hospitalization and perinatal mortality of a population served by medical groups under contract with the insurance plan compared favorably with that of the New York City population.[30] That study, however, was concerned with an additional element in the arrangement of medical care—the prepaid service contract. It is believed that when people can be insured so that no financial barrier stands between them and medical care, they will not hesitate to use services and so can obtain the care they need early in the course of illness, thus preventing complications. Consequently, a comprehensive prepaid service contract is believed to be—of itself—conducive to better medical care. With insurance and organizational variables undifferentiated, the influence of either on quality of care is difficult to establish.

[29] Health Information Foundation, "Physicians Who Perform Surgery," *Progress in Health Services,* X (1961).

[30] S. Shapiro, L. Weiner, and P. M. Densen, "Comparison of Prematurity and Perinatal Mortality in General Population and in Population of Prepaid Group Practice," *American Journal of Public Health,* XLVIII (1958), 170–187.

The same difficulty holds when the mode of compensating the physician is undifferentiated from organization. A study by Densen and his associates compared the hospital utilization of members of a single union who were under two different medical insurance plans—one involving medical group practice compensated on a per capita basis, and the other solo fee-for-service practice. Hospital utilization in the former proved to be lower, even though the comprehensiveness of insurance was much the same.[31] But it is difficult to tell whether the lower utilization resulted from group practice as such or from the fact that the group plan provided no additional compensation to the group physician for in-hospital surgery.[32] Clearly, present evidence is inadequate.[33]

Whether or not people are deeply involved emotionally with their doctors, they must in any case be sufficiently happy with the care they receive to make use of their doctors. Patient satisfaction assumes additional importance when medicine becomes a political issue. In a number of national sample surveys in the United States, most people have expressed general satisfaction with medical services which typically are organized on only a loosely cooperative, fee-for-service basis, and the solo general practitioner is part of the national folklore. In spite of this, fairly large proportions of the population cite grounds for dissatisfaction. They complain that doctors keep them waiting too long, are difficult to reach on nights and weekends, and do not give enough time to them. Koos's studies report the largest proportions of dissatisfaction,[34] while the Gaffin study showed that people are less likely to complain about their own doctors than about doctors in general.[35]

[31] P. M. Densen, E. W. Jones, E. Balamuth, and S. Shapiro, "Prepaid Medical Care and Hospital Utilization in a Dual Choice Situation," *American Journal of Public Health,* L (1960), 1710–1726.

[32] For some evidence bearing on this see Robin F. Badgley and Samuel Wolfe, *Doctors' Strike: Medical Care and Conflict in Saskatchewan* (New York: Atherton Press, 1967), pp. 115–118.

[33] For a recent review of the evidence bearing on these difficult questions, see Avedis Donabedian, "A Review of Some Experiences with Prepaid Group Practice," *Bureau of Public Health Economics, Research Series,* No. 12 (Ann Arbor: School of Public Health, The University of Michigan, 1965).

[34] E. L. Koos, "Metropolis—What City People Think of Their Medical Services," *American Journal of Public Health,* XLV (1955), 1551–1557.

[35] Ben Gaffin Associates, "What Americans Think of the Medical Profession," American Medical Association brochure, n.d.

This material, however, like the data on in-hospital surgery, bears on solo practice only insofar as it is the most common and most characteristic form in the United States. Again, comparative studies provide the most useful evidence. Anderson and Sheatsley compared two groups of socioeconomically equivalent, insured patients, one being served by solo physicians compensated by an insurance organization on a fee-for-service basis, the other by physicians in medical groups, paid on a per capita basis.[36] The finding was that the solo fee-for-service program elicited more patient satisfaction than did the capitation group practice. Patients of the latter were prone to complain of lack of personal interest, insufficient explanation of their condition by the doctor, waiting in office, and difficulty in getting house calls. In Freidson's study, where patients contrasted their experience with these two types of practice, there was also a tendency to feel that the sense of "personal interest" was more likely to be obtained in solo fee-for-service practice than in capitation group practice. But there was some feeling that medical care of a technically higher quality could be obtained from the medical group.[37] In both studies, however, solo fee-for-service practice is compared to capitation group practice, and no way is provided to control the financial variable and compare forms of practice as such. Plainly, the material on patient satisfaction is equivocal, but none contradicts the idea that emotional satisfaction on the part of the patient seems more likely to be gained from a physician who is in a position to be more immediately responsive to (and dependent on) the patient than are group physicians who have obligations to a work organization.

Physician satisfaction, too, may be more influenced by the arrangement of work than by the arrangement of payment. In assessing job satisfaction, however, we must first recognize that it is much easier for the physician to "free-lance" than for the professor or

[36] Odin W. Anderson and Paul B. Sheatsley, "Comprehensive Medical Insurance," *Health Information Foundation Research Series,* No. 9, 1959.

[37] Eliot Freidson, *Patients' Views of Medical Practice* (New York: Russell Sage Foundation, 1961). See also the review of Weinerman, "Patients' Perceptions," *op. cit.,* and of Avedis Donabedian, "A Review of Some Experiences with Prepaid Group Practice," *Bureau of Public Health Economics Research Series,* No. 12 (Ann Arbor: School of Public Health, The University of Michigan, 1965).

the minister, since both of the latter require congregations rather than an assortment of successive individuals, and neither can count on the fairly strong motivation provided by illness. This by itself means that even in an environment where the state sets the terms of work for the average practitioner—as in England and the Soviet Union—it is possible for the physician to stay outside the scheme if he wishes. Hence, a physician in any organized scheme of practice can always find some way to work outside, even if at some personal risk or sacrifice.

It may be noted furthermore that job satisfaction is inevitably a function of the career alternatives that exist at any particular time and of the symbolic and material rewards of these alternatives. In medicine in the United States today, for example, the symbolically valued work setting is the successful, fee-for-service, solo specialty practice. The general practitioner may genuinely enjoy the procession of minor cases (called "garbage" by specialists), the laying-on of hands, and the genial calls at humble homes—the human rather than the scientific side of medicine. But in depressed moments he may realize that he is not a social or professional success because he is not a specialist with limited practice and prominent clients. Thus, environment must be considered a partial influence on satisfaction, both in the way it defines any form of practice and in the way it offers alternative possibilities.

No matter what the tyranny of the patient, the solo work setting has the quality of potentially complete autonomy. The physician working in the privacy of his own consulting room can examine, prescribe, diagnose, and treat as he sees fit. There is no one to soften patient pressure to honor lay prejudices, of course, and when practice is insecure it is likely that the doctor will feel obliged to do what he does not really want to do, but theoretically, the solo physician may dismiss his patients rather than give in to them. Autonomy perhaps more extensive than in any other profession thus exists, at least *in potentia,* in solo practice. This is what was stressed by medical students in response to survey questions on why they would reject salaried positions in organizations. In contrast to this apparently gratifying side of solo entrepreneurial practice are a number of potential handicaps: isolation from one's colleagues and their information and support, the necessity to be preoccupied daily with the financial basis of practice, the leanness of early and late stages of the career, and the difficulty of controlling and regularizing work hours. These are the very things which are said to be solved by group practice. Indeed, medical students who preferred salaried positions stressed opportunities to work in close association with colleagues, to obtain a regular income, and to work regular hours.[38]

On the whole, one should expect that a doctor-owned, fee-for-service partnership or group practice would provide most of the gratifications and fewest of the deficiencies of the two extremes of solo and bureaucratic practice. It seems to allow the greatest amount of room for self-determination without in turn sacrificing the major virtues of cooperative practice. It is a very popular form in the Midwest and Southwest of the United States. The Cahalan survey of medical students reported that of those who preferred a non-salaried form of practice, only 26 per cent preferred solo to group practice, partnership, or some other form of formally cooperative practice.[39] Since more freshmen than seniors preferred solo practice, we can assume that interest in cooperative forms increases as the medical students come closer to being a physician. However, the Cahalan study notes that those students expressing a preference for group practice were less likely to expect that their preferences would be realized than were those preferring the solo form. Testimony to the realism of their expectation is provided by Weiskotten's finding that 64 percent of those in the class of 1950 engaged in private practice were practicing alone.[40]

Analytical Types of Practice Organization

Thus far, we have discussed medical work settings as a variable *quantity* of professional cooperation and organization, from the isolated solo practitioner to the member of an elaborate medical bureaucracy. However, this simplistic mode of analysis does not pick out some of the important analytical qualities of practice, particularly those bearing directly on the differential performance of physicians in practice. For example, as has already been noted, the solo practitioner is not generally considered to give as good techni-

[38] Cahalan *et al., op. cit.*
[39] *Ibid.*
[40] Weiskotten, *op. cit.*

cal care as the man in group practice but is generally considered to have better interpersonal relations with his patients. And on another level, the specialist is reputed to give better technical care than the general practitioner, though he is considered to be more cold and impersonal. And finally, different specialists—for example, obstetricians as opposed to pathologists—are reputed to have different "personalities" and certain significantly different practices.

How can we explain such differences? We can explain them by assuming that people select themselves—that they know enough about practices in advance, and can assess themselves precisely enough to select their practices to fit their capacities. Certainly self-selection is one element to be taken into account, but to use it as the prime explanation is to put faith into a miraculously precise prescience and self-knowledge that surpasses reason. We can, alternately, assume that some individuals, after experiencing one kind of practice, try another, and perhaps even another. It is certainly true that there is some degree of trial and error in medical practice. Some move from general to specialty practice, others from solo to group practice, or vice versa. But the personal and economic cost of such movement, particularly from one *specialty* to another, is so great that this kind of self-selection simply cannot be very common.

Quite another kind of explanation lies in the press of the situation on the individual after he has landed in a position—on the influence of the setting of work on transforming the individual who has become committed to adjusting to it, on the consequences of being in a situation in which persistent and powerful demands cause the individual to behave in a certain way regardless of his personal qualities. The structural contingencies of practice that would seem to have the greatest significance for the profession are those that influence the maintenance, raising, or lowering of the standards of ethical and technical performance. These are established and assessed by members of the profession as such and may be labeled "colleague" standards. Many such standards are by no means universally agreed upon by all members of the profession, but we can distinguish them grossly by contrasting them with lay standards. We may take it as axiomatic that the patient has a different perspective on health services than does the physician and that on occasion he will almost certainly ask for medication or procedures which colleagues would not approve. Opposing laymen and colleagues to each other, then, we may distinguish practices by *the degree to which they are amenable to lay or colleague control.*

On this basis we can distinguish two logically extreme types of practice for purposes of analysis.[41] On one extreme is a work setting that is wholly dependent for its economic continuance on lay evaluations—client-dependent practice. When he first feels ill, the patient feels he is competent to judge whether he is actually ill and what general class of illness it is. On this basis he treats himself. Failure of this and other informal modes of treatment leads him to a physician. This physician, it should be clear, is chosen on the basis of lay conceptions of what is needed, not by professional criteria. In order to be chosen—in order to stay in practice—he must offer services of a sort that laymen themselves feel they need: he must give antibiotics for colds, vitamin injections for being "run down," and sedatives or tranquilizers for "nerves." And to be chosen again and survive, he must be prepared to provide services that honor the client's prejudices sufficiently to make him feel that what he thinks bothers him is being treated properly. Furthermore, if it is wholly dependent on client choice, this type of work setting is unlikely to be either very observable to or dependent upon colleagues. Its professional standards are therefore likely to be comparatively low. At the other extreme may be seen a colleague-dependent practice that does not in and by itself attract its own clientele but that instead serves the needs of other colleagues or professional organizations that do attract such clientele. It is dependent for its clientele on colleagues rather than laymen: colleagues transmit clients to it. In this sense, in order to survive, it must honor the prejudices of colleagues more than those of clients. Here, obviously, we should expect that the degree to which it honors professional standards will be relatively great.

The logical extreme of client-dependent practice does not seem fully applicable to any professional work setting, if only because the license of a professional practitioner ultimately depends upon the

[41] This criterion was first suggested in my "Client Control and Medical Practice," *American Journal of Sociology,* LXV (1960), 374–382, and elaborated in my *Patients' Views, op. cit.*

approval of his colleagues. The quack, however, seems most usefully defined as a practitioner who fits this extreme, having no obligations to or identity with an organized set of colleagues. Close to this extreme in the United States is the independent solo neighborhood or village general practitioner, with at best loose cooperative ties to colleagues and local medical institutions. Also close to this extreme are specialists who must attract a clientele directly and who do not need to make everyday use of hospitals—for example, in urban areas in particular, some internists and pediatricians, as well as some ophthalmologists and gynecologists. At the other logical extreme of colleague-dependent practice, empirical cases are easier to find. Such medical specialties as pathology, anesthesiology, and radiology are almost completely dependent upon colleague referrals and have little significant need for such client-oriented techniques as bedside manners. Somewhat less pure, but moved toward that extreme nonetheless, are practices to be found in hospitals, clinics, and other professional bureaucracies. Here, while the client very often does exercise choice, organizational requirements minimize his influence. By and large, practice is dependent upon organizational auspices and equipment. And while practitioners within the organization may be chosen by clients, the practitioner's visibility and vulnerability to his colleagues in the organization should lead him to minimize his responsiveness to clients.

This classification of medical practice provides a foundation for understanding some of the mechanisms involved in creating observed differences in performance among physicians in one setting rather than another. If the physicians are as individuals unusually conscientious and ethical, we are in a position to understand what practice settings can make them uncomfortable if not significantly change their performance. If the physicians are individuals who are only ordinarily conscientious and ethical, we can understand why, in one setting, they fail to apply the standards taught them in school, and why, in another, they are more likely to maintain such standards. And, given physicians who are equally "cynical" upon graduating from medical school, we can predict the degree of "cynicism" they maintain when they disperse into practices that pose distinctly different structural pressures on them.[42]

[42] Gray, *op. cit.*

6.

PATTERNS OF PRACTICE IN THE HOSPITAL

IN the last chapter I discussed primarily the characteristics of the American physician's office practice—that is, the work setting which constitutes his professional address, where patients may call him, come to consult him, and pay him. As I indicated, the organization of office practice can vary greatly, as can the nature of the interaction that it allows between doctor and patient. Furthermore, it can take place in the living room of the physician's home or in a separate office or in a large clinic or hospital. As varied as everyday medical practices are, however, few can avoid taking into account the unusual but routine occasions when the patient becomes so incapacitated that he cannot walk in to see the physician, when the patient's condition is thought to require a regimen too precise or dangerous to trust to laymen at home, and when he is thought to need services requiring the coordination of a variety of special skills and machines.

Given the development of medical technology over the past fifty years, the hospital has become the place in industrial and post-industrial countries where those unusual but routine cases are treated. Thus, the hospital constitutes a major work setting for medical practice—a facility which the organization of every practice must, in one way or another, take into account. The everyday practitioner who does not or cannot personally hospitalize his patients and supervise their care in hospital must be prepared to see some of his patients transfer to practitioners who can see them through the hospital. If he is to have a stable practice he must participate in an arrangement that encourages his patients to return to him after leaving the hospital. Such arrangements are many and varied: in many European hospitals there is a rigid separation between community and hospital practice which prevents the community practitioner from caring for the patient in hospital but which also prevents the patient from seeking everyday care from hospital practitioners. While the community practitioner "loses" his patients upon hospitalization, he is assured of regaining them on discharge.

Thus, even the community practitioner without any hospital ties must incorporate arrangements into his practice that take the hospital into account. In this sense, virtually all types of medical practice in industrialized societies include within them systematic accommodations to hospitals. From this point of view, the hospital may be seen as part of medical practice as such, serving as a setting where cases inappropriate for office or home practice may be taken and treated. Historically, the hospital developed separately from conventional medical practice, being a place where the poor and the stranger, both without access to the community medical practice of the time, could find (or share) a bed and nursing care.[1] While the hospital is in reality something more than a mere creature of medical practice, nonetheless a great many of its problems can be better understood by emphasizing its status, particularly in the average community hospital in the United States, as an appendage of medical practice, struggling for greater autonomy in establishing goals and policies separate from those of the entrepreneurial community practitioner.[2]

1 For an excellent history, see Brian Abel-Smith, *The Hospitals, 1800–1948* (London: William Heinemann, 1964). For a brief history of the development of the hospital, see George Rosen, "The Hospital: Historical Sociology of a Community Institution," in Eliot Freidson, ed., *The Hospital in Modern Society* (New York: The Free Press of Glencoe, 1963), pp. 1–36.

2 "For the paying patient and his physicians, the hospital is primarily a service institution where the physician arranges to treat his patient," Ivan Belknap and John G. Steinle, *The Community and Its Hospitals* (Syracuse: Syracuse University Press, 1963), p. 39.

Hospitals as Medical Practices

In examining the hospital for the degree to which it is an appendage of medical practice, we first consider the range of variation in the extent to which hospital policies and procedures are controlled by the physicians who use it as a place in which to bed and treat their patients. In the United States this range is wide, though comprehension of it is severely handicapped by a lack of systematic, empirical information about many varieties in that range. To discuss this range intelligently we must limit our definition of the word "hospital" in such a way as to exclude nursing homes, homes for the aged, "rest homes," "sanitaria," and other domiciliary institutions that may provide some nominal health care but not medical care on an intensive or daily basis. Thus, I limit myself to considering a hospital to be "an institution in which patients or injured persons are given medical or surgical care." [3]

At one extreme of the range is the *proprietary hospital*—one owned privately and run for profit. Insofar as the proprietary hospital is devoted to providing services that only physicians are licensed to give, and insofar as physicians are the gatekeepers who persuade patients to be hospitalized and decide what shall be done with them, it follows that whether or not physicians own the proprietary hospital (as is apparently common), its policies are likely to be focused on accommodating to the needs and desires of the physicians, tempered somewhat by the demands of the customer, economics, and other requisites of profit. The physician who brings in the most patients or the best-paying patients will have the greatest influence on policy. And policy in general will be dominated by the principle of laissez faire: the physician will be free to do more or less what he pleases, medically, with little or no supervision of his medical performance.[4] This kind of hospital is a literal extension of medical practice.

A somewhat similar situation was once very common in the

[3] *Webster's New Collegiate Dictionary* (Springfield, Mass.: G. & C. Merriam Co., Publishers, 1959), p. 400.

[4] See the findings on the quality of care in proprietary hospitals in New York City in "The Quantity, Quality and Costs of Medical and Hospital Care Secured by a Sample of Teamster Families in the New York Area," Columbia University School of Public Health and Administrative Medicine, n.d.

voluntary or community hospital in the United States. Such hospitals are by definition not run for profit.[5] Frequently running on less than a cost basis, they receive significant amounts of support from charitable contributions and subsidies. Until recently, when hospital compensation by private and later public health insurance became the rule rather than the exception, many of the patients of the American voluntary hospital were "charity" cases, contributing little to the cost of their services. To balance the cost of the care of such "charity" cases, well-paying patients were obviously desirable to the hospital. The physicians who could bring such well-paying patients into the hospital were obviously of great importance to its survival and, as might be expected, were dominant in setting hospital policy in spite of the fact that they were neither owners of the hospital nor committed to it by employment or capital investment.[6]

More recently, however—in part because of the increased likelihood that, by private or public health insurance devices, every patient is a "paying patient," and in part because of the development of full-time, hospital-based practice—much of the control of voluntary and community hospital policies has been passing out of the hands of the community practitioner and into those of the boards that "own" and the administrators who manage the day-to-day affairs of the hospital. Policy has become divided into several spheres, medical boards controlling much of the policy specifically related to their work, and administrative staff controlling the rest, including access to the governing board. Even before such changes occurred, the voluntary hospital played an important part in shaping medical practice. Whereas in the proprietary hospital the physician could come and go at his own convenience, the physician was obliged to "donate" his services to some of the "welfare," "clinic," or "service" patients in return for the "privilege" of hospitalizing his patients in the voluntary hospital. Furthermore, because the voluntary hospital had a general aim of community service rather than the narrow one of "servicing" practitioner's needs for beds, and sometimes had nonmedical goals, it was likely to impose rules of its

[5] Such a definition is much too simple, as the discussion in Belknap and Steinle, *op. cit.*, indicates.

[6] See the discussion of this period of medical domination of hospital policy in Charles Perrow, "Goals and Power Structure: A Historical Case Study," in Freidson, *op. cit.*, pp. 112–146.

own on physician behavior—as for example, that the physician must conform with religious dictates in hospitals run by religious orders or run under orthodox religious auspices.

In both of the cases I have discussed so far, medical practice is distinct from the hospital as such. In other cases, medical practice becomes wholly encompassed by the hospital, not standing apart from it. The most clear-cut example of this is to be found in the *military hospital,* where physicians are full-fledged members of the organization, as committed to it and subject to discipline as other performing members. Another example is to be found in those federal, state, and municipal hospitals that are staffed by exclusively full-time medical personnel. The physician's practice lying entirely within the organization, his career is formed by his relationship to it and its personnel, like that of a civil service employee. A somewhat more complicated example of this type of relationship is to be found in the increasingly common practice of full-time medical staff members in medical schools and teaching hospitals [7]—a practice that is not as dependent upon the organization for resources as is implied by the fact of employment. Like the university professor, the full-time staff member of the medical school and the teaching hospital tends to have a national or even international "clientele": while his "practice" depends upon holding a position in an organization, his career tends to be one of high mobility, moving from one organization to another. Interestingly enough, it is the very fact that full-time practice in the hospital does not have to attract a *personal* following of clients—rather, merely serving the clients attracted by the hospital—that liberates it from the local community so as to become transferable (and marketable) to other hospitals and communities.

Finally, it is necessary to discuss a special case of hospital practice that is not "pure" but that is critical to many hospitals' supply of skilled medical work—the work of the postgraduate physicians—interns and residents, or "house staff." Much of the medical care that the house staff gives to patients in hospitals is part of what it

[7] See Patricia Kendall, "The Relationship Between Medical Educators and Medical Practitioners," *Annals of the New York Academy of Sciences,* CXXVIII (1965), 568–576, for a report of a study of the frictions between those who practice in teaching hospitals and those who practice in the community. See also the material in Raymond S. Duff and August B. Hollinghead, *Sickness and Society* (New York: Harper and Row, 1968), pp. 44–65.

must do in order to develop its skills for both general and specialized practice.[8] However, the work is of great value to the hospital itself, for it is medical work that no one else in the hospital can do. Whether because of their commitment to affairs outside the hospital or to research, or whether because they are in absolute short supply, the medical staff is in no position to do the work of the house staff should the latter suddenly disappear. One might expect that in hospitals without house staff—for example, proprietary hospitals and small isolated community general hospitals—most of the *medical* work that the house staff would do elsewhere must instead be performed by nurses and even aides or attendants, only the most critical being taken over by the medical staff.

A characteristic of perhaps greater sociological importance for understanding the functioning of hospitals, however, is the *transience* of house staff. Like students in a college, their orientation is toward obtaining what they feel they need from the institution (which is not necessarily the same as that needed by the staff and patients) in order that they may leave and begin their "real" life of practice. It is of course true that some interns wish to stay on to be first-year residents, some of the latter wish to be second-year residents, and so on. Furthermore, it is true that some of the house staff wish to join the medical staff of the institution in which they work. Nonetheless, their commitment to their hospital work is different from that of the commitment of others, being perhaps less intense than that of the full-time staff and more intense than that of attending staff but, in any case, of a shorter term than either. The consequences of such limited commitment may not be significant to their work in instances where episodic or short-term care is necessary. But the mere fact of their constant rotation or turnover may have serious consequences for the care they give patients who require a sustained personal relationship with a therapist. The most obvious example of this is the mental hospital, public or private: assuming that verbal psychotherapy is an efficacious method of treatment and that for its success it requires fairly close rapport between patient and therapist, turnover among individuals' therapists is patently undesirable therapeutically.

[8] See Cecil Sheps *et al.*, "Medical Schools and Hospitals," *Journal of Medical Education*, XL (1965), Part II, pp. 1–169, for extensive discussions of teaching hospitals and their programs.

I have dwelt at length on the issue of hospital practice in order to link my discussion of medical practice in with my discussion of the hospital, but more importantly I wish to emphasize a fact that is frequently overlooked in discussions of the organization and operation of hospitals. In circumstances most commonly studied *in the United States, the physician is not so much part of the hospital as the hospital is part (and only one part) of the physician's practice.* In the most common type of American hospital—the community general hospital—the medical staff that hospitalizes patients and supervises their care is not committed to the hospital in the same way as are such full-time employees as nurses. While they are part of the hospital, as are patients, they are part of it in a very special way that is markedly variant from that of the members of such clearly bureaucratic organizations as armies, factories, and civil service bureaus.[9] By the same token, however, this hospital segment of their medical practice is markedly different in organization from the office segment. In his office practice the physician makes use of workers from other occupations but on the whole controls the initiation and maintenance of his relation with such workers. In the hospital, however, the physician is confronted with a division of labor organized and administered independently of his own individual practice and carried out by workers with occupational aspirations and perspectives which may conflict with his own. He can work alone in his office, but in the hospital he cannot fail to come into sustained contact with the larger division of labor of which he is a part. Thus, the hospital is one major proving ground for his place in that division of labor.

Ordering the Hospital Division of Labor

What groups are involved in the hospital?[10] In my definition I stressed the centrality of medical and surgical work. But while

[9] For discussions of organization and function, see C. Wesley Eisele, ed., *The Medical Staff in the Modern Hospital* (New York: McGraw-Hill Book Co., 1967).

[10] The most comprehensive sociological treatise on the hospital is Johann Jürgen Rohde, *Soziologie des Krankenhauses* (Stuttgart: Ferdinand Enke, 1962). A very accessible introduction to the American hospital is Temple Burling *et al., The Give and Take in Hospitals* (New York: G. P. Putnam's Sons, 1956). A standard textbook on hospital administration, covering hospital operations very thoroughly, is M. T. McEachern, *Hospital Organization and Management* (Chicago: Physicians Record Co., 1957).

physicians and surgeons may control the performance of such work as befits a profession, they cannot do it all themselves. Furthermore, various supportive services, some domestic and some technical, are necessary for the continued operation of an institution which combines domiciliary with therapeutic services.

Recalling the discussion of the medical division of labor in Chapter 3, it is possible to distinguish (1) physicians from (2) those workers who give direct and indirect medical services under "orders" of or supervision by physicians—medical and paramedical personnel, respectively. In the latter case we must distinguish between (a) those who serve the patient directly—primarily nursing and ward personnel but also various "therapists" and (b) those who provide technical services contributing to medical service—laboratory and other technicians. We must also mention (3) those service workers who care for the physical plant of the hospital and perform the other tasks connected with maintaining the plant and managing the food, laundry, and other services necessary for its survival, and (4) the clerical personnel who prepare, transmit, and store the written communications of the institution. We must also mention (5) those whose task is to organize, supervise, and coordinate the work of all workers in the light of the over-all objectives of the organization itself—the "administrators." In addition to these major types of everyday hospital worker, there are, of course, (6) the legal governing board of the institution, which is not a continuously working group, and (7) the patients or clients, who, while more or less passive and frequently transient, are nonetheless members of the organization. How are these relationships ordered?

In the conventional industrial organization that tends to be our commonsensical model of what an organization "really" is, the workers whose skill is used in industrial production are subordinate to the administration.[11] The plant manager or the vice-president in charge of production is naturally a key man, but the qualifications he must have to obtain and perform his job satisfactorily do not include among them the training for and capacity to be a production *worker*. Furthermore, while he does tend to be key man in the

[11] One excellent introduction to sociological approaches to the factory is Delbert C. Miller and William H. Form, *Industrial Socology*, 2nd ed. (New York: Harper and Row, 1964).

organization, his rank is shared by other vice-presidents with such other concerns as sales, finance, public relations, labor relations, and the like. In this sense, the worker who performs the primary, core task of production in the industrial organization is neither in control of the organization nor represented by an especially powerful superior. The organizational chart of the industrial organization is thus fairly logical and symmetrical, each "function," including that of production, responsible to coequal administrators who are in turn responsible to a single coordinating head or president. There is nominally, then, a single line of authority, delegated and differentiated by task—a monocratic model like that analyzed by Max Weber.

Recent discussions of organizations by such analysts of conventional corporate enterprises as Victor Thompson[12] claim that when creative and complex work is required, the monocratic model of organization is inappropriate. Those concerned with the role of the professional in the organization have suggested that something quite other than a monocratic form of organization is appropriate to the creative and complex work imputed to the professional—a company of equals, a professional organization, or, in Weber's terms, a collegial form of organization.[13] And, indeed in the hospitals discussed by Smith,[14] there is not just one line of authority but two. Essentially, Smith notes that the physician can intervene in many areas of the hospital over which he has no formal administrative jurisdiction or authority. Unlike the foreman, who is caught "in the middle" between his legitimate superiors and subordinates, the nurse is caught between two superiors, administrative and medical. The latter, however, is not her bureaucratic superior; that is to say, while the floor nurse is subject to the orders of her supervisor, who is her official superior in the hospital hierarchy, she is also subject to the orders of the physician involved in the care of her patients by virtue

[12] Victor A. Thompson, *Modern Organization* (New York: Alfred A. Knopf, 1961).

[13] See Bernard Barber, *Science and the Social Order* (New York: Collier Books, 1962), pp. 195–198. Erwin O. Smigel, *The Wall Street Lawyer* (New York: The Free Press of Glencoe, 1964), pp. 275–286; and Max Weber, *Theory of Social and Economic Organization* (New York: Oxford University Press, 1947), pp. 392–407.

[14] Harvey L. Smith, "Two Lines of Authority Are One too Many," *Modern Hospitals*, LXXXIV (1955), 59–64.

of his superior knowledge and responsibility. Similarly, justifying his demands by reference to the well-being of his patient, the physician can and does give "orders" to other hospital personnel even though he is not a bureaucratically defined superior. In this way the functioning of the hospital is seen to be disrupted and broken, lacking the clear, unilinear authority upon which Weber predicates efficiency and reliability in organizational performance.

However, one may ask why this situation exists so markedly in American hospitals and so much less so in industrial organizations. In the latter there are an increasing number of professionals, first as staff which plans the work performed by the line, and increasingly as research and development scientists. But if we can believe such writers as Kornhauser,[15] rather than being free to intervene in others' work as do doctors, scientists in industry are hardly free to do their own work as they please. The tribulations of staff in industry thus teach us that it is not expertise as such that grants the "authority" to intervene in others' work and immunity from retaliation by those in formal authority. Rather, we might suspect that the physician in American hospitals is in a very special position, different from that of other contemporary experts by virtue of the *content* of his expertise, the organization of his practice, and the position of his profession.

As Hall pointed out, the physician is able to intervene in many places in the hospital and justify his intervention on the basis of a "medical emergency"—a situation in which the well-being of a patient is said to be seriously in jeopardy and in which it is the physician alone who knows what is best done.[16] We all are familiar with the dominant symbolic image: the interruption of orderly routine by a violent convulsion, heart failure, a hemorrhage; the suspension of ordinary relationships and their reorganization around the masterful physician who, by his intervention, saves a life. While this no doubt happens on occasion, far more common in the hospital is the *labeling of ambiguous events as emergencies* by the doctor so as to gain the aid or resources he believes he needs. The recent

[15] William Kornhauser, *Scientists in Industry* (Berkeley: University of California Press, 1962).

[16] Oswald Hall, "Some Problems in the Provision of Medical Services," *Canadian Journal of Economics and Political Science*, XX (1954), 456–466.

creation of emergency admission committees in some hospitals—committees that review the justification of suspending ordinary procedures and priorities for admitting a doctor's patient to the hospital—suggests both that the label is not always used by individual physicians in circumstances that his colleagues would agree is "really" an emergency and that it is a powerful source of leverage in the hospital which cannot be effectively contested by any other than medical men. It is his ability to invoke life-threatening emergency and to claim exclusive capacity to evaluate and solve it that marks the physician off from many other experts in other organizations.[17]

When Does the Second Line of Authority Operate?

As I have noted in a number of contexts, "the physician" is at best a very general occupational type that can be only vaguely contrasted with "the lawyer," "the scientist," and "the engineer." There are many kinds of physicians, in the sense that systematic variations of some significance occur within the general profession. The content of the physician's work influences the kind of emergency he is likely to meet and indeed whether or not his "typical emergency" will have the rhetorical force of "a life-and-death-matter" to those he must persuade. I suggest that while all specialties (and indeed all kinds of work) have their typical emergencies, they vary in the degree to which the emergencies are generally believed by others to be critical enough to warrant suspension of everyday routine, and they vary in the degree to which such emergencies are frequent and characteristic, almost routine. In the specialty of public health, for example, the typical dramatic emergency is the outbreak of a lethal epidemic or of virulent food poisoning, a circumstance that would give the public health officer justification to breach ordinary lines of authority. However, in the United States such outbreaks are so rare and so comparatively mild that the public health officer may

[17] The invocation of "emergency" is a strategic action of some consequence in more than medical affairs. Successful claim of emergency suspends, if not destroys, the normal, the routine, the rational, and the legal. In the most obvious instance, the successful claim of emergency by a government justifies the suspension of civil liberties and due process of law. No one has yet made an extensive sociological analysis of the emergency.

be expected to conform to the usual routines, bureaucratic and otherwise. And his "image" is similarly safe and bureaucratic, as the North Carolina study of specialty choice has clearly shown.[18]

In the hospital we can, holding all else equal, predict the likelihood of the intervention of this "second line of authority" (and the disordering of decision-making) by the degree to which the specialty of the physician involved permits the plausible and regular claim of "critical emergency." While the distinction may be too broad to be significant, one might suspect that the surgical specialties may be able to claim more emergency than the medical. Within medicine, obviously physical medicine is *less* likely to permit such a regular claim than is cardiology. Within surgery, ophthalmology and otolaryngology are less likely to be able to make a plausible claim of emergency than neurosurgery or orthopedic surgery. And the service specialties of pathology, roentgenology, and anesthesiology are considerably less likely to claim their own emergencies than to attach themselves to the emergencies defined by medicine and surgery.

As important as the content of work (and the claim of expertise) may be, though, I would insist that much of the problem posed by the second line of authority stems not from the substantive element of professional expertise but from the combination of his sociolegal responsibility for hospital patients with the socioeconomic independence of the physician from the hospital in the United States. As a volunteer worker, or as a guest both serving and being served by the hospital, the physician is in a position to escape many of the obligations of any member of a bureaucracy, including the exercise of bureaucratic authority: he is a relatively free agent, unrestrained by subordination to a clear organizational hierarchy. In contrast, the staff expert in the industrial organization is an employee of the organization with no necessary outside career alternatives. Furthermore, the practicing physician is recognized to be responsible for the treatment of the patient: if he were responsible but could not order about those engaged in the treatment, he would be in an intolerable position. In contrast, the staff expert in industry is responsible for his own work but not for the work of others, including

[18] See R. E. Coker *et al.*, "Public Health as Viewed by the Medical Student," *American Journal of Public Health*, XLIX (1959), 601–609.

those engaged in the organization's central task of production: that the expert cannot order production workers about is hardly crucial to his work. Analogous to the staff expert in industry is the pathologist in medicine: he is not responsible for the treatment of patients (production) but only for his own expert work which, while having some bearing on treatment, does not constitute treatment. It is the special responsibility of the practicing physician that inevitably involves him in the varied levels of the division of labor. Whenever the practicing physician has such personal responsibility, we will find him intervening no matter what the hierarchical and functional organization of the hospital. But the *amount, content,* and *success* of such intervention will vary with the physician's commitment to and dependence on his position in the hospital.

In brief, I would hypothesize that, all else being equal, the greater the physician's commitment to his position in the hospital, the greater his inclination to use the regular channels of authority and the more orderly the transmission of information and "orders" bearing on patient care. Empirically, the simplest example of such commitment is full-time employment with no other career alternatives, though instances do occur in which a "voluntary" staff position is so crucial to the practice of a physician as to commit him to the hospital as much if not more than employment as such. This means that we should find far more evidence of the confusion described by Smith in American hospitals than in English and European hospitals where full-time hospital practice is more common. And it means that the problem is not generic to the hospital as such, nor to those bureaucratic organizations in which professionals work. Rather, the problem stems from the special characteristics of the medical profession, from the circumstances of medical practice in general and in the United States in particular.

Conflicting Perspectives in the Hospital

We usually assume that those who are administratively responsible for an organization possess the resources to make that organization pursue the officially approved goals set for it—that is, that actual behavior in the organization will be in accord with the official view of what the organization *should* be doing. But frequently it is not. The classic study of a state mental hospital by

Ivan Belknap [19] showed how an institution supposedly devoted to curing illness was instead devoted to maintaining a cruel custodial order among inmates, without making significant attempts at therapy. Furthermore, even when an official goal is more or less pursued, it is pursued in the context of interaction between the conflicting perspectives of the participants. A surgical ward, or a lying-in hospital, may be run like a tight ship by the surgical captains, but not without the friction created by the resistance of patients who may want more deference, personal service, and emotional support.[20] To understand what actually goes on in the ward, therefore, one must understand the perspectives of the participants, how they conflict with each other, and what resources each has available to allow him to assert his perspectives over the others. We may mention four perspectives here—that of the patient, of the nonprofessional aide, of the professional nurse, and of the physician in charge.

The patient. A great deal has been written about the personal anxiety attached to being ill and about the consequent irrational character of much of the patient's behavior on the ward. The staff is less involved in the illness than is the patient. Furthermore, as a layman the patient is also less capable of arriving at the proper diagnosis of his complaint than those who take care of him and is less likely to be able to evaluate his treatment. Finally, the individual patient is concerned with his own fortunes. In contrast, the staff is concerned with the fortunes of all patients, balancing off the relative need of one patient against the need of another, in the context of the limited time and energy available. While patients may certainly vary as individuals in the degree to which they are marked by such characteristics, those characteristics distinguish patients as a group from the staff as a group.

By the nature of the situation the perspective of the patient is in

[19] Ivan Belknap, *Human Problems of a State Mental Hospital* (New York: McGraw-Hill Book Co., 1956).

[20] Note Cartwright's finding that British maternity patients more than others are critical of the care they receive in hospital—apparently because they are often left alone during labor. Medically, maternity patients are not in so critical condition as to be believed to "need" the company of nurse or physician. Ann Cartwright, *Human Relations and Hospital Care* (London: Routledge and Kegan Paul, 1964), pp. 177–188.

conflict with that of the staff, and some of the staff effort will be devoted to controlling behavior that disrupts the ward routine. Depending on its mandate and ideology, the staff may seek to control such conflict by physical means (mechanical, electrical, chemical, or whatever), by efforts at rational explanation, pedagogy, and training, and by the techniques of psychotherapy. However, all members of the staff are not able to use all techniques of control if only by virtue of the division of labor that limits each level of the staff to the use of techniques appropriate to its "level of skill" or occupational jurisdiction. Furthermore, the resources of the patient himself can impose constraints on staff behavior.

From the accumulation of studies of interaction on the ward, a number of patient attributes seem to have important bearing on what techniques of control can be exercised by staff members seeking to order their work.[21] The grossest attribute is physical incapacity: an unconscious patient obviously poses fewer problems to the staff than a conscious one; a weak and bedridden patient fewer than an ambulatory. Another critical attribute is the patient's sociolegal identity: if he is a public charge by virtue of his "welfare" status, or a prisoner by virtue of legal commitment (in the case of drug addiction, tuberculosis, or psychosis), or something less than a responsible human being by virtue of being labeled psychotic, senile, retarded, or otherwise deficient in the qualities that grant one the right to be taken seriously, then he will have difficulty asserting his perspective in interaction on the ward. Also may be mentioned his socioeconomic resources: if he has the money (or, in Socialist countries, the political importance) to gain special care—a private-duty nurse or a hospital with a low patient-staff ratio, for example—and if he has the active support of healthy, knowledgeable, and influential friends or relatives outside the institution, he is a special problem of management. Finally, it is probable that organized and persistent problems of patient management are most likely to occur when patients are able to be in regular social inter-

[21] Perhaps the most important work bearing on the patient's perspective on and resistance to staff procedures is that of Julius A. Roth. See Roth and Eddy, *op. cit.*, Julius A. Roth, "Information and the Control of Treatment in Tuberculosis Hospitals," in Freidson, *op. cit.*, pp. 293–318; and Julius A. Roth, *Timetables* (Indianapolis: Bobbs-Merrill Co., 1963).

action with each other, when they all have the same general class of ailment about which they can exchange information, and when they share a relatively long-term, chronic prognosis. Under such circumstances they are likely to form their own little society which, whether it involves "living in the cracks" or "colonizing," nonetheless becomes a source of social strength which staff must take into account.[22]

Aides, orderlies, attendants. Empirically, many differences may be expected among patients on wards due both to variation in patient values and knowledge and to variation in the social resources which allow the patients to assert their own perspective. Such variation exists to a much lesser degree among the staff whose function it is to get done the necessary housekeeping jobs of the ward—at least so far as values and knowledge go. It seems no accident that attendants in mental hospitals, who are lower class in the United States and the United Kingdom, and lower-class but *not* middle-class mental patients, both have a high "custodial" orientation to the management of mental illness.[23] These poorly paid, essentially untrained workers, whose job it is to handle the dirty work of the wards, cannot be expected to hold, much less to exercise, the complex conceptions of treatment espoused by professionals. However, this is not to say that they have *no* conception of treatment. Their sin is in having a lay conception that is not shared by some influential professionals. As the "Custodial Mental Illness Ideology Scale" implies, their conception of mental illness is that it is so abnormal, hopeless, irrational, and dangerous as to surpass human understanding and to require close surveillance and control in hos-

[22] The tuberculosis patients studied by Roth were of this character, which is perhaps what made them such effective antagonists. For a very useful general discussion of the organized contingencies bearing on the degree to which patients could learn from each other how to manage the ward setting (by resistance or cooperation), see Stanton Wheeler, "The Structure of Formally Organized Socialization Settings," in O. G. Brim, Jr., and Stanton Wheeler, *Socialization after Childhood, Two Essays* (New York: John Wiley & Sons, 1966), pp. 53–113.

[23] See D. C. Gilbert and D. J. Levinson, "Role Performance, Ideology and Personality in Mental Hospital Aides," in M. Greenblatt *et al.*, eds., *The Patient and the Mental Hospital* (Glencoe, Illinois: The Free Press, 1957), pp. 197–208; and G. M. Carstairs and A. Heron, "The Social Environment of Mental Hospital Patients: A Measure of Staff Attitudes," in M. Greenblatt, *op. cit.*, pp. 218–230. For patients, see E. Gallagher and D. J. Levinson, *Patienthood* (Boston: Houghton Mifflin Co., 1965).

pital. This conception is quite similar to that described by the Cummings among the citizens of a Canadian community.[24] Nonetheless, as Strauss and his associates have pointed out, the view does not imply merely punitive reactions on the part of aides: their lay orientation to the management of the mentally ill contains within it specific modes of "training" and otherwise helping patients.[25]

By definition as nonprofessional workers, then, aides, orderlies, and attendants have nonprofessional perspectives on their work. This, however, is not a terribly important practical issue for interaction on the ward unless the aide is in a position to impose his perspective on others in the ward. By virtue of being involved in work on the ward day and night, he is in a position to exercise some leverage over the patient, both by physical restraint, and by the age-old evasive tactics of the underdog everywhere—"not hearing," "forgetting," and otherwise evading the demands of the more powerful. This certainly gives him a position of some influence on any ward. What apparently consolidates and strengthens the aide's position in the state mental hospital, however, is the effective absence from the ward of other workers, combined with circumstances that effectively neutralize patient demands. It seems no accident that these "first-line" workers are powerful precisely in those settings where the patients are stripped of their identity as responsible, adult human beings, and where there is no extensive and continuous participation by professional workers in some regular, effective therapeutic process on or off the wards. The aide's role has been powerful enough to warrant extended attention only in those institutions so underfinanced as to support at best a skeleton staff of professional workers, and in those institutions filled with patients with ailments for which there is no straightforward therapy with any immediate and definite results. In the former case, there are insufficient professional staff to allow effective supervision and control of aides: they must rely on what the aide reports to them. In the latter, there is insufficient foundation of observable, unambiguous results (such as frequently follows medical or surgical treatment) to persuade

[24] Elaine Cumming and John Cumming, *Closed Ranks, An Experiment in Mental Health Education* (Cambridge: Harvard University Press, 1957).

[25] Anselm Strauss *et al., Psychiatric Ideologies and Institutions* (New York: The Free Press of Glencoe, 1964), pp. 54–57. See also the excellent discussion in Richard F. Salisbury, *Structures of Custodial Care* (Berkeley: University of California Press, 1962), pp. 37–40.

attendants that there are professional techniques whose outcomes surpass lay common sense.

The nurse. As I have already observed in my discussion of nursing in Chapter 3, the professional qualities of the nurse are, particularly in the hospital, contingent on her relation to the physician.[26] She is the agent of the supervising physician in carrying out treatment and patient care. In this sense, she represents the professional perspective on the ward. However, insofar as she represents the day-to-day administration of the ward, she is also concerned with patients as a batch—something that, in the United States, at least, the physician is less concerned with. She must, therefore, balance individual physicians' orders for the care of individual patients against the independent demands of the patients as such and against the need to manage an aggregate of cases in an administratively acceptable way. It is because, unlike the aide, the nurse serves as an adjunct of both medical and administrative authority, that she seems to be the intense focus of conflicting perspectives. Unlike the aide, the nurse is imputed professional identity, and so she is likely to be engaged in a considerably more complex system of bargaining. In bargaining with physicians, one of her prime resources lies in her first-hand knowledge and professional evaluation of what goes on in the ward through her continued presence—a strategic advantage no doubt lost in such hospitals as those in the Soviet Union, where physicians are also present in enough number on a full-time basis to make a difference. In bargaining with patients, her prime strength lies in her access to the physician, both in knowing his inside information and in being able to discuss cases with him. Thus, while she may serve as a troubled focus of conflicting perspectives, she also may very well hold the balance of power in determining the outcome of bargaining among patient and staff.

The physician. As I have already noted, in an active treatment setting the physician largely determines what therapeutic efforts are made and, if he does not make all such efforts himself, he orders

[26] There is a huge literature on the nurse and her role conflicts, some of which has already been cited in Chapter 3. For a recent excellent statement, see Hans O. Mauksch, "The Nurse: Coordinator of Patient Care," in James K. Skipper, Jr., and Robert C. Leonard, eds., *Social Interaction and Patient Care* (Philadelphia: J. B. Lippincott Co., 1965), pp. 251–265. And see the extensive discussion in Duff and Hollingshead, *op. cit.*

and supervises the efforts of others. Aside from preventing interaction in the ward from damaging his relation with those patients for whom he is responsible, his problem is to obtain conformity with his orders by the other staff. But while it is relatively easy to have orders followed to the letter, the spirit is more difficult. When the lay common sense of aides, orderlies, or attendants is contradicted by the physician's philosophy of treatment, there is trouble. And when the physician's philosophy of treatment threatens the routine order of the ward, his approach is even less likely to be followed. The nurse may be involved in these difficulties when her training leads her to hold a "professional" philosophy of treatment that is at variance with that of the physician. Should such conflict in philosophy exist, a considerably more delicate process of manipulation and bargaining must occur for the physician to get his way, as Strauss and his associates have shown.

When all is said and done, however, it is the physician's expertise that is his ultimate resource in his interaction with others. As the final arbiter of practice in the medical division of labor, sustained by prestige and legal mandate, he has an "authority" that is independent of administrative authority as such.[27] The "authority" of his knowledge, judgment, and responsibility being ultimately exercised in the division of labor, it follows that a "hierarchy" of expertise exists independently of the administrative hierarchy in the hospital, the physician ordering and supervising those below his superior level of skill. This leads to hierarchical behavior even in those settings where the philosophy of treatment involves attempts to set up "democratic" or "therapeutic communities" which, while nonhierarchical in intent, turn out to be hierarchical in practice. There is no court of appeal from superior training, knowledge, and judgment; technical decisions are not made by vote.

Medical Tasks and Ward Behavior

These remarks about the perspectives of participants in the ward have had to take into account such variables as the medical specialty involved and the illness being treated. Clearly, one cannot under-

[27] See my discussion of the authoritarian implications of expertise in Eliot Freidson, *Professional Dominance* (New York: Atherton Press, forthcoming), Ch. 6.

stand the regularities to be found in the hospital without bearing in mind the specialties involved, the consequences of their technical jobs, and their different demands of and from patients. One can argue that one cannot discuss the general hospital as a single organization. While we may discuss the lying-in hospital, the mental hospital, and others that specialize in particular conditions or problems of treatment as relatively homogeneous organizations, we cannot discuss the general hospital in the same way because of the varied illnesses, patients, and procedures to be found in its special wards.[28] Instead, we must break down discussion of the general hospital into the various special services and wards, each of which has its own characteristics.

There is a fair amount of evidence of significant variation in the organization of interaction and performance within the wards of the general hospital, differences apparently stemming from the presence of different specialties, which is to say different practices, different tasks, and different requirements for the performance of those tasks (or "technologies"). Perhaps the most marked difference in task that one may observe in the everyday setting of the general hospital is the difference between medicine and surgery. Burling, Lentz, and Wilson have given an excellent description of the general differences.[29] In a somewhat more analytical paper, Coser noted some of the consequences of these differences.[30] Coser pointed out that surgical tasks are more frequently of an emergency character than are medical tasks. An emergency task must be performed quickly, undelayed by debates among the participants. The responsible surgeon must make his decisions quickly, and he must be able

[28] For discussion of classification by "technology," see Charles Perrow, "Hospitals: Technology, Structure and Goals," in James G. March, ed., *Handbook of Organizations* (Chicago: Rand-McNally and Co., 1965), pp. 910–971. And see the comments on the noncomparability of hospitals with varying interests in the patient in Mark Lefton and William R. Rosengren, "Organizations and Clients: Lateral and Longitudinal Dimensions," *American Sociological Review*, XXXI (1966), 802–810. It is their lack of recognition of this problem that makes it difficult to evaluate the findings by Basil S. Georgopoulos and Floyd C. Mann, *The Community General Hospital* (New York: The Macmillan Co., 1962).

[29] Burling *et al.*, *op. cit.*, Ch. 16.

[30] Rose L. Coser, "Authority and Decision-Making in a Hospital," *American Sociological Review*, XXIII (1958), 56–64.

to expect unquestioning, immediate aid. This quality of the surgical task was found to be reflected in differences in the way the exercise of authority and performance varied between the medical and surgical wards Coser studied. While the formal line of authority was much the same in both cases, in medicine there was consistent delegation of authority from the chief resident to the interns. But in surgery the chief resident did not delegate authority to his surgical subordinates. Furthermore, the social distance between the chief resident and the residents and interns under him was much greater in surgery than in medicine. Without delegated authority, the subordinate residents, interns, and even nurses on the surgical ward were all more or less "equal" in that all followed the decisions of the chief resident: the interaction among them was fairly free and informal. In contrast, on the medical ward, where the medical men but not the head nurse participated in decision-making, authority to do such was delegated down the medical hierarchy. Interaction among all participants was more formal, social distance dividing each rank from the other, rather than all from the chief resident.

Now clearly, daily routine on both medical and surgical wards can vary a great deal independently of the task, depending on the policies of the hospital administration and of the physician who serves as chief on the service. Coser's example is thus only an example, suggesting ways in which the consequences of task difference may be discerned. In another case, Seeman and Evans found surgical wards in one hospital on which the head physician tended to maximize his monopoly over decision-making, his social distance from subordinates, and his symbolic rank, and also, in the same hospital, surgical wards in which such "stratification" was low.[31] Their measure seems to refer to variations in the personal "leadership" style of the physicians in charge of the wards and does not seem addressed to the issue of task discussed by Coser and expanded on by Perrow.[32]

The "leadership style" of a superior may stem from his qualities as a person. On any ward, a physician who shares in decision-

[31] Melvin Seeman and John W. Evans, "Stratification and Hospital Care: I. The Performance of the Medical Interne; II. The Objective Criteria of Performance," *American Sociological Review,* XXVI (1961), 67–80, 193–204.

[32] Perrow, "Hospitals," *op. cit.*

making and minimizes his social distance from subordinates may very well be a warm, accepting person. However, if he is a "warm" person he may subscribe to a "warm philosophy." And even if he is not personally "warm" he may subscribe intellectually to a treatment ideology which emphasizes the importance of social and psychological variables in influencing illness and its therapy. The ideology defines the task as something quite different than the "mere" surgical removal or repair of some troublesome condition. In this sense, the task does not stand by itself, independent of the conceptions of the participants: holding such a "routine" surgical task as an appendectomy constant, behavior on the ward may vary according to the ideology as well as to the personal qualities of the workers. It may very well be that the *outcome* of the work in the form of rates of "cure" is not much different no matter what the operative ideology or philosophy, but the organization of interaction among the workers on the ward and between workers and patients, as well as the concrete work performed, does seem to vary significantly. As sociologists, we are interested in the interaction of treatment, so that to us, the variation in *interactional outcome* by ideology as well as by task is perhaps more important than the "disease outcome."

The importance of ideology to the organization of hospital work is illustrated by another case study by Coser, which contrasts the behavior of the nursing staff on wards whose patients are held by the staff not capable of improvement with a rehabilitation center of the same hospital whose patients the staff believes can be cured.[33] In the former case, the task was defined in custodial terms —to run a neat and orderly ward. In the latter case the task was defined in therapeutic terms—to improve the patient's condition to such an extent as to allow his discharge. While the "objective" physical capacities of the patients in both instances overlap—some in the custodial wards believed improvable by hospital physicians, and some in the rehabilitation center having irreversible conditions —the ideology dominant in each seemed to govern a great deal of staff behavior.

In the "custodial" wards the nursing staff found plans to dis-

[33] Rose L. Coser, "Alienation and the Social Structure: Case Analysis of a Hospital," in Freidson, *op. cit.*, pp. 231–265.

charge a patient disruptive, for they assumed that the patient would be back after a short absence in any case. Emphasis was on orderly housekeeping and routinized records and on the mechanical side of nursing tasks. There was comparatively little staff interaction with the patients. Indeed, the high patient-staff ratio on the custodial wards seemed to lead to withdrawal from therapeutic tasks on the part of both nurses and physicians including not only withdrawal from the patients but also withdrawal from interaction with other staff members over problems of patient management. Without interaction, there was little occupational conflict on the custodial wards. In contrast, in the rehabilitation center, where an active treatment ideology prevailed (supported, we should not forget, by a very low patient-staff ratio), a great deal of patient-staff interaction took place as did a great deal of conflictful interaction among the various occupations. "Treatment philosophy" thus has clear consequences for ward interaction, consequences which can be dealt with by specifying three patterns of ward care.

Patterns of Ward Care

In my discussion thus far I have pointed, sometimes glancingly, to a number of variables which seem to have strategic relevance to understanding the performance of the staff of American hospitals. Given significant differences in the social consequences of various medical and surgical tasks, and in the consequences of various ideologies of treatment guiding how tasks are actually performed, it seems useful to distinguish among several patterns of performance to be found in hospitals or some of their wards. At one extreme may be found the *domestic service pattern*, which is not appropriate, strictly speaking, to our definition of a hospital, but which is nonetheless found in "hospitals" which have official recognition as medical treatment institutions. This pattern involves the performance of essentially housekeeping tasks—feeding, clothing, bedding, amusing, and otherwise managing the lives of the inmates—with little effort at anything more than the routine episodic medical care that a "house doctor" resident in a hotel or on board ship may be expected to give.

The domestic-service pattern of management is founded on the assumption that nothing more can (or should) be done for the inmates than to make them comfortable or keep them out of trouble while they are residents. They are in some way inappropriate subjects for intensive therapeutic efforts—they are, for example, hopelessly retarded, crippled, or psychotic, or irreversibly helpless physically, whether by virtue of age or impairment.[34] Given this assumption, it follows that there is no need for a treatment staff. Furthermore, it follows that the quality of the staff-"patient" retionship is likely to have few of the attributes said to be characteristic of that of a professional to his client. Rather, it is likely to resemble that of a protective servant to his master or of a keeper to his charge. The former relationship seems to exist in expensive private "rest homes" and nursing homes,[35] perhaps in the Japanese mental hospital with *tsukisoi.*[36] The latter pattern, often called custodial in an invidious tone by those who feel that therapy is indicated,[37] seems to exist in the underfinanced and understaffed public mental hospitals. Whether "custodial" or otherwise, the domestic-service pattern is not one dominated or closely supervised by the medical man, whether by design or by the default of underfinancing and understaffing.

The second pattern has been called "the classical hospital care model" by Wessen,[38] though I prefer the term "*medical-intervention pattern.*" Unlike the domestic-service pattern, it is dominated by the medical man. The medical man is prone to see the patient's difficulty as a transitory technical problem that can be overcome by

[34] See Julius A. Roth and Elizabeth M. Eddy, *Rehabilitation for the Unwanted* (New York: Atherton Press, 1967), for a study of physically handicapped inmates.

[35] See the British survey of homes for the aged—Peter Townsend, *The Last Refuge* (London: Routledge and Kegan Paul, 1962).

[36] William A. Caudill, "Around the Clock Patient Care in Japanese Psychiatric Hospitals: The Role of the *Tsukisoi,*" *American Sociological Review,* XXVI (1961), 204–214.

[37] The value of the invidious word "custodialism," most closely identified with the work of Daniel Levinson, is unfortunately weakened by its confusion of two separate notions. The first notion is a moral one with which all must agree—that no matter how poor or deficient in ordinary human attributes, inmates should receive humane care. The second notion is an article of faith in the therapeutic results of humane management, results by no means established on a sound scientific basis. See Perrow, "Hospitals," *op. cit.*

[38] Albert A. Wessen, "The Apparatus of Rehabilitation: An Organizational Analysis," in M. B. Sussman, ed., *Sociology and Rehabilitation* (Washington: American Sociological Association, 1966), pp. 170–173.

some physical or biochemical intervention which only the physician is qualified to perform. The assumption is that the patient can be cured and discharged. But the patient is incompetent to judge what is needed and in order to be cured must put himself passively into the hands of the staff, obeying them without question and allowing them to do to him what they see fit. Similarly, the staff's work is organized by the physician's orders, initiating little itself, and primarily serving as his agent in dealing with the patient. Interaction between patient and staff thus takes on an impersonal quality, and interaction among various members becomes ordered by a professional chain of command, from the supervising physician to the registered nurse to the practical nurse and so on. This pattern is most marked on surgical floors but is also present in medicine and, in the form of the "somato-therapeutic ideology," in psychiatry.

Over the past few decades, the classical intervention pattern has been under intensive attack by many, both in and out of medicine. Quite apart from the special problem of mental illness, growing interest in psychosomatic medicine and in the theory of stress has led to seeing even superficially simple illnesses to be influenced by the feelings and motives of the patient, the illnesses no longer being considered discrete, delimited entities that can be managed independently of the patient as a person. The phrase "comprehensive care" has risen to serve as a label of the view that ailments should not be managed discretely, separately from each other by individual specialists.[39] These developments, while still more programmatic than actually realized, have come to make ambiguous the character of the classical intervention pattern, particularly in the university-affiliated hospitals where they flourish. They blur the empirical sharpness of the distinction that logic can make between the classical intervention pattern and the newer pattern of therapeutic interaction.

The pattern of *therapeutic interaction* is one that is commonly used, in its essentials, in psychotherapy. It is also, however, a pattern of organization for hospital services, much of which is referred to by psychiatric ideas of a "therapeutic" milieu, and which is implied

[39] For a description and evaluation of a training program, see George G. Reader and Mary E. W. Goss, eds., *Comprehensive Medical Care and Teaching* (Ithaca: Cornell University Press, 1967).

by Wessen's discussion of the "rehabilitation model."[40] In this pattern, the patient must be persuaded to become an active participant in a process of interaction around therapy; his own motivated activity is an essential part of the pattern. Furthermore, while none but the most radical or most self-deceiving proponents of the pattern would relegate him to a subordinate or even merely equal position, the physician's position is more ambiguous than in the classical intervention pattern. He is legally and usually institutionally in charge of the case, true, but he is not held to have a monopoly over relevant treatment skills, and insofar as he recognizes that all paramedical members of the staff in interaction with the patient have access to information of value to planning therapy and that they cannot fail, in their interaction, to have influence on the patient's response to treatment, the physician must at least act like a member of a therapeutic team. He is likely to have comparatively little on-the-job social distance from his "subordinates," being less the chief and more the first among equals. Indeed, the patient himself is sometimes even held to be a member of the "team," though never to the extent of participating in all staff meetings.[41] The absolute character of the authority of expertise makes itself felt even in this pattern.

Medical Performance in the Hospital

In this chapter I have emphasized the influence on hospital affairs, and the division of labor embodied in the hospital, by medicine and medical practice. I have done this in spite of the fact that the physician-owned hospital is increasingly rare in modern societies, that community and state are increasingly dominant in setting general hospital policies, that hospital administrators become increasingly the strategic force in setting everyday operative policies in the hospital, and that an increasing number of nonphysician

[40] Wessen, *op. cit.*, pp. 176–178. Obviously relevant here are some of the presently fashionable psychiatric notions of therapeutic "communities." See, for example, Maxwell Jones, *The Therapeutic Community, A New Treatment Method in Psychiatry* (New York: Basic Books, 1953).

[41] This "failure" was reported in Robert Rubenstein and Harold D. Lasswell, *The Sharing of Power in a Psychiatric Hospital* (New Haven: Yale University Press, 1966).

workers in the hospital lay claim to being "professionals" and attempt to behave accordingly.[42] I have adopted this emphasis in part because of my interest in medicine rather than the hospital. More importantly, I believe this emphasis is justified because of the dominant role the physician plays in determining the character of the essential activities that provide the very raison d'être of the hospital —what is done to and for the patient. Increasingly, the physician does not control the financing or the constitutional organization and administration of hospital care, but he nonetheless retains the right to determine what technical and occupational resources are needed by the patient who is under his care. This is, as I have already noted, typical of a profession. Furthermore, his determinations are not subject to direct evaluation or review by any other occupation: they may be limited by purely administrative or financial decisions made by others, but they may not be directly questioned except by other physicians. This, too, is typical of a profession. His medical performance, therefore, is most likely to vary according to the role his colleagues on the medical staff play in his work and only secondarily in the special characteristics of his work, and in special circumstances of hospital practice, according to the role played by other workers in the division of labor in the hospital. Here, too, as in types of office practice, interaction with his colleagues is the critical variable in the control of his performance.

In this chapter and in Chapter 5, I have tried to show how variations in the organization of office and hospital practice may exert systematic influence on the performance of medical work. Such variation is hypothesized on a statistical basis, predicting that the *average* performance of the total aggregate of physicians in one work-setting will conform to higher or lower medical standards, or lay standards, than the average performance of the medical population in another work-setting. I have emphasized the importance of the individual's dependence on and close interaction with his medical colleagues. While, particularly in this chapter on the hospital, I have also suggested other factors, including variation in the work itself, which seem to play a part in influencing his performance,

[42] For data on these and other cross-national trends, see the important essay, William A. Glaser, "American and Foreign Hospitals: Some Sociological Comparisons," in Freidson, *Hospital in Modern Society, op. cit.*, pp. 37–72.

colleague interaction is central: the more there is, the more likely medical rather than lay or individual standards will be met.

Nonetheless, in spite of the fact that this kind of reasoning should be able to predict and perhaps explain *relative* differences in performance, it cannot predict or explain *absolute levels* of performance. This is to say, if we arbitrarily assign numerical values of one through seven to performance, seven representing the optimal, we should find that a population of isolated general practitioners will perform on, say, an average level of two, and a population of hospital-based anesthesiologists on an average level of four. But why those values? Why should they be at the level they are? Most particularly in the case of men working in a colleague-dependent and colleague-controlled setting, why should not performance be at a level of five or six? It is useful and important to understand the source of relative differences, but surely it is at least as important to understand the source of the absolute level of performance.

Obviously, a number of variables figure in an answer, including the absolute level of skill and capacity of the individuals involved and the effectiveness of the knowledge and equipment available to perform various tasks. Psychologists can no doubt tell us much about the former, and physicians about the latter. There is, however, another variable about which the sociologist might properly inquire: given whatever skill and capacity are available, and given current knowledge and equipment, is the interaction among colleagues which is believed to raise the *relative* level of performance of such a nature as to encourage the *absolute* level that individual and scientific capability allows? This question raises a number of others: What, exactly, is involved in the colleague interaction surrounding the control of performance? What information about performance is reviewed and how is it used? What is done when information about suboptimal performance comes to hand? What, in short, is the nature of the process of self-regulation to be found among physicians and how extensive is it? These are the questions I shall attempt to answer in the next chapter.

7.

THE TEST OF AUTONOMY: PROFESSIONAL SELF-REGULATION

As I noted in my analysis of medicine as a profession, autonomy is the test of that status. Professional people have the special privilege of freedom from the control of outsiders. Their privilege is justified by three claims. First, the claim is that there is such an unusual degree of skill and knowledge involved in professional work that nonprofessionals are not equipped to evaluate or regulate it. Second, it is claimed that professionals are responsible—that they may be trusted to work conscientiously without supervision. Third, the claim is that the profession itself may be trusted to undertake the proper regulatory action on those rare occasions when an individual does not perform his work competently or ethically. The profession is the sole source of competence to recognize deviant performance, and it is also ethical enough to control deviant performance and to regulate itself in general. Its autonomy is justified and tested by its self-regulation.

Patently, the processes of self-regulation to be found in a profession are of great practical and analytical importance. The difficulty is, however, that there is very little information available about the way they operate. To be sure, there is some information to be had about formal review institutions. In Chapter 2, for example, I noted the British arrangement for reviewing charges made by patients against physicians. In the United States, county medical societies are supposed to review both patient and colleague charges, and, as we saw in the case of physicians violating prevailing norms of "ethicality" by practicing on other than a solo fee-for-service arrangement, they do sometimes perform disciplinary functions, reviewing charges of incompetence as well as of unethicality. Their activities are secret, and it is hard to say much about them except that some county societies are fairly active and many are inactive. In any event, the county society review boards are a form of private law court; they hear charges whenever they are made. A civil court could presumably review the same charges and perform the same function should civil suit be instituted. But unlike legal institutions in general, county society judiciary councils do not have any formal agents whose job it is, like that of the police, to actively look for violations of the law, to inspect or review everyday behavior for deviance, and to institute charges on behalf of the public. In short, they lack formal screening and review procedures.

More important than the county medical society judicial committee in the United States are the review committees that have arisen in some medical groups and hospitals. In "accredited" hospitals—that is, those meeting the minimum standards of the Joint Commission on the Accreditation of Hospitals—committees reviewing the credentials of physicians seeking staff privileges, the medical records, and laboratory analysis of tissue removed by surgery are most common. McNerney's survey of "control" in hospitals, even if limited in many instances to some thirty-three institutions in Michigan, provides us with an invaluable guide to regulatory procedures in medicine.[1] Only 26 per cent of small hospitals and 47 per cent of those of between 100 and 500 beds, he noted, impose restrictions on the work that members of the staff may perform, according to their qualifications. Most large hospitals placed limits on "privileges." In the case of the review of medical records, only 37 per cent of the medical-record committees used the records to determine whether or not the care given by the physician was adequate, while the remainder merely reviewed the record to make sure it was filled out completely. Sixty-one per cent of the tissue committees, however,

[1] Walter J. McNerney *et al.,* Hospital and Medical Economics, 2 vols. (Chicago: Hospital Research and Educational Trust, 1962), especially pp. 1205–1459, on "controls within and upon the voluntary health system."

operate correctively. Surveillance and control are commonly exercised over major surgical procedures and less often over complicated obstetrical procedures. Control over complex medical problems, minor surgery, and simple medical and normal obstetrical tasks is quite uncommon.

With McNerney's evidence in mind, we may note that in 1967, 66 per cent of the hospitals in the United States were accredited. This means that there is no assurance that even the minimum standards of review of credentials and performance are met in one of every three hospitals in the nation. Clearly, extensive *formal* self-regulatory mechanisms for the review of performance even in such organized settings as hospitals do not predominate. Indeed, as McNerney states, physicians are highly resistant to restrictions on the independence of their decisions.[2] There has, in fact, been persistent criticism of the profession's lack of support of such restrictions.

It seems clear that *formal* review procedures are not very common in most medical work settings. They are, however, more common in hospitals than in office practice and considerably more common in teaching hospitals—that is, those accredited for providing the postgraduate training of interns and residents—than in hospitals without approved programs of training. Furthermore, they are said to be more common in university or university-affiliated hospitals than in those without university connections. Indeed, the quality of staff performance is said to be higher in university-affiliated hospitals than in others, a finding we might expect from their formal review procedures as well as from the quality of their staff as individuals.

It may be noted from the above discussion that attention has been focused entirely on the mere *existence* of formal standards and review procedures. It is plausible to believe that where they exist, performance will be on a somewhat higher average level than where they do not. However, until we know how those formal procedures are actually used, we have no way of knowing whether or not *optimal* performance is being encouraged. But outside of anecdote and tactfully vague official reports, there is virtually no in-

[2] *Ibid.*, p. 1325.

formation available on how those regulatory committees work. Furthermore, the sociologist is well aware of how much social control goes on outside of formal bodies and of the important role of the unofficial or informal regulatory processes in bringing deviant performance to the attention of formal bodies. Indeed, I would argue that adequate *informal* devices of regulation are necessary for the effective operation of formal institutions and, under some circumstances, both necessary and sufficient for optimal regulation of performance. Since there is some systematically collected empirical information available about those informal devices, I believe it is worthwhile to concentrate on them here. It is necessary to treat of relatively detailed data from only one practice setting, supplemented by a few other studies. While this information is hardly enough to exemplify all of American medicine, I believe that the setting is strategic enough to be instructive. The setting is highly academic in character, representing one of the more advanced and prestigious types of practice in the United States. Tied in with a university-affiliated hospital, its practitioners all have staff privileges and the training that goes with them. Thus, it should manifest a higher average level of performance than is to be found in ordinary office settings and even ordinary hospital settings. Furthermore, the regulatory processes to be found within the setting studied should represent some of the best, not merely the ordinary, usages of self-regulation.

The Work Setting[3]

The observations described here were made during the course of an intensive study of an urban medical clinic staffed by exception-

[3] Portions of this section are reprinted from Eliot Freidson and Buford Rhea, "Processes of Control in a Company of Equals," *Social Problems*, XI (1963), 119–131, reprinted by permission of the Society for the Study of Social Problems, and Eliot Freidson and Buford Rhea, "Knowledge and Judgment in Professional Evaluations," *Administrative Science Quarterly*, X (1965), 107–124, and reprinted by permission of the *Administrative Science Quarterly*. Support for the study and its analysis was provided by U.S. Public Health Service Grants CH–00025 and CH–00414.

Throughout this report the past tense is deliberately used to emphasize that many changes in the clinic have taken place since 1961–62, the time of the study.

ally well-trained, experienced physicians, all of whom were either board-certified, or eligible, by virtue of their training, to take specialty board examinations. In this sense they had better professional credentials than the average run of doctors. And while it was a fairly large clinic of about fifty doctors, equipped with a fully developed administrative staff, numerous clerks and paramedical personnel, and all doctors were on salary rather than being partners, it was considerably less bureaucratic than, for example, a college.

The files of the organization were examined, both confidential and routine, official and unofficial. All of its meetings including those of the executive body were attended during the time of the study. In addition to interviewing all of the doctors in the clinic, most of them three or four times, a sample of thirty doctors who were once associated with the clinic was interviewed. The chief administrative personnel were also interviewed a number of times. By these devices, a large accumulation of data was made, ranging from verbatim interview transcripts to notes on luncheon gossip, and including sociometric ratings, minutes of meetings, and extracts from both medical and administrative records.

Like the university, the clinic followed the principle of hierarchy, although unusually simply. The Medical Director was responsible for the conduct of the organization in general, including that of the physicians, and the Administrator was responsible for everyday operations, particularly but not exclusively for the conduct of the paramedical and clerical staff. The latter was organized into offices and departments, with clear lines of authority, but whereas the physicians were divided into various medical specialty departments, there was little division into vertical ranks. There were titular chiefs of some departments, but it was not at all clear what their duties and prerogatives were, not even to them. Aside from this, there was no system of graded ranks analogous to those found at universities, and whereas seniority was an important source of influence, it was not a consistent locus of hierarchical authority. Furthermore, the workers have had the long period of training characteristic of professionals, their professional freedom was protected by tenure, and formal subordination and superordination among colleagues were almost nonexistent. Hence, the clinic came close to being the "company of equals"[4] that professionals consider optimal for work: an organization in which little other than colleague controls exist.

Rules

In most models of bureaucracy, subordinates are said to be so placed by virtue of the obedience they must render to superiors and their obligation to conform to various rules and regulations. This was also partially the case for the clinic. In the first place, the physician had "contractual" obligations, such as the number of hours he must spend in his office seeing patients, which were spelled out in some detail and which he accepted as conditions of his employment. All physicians recognized (even if unwillingly) the legitimacy of these administratively determined regulations. In addition, there were intramural rules whose purpose it was to insure coordination of effort: for example, whether the obstetrician or the generalist[5] would be responsible for providing emergency care for spontaneous abortions. Some of these rules were worked out by the physicians; some were suggested by the administration; and others were agreed upon in joint administration-physician discussion. In all cases they were seen as mutually agreeable expedients to solve unavoidable and obvious problems. Finally, there were some rules which should but in fact did not affect the physicians. Some of them came from external sources, and if they conflicted with medical or organizational efficiency and there was small chance of detection, both administration and collegium tacitly agreed to ignore them.

The variety of rules thus far parallel those which are common to most formal organizations. However, I must note that none of the rules bearing on the purely technical core of medical practice—examination, diagnosis, prescription, and treatment—may be classified as formally binding. By and large, the most important rule bearing on the purely technical core of medical practice was more a policy statement than a regulation: it asserted that the highest possible medical standards would be maintained regardless of cost.

[4] Cf. Bernard Barber, *Science and the Social Order* (New York: Collier Books, 1962), p. 195.

[5] All physicians were "specialists," but those internists and pediatricians who provide primary care are here called "generalists."

Like many another organization in which unusually skilled work is performed, the clinic did not specify the technical procedures to be used, but it did attempt to specify that procedures generally approved by the professional community should be used. When the doctors of the clinic disagreed, determination of what was proper lay with members of the extra-clinic professional community who might be called in. Conflict observed in technical affairs was between professional opinions—for example, between that of the clinic doctors, and of professional consultants from outside the clinic—and not between the physicians and the clinic administration.

Mention of technical affairs brings up the need to distinguish the areas of work over which control may be exercised. The technical core of medical practice was one major area. The other was the degree to which effort was exercised and the way effort was organized. It was in the latter area, which had no necessary relationship to technical expertness, that conflict was most likely to occur between administration and physician and among physicians. For example, the organizational need for calculability and coordination in the provision of services led to administrative pressures on the doctor for punctuality. Organizational responsibility for the patient led to the creation of administrative channels for patient complaints. Neither the need for punctuality nor that for responsibility for the patient was questioned by most physicians, but being accountable to the organization for one's time and for one's difficulties with patients was seen to be undignified, the equivalent of being treated like a factory worker or a clerk.[6] Conflict between administration and collegium, and even among colleagues, in such areas as these was persistent and was based on quite different rules and norms than was the conflict that occurred about technical procedures.

Administrative Collection of Supervisory Information

If control over workers is to occur, information about performance must be collected. Obviously, rules would be meaningless if

[6] It should be noted that while professionalism as an expression of *expertise* requires only control over the *content* of work (as I have already indicated in earlier chapters), professionalism as an expression of *prestige* presses for control over the *organization* of work. While there are certainly areas in which organization bears on content, the two are not synonymous analytically or pragmatically.

one never knew when they were broken. How can conformity to the rules be ascertained by the administration when the physician does so much of his work in the privacy of his office? First, certain gross aspects of the physician's organization of effort were noted in routine ways. Receptionists were supposed to notify the administration in the event that a physician changed his hours, did not allow her to make an appointment for an open scheduled time period, or was habitually late. Similarly, when a physician rushed through his patients to finish early or booked patients earlier than he could actually see them to make sure they would be ready for him whenever he was ready, these and like behaviors were visible to all who would take the trouble to look. Judicious tapping of the paramedical grapevine, plus inspection of appointment books, constituted fairly regular devices for checking on the organization of physicians' efforts. But this was the only regular and continuous administrative check on performance, and it yielded information primarily about punctuality and speed of work, nothing about technical performance.

The patient was directly in contact with the physician during his work, and the clinic was organized to provide regular channels for patient complaints to the administration. Therefore, the patient could be a source of information about performance. But the patients' opinions were something few physicians would accept as valid indication of technical performance, and although some complaints did stimulate investigation, instances were fairly rare and provided only random bits of evidence.

Interestingly enough, an accurate source of information about all physicians existed, but it was used only after it was suspected that something might be wrong. The medical record for each patient was, in its wealth of detailed information, a bureaucratic delight (though its unsystematic character also makes it a researcher's nightmare). Perhaps because of the legal liability of the work, as well as because of the needs of treatment, information was continuously recorded but not routinely scrutinized by anyone. The medical chart was a working tool, becoming a supervisory device only when interest in the case had been triggered by some event suggesting the necessity of investigation—a patient complaint, a lawsuit, an accidental observation, or the like. It was thus only latently supervisory, used after the fact to reconstruct past performance in damning or exonerating detail.

Colleague Collection of Supervisory Information

The clinic administration was obviously only tangentially involved in any activities that could form the basis for exerting control over the core technical activities of the physicians. This was as it should be in the professional view of things, for only colleagues should be so involved. But how far were colleagues involved? How, without routine review of the charts, could information about a doctor's technical performance be gathered? How much did colleagues know about each other? To answer this, I may cite some data drawn from the segment of the study in which physicians were asked to rate each other by competence and other criteria. Statements of ignorance about the performance of *some* colleagues were accepted at face value, though if a rater gave this response for every one of his colleagues it was assumed that he was being evasive rather than entirely honest.

What was the state of mutual knowledge and ignorance among the doctors of the clinic? [7] First of all, referral relations must obviously be involved in order for one doctor to be in a position to observe another. In the clinic studied, fourteen specialties were represented. The largest department, internal medicine, was composed of twenty internists, all of whom functioned in the clinic as "family doctors" treating adults. Six pediatricians composed another generalist department, devoted to the general care of children. All but one of the remaining departments were clearly consulting specialties devoted to particular organs, pathologies, or procedures. The exception, obstetrics-gynecology, occupied an ambiguous position in the medical division of labor, because as obstetrics it assumed prime responsibility for treating pregnant women for most medical problems while they were pregnant, but as gynecology it treated only those special problems connected with female organs. Excluding obstetrics-gynecology, tabulation of statements of ignorance established a clear relationship between the capacity to rate a colleague and a general referral relationship. This is to say, more

[7] Statistical details appear in Freidson and Rhea, "Knowledge and Judgment," *op. cit.*

ignorance about the abilities of colleagues was reported by internists and pediatricians about each other, and by the various consulting specialists about each other, than by specialists about generalists and vice-versa.

The gross distinction between referring and consulting specialties, however, may be refined by the character of the specialty and its place in the division of labor. Ophthalmology, for example, is a very limited technical specialty: it was known relatively little by the men in seven other specialties, and itself knew very little about seven of the specialties. Allergy was relatively little known, as was orthopedics. The best known and most knowledgeable specialties were internal medicine and surgery.

These remarks have been restricted to knowledge about technical performance alone, but of course there are other areas of performance. Even before ratings of colleagues by competence were asked for, all physicians were asked to rate the generalists by the relative number of house calls they made, their popularity with patients, their tendency to finish scheduled hours on time, and their tendency to refer their cases to consultants rather than to handle them themselves. Since pediatrics and internal medicine were by and large parallel to each other in the division of labor, and pediatrics was a considerably smaller service, it is necessary here to focus solely on the internists and compare what they knew about each other with what consultants knew about them. Among the internists, it was found that very few could not rate both their colleagues' patient popularity and their willingness to make house calls. But little more than half could rate their colleagues' capacity to finish hours on time, and only a third could rate referral habits. Consultants, on the other hand, were considerably less able to rate internists' house-call habits and were unable to rate their ability to finish their hours on time. Somewhat over half could rate the internists' popularity with patients. This may be taken as a demonstration that what one man knows about another is pretty much a function of the division of labor, but that *the visibility of performance granted by the division of labor is not holistic but fragmentary*. One man will only know some things about the performance of another, not everything. He will only know what is important to *his* relationship and not necessarily what is important for others, or important for assessing the over-all performance of the individual concerned. As I shall point out later on, there is in this particular clinic little communication of such information by gossip, so the barriers to a widespread flow of information about performance established by the division of labor stand out clearly.

In addition, it is possible to observe that there were structured biases in the way one man evaluated another—that the standards for assessment of performance varied. Aside from the fact that younger men were generally more critical in their evaluations than older men—that is, gave lower ratings—and that long-tenured men were generally rated higher than those with short tenure, the different perspectives men had in the division of labor led to different assessments of competence owing to different expectations.

The bias of perspective may be illustrated by comparing the ratings of obstetrics-gynecology given by pediatricians and those given by internists. The pediatricians rated the obstetricians higher than most of the specialists; the internists rated them lower. This seemed to be explained by the fact that the pediatricians did not really work with the obstetricians but merely received generally healthy babies from them. The internists, however, sent their gynecological problems to the obstetricians, many of which were troublesome and difficult to solve, and so the internists had occasion to obtain a somewhat more jaundiced view of the capacities of the gynecologists. Differences in assessment, then, occurred according to variation in the type of work being referred.

Finally, it might be observed that, in the clinic studied, men did not seem to gossip much about each other's experience with colleagues. This means that there was nothing to compensate for the limited and fragmented distribution of information or the biasing of assessment by the division of labor and that very few people would share much information about any single person.

Transmission of Supervisory Information

It should be clear that neither the administration nor the collegium observed both the doctor's organization of effort and the technical quality of that effort. Furthermore, what work was observed was fragmentary and rather specialized; each class of data was insulated from the others. The administration collected information about office hours that was not very accessible to the collegium. The consultant collected information about the generalist that was not very observable to generalists. Obviously, the colleague group could not behave as a collectivity as long as these bits of information were scattered discretely through its ranks. They must in some way share the same information by pooling it. This could occur when a man practiced such persistent and thoroughgoing deviance that in one way or another it became apparent to every individual in the clinic; it was more likely to occur quickly when individual bits of information were passed around among the doctors.

By and large, although communication of observations did occur, it was slow and limited, most often occurring by innuendo rather than directly, and within rather than between specialties. While colleagues in the clinic did gossip about each other, they were generally not inclined to communicate their observations bit by bit, as they collected them. There was little continuous revelation of observations. Rather, each individual tended to store up his own observations, saying little or nothing about them until he could no longer contain his indignation or until he discovered from others' hints that they too had doubts about the same individual. If his observations were few, and he had no strong opinion about them, he might never communicate them. Given the accidental character of many disclosures and given the necessity for them to accumulate before they were shared, a considerable period of time could elapse before any widespread opinion about a man emerged. And obviously the time would vary with the strategic visibility of the specialty. Several instances were observed of rather long-tenured people who were thought to be below the clinic average of competence by those in their own specialty but who were thought to be above average or at least average by all others.

In unusual cases, a sufficiently large number of observations had been stored in the memories of a sufficient number of physicians to allow a coalescence of opinion. Arriving at a certain critical mass of discontent with an individual seemed to be necessary before most physicians would begin complaining about him to each other and the administration. One physician might make a rather neutral but probing remark to a second about a third, whereupon the second would have his story to contribute, and so forth. But this collective definition formed only among groups of physicians who had the opportunity to discuss such matters, and as a result there could be different pockets of opinion about the same man within the clinic.

Negative Sanctions

Slowly and selectively, some information about misbehavior did come to light. How was it handled? When physicians were asked what they would do about an offending colleague, the usual response was: "Nothing." Asked what they would do if the offense were repeated, however, they answered: "I'd talk to him." "Talking-to" was, in fact, the most ubiquitous sanction in the clinic and was used by both colleagues and administration as virtually the only means of sanction. From the examples we collected, talking-to seemed to involve various blends of instruction, friendly persuasion, shaming, and threat.

The incidence of talking-to varied with social distance. A colleague was more likely to talk-to someone in his own department than to someone outside and to a peer or junior more than to a senior man. He was likely to say nothing to an individual outside his department or to his senior, and when he got angry enough he would complain instead to his peers or even to the administration. Talkings-to were also graded according to severity. The mildest (and by far most common) talking-to was a simple man-to-man affair—one person informally raising the issue with another. If the offender did not mend his ways the offended man might enlist the aid of other talkers, either the administrator or one or more colleagues. Eventually, if misbehavior persisted and there was strong feeling about it, the offender might be talked-to by the Medical Director or a formal committee of colleagues.

Talking-to is of course a very common informal sanction among peers in all work groups and is used by superiors everywhere. What is interesting about talking-to in the clinic is that it was the only institutionalized punishment short of dismissal. There were no intermediate forms of punishment. And since dismissal was almost impossible once a man was tenured, talking-to was virtually the only sanction available. Tenure regulations required a vote of three-quarters of the members of the clinic: a decision by a company of equals was necessary for dismissal. As we have already seen, the conditions for the formation of a collective opinion were not generally present in the system. Given the unevenness of the distribution of information in the clinic we have described, even a simple majority of the doctors was unlikely to have had personal experience with an individual's deficiencies. Without such personal experience, most physicians were loath to vote for expulsion on the basis of the complaints of the few colleagues or patients who did experience them. Only the most gross and shocking deficiencies would do. The practical impossibility of dismissing a tenured physician was thus inevitable. In a fifteen-year period, about eighty doctors had resigned from the clinic, most of them for their own reasons, some with encouragement, but none who were tenured were formally dismissed.

Talking-to was thus the only practical form of negative sanction in the clinic. Aside from this, there were only rewards to motivate the physicians. Most of those rewards were bureaucratized so as to operate automatically, independent of the physician's deportment. There was, for example, a system of automatic increments, vacation with pay, bonus increments for obtaining specialty board certification, and the like. And at a certain age a man could buy his way out of making night and weekend emergency calls on patients. These rewards were rights of which an offender could not be deprived. There were, however, other rewards which were particularly important because they were not bureaucratically guaranteed and because they were characteristically indirect and discretionary. Insofar as they were not mandatory, an individual could be "punished" by being "passed over" in their assignment. Some were controlled by colleagues and some by the administration.

The set of such discretionary rewards might be called a privilege system: special tokens, sometimes rather trivial in character, which have not been codified and bureaucratically guaranteed as rights or increments, and which, taken individually, may be unique and nonrecurrent, even subject to invention by the administration. In the clinic, some of the more stable privileges involved extra money for performing such tasks as supervising the laboratory, handling official correspondence about patient complaints, serving as a special consultant, and supervising a research program. Others were more symbolic in character: for example, being invited to represent the organization to a group of distinguished visitors, being chosen to travel at clinic expense, or being allowed to take a leave of absence. The most strategic privileges played upon the physician's self-image. They constituted recognition of what he felt was due him at his stage of career or level of attainment.

In sum, the characteristic sanctions were never so strong as to reduce income and minimize or prevent work on the part of offenders, and they were rarely organized. By and large, offended colleagues used the technique of *personal* exclusion. They attempted to bar a man from working with them individually or with their own patients, but they did not attempt to bar him from working with or on the patients of others. This is similar to the principal method of control used in solo practice. The offender is not referred patients or, if referral must be made, only unimportant cases are sent to him. He is not consulted about problems in his specialty or sub-specialty: his advice is not sought, and he is not called in to look at an interesting or peculiar case. Finally, he is not included in the system of exchanging favors that is so important and common in professional work: if he asked someone for a favor, he would probably not be refused, but others would not ask him for favors and so would refuse him the credit that would allow him to ask with impunity for another favor in the future. It is important to note that all these methods of exclusion are practiced by *individuals:* they are not actions of the collegium. Therefore, they do not prevent an offender from working and maintaining his work relations with colleagues whom he has not offended. *They punish him only insofar as he is sensitive to the good opinion of those particular individuals who exclude him.*

Characteristics of the Process

I have noted that the elements involved in the process by which control was exercised in this company of equals were fairly unbureaucratic in character. Access to information about work performance was not, by and large, hierarchically organized. At best it was a selective function of the division of labor; at worst it was a function of unsystematically random, accidental revelations to accidental observers. This state of affairs was a consequence of the fact that for most areas of performance the administration did not exercise ordinary bureaucratic methods of gathering information systematically, leaving the matter instead in the hands of the colleague group. And while the physicians' access to information about each other's performance was spotty, this would not be so significant if they were not also disinclined to share this information with each other. In consequence, the formation of a collective colleague opinion and the initiation of collective colleague action were made rather difficult. Indeed, deviance was controlled by administrative exercise of discretionary rewards and in other respects almost entirely on an individual rather than collective professional basis. Furthermore, what methods of control there were, were largely normative in character.

I have implied that much technical performance goes generally unobserved and, even if observed, uncommunicated and, even if communicated, uncontrolled. The problem is to reach some consensus on the *kind* of performance that should be observed and controlled. Some of the clinic doctors conceded that they did not know very much about their colleagues, but they believed that if someone did something "really serious"—like kill a patient—they would know about it very quickly. They believed that if a colleague were shown to be grossly and obviously incompetent or unethical there would be no question but that he would be dismissed. And they pointed out that the really serious forms and consequences of work are brought to the hospital, where a system of professional surveillance does operate self-consciously. They argued, then, that the important areas of performance *were* controlled. However, their idea of what is "really serious" was so extreme as to be removed from their everyday experience. What they were saying, in essence, was that butchers and moral lepers would be spotted and controlled quickly: to that extent the system works remorselessly. However, almost all forms of deviance lie somewhere between the performance of the moral leper and that of the saint. And it is precisely in that middle ground that the observed controls were problematic.

The process described here had several characteristics. First of all, the system of control was not characteristically either collective or hierarchical in its operation. It was inclined to operate like the economist's free market, private individuals being brought into interaction at the points where their individual work interests were involved. This was so in spite of its taking place in a consciously organized group-practice setting. Second, the process worked slowly, for a system of control can work only as rapidly as the information necessary for control can accumulate readily. Finally, the process had a characteristic vulnerability. In the nature of the case, in order to be effective the sanctions used required that all participants be fully responsive to the norms involved. The system was quite helpless in the face of a man who did not depend upon the esteem and trust of his colleagues and who did not respond to the symbolic values of professionalism. Confronted by a man who is not so incompetent or unethical as to be grossly and obviously dismissable and who fails to show any respect for his colleague's opinions, the administration and the colleague group are helpless. He cannot be flattered, shamed, or insulted and so cannot be persuaded to mend his ways or resign: all that can be done is to seal him off and try to minimize whatever damage he is believed to do.

Regulation in Other Settings

What has been presented thus far has been a study of a single case. It would of course be foolish to characterize an entire profession and the varieties of its practice by this one example. This is particularly so in the light of what is known, and even required to be the case, about practices that are embedded in the teaching hospital. A very useful study of such a practice was made by Goss,[8] who studied the operations of a teaching program of a university medical center by which about twelve thousand ambulant clinic patients were cared for annually by some eighty practicing physicians, and which provided clinical instruction for all fourth-year medical students of the college. Unlike the medical group already described, it was clearly organized into a hierarchy of professionals, with a director, four assistant directors, the prac-

[8] Mary E. W. Goss, "Influence and Authority Among Physicians in an Out-Patient Clinic," *American Sociological Review,* XXVI (1961), 39–50; and Mary E. W. Goss, "Patterns of Bureaucracy among Hospital Staff Physicians," in Eliot Freidson, ed., *The Hospital in Modern Society* (New York: The Free Press of Glencoe, 1963), pp. 170–194.

ticing physicians with varying hospital or faculty ranks, and finally the medical students.

Goss distinguished two types of supervisory control exercised along the hierarchy. First, there were what might be called administrative decisions that allocate and schedule the work a man will do: for example, preparing a master schedule in which instructors were assigned students to work with at certain hours, with certain patients, and in particular examining rooms. To put it crudely, a superior tells the practicing physician when and where to work, how much to work, and with whom. These decisions and "orders" were accepted without question, the right of the superior to make them and the obligation of the subordinate to follow them being generally recognized and conceded. However, no formal method of determining compliance seemed to be exercised, and no specific formal penalties for noncompliance existed.

These administrative "orders" established the pacing and tempo of practice in the teaching clinic but did not bear on practice as such. A supervisor was not given the right to order someone to use some procedure on his patient. The superior did have the right, if not obligation, to give advice about the handling of cases to the subordinates responsible for them. But while the supervisor had the formal right to give orders about the care of the subordinate's patient, if only because "they were officially responsible for the professional care given to patients in their units," [9] this was done so rarely as to be atypical. Most characteristic of the system was the giving of advice rather than orders—often writing advice out and clipping it to the medical chart but rarely writing it into the medical chart proper. In contrast to advice often given in private practice, however, this advice was given without solicitation, even when the advisee felt no need for it.

Insofar as it may be called advice rather than an order, there was no obligation to follow it. The clinic physicians "considered it their duty to take supervisory suggestions about patient care into account, and in this sense they accepted supervision. But they also felt obliged . . . to examine such suggestions critically, and to follow them only if they appeared to be in the patient's best interests

[9] Goss, "Influence and Authority," *op. cit.*, p. 46.

according to their own professional judgment."[10] Indeed, there was no evidence of formal sanctions for noncompliance, though in the event of continued concern by a supervisor about a case's treatment (presumably when his advice is not followed) he would make a point of discussing the technical problems of the case personally with the responsible physician, or perhaps arrange to have the case presented and discussed by students and faculty at a teaching conference. But as long as the recipient of advice could justify his own management of a case by reference to medical technique and knowledge, neither punitive nor "educational" pressure is put on him, his obligation being only to review the advice seriously in the light of available medical knowledge and his personal, clinical experience of the patient and his difficulties. Since it is he who takes personal responsibility for the outcome, it was his decision that was accepted as final so long as he could justify rejecting the advice.

Comparing the teaching clinic to the medical group, what is distinct about the former is the way medical performance is made observable by the systematic review of medical charts by supervisors and, second, the exercise of supervisory influence by hierarchical superiors who give unsolicited advice. Both characteristics, I believe, are rare in medical practice in general and reflect the peculiar attributes of teaching institutions, where are to be found students, who by definition are not full-fledged practitioners and who therefore must be supervised and must submit to guidance. The possibility of supervision is enhanced even more in teaching *hospitals,* where patients are laid out in beds open to the observation of anyone passing by on rounds, and, what is more important, where patients remain present for examination by others, rather than going home after consultation, as is the case for ambulatory care. In this, the hospital allows direct, firsthand observation, rather than merely the review of records. This is only a potentiality of course, for even in teaching hospitals it is only the public or ward patient who is readily observable by students and staff; in some teaching hospitals, "private" patients are inaccessible. Nonetheless, the possibilities for observation and supervision of medical performance are greatest in hospitals and particularly in teaching hospi-

[10] *Ibid.,* p. 44.

tals.[11] And as I have already noted, a number of formal review procedures are present in American hospitals.

But neither medical groups nor hospital teaching clinics, let alone hospitals, are typical of the practice of the bulk of physicians in the United States. Most physicians spend most of their time in their own individual offices. Except when they refer, or obtain a referral, their work is observable by and subject to the influence of only their patients. Even when their work is observed and evaluated by a colleague, he is unlikely to respond to it. Certainly, unsolicited advice is not likely to be offered unless a sufficiently senior and non-competing man felt fatherly, or unless a man wanted to insult another, for unsolicited advice violates ordinary medical etiquette. The only response to observed or reported performance is likely to be either maintaining a referral relationship or avoiding one. In these days of relatively high demand for physician services, such a response is of general importance only insofar as the judged individual is in some fashion dependent on the other's esteem. All a man does by avoiding working with another whose work he does not value is to protect his patients and practice: his avoidance is unlikely to change the other. Indeed, the other may not be aware of being avoided, and if aware, is unlikely to know why. Since in "private practice," unlike in medical groups or hospitals, cooperation with another is rarely obligatory, there is nothing to encourage some form of "talking-to," "advice," or influence designed to modify the other's performance. In this sense, in the laissez faire system of private, solo practice we are likely to find the least conscious and systematic regulation of behavior.

Observability, Leverage, and Norms

In this chapter I have been concerned with the way the individual physician's behavior can be controlled by his colleagues—the way the profession lives up to its promise to police itself. By and large, the focus has been on assessing the way the organization of practice makes colleague regulation *possible*. The assumption has been that

[11] There is great variation in teaching hospitals, also. See, for example, Patricia L. Kendall, "The Learning Environments of Hospitals," in Freidson, *op. cit.*, pp. 195–230.

observability [12] of performance is a structural prerequisite for regulation, limiting the degree to which work performance can be overseen and the quality of information about performance that may be collected. Therefore, observability limits the kind of assessment of work that can be made. Some attempt was made in this chapter to describe how, given the structuring of observability, controls were exercised.

The material presents us with an important problem of understanding. By and large, it seems that the controls that were exercised were *less* than what the given degree of observability allowed. In the medical group, an observer had to be virtually driven to communicate his observations to others, and while controls other than avoidance or talking-to were possible, they were not used. In the teaching clinic, an observer would give advice if he were a supervisor, but was loath to do more even if advice-giving failed. Clearly, the structural limits on control imposed by observability and dependence in different work settings were not enough to explain or predict the controls actually applied. That is, they do not seem to explain the source of variation in the *absolute* level of performance. However, I believe that the pattern of regulatory behavior described in this chapter strongly suggests the nature of the variables which can explain the source of variation. These variables are normative in character, not structural, and arise in the course of consulting or applied work like medical practice. In the next chapter I shall discuss them and, in doing so, try to illuminate further the problem of professional self-regulation.

[12] For some useful comments on observability, see Robert K. Merton, *Social Theory and Social Structure* (New York: The Free Press of Glencoe, 1957), pp. 336–357. And see Rose L. Coser, "Insulation from Observability and Types of Social Conformity," *American Sociological Review*, XXVI (1961), 28–39.

8.

THE CLINICAL MENTALITY

In the last chapter I suggested that the organization of medical work settings—particularly those connected with high-prestige, academic practice situations—was such as to allow more colleague regulation of work performance than in fact seemed to occur. I asserted that when deviant performance was observed it was not always attended to, not often communicated to others, and rarely subject to regulation. Such a finding points to the limitations of a "pure" as well as a formal organizational or structural analysis: it requires that I turn my attention to the norms or values of the individuals who are working in the organized settings, for when these settings permit regulatory behavior, and when that behavior does not occur whenever it is possible, I assume that the values of the participants figure in discouraging self-regulation. The problem, then, is to sketch out those medical norms which seem to be most closely connected to the behavior I have described.

As I noted in Chapter 4, it is conventional to distinguish the profession from other occupations by its service orientation. This is to say, professions are supposed to be distinctive by virtue of their dedication to the service of mankind or society. In Parsons' terms, the profession's role is supposed to be "collectivity oriented" rather than "self-oriented." Parsons also notes other norms, as follows:

> As an occupational role it is institutionalized about the technical content of the function which is given a high degree of

> primacy relative to other status-determinants. It is thus inevitable both that incumbency of the role should be achieved and that performance criteria by standards of technical competence should be prominent. Selection for it and the context of its performance are to a high degree segregated from other bases of social status and solidarities. In common with the predominant patterns of occupational roles generally in our society it is therefore in addition to its incorporation of *achievement* values, *universalistic, functionally specific,* and *affectively neutral.* [1]

Put more simply, it is expected that physicians be recruited and practice on the basis of ability rather than ascribed characteristics, that they rely on generally accepted scientific standards rather than on particularistic ones, restrict their work to the limits of their technical competence, work objectively without emotional involvement, and finally, put the patient's interests before their own.

However, as Parsons himself has observed, these attributes are not peculiar to the physician: they apply to all so-called professionals including those, like scientists, who do not characteristically perform services for a lay clientele. Furthermore, as Parsons observed, most of the characteristics are not even restricted to professions alone.[2] It could be argued quite forcibly that they apply to virtually all occupations providing a service involving technical skill. Plumbers, too, are supposed to be selected on the basis of achievement, to employ universalistic standards, and to be functionally specific and affectively neutral. And while it is expected that the plumber would make a profit on his services (just as that the physician should be able to earn a decent income), the plumber is supposed to do good work within the financial limits imposed on him, without cheating. While the plumber may not be expected to be dedicated to humanity, neither is he expected to be dedicated to self alone.

It is precisely by bringing plumbers into the discussion that we are brought face to face with the character of Parsons' specifica-

[1] Talcott Parsons, *The Social System* (New York: The Free Press of Glencoe, 1951), p. 434, italics added.

[2] *Ibid.*, p. 435.

tions, for those defending the profession will say, "Yes, but plumbers do not *really* manifest such norms, while professionals do." The response to this statement can only be one distinguishing expectation from performance. Parsons does not specify performance at all, but only expectation. Furthermore, those expectations are part of the broad institutional norms connected with professions as officially organized occupations. They are, in fact, the normative segment of the formal organization of professions, expressed by codes of ethics, public statements of spokesmen for the profession, and the like. They are quite distinct, analytically and empirically, from the actual norms of individual professionals. Like such abstractions as the Judeo-Christian ethic, they are formal claims and officially held expectations, perhaps ideals, but not necessarily the operative norms of performance. Furthermore, even if they can explain adequate performance by reference to the effectiveness with which the performer was "socialized," they cannot explain the particular kind of deviant performance into which an "undersocialized" worker is led. And finally, it should be noted that the norms or values are themselves so broad and general (like the Judeo-Christian ethic!) as to be difficult to relate to even so critical an issue of performance as the process of self-regulation. More concrete norms seem necessary for the analysis of medical work.

In this chapter I shall attempt to sketch the norms that seem to play an important part in the work of the physician, particularly those norms with some relation to the physician's response to deviant performance. Consonant with the interest of my analysis, I shall be concerned with the practicing or consulting physician, not the researcher. I shall, furthermore, be concerned mostly with the consultant whose primary experience is rooted in full-time community practice. I explicitly rule out preoccupation with the type of medical man and medical work to be found in the highly visible prestigious teaching and research institutions of medicine and concentrate instead on the vast majority of medical men who work in the obscurity of a full-time everyday practice. The former are the formal spokesmen, the leaders and sometimes the models of the profession. The latter *are* the profession. I shall concentrate on the latter, on the demands their work makes on them, and on the characteristic perspective arising from those demands. My focus shall be on understanding how that perspective influences the way processes of control are exercised in medical work.

Professional Responsibility

Carr-Saunders and Wilson provide a starting point for analysis by stating that while in their view the possession of a specialized intellectual technique acquired as a result of a prolonged period of training is the essence of a profession, "this is because it gives rise to certain attitudes and activities." [3] The most critical attitude is manifested in a sense of responsibility for the integrity of that technique, particularly insofar as practice involves "a direct and personal relation to clients." [4] The most important activity connected with it lies in the institutionalization of methods of "enforcing the observance of . . . standards of conduct." [5] Thus, they assign primacy to a special sense of responsibility for the integrity of practice and its consequences for the patient. This sense of responsibility, one might suppose, has some relationship to service or collectivity orientation. But how is it manifested?

Carr-Saunders and Wilson point out that, in the case of British medicine, formal disciplinary powers are used solely to encourage the observance of moral rather than technical standards, and that in any case expulsion from the profession is rare.[6] Parsons also observes the minor role of formal discipline in American medicine,[7] and, somewhat more authoritatively, a recent report of the Judicial Council of the AMA stated that "all too seldom are licensed physicians called to task by boards, societies or colleagues." [8] The hypothesized profession-wide "sense of responsibility," then, is manifested almost wholly in standards for training and admission to practice, without any active, formal mechanism for assuring that standards are maintained in practice. Superficially, this does not

[3] E. M. Carr-Saunders and P. A. Wilson, *The Professions* (Cambridge: Clarendon Press, 1936), p. 286.

[4] *Ibid.*, p. 285.

[5] *Ibid.*, p. 284.

[6] *Ibid.*, pp. 396–98.

[7] Parsons, *op. cit.*, p. 472.

[8] Judicial Council of the AMA, "Disciplinary Action in the Medical Profession," *Journal of the American Medical Association*, CLXXXIII (1964), 1077–1078.

seem to manifest a sense of responsibility for the integrity of practice. However, Carr-Saunders and Wilson as well as Parsons suggest that discipline is indeed carried out, but on a more informal basis by means of colleague boycotts [9] or loss of professional reputation among colleagues.[10] Such informal control does not, as I have noted in the previous chapter, prevent an offender from working; instead it merely keeps away from him the patients of those who think little of him: they do not keep other patients away from him and therefore do not protect the integrity of practice. Clearly, we must elaborate in more detail the peculiar character of this "sense of responsibility."

The Nature of Medical Work

Carr-Saunders and Wilson explain such a loose system of control in an ostensibly responsible profession by reference to the kind of work involved. They note that in many kinds of potentially dangerous work (such as marine or air navigation) what is required for public safety is the proper observance of a routine, without deviation. Medicine, however, requires not a set routine but the exercise of complex judgment, and instead of caution it sometimes requires the taking of risks. Furthermore, judgment as such cannot be objectified because it is at least in part a matter of opinion: it would not be wise to create formal codes or rules placing one opinion, theory, or school over another.[11] This explanation seems true enough in kind, but not in degree. Medicine is of all the established professions based on fairly precise and detailed scientific knowledge, and it entails considerably less uncertainty than many other technical occupations. There are some very clear rights and wrongs, as the success of negligence or malpractice suits suggests: simple precautions against infection or anaphylactic shock, for example, routine laboratory tests indicated for specific complaints, and simple rules about removing drains, sponges, or utensils from body cavities before sewing up an incision. There is really no question of judgment in such routine procedures, and so there is really no explanation of the lack of formal discipline within the profession

[9] Carr-Saunders and Wilson, *op. cit.*, pp. 403–404.
[10] Parsons, *op. cit.*, p. 472.
[11] Carr-Saunders and Wilson, *op. cit.*, pp. 399–400.

by reference to judgment. Without denying the facts of a degree of uncertainty, of the necessity for the exercise of judgment, or of legitimate differences in opinion, the precision of much modern medical knowledge and the trivial routine of much everyday medical practice preclude explaining the peculiar loose charity characteristic of professional self-regulation in medicine by reference to objective uncertainty and conflict of opinion. Rather, it seems more plausible to say that practitioners express a characteristic *subjective sense* of uncertainty and vulnerability, whatever the objective foundation.[12] Indeed, I wish to suggest that this subjective sense can be seen to be a function of the nature of practical medical work, part of the perspective of the worker rather than a consistent reflection of the scientific and technological inadequacy of medical knowledge.

What is the work of the profession? It is the attempted solution of the concrete problems of individuals. As I have already pointed out, it is by its nature applied rather than theoretical in character, and so it is markedly different from the work of the scientist. At best, the practicing physician may use general principles to deal with concrete problems: the scientist typically investigates concrete phenomena in order to test, elaborate, or arrive at general principles. Insofar as the practice of medicine at all uses science, then, it is characteristically oriented to *applying* rather than creating or contributing to it. Indeed, since its focus is on the practical solution of concrete problems, it is obliged to carry on even when it lacks a scientific foundation for its activities: it is oriented toward intervention irrespective of the existence of reliable knowledge. The practitioner is more comfortable in doing something—being, as Dowling suggested, inclined to fear doing nothing—and so is led to use drugs and other procedures more than might be indicated by academic (and scientific) standards.[13]

[12] In some circumstances, as Davis noted, physicians may deliberately indicate uncertainty to patients in order to minimize their own "management" problems. See Fred Davis, "Uncertainty in Medical Prognosis, Clinical and Functional," *American Journal of Sociology,* LXVI (1960), 41–47.

[13] Harry F. Dowling, "How Do Practicing Physicians Use New Drugs?" *Journal of the American Medical Association,* CLXXXV (1963), 233–236. As a Russian surgeon put it, "One can't wait until medicine becomes exact and faultless." N. Amosoff, *The Open Heart* (New York: Simon and Schuster, 1966), p. 44.

Furthermore, medical practice is typically occupied with the problems of *individuals* rather than of aggregates or statistical units. Probabilities can only guide the determination of whether a patient does or does not have a disease. Thus, even when general scientific knowledge may be available, the mere fact of individual variability poses a constant problem for assessment that emphasizes the necessity for personal firsthand examination of every individual case and the difficulty of disposition on some formal, abstract scientific basis.

It may be noted that these remarks point, though in a somewhat different way, to the taking of risks in the course of intervention, and to the necessity for judgment discussed by Carr-Saunders and Wilson, and by Parsons. But the actual amount of such risk and opinionated judgment can vary a great deal. What does not vary is the fact that the work is applied, involving intervention irrespective of available knowledge, and revolving around experience with individual, therefore somewhat variable, cases. These characteristics of everyday medical work, I wish to suggest, are responsible for the development of norms or attitudes that encourage a very special, limited sense of responsibility. In brief, they encourage in the practitioner an emphasis on *personal* rather than general or communal responsibility, which in turn leads to only limited attempts to assure adequate performance. And they encourage emphasis on the primacy of firsthand clinical experience rather than of scientific laws or general rules, which has the consequence of exaggerating the acceptability of varying opinions and thus sustaining well-intentioned resistance to forsaking one's own practices in the face of others' disapproval. These two emphases seem to intervene between the structural possibilities for professional regulation and the actual form of regulation. They seem to form the foundation for norms discouraging general collegial control of individual physician behavior. While I believe that they are sustained and reinforced primarily by experience at medical work in everyday practice, there is some evidence that medical students are brought into contact with those values even before they enter practice.

Medical Responsibility and Clinical Experience in Training

In their study of students at the University of Kansas Medical School in the 1950's, Becker and his associates found that the two norms of responsibility and experience were critical in guiding the way the medical students managed the level and direction of their efforts.[14] During the years of clinical training they were confronted by the overwhelming detail and variety of the curriculum and had to deal with the problem of deciding what was important to memorize, to practice at or work hard on, and what to ignore. Becker and his associates argue persuasively that the students solved their problem by adapting to their own needs two values that were strongly emphasized by the staff of the medical school. These were the values of *medical responsibility* and *clinical experience.*

Basically, the term "responsibility" refers to "the archetypal feature of medical practice: the physician who holds his patient's fate in his hands and on whom the patient's life or death may depend. Medical responsibility is responsibility for the patient's well-being, and the exercise of medical responsibility is seen as the basic and key action of the practicing physician. The physician is most a physician when he exercises this responsibility."[15] This responsibility is *personal* and *direct,* in that it belongs to the physician who is working directly with the patient. It is *consequential* in that it requires the physician to take the blame for bad results. The idea was impressed on the student by his teachers in many ways, not the least of which were frequent informal lectures about "getting into trouble" (putting the patient's welfare in jeopardy) by omitting some precaution, procedure, or whatever. When questioning a student, teachers were also fond of using the pedagogical device of hypothesizing an emergency and asking how it should be handled. Furthermore, the idea figured prominently in the organization of the university hospital, where the hierarchy of junior and senior students, intern, resident, and junior and senior teaching staff could be seen to be ordered by differential access to such responsibility. The lowest members were restricted to the routine, whereas the highest were free to do the most complicated and dangerous procedures. Indeed, the students in the first two (preclinical) years of medical school were hardly allowed to assume even routine responsi-

[14] Howard S. Becker *et al., Boys in White, Student Culture in Medical School* (Chicago: University of Chicago Press, 1961).

[15] *Ibid.,* p. 224.

bilities, which was one reason why they did not consider their experience to be relevant to medical practice.

"Clinical experience" refers to "actual experience in dealing with patients and disease . . . [which] even though it substitutes for scientifically verified knowledge, can be used to legitimate a choice of procedures for a patient's treatment and can even be used to rule out use of some procedures which have been scientifically established." [16] In part, the idea depends upon the fact that contemporary medical diagnosis still requires the direct use of several of the physician's senses, which by the nature of the case can only be schooled by direct practice at using them. The idea also seems to depend in part upon the inadequacy of "book" and scientific knowledge in the face of the practical contingencies and complexities of the individual case. Whatever its source, the student's nose was rubbed into the primacy of the idea at Kansas. He may have answered a faculty member's question on the basis of something he read in a textbook or a journal only to find it rejected because it had never been found to be the case in the faculty member's own experience. Indeed, "argument from experience was quite commonly used and considered unanswerable. . . . The only counter-argument that can prevail is . . . by someone who can claim greater experience in the area discussed." [17] Furthermore, the hierarchy of the school could be roughly differentiated by the possession of varying amounts of such experience, which is implied by the rule of seniority so critical to medicine.

The Kansas study reported that the idea of clinical experience organized the student's selectivity in that he devoted himself to picking up all the practical experience he could at the expense of abstract knowledge. Thus the students discounted most of their basic science work because it failed to provide the clinical experience they thought useful to their future practice. Training that provided them with the opportunity to gain clinical experience directly, or vicariously through their instructors, was valued greatly. Instructors were not only judged by the degree to which what they taught was concrete enough to be memorized in the event of examination, but also by their tendency to throw out little pearls of practical information.

[16] *Ibid.*, p. 225.
[17] *Ibid.*, p. 234.

Courses and assignments were also judged by the criterion of medical responsibility. For a student to obtain responsibility was to obtain a privilege reflecting positive evaluation of his capacities by his superiors. The student did get increments of responsibility as he moved through school, in the handling of patients, for example, and in the opportunity to perform minor diagnostic and therapeutic tasks. But the student was irritated and depressed by the denial of responsibility, and since the idea of responsibility is by the nature of the case relative, what was gotten with pleasure yesterday could be rejected as too minor and unimportant tomorrow. Jobs like catheterization, lumbar puncture, and pelvic examinations were doled out so slowly that they looked attractive, and the first opportunity to do them was welcomed eagerly, but they were gradually rejected as merely scut work. After a while, performing a pelvic or rectal examination seemed dull and disagreeable—a bad way to spend the afternoon. It, and particularly work involving no responsibility at all, like doing a blood count or a uranalysis, might actually be shirked. The faculty, of course, claimed that the student was not yet ready to assume some responsibilities in his last year and even in his postgraduate internship. The student, however, claimed that he had better get the experience under supervision than have to get it by himself in practice.

The Kansas study was of but one medical school. Furthermore, it was of a medical school which did not at the time reflect either the experimentation in training or the emphasis on careers in research to be found in other schools.[18] For this reason it cannot be argued that the values specified by Becker and his associates are characteristic of those emphasized at all American medical schools. However, the school at that time emphasized the training of practitioners to serve the needs of rural areas, and many of the students

[18] For a discussion of the way medical schools in the United States vary, see Paul J. Sanazaro, "Research in Medical Education: Exploratory Analysis of a Blackbox," *Annals of the New York Academy of Sciences,* CXXVIII (1965), 519–531. For studies of more academically oriented medical schools, see Robert K. Merton *et al.,* eds., *The Student Physician* (Cambridge: Harvard University Press, 1957). For a review of sociological studies in medical education, see Samuel W. Bloom, "The Sociology of Medical Education, Some Comments on the State of a Field," *The Milbank Memorial Fund Quarterly,* XLIII (1965), 143–184.

planned to be rural practitioners. While there is little evidence to support the assumption that students adopt the values of their teachers or that they can accurately anticipate the demands of work after graduation, the particular values discerned among the Kansas students do fit into the nature of everyday practice and, in association with other conceptions of professional dignity and independence, go far toward explaining the norms of medical work, particularly those governing the process of self-regulation. As I shall point out later, all physicians are not likely to emphasize them to the same degree because not all do the same work with the same demands.

The Clinical Mind

By and large, I think it can be said that the practitioner has a different view of his work than the theoretician or investigator. In fact, he has a different way of looking at the world. First, the aim of the practitioner is not knowledge but *action.* Successful action is preferred, but action with very little chance for success is to be preferred over no action at all. There is a tendency for the practitioner to take action for its own sake on the spurious assumption that doing something is better than doing nothing. I have already noted that this tendency to prefer action seems to underlie the prescribing habits of practitioners. Second, the practitioner is likely to have to *believe in what he is doing* in order to practice—to believe that what he does does good rather than harm, and that what he does makes the difference between success and failure rather than no difference at all. He is himself a placebo reactor who is developing faith in his remedies and so modifying his behavior toward his patient.[19] Insofar as work characteristically revolves around a series of concrete and individual problems, both success and its cause are rarely unambiguous. Given a commitment to action and practical solution, in the face of ambiguity the practitioner is more likely to manifest a certain will to believe in the value of his actions than to manifest a skeptical detachment. (How could a present-day psychiatrist work if he really believed the careful

[19] See Arthur K. Shapiro, "Factors Contributing to the Placebo Effect," *American Journal of Psychotherapy,* XVIII (1964), 73–88, and Chapter 12 of this book.

studies which emphasize the unreliability of diagnosis and the undemonstrability of success of psychotherapy? And how could physicians work one, two, or five centuries ago?) Third, perhaps because of his action orientation, perhaps because of the complexity and variety of the concrete, the practitioner is a fairly crude *pragmatist*. He is prone to rely on apparent "results" rather than on theory, and he is prone to tinker if he does not seem to be getting "results" by conventional means. Fourth, the clinician is prone in time to trust his own accumulation of personal, *first hand experience* in preference to abstract principles or "book knowledge," particularly in assessing and managing those aspects of his work that cannot be treated routinely. As Sharaf and Levinson noted in the case of psychiatrists in training, "The dangers of 'intellectualizing' and 'book learning' are stressed. The highest value is placed on emotional experience, on widening the range of the 'gut response' as a means of understanding what is going on in oneself and in the patient." [20] This represents a certain subjectivism in his approach. And finally, the practitioner is very prone to emphasize the idea of *indeterminacy or uncertainty*, not the idea of regularity or of lawful, scientific behavior. Whether or not that idea faithfully represents actual deficiencies in available knowledge or technique, it does provide the practitioner with a psychological ground from which to justify his pragmatic emphasis on firsthand experience.

In his commitment to action, his faith, his pragmatism, his subjectivism, and his emphasis on indeterminacy, then, the practitioner is quite different from the scientist. One whose work requires practical application to concrete cases simply cannot maintain the same frame of mind as the scholar or scientist: he cannot suspend action in the absence of incontrovertible evidence or be skeptical of himself, his experience, his work and its fruit. In emergencies he cannot wait for the discoveries of the future. Dealing with individual cases, he cannot rely solely on probabilities or on general concepts or principles: he must also rely on his own senses. By the nature of

[20] Myron R. Sharaf and Daniel J. Levinson, "The Quest for Omnipotence in Professional Training," *Psychiatry*, XXVII (1964), 141. And see the discussion of the finding that GP's were impatient with the theoretical aspects of medicine in Osler L. Peterson *et al.*, "An Analytical Study of North Carolina General Practice, 1953–1954," *Journal of Medical Education*, XXXI (1956), Part II, 89–90.

his work the clinician must assume responsibility for practical action, and in doing so he must rely on his concrete, clinical experience. Contrary to Parsons, I would suggest that the practitioner is particularistic, *not* universalistic.

In assuming responsibility for the practical action he takes, the practitioner also assumes a degree of vulnerability, for while he may gain the gratitude due the miracle worker, he may also gain the reproach due the man who fails to work miracles. In assuming responsibility for virtually any concrete and practical action, one also assumes a risk and thus is always vulnerable to reproach, legal or otherwise. It seems appropriate that the clinician should feel a certain righteousness and pride in being willing to assume responsibility and a certain defensiveness and paranoia about the risk of reproach. This peculiar blend of paranoid superiority is closely akin to the response of politicians to "armchair" intellectuals and of the businessman to those "who never had to meet a payroll"; in short, it is the response of all practical men. Like political or economic power, professional authority teeters between glory and ruin and is prone to claim its glory more because of its risk of ruin than because of its accomplishment.

In having to rely so heavily upon his personal, clinical experience with concrete, individual cases, however, the practitioner comes essentially to rely on the authority of his own senses, independently of the general authority of tradition or science. After all, he can only act on the basis of what he himself experiences, and if his own activity seems to get results, or at least no untoward results, he is resistant to changing it on the basis of statistical or abstract considerations. He is likely to need to see or feel the case himself. As the Coleman study of drug adoption indicated, the practitioner must try out a new drug himself on a patient, not take someone else's word about its use.[21] This, along with the loose system of "discipline," allows many ineffective or insidious practices to persist quite long among clinicians.

Thus, a rather thoroughgoing particularism, a kind of ontological and epistemological individualism is characteristic of the clinician. In part because he is so absorbed in and isolated by his own work,

[21] James A. Coleman *et al., Medical Innovation* (Indianapolis: Bobbs-Merrill Co., 1966), p. 32.

he is likely to see and evaluate the world more in terms of his own experience than in terms of what authorities tell him. As Marmor put it, his "inability to observe directly the techniques of others may in time lead to a tendency to overestimate the virtue of his own particular approach and ability in contrast to those of his colleagues."[22] Indeed, so impressed is he by the perplexity of his clients and by his apparent capacity to deal with those perplexities that the practitioner comes to consider himself as expert not only in the problems he is trained to deal with but in all human problems. Like many occupational groups dealing with the seamier side of life—janitors, policemen, prostitutes, taxi drivers, bartenders—he is prone to believe that his work equips him better than others to be wise about life and human nature.[23] But unlike other workers, the professional clinician's belief in his functionally diffuse wisdom is reinforced strongly by the respectful receipt of his opinions by a lay world that does not discriminate between what is functionally specific to his training and what is not. Thus, he manifests a strain toward functional diffuseness, again contrary to Parsons' expectation.

The particularism and the moral subjectivity characteristic of the clinical man's work does not mean that he is not rational. Much of the medical man's activity can be represented by the process of differential diagnosis: a succession of diagnoses in the form of hypotheses is tested against the available signs and symptoms. Rationality is a significant attribute of the physician now just as it was among some Hippocratics in ancient Greece. The rationality is particularized and technical; it is a method of sorting the enormous mass of concrete detail confronting him in his individual cases. The difference between clinical rationality and scientific rationality is that clinical rationality is not a tool for the exploration or discovery of general principles, as is the scientific method, but only a tool for sorting the interconnections of perceived and hypothesized facts. "Principles" are generated in the course of clinical practice, but

[22] Judd Marmor, "The Feeling of Superiority: An Occupational Hazard in the Practice of Psychiatry," *American Journal of Psychiatry*, CX (1953), 371.

[23] The myth is occasionally advanced that physicians are better equipped to be creative novelists because of their "wide acquaintance with mankind." E.g., Claude E. Jones, "Tobias Smollett (1721–1771)—The Doctor as Man of Letters," *Journal of the History of Medicine and Allied Sciences,* XII (1957), 337–348.

they are generalizations from clinical experience, which is to say, generalization from personal and systematically biased experience. As Oken has stated, "clinical experience" is frequently personal mythology based on one or two incidents, or on stories by colleagues.[24]

It follows from this discussion of the clinical mentality that individualism is a dominant element in orientation and behavior. Each man builds up his own world of clinical experience and assumes personal, that is, virtually individual, responsibility for the way he manages his cases in that world. The nature of that world is prone to be self-validating and self-confirming, if only because by hypothesizing indeterminacy the role of scientific (that is, generally agreed or shared) knowledge and the role of others' opinions in practice are minimized. This is not to say that such knowledge and opinion are not used, only that thinking in terms of unique individual cases places the burden of proof on the particular rather than on the general. A certain individualism, therefore, flows out of the nature of clinical work, and it is reinforced by social elements having little to do with the work itself.

Professional Status and Values

"Clinician" and "practitioner" are words referring to consultants whose work requires the application of available knowledge to the solution of some concrete problem: they are neutral words in that they emphasize what is technically special about a job. "Professional," however, is a word that is not neutral. It may refer to a special kind of complex work, but it also connotes a highly prestigious occupation. Thus, while "clinician" or "practitioner" can denote a pure situs—a specific technical position in a division of labor, without hierarchical implications—"professional" combines situs with status. Part and parcel of professional performance and the ideology surrounding it are the historical accretions of an occupational status and the social origins of its incumbent. Being predominantly from the bourgeoisie, the professional emphasizes inde-

[24] Donald Oken, "What to Tell Cancer Patients: A Study of Medical Attitudes," *Journal of the American Medical Association,* CLXXV (1961), 1120–1128.

pendence, social and economic individualism, and class dignity in his status.

Throughout the Western world, the physician seems to be recruited from predominantly middle-class families. This seems no less true of political economies like that of the U.S.S.R.[25] than of nations like France[26] and the United States.[27] A 1960 study of 1,000 medical school graduates selected randomly from each of twenty-five American medical schools found that 56 per cent were sons of professional, proprietor, or manager-official fathers.[28]

Scattered materials from American studies suggest some of the ideological components of the professional status of the physician. A fairly extensive study of the occupational choice of college students found that, like prospective social workers, prospective physicians valued highly the "opportunity to work with people rather than things" and the "opportunity to be helpful to others." However, prospective physicians were more like prospective lawyers and businessmen and less like social workers in emphasizing the desirability of earning a great deal of money and obtaining social status and prestige. Like prospective businessmen and such other practical clinical professions as social work and law, prospective physicians did not (as did prospective scientists) place high value on the opportunity to be creative and original or "to use my special abilities or aptitudes."[29] They also had relatively low faith in the degree to which people could be trusted.[30] There is, therefore, a

[25] See the comments on the bourgeois origins of Soviet physicians in Mark G. Field, *Doctor and Patient in Soviet Russia* (Cambridge: Harvard University Press, 1957).

[26] J. D. Reynaud and A. Touraine, "Enquête sur les étudiants en médécine," *Cahiers Internationaux de Sociologie*, XX (1956), 124–148.

[27] S. Adams, "Trends in Occupational Origins of Physicians," *American Sociological Review*, XVIII (1953), 404–409. Adams' argument is that the lower socioeconomic groups have been supplying relatively more physicians than in the past, but his figures nonetheless show predominant middle-class origins. Cf. James A. Davis, *Undergraduate Career Decisions* (Chicago: Aldine Publishing Co., 1965), p. 12.

[28] Charles F. Schumacher, "The 1960 Medical School Graduate: His Biographical History," *Journal of Medical Education*, XXXVI (1961), 401.

[29] Davis, *op. cit.*, also found this comparatively low emphasis on "being original and creative."

[30] See Morris Rosenberg, *Occupations and Values* (New York: The Free Press of Glencoe, 1957), pp. 10–35.

curious ideological ambivalence in the premedical student, certainly composed in part of an inclination to assume a service orientation in the form of wishing to help people, but countered by an inclination to desire prestige and money as well. The former is supposed to be characteristic of the professional, while the latter is supposed to be more characteristic of the businessman, but in reality both are present in the premedical student and the physician. And compared to prospective social workers, their "service orientation" was weaker. A later comparison between a group of college males and entering medical students found that the latter were higher in theoretical and esthetic interests and lower in economic, social, political, and religious interests.[31] Without comparison with subgroups aspiring to specific occupations, it is difficult to make very much of this data, but they do seem to reflect a trend toward an increasingly scientific orientation among students entering medicine, and, again, present little evidence that those aspiring to medicine have a stronger service orientation than those aspiring to other occupations.

Apart from comparisons between medical students and others, which are essential for preserving an adequate perspective on the comparative characteristics of medicine itself, a number of studies of medical students tell us something about which values predominate among them. Cahalan's study of a stratified random sample of male medical students found that "helping others, being of service, being useful" and "working and dealing with people"[32] were valued highly, as was the clinical situation of working directly with patients as opposed to working "at medical problems that do not require frequent contact with patients." "Intellectual stimulation" was emphasized rather little as a principal career satisfaction, though it did figure importantly in choosing to work in a specialty rather than in general practice. And finally, 30 per cent specified "financial return or economic security as one of the things they

[31] Edwin B. Hutchins, "The AAMC Longitudinal Study: Implications for Medical Education," *Journal of Medical Education,* XXXIX (1964), 265–277. However, Davis, *op. cit.,* found that undergraduates choosing medicine emphasized "working with people" more than those choosing most other occupations.

[32] Don Cahalan *et al.,* "Career Interests and Expectations of U.S. Medical Students," *Journal of Medical Education,* XXXII (1957), 558.

expect to like best about being a doctor."[33] We may take this to be a significant proportion because the question did not treat money as merely one of the many fringe benefits or correlates of being a doctor, but rather as one of the things liked best about being a doctor.

Supporting data are found in later studies. Phillips' study of 2,674 students in a sample of eight medical schools found the predominant emphasis on the value of close patient relations (43 per cent), less emphasis on learning (27 per cent) and research (24 per cent), and still less emphasis on other values. However, those choosing general practice emphasized close patient relations and helping people far more than those choosing specialties, the latter emphasizing intellectual and economic values more.[34] Schumacher reported somewhat similar (though not entirely consistent) differences between choices of one type of practice rather than another. He emphasized, however, the difference between those with plans for full-time practice, general or specialized, and those who are academically oriented, planning to practice only part-time and otherwise engaged in teaching and research. The latter valued scientific discovery and were prone to be interested in social welfare; the former were more inclined to value practical knowledge and economic rewards.[35] The former, of course, plan to be the everyday practitioners I discuss in this chapter.

It should be noted that the studies I have cited are all of medical students or would-be students, not actual practitioners. The relevance of such data to predicting the characteristics of practitioners is uncertain, for I have already noted the extent to which both values like "cynicism" and the quality of medical performance may change markedly once the student is engaged and committed to medical work. Unfortunately, there have been very few studies of practicing physicians. Even more unfortunately, a recently reported

[33] *Ibid.*, p. 560.

[34] Bernard S. Phillips, "Expected Value Deprivation and Occupational Preference," *Sociometry*, XXVII (1964), 151–160.

[35] See Charles F. Schumacher, "Interest and Personality Factors as Related to Choice of Medical Career," *Journal of Medical Education*, XXXVIII (1963), 932–942, and Charles F. Schumacher, "Personal Characteristics of Students Choosing Different Types of Medical Careers," *Journal of Medical Education*, XXXIX (1964), 278–288.

study of practitioners in the county surrounding Cleveland, Ohio, presented its findings in factor analytic form, making it difficult to determine how widespread among the respondents were given values.[36] Of the values I have discussed, however, factors were found which emphasized a concern for individual patients "rather than a broad concern for humanity,"[37] personal responsibility, and "temperate individualism."[38] In the case of valuing financial rewards, the authors, in the course of deprecating its importance, note that "evidently money is significant to the doctor chiefly as a symbol of appreciation and status, and he is more aware of it when it is withheld!"[39] One may suspect that money is valued as money by physicians as it is by everyone else.

One more value remains to be noted, related to the others but pointing to a specifically entrepreneurial dimension in the physician's values. Cahalan reported that in choice of practice arrangements seven out of eight students reported a preference for fee-for-service or nonsalaried practice. Among those preferring individual practice, with or without the pooling of facilities with other doctors, 62 per cent attributed their preference to their desire "to be my own boss."[40] This desire seems to be pervasive in America, where emphasis is placed on independence and self-determination for their own sake. The value seems to extend even across part of the stable working class, members of which aspire to leave salaried positions in order to be their own bosses in their own small businesses.[41] It seems quite impossible to explain much of the American physician's persistent emphasis on and seeming preference for economic circumstances comparable to small shops or owner-operated businesses except by reference to bourgeois values of independence that

[36] Amasa B. Ford *et al., The Doctor's Perspective* (Cleveland: The Press of Case Western Reserve University, 1967).

[37] *Ibid.*, p. 78.

[38] *Ibid.*, pp. 141–143.

[39] *Ibid.*, p. 110, exclamation point added.

[40] Cahalan, *op. cit.*, p. 558. It may be noted that valuing a job "that leaves me relatively free of supervision by others" was one of the dimensions on which data were obtained in Rosenberg's study, but cross-tabulations were unfortunately not published.

[41] "Autonomy" was greatly emphasized in the findings on dentistry. See D. M. More and N. Kohn, Jr., "Some Motives for Entering Dentistry," *American Journal of Sociology*, LXVI (1960), 48–53.

are quite distinct from if not actually incompatible with the technical requirements for the practice of medicine. High valuation of independence expresses at the same time the ideology of the entrepreneur and of the professional, combining in an undifferentiated fashion notions of economic freedom and of intellectual or technical autonomy.

The North Carolina study of specialty choice obtained some useful information on the attitudes of medical students toward "independence." It found that 28 per cent preferred a career offering independence but little money over one offering a good income but little independence, 17 per cent preferring the latter, and the remainder of the respondents taking an intermediate position. Tabulating preferences for these and other values, they found five distinct clusters of choice in three of which independence figured prominently.[42] In this study, independence as a value was opposed to money as a value by virtue of the study design and the method of analysis, one having to be chosen to the exclusion of the other, so the exact interrelationship of the two was difficult to determine from the report. The same may be said for the study of physicians in Ohio: autonomy and independence figured in the physicians' responses, but in a way difficult to assess.[43] And the program of studies of the Association of American Medical Colleges indicated that while students from medical schools which are academically oriented rank independence fifth as what they like best about being a doctor, students from schools whose graduates primarily enter full-time practice rank independence 2.5, tied with helping other people.[44] Finally, I may note that Davis [45] noted that valuing "freedom from supervision in my work" was associated to about the same degree with *both* wanting "opportunities to be creative and original"

[42] See Robert E. Coker, Jr., *et al.*, "Medical Students' Attitudes Toward Public Health," *The Milbank Memorial Fund Quarterly*, XLIV (1966), 170–175. Unfortunately, over-all figures were not presented, so the over-all importance of the value of independence was not clear. In the three clusters where "independence" was prominent, it was so because it was chosen more often than average. The average, however, was not specified, so "independence" could have been quantitatively important in all cases, even when chosen *less* often than average.

[43] Ford, *op. cit.*, pp. 96–111.

[44] Personal communication, Paul J. Sanazaro, November 21, 1966.

[45] Davis, *op. cit.*, pp. 222–224.

and with wanting to "make a lot of money." The desire for independence or autonomy is obviously a complex phenomenon which requires considerably more detailed analysis than it has obtained thus far.

In summary of this review of data on the values of physicians, it seems fair to say that while physicians do not lack a service or collectivity orientation, it does not seem to be a very prominent value compared to others. Furthermore, the value is addressed to concern for helping individuals rather than to serving society or mankind. Second, physicians have some intellectual investment in their work, everyday practitioners having less than others, emphasizing instead practical knowledge and action. Third, physicians emphasize the value of the income and prestige connected with their occupation. And finally, everyday practitioners more than others emphasize the value of independence and autonomy. These values, I believe, stem from the social background of the practitioner more than from his work, reflecting both the values of his bourgeois origins and the special intent of his career choice. The work of medicine is something else. Being applied, involving active intervention in individual cases, it gives rise to a special frame of mind oriented toward action for its own sake, action based on a radical pragmatism. Such action relies on firsthand experience and is supported by both a will to believe in the value of one's actions and a belief in the inadequacy of general knowledge for dealing with individual cases. I believe that these two sets of values, one stemming from social background and aspiration, and the other from the demands of the work itself, together allow us to understand the practitioner's response to having others look critically at his performance of medical work. Critical evaluation by others is, after all, the first step to the regulation of performance.

Criticism and Criticizing

The physician's attitudes are marked by a profound ambivalence. On the one side he has a more than ordinary sense of uncertainty and vulnerability; on the other, he has a sense of virtue and pride, if not superiority. This ambivalence is expressed by sensitivity to criticism by others. In most cases he is prone to feel that he is above reproach, that he did his best and cannot be held responsible for untoward results. "It could have happened to anyone!" or "How could I have known?" are commonly used remarks. In relatively few cases he personally concedes error; these he punishes himself for, but even so he must find them excusable in some way—"a bad break," "just one of those things." Self-criticism is more likely to be observable than other forms of criticism, for it is often verbalized in order to get reassurance from friendly colleagues. By conceding error to friends who will not themselves criticize, one gains the cathartic benefit of confession while avoiding the price of penance.

While self-criticism is acceptable, criticism by others is not. The practitioner is prone to believe that mistakes are bound to be made by the very nature of clinical work, so that every practitioner at one time or another is vulnerable to reproach. This belief is used to excuse oneself and also to restrain one from criticizing others and them from criticizing him. In looking at others' apparent mistakes the physician is inclined to feel that "there, but for the grace of God, go I" and that "it may be my turn next." When he "gets into trouble," he expects colleagues to cultivate the same sense of charity and is inclined to feel that those who are not so charitable are dogmatic fanatics, to be distrusted and avoided.

Suspension of criticism is considered necessary in the light of the imputed inevitability of mistakes and also in the light of the ascribed inability of laymen to accept the inevitability of mistakes. All practitioners are vulnerable to the reproaches of their clients who, quite understandably, cannot philosophically accept the contingencies of practical action when they are the ones who suffer the contingencies. Thus all practitioners should stick together, preserving a united front against criticism by outsiders. If one practitioner cannot restrain himself from criticizing another, he should at least do it in private, to the man's face, or at worst within a closed professional circle. Laymen cannot understand the character of clinical work well enough either to be allowed to hear professionals criticize others or to permit much credence to be given their own criticism of a colleague. The dangers of malpractice suits quite naturally reinforce this tendency to keep criticism within the professional family.

Criticism, however, presupposes some direct or indirect visibility of work. As I have suggested already, the visibility of performance is itself problematic in clinical work involving a personal and confidential service. Furthermore, there is resistance among professionals to observing others or being observed by them. The clinician feels that his work is unique and concrete, not really assessable by some set of stable rules or by anyone who does not share with him the same firsthand experience. And he emphasizes his own personal responsibility. On both grounds he asserts his autonomy. In addition, perhaps reacting to the extended period of supervised practice he went through in the course of his professional training, he stresses his maturity: "I'm a big boy now," he is wont to say. Being supervised is synonymous with being a student. It implies not being trusted with one's responsibility. Indeed, to be granted freedom from supervision is a mark of being trusted, of being autonomous; in short, of being a professional. Being visible when the work itself requires it or where one himself so requests is acceptable, but anything more is uncomfortable, if not demeaning. A professional does not lower himself by snooping into the affairs of colleagues and expects his colleagues to respect the privacy of his affairs.

Personal and Communal Responsibility

I have tried to deal with what seems to be the practitioner's own view of his work without assuming the view to be either true or false. I have, however, implied that if it is not false, it is at least a bit distorted, for in medicine there is more certainty and precision than is usually emphasized by the practitioner whenever the accusation of error is defended. Thus, insofar as error or incompetence can be objective concepts, I would argue that more exists than practitioners are inclined to recognize.

But truth or not, the proof of professionalism comes when bad performance *is* recognized by practitioners: on perceiving errors or incompetence, what do they do? There is first of all the very special and comparatively rare case of incontrovertible misbehavior. I refer to the response to an unambiguously outrageous offense—the drunken surgeon, for example, who cuts into more than was bargained for, or the addict, who makes off with too many narcotics from the hospital stores. Even when clear and unequivocal incompetence or unethicality is revealed, there is considerable reluctance to exert controls. After a certain period of time, however, those with whom he works feel they must bar him from their company. This is done most often by allowing the man to resign rather than by any outright expulsion that would call attention to his departure, and news of the circumstances of his resignation may not be circulated widely.[46] By this I mean that while a physician-addict may be expelled from a hospital for stealing drugs, it is not likely that his departure will be publicized as a dismissal or even that other hospitals to which he may seek access will be warned. It will be left to others to find out for themselves. Thus, in gross cases a man is likely to be expelled from the company of his present colleagues but not from his profession. Data for medicine are very scarce, but it seems plausible that, as was found to be the case in law, actual loss of license for gross and obvious instances of unethical or incompetent behavior is the consequence of publicity that forces the professional group to act rather than the offense as such.[47]

Professional handling of such cases is marked by ambivalence and pain.[48] Colleagues recognize that the man is likely to do harm to others unless he is stopped. However, to do this requires having his license suspended, an activity that, in their mind, ruins the man's life. After so many years of preparation for medicine, a man is middle-aged by the time he begins to practice. At that age, when it is difficult to start all over again, it is virtually unthinkable to force him to leave his profession. While one might do him out of a job, one would not want to do him out of his very work. In consequence, his colleagues settle for what their very individualism would see as their first duty—keeping their own nests clean. He is encouraged to resign from their company, but he is not expelled from the profession. They protect themselves and their patients,

[46] As a Soviet physician put it to an offender, "Unless you resign now, I'll have no alternative but to ask for your dismissal through official channels." Amosoff, *op. cit.*, p. 70.

[47] See the analysis of the bar in Jerome Carlin, *Lawyers' Ethics* (New York: Russell Sage Foundation, 1966).

[48] "Everyone is ill at ease and ashamed. To dismiss a physician like this! But what can one do in such cases? The man is at fault. He pretty near killed a patient. This is not the first time he has made this same mistake." Amosoff, *op. cit.*, p. 71.

which they see to be their first duty, but yet avoid ruining his life.[49]

Their actions point to a characteristic limitation of the practitioner's sense of responsibility. As I have said, the clinician not only assumes responsibility for his work, but even revels in it. However, that responsibility is personal rather than communal.[50] There is a considerable difference between having a sense of personal responsibility for the particular task or client and having a sense of communal responsibility for all tasks and clients of all members of one's profession. Although professional societies do have a general sense of communal responsibility manifested in the enforcement of minimal standards for training and practice, this tends to be as far as they go. It is the sense of personal responsibility that lays the heaviest qualification on the behavior of the individual practitioner in his everyday work. The physician is likely to take personal responsibility for his own work and not to be concerned with the work of colleagues *unless* it has direct bearing on his own. This is why he feels he need not snoop into the affairs of others.

A man is likely to assume personal responsibility for the care he actually gives his patients as well as for the care his patients get from colleagues to whom he has referred them. But, for example, when he refuses to care for an obnoxious patient and does not wish to unload him on a known colleague, he sends the patient away assuming that he will receive good care from anyone else, or that, in any case, so long as he is not willing to take responsibility for the patient, whatever happens to the patient is none of his concern. Only the immediate demands of his personal responsibility seem able to counterbalance his attitudes of distaste for controlling or being controlled by others. The sense of vulnerability already referred to, as well as the tendency to suspend judgment when one

[49] "Stepan's hurt pride is insignificant compared with that. He will live through it. Let him work somewhere else and not hurt *my* patients. This is how I argue with myself." Amosoff, *op. cit.*, p. 75. Note that there, in the Soviet Union, where "society" is supposed to be more important than the individual, it never occurs to such a humane and conscientious surgeon as Amosoff that by letting the offender, Stepan, work elsewhere, *other* patients may be hurt. This curious blindness is, I believe, characteristic of practitioners everywhere.

[50] For some sensible and perceptive remarks about professional individualism and its relation to the commonweal, see T. H. Marshall, *Class, Citizenship and Social Development* (Garden City: Doubleday and Co., 1965), pp. 165–175.

lacks firsthand experience with a case, limit the motive to intervene. And of course the very ambiguity of most everyday circumstances provides little stimulus for strong moral outrage.

The Personal Boycott

If a practitioner is dissatisfied with another's work, and talking to him does not lead to desired changes in his behavior, he is not likely to move to ruin the other's life. All he will do is protect his own personal responsibility. This is done not by any direct effort at control, but by avoidance, by what, in rather dramatic politico-economic terms, Carr-Saunders and Wilson called the boycott. But it is an individual or at most a special colleague-group boycott, not a profession-wide boycott. The tendency is not to try to change an offender's performance so much as to avoid choosing him to work with, and keeping one's own patients away from him. When a man can avoid cooperation and exchange of patients with a colleague he does not think highly of, he avoids having to assume responsibility for the culprit's actions (or at least having to deal with their consequences) while at the same time he avoids having to assume responsibility for the culprit's professional life.

The personal boycott is, I suggest, the most analytically important mechanism of control to be found among physicians and other professionals. It is important because it allows us to understand how one man can be personally ethical and conscientious and another not, yet both exist within the same profession without causing any great tension or conflict between the two. It expresses both the ethical success and failure of the profession, representing as it does the peculiar outcome of the professional's way of looking at his work, himself, and his responsibility.

Variations in Professional Values

The most important point I have made in this chapter revolves around an extension of the distinction between consulting and scholarly professions—the technological and social distinction between "professionals" who do everyday consulting work and those who do not. My argument was that both the contingencies of clinical work and the social characteristics of the people who perform it make for critical differences in values. The clinical practitioner is inclined to use particularistic standards in evaluating his own work and is typically led by his relation to laymen to play a pontifical, functionally diffuse role, one not modestly limited by training or qualification. Although he does not lack a service orientation, he is inclined to stress the symbolic and material perquisites of his official status as a professional more than the intrinsic rewards of his expertise. Thus, the clinical practitioner is less likely than the scholar or researcher to manifest the whole set of "professional values" described by Parsons and discussed at the beginning of this chapter.

The autonomy of his status and the individualism encouraged by the demands of his work make it difficult for the clinician to either submit to or participate in regulatory processes that attempt to assure high ethical and scientific standards of performance in the *aggregate* of practitioners. He wants to control the terms and content of his own work and is not inclined to want to lose that control to profession-wide, systematic auspices. In science and scholarship the obligation and necessity to publish keeps one's work public and under the scrutiny and evaluation of colleagues. But to the consulting practitioner, his work and its results are seen almost as a form of private property.

It follows from the discussion that within medicine itself, which encompasses a variety of individuals and forms of work, values connected with the regulation of performance will vary by the kind of work performed and by the lay values of its performers. Supervision and regulation, therefore, are more likely to be participated in by those who do not work with a lay clientele, by those whose work is objectified into material procedures and outcomes, and by those who have in some way avoided commitment to the values of the entrepreneur. These variables, in conjunction with the way work settings minimize or maximize the observability of work, seem to go far toward explaining the varied levels of performance to be found in the profession. Taken together, they allow us to match the way the performance of professional individuals is organized with the way the profession is constituted as an official organization. These two sides of professional organization, formal and informal, may now be brought together for a more comprehensive view of the nature of the profession.

9.

PROFESSION AS ORGANIZATION—FORMAL AND INFORMAL

IN Part I of this book I dealt with the formal characteristics of the profession of medicine. Taking the profession as a whole, without reference to individuals or to concrete work settings, I discussed the legal and occupational foundations upon which professions rest. I tried to analyze what distinguishes physicians from others who participate in the medical division of labor and what is common to physicians working in a variety of political and economic circumstances. I had occasion to discuss the difference between a position of legal and technical authority in a division of labor (professional status) and a set of attitudes toward work (professionalism), and the difference between control over the content of work and control over the social and economic methods of organizing the performance of work.

I suggested that what is critical for the status of medicine and any other profession is its ultimate control over its own work. Given such control, the status of other occupations participating in a medical division of labor can only be subordinate, however much their faces may be smoothed by such cosmetics as a code of ethics, a long period of schooling that includes instruction in a body of theory, and a claim to serve humanity. I suggested further that control over work need not be total: what is essential is control over the determination and evaluation of the technical knowledge used in the work; important but secondary is control of the social and economic terms of work. Thus, a professional may remain a professional when he is socially subordinate to someone who does not belong to his profession so long as he is not technically subordinate. I distinguished the profession from the paraprofessional occupation by the place of each in an organized division of labor, the profession being technically subordinate to no other occupation, and the paraprofessional occupation being technically subordinate to a profession.

Distinction between a profession as an occupation with a special position in a division of labor and professionalism as the possession by individual members of an occupation of certain attitudes toward work allowed further clarification. In the usage I suggested, whether or not an occupation is a profession is established by the analysis of the relation of occupations to each other in a social structure. Whether or not professionalism exists in an occupation is an entirely different question, answered by study of the attitudes of individual members of occupations. There is no necessary or substantive relationship between the position of an occupation and the attributes of its members. It is the former, I suggest, that is the most useful core of a definition of profession. It is useful because by defining a profession structurally, as a position in a division of labor, one can, without embarrassment and apology, deal with the difference between what a group typically claims its members to be as opposed to what they actually are, and between what is generally believed about a group by others and what is actually the case. And it can distinguish between a process of "professionalization" which is not successfully completed and one which is.[1] A code of ethics, for example, is an important device for persuading the general public to believe that the members of an occupation are ethical, but it does not guarantee public belief. It has no necessary relationship to the actual behavior of members of the occupation any more than legal codes, taken independently of the operation of law enforce-

[1] This is the problem confronting Vollmer and Mills, who seek to avoid defining "profession" by dwelling instead on a process of "professionalization." In default of a definition of profession, however, one does not know where the process is headed, and one cannot assess its progress by any stable criterion. See Howard M. Vollmer and Donald L. Mills, eds., *Professionalization* (Englewood Cliffs: Prentice-Hall, Inc., 1966), pp. 1–2.

ment and the substance of public morality, have any necessary relationship to the behavior of members of a society. In this sense, a code of ethics may be seen as one of many methods an occupation may use to induce general belief in the ethicality of its members, without *necessarily* bearing directly on individual ethicality. Similarly, even if it were clear in other than an intuitive fashion what a "systematic body of theory" is, this criterion too may be treated as part of the process by which an occupation seeks to sustain or create public belief about it without having any *necessary* bearing on the objective prerequisites for the occupation's real work. Indeed, the reasons for inventing courses in theory in the training schools of ambitious occupations are utterly transparent, the popularity of courses in theory in professional schools is notoriously low, and the actual work of professional practitioners is far more often concrete than abstract.

Thus, the formal status of a profession reflects what Hughes called its license and mandate to control its work, granted by society.[2] This is what is unique and central to the notion of profession. The profession's position in society does not necessarily (though it may) reflect a distinctively and especially superior skill, theoretical learning, or ethical behavior on the part of all or most members of the occupation. There are always occupations with such characteristics that are not granted the status of profession, and there are occupations granted the status which lack such characteristics. What the status reflects is society's *belief* that the occupation has such attributes and society's belief in the dignity and importance of its work. The conformity of the real characteristics of an occupation with all the beliefs about them is not presumed by my emphasis and is a matter for empirical determination. The emphasis of the definition is the status.

Once we define the profession primarily as a special status in the division of labor supported by official and sometimes public belief that it is worthy of such status, we are liberated from the confusion and special pleading which permeates most discussions of professions. We need not be embarrassed that a code of ethics is not conspicuous in such a recognized profession as college teaching nor

[2] Everett C. Hughes, *Men and Their Work* (New York: The Free Press of Glencoe, 1958), pp. 78–80.

upset by lack of a systematic body of abstract theory in such an established profession as law (jurisprudence notwithstanding), for these no longer become necessary elements of definition. And we can understand that while such institutional attributes need have at best modest relationship to the way their participants behave, they are not meaningless because they are part of a dialogue between an occupation and society and between reality and desire. Thus, we ask what it is that persuades society to grant professional status. Codes of ethics may persuade in some cases and not others; the existence of what seems to be systematic theory may persuade in some cases and not others. Some of the formal institutional attributes of occupations, then, are analyzed as devices mediating the relationship between the occupation and society. The most critical formal characteristics establish and maintain the occupation's status in society and in the division of labor.

To this emphasis on the status of autonomy in a division of labor must be added a distinction which conditions the character of that status and the way in which it is obtained, as well as the character of performance in that status. I refer to the distinction between work oriented toward solving the problems posed by laymen, and those posed by coworkers—in short, between consulting and scholarly or scientific professions. I suggested that scholarly or scientific professions may obtain and maintain a fairly secure status by virtue of winning solely the support of a political, economic, or social elite, but that such a consulting profession as medicine must, in order to win a secure status, make itself attractive to the general public which must support its members by consulting them. The contingency of the lay public was thus critical to the development of medicine as a profession. And similarly, as I went on to show, the contingency of the lay client is critical to the professional performance of physicians.

Work Settings and Professional Performance

In Part II of this book I moved from the formal status of the profession in society, sustained by its political and legal organization, to the varied settings in which individual members of the profession work and which themselves, by their organization, encourage or discourage physicians to perform their work in particular ways.

In short, I moved from the official claims of and for the profession to the everyday performance of its members. Consonant with the situational approach I use in this book, I emphasize how much greater is the influence of the work setting on the performance of the professional than is his prior formal training in knowledge and ethics. Given the autonomy of the profession at large, the general question guiding my analysis was: How is that autonomy exercised? More specifically: How is variation in professional performance related to the settings in which work takes place, and how, under the formal condition of autonomy, do colleagues regulate each other's performance?

Restricting myself there as elsewhere primarily to the United States, I had occasion to distinguish a number of types of work settings for their bearing on performance. In the case of everyday office work settings, I suggested that a critical variable lies in the physician's isolation from and independence of his colleagues. In a "solo" practice, the prime source of pressure on the physician's performance comes from his patients who, as laymen, are likely to encourage him to please them, and in doing so, to deviate from the standards of other physicians. Isolated from his colleagues, there is little likelihood of countervailing pressures toward professional standards. Logically distinct from such "client-dependent practice" is "colleague-dependent practice," where interaction with colleagues and their cooperation and approval are necessary for work. There, performance is more likely to conform with that of other physicians rather than the expectations of patients. I suggested that solo, fee-for-service practice in a competitive situation was more likely to be client-dependent than colleague-dependent, and that some specialties were likely to assume the characteristics of the former and others of the latter. Thus, on the basis both of my logic and of available evidence, I predicted systematic variation in the quality of work performance of members of the profession by reference to the structured pressures that an organized work setting contains. These variations in performance have little direct relationship to the formal characteristics of the profession, nor are they predicted by them. Nor are they related to prior professional training. They flow from variations in the contingency of the client, a contingency with which every consulting profession must cope.

Turning from office work settings to those that hospitals represent, I tried to review some of the issues bearing on the performance not only of physicians but also of other participants in the hospital care process. Given the many occupations involved in the division of labor in the hospital, and given the varied sources of support and control of the hospital, my treatment was of necessity more complex than was the case for office practice. I discussed how the autonomous but authoritative expertise of the physician, in the context of the organization of medical practice in the United States, allows him to exert remarkable influence on the operation of the hospital, an influence based only in part on his expertise. I then went on to discuss how patterns of staff performance vary in the hospital as tasks and treatment philosophies vary, as patients vary, and as paraprofessional staff varies.

Having sketched out the more common variety of work settings in which members of the profession are found in the United States, I then turned to what is, I believe, the most critical question one may ask about a profession: Given the fact that society grants it autonomy from regulation or intervention by laymen, how does it regulate itself? From the evidence available, I concluded that in ambulatory more than residential settings, and in individual and "private" more than in organized group settings, observation and regulation are minimized. Even in the well-organized work settings which most allow and encourage the observation and regulation of medical performance, however, a large measure of permissiveness seems to exist, the process of regulation at its most strenuous serving to exclude the offender from the concrete setting in which his performance is criticized, but not to exclude him from performing similarly in other settings and on other patients.

This finding is contrary to the usual assumption that when physicians or any other professionals are left free of outside intervention to control themselves, their performance will be optimal. Furthermore, the organization of work settings failed to be adequately explanatory of the outcome, because the organization analyzed permitted far more regulation of performance than seemed to be actually practiced. In the light of this deficiency in the explanatory value of the situational approach, I turned to close examination of working professional norms, particularly those likely to explain why regulatory opportunities were not used. Rejecting the value of the general norms usually said to be connected with professionalism, I sketched out the values which seem to arise from the contingencies of consulting, or clinical work. Being by the nature of the case concerned with practical action for a lay clientele, clinical work, I suggested, leads to an exaggerated sense of limited personal responsibility along with emphasis on the primacy of personal work experience. When these norms are combined with those of class dignity and independence stemming from the bourgeois origins of professionals, they lead to an individualism which is as intellectual as it it social. That individualism minimizes the value of basic scientific knowledge and the methods by which it is established, and maximizes the value of individual opinion based on close personal experience with individual cases. The outcome of such an ideographic mentality is reluctance to criticize or be criticized by another. When confronted by a colleague whose work seems improper, the solution is to exclude him from one's own patients, but not from others. Within the freedom of action granted by professional autonomy, then, the characteristic mechanism of control stemming from normative responses to consultative or clinical work is the personal boycott, designed more to regulate one's own work than the work of the profession as a whole.

Linking Performance with Organization

My discussion of medical norms and the regulation of professional performance has been, at most, a discussion of the reality of professional work compared to the hopes and claims of official spokesmen for the profession. Analytically, the two are not yet connected into a coherent system. There is in the picture I have drawn no link between the reality of professional practice and the reality of formal professional organization. The formal professional association provides a view from above, an official view, of the links between local associations of individual practitioners in different communities. Since such a view does not allow anticipation of variations in performance among practitioners, however, it is patently inadequate. On the other hand the view from below, from the perspective of performance at work, has provided a systematic view of variations in performance, but it has not provided a view of how those variations are organized into patterns of human association, and what the link is among various patterns.

The link, I believe, lies in the personal boycott. The mechanism of the personal boycott, while expressing professional norms, also has specific interactional and organizational consequences for the ordering of relationships among the concrete individuals and institutions distributed through local communities—the everyday social reality upon which the general and formal idea of the profession is imposed. It suggests that running separately from the formal organization of the profession is another organization. Since it is neither publicly codified nor officially recognized by the formal professional associations (though I do not mean to imply that its existence is therefore the result of a conspiracy), it might be called the informal organization of the profession. Knowledge of the characteristics of the informal organization can explain what the formal organization of the profession does not concede and cannot explain—namely, how a diversity of technical and ethical practices can persist without strain in a nominally ethical and competent profession composed of men all trained according to minimal standards. Specifying the formal organization of medicine allows us to understand what *structured uniformity* there is in medical performance, largely by reference to legally supported minimum standards of licensing. Specifying the informal organization of medicine allows us to understand the sources of *structured variation* in medical performance, largely by reference to the interaction of practitioners organized by specific settings. In order to round out my picture of the operative organization of the profession, I shall attempt a sketch of its informal organization.

The Creation of Informal Organization

In his fine-grained study of physicians, Oswald Hall was able to distinguish three types of medical career by the kind of relation a young medical graduate had to senior men already in practice: an "individualistic career," in which a young man struggles for his own clientele independently of others; a "friendly career," in which a man is helped by and helps a few colleagues who are close friends; and a "colleague career," in which a young man works under the patronage of highly successful older men who control hospital appointments and access to the most desirable clientele.[3] In the course of discussing the latter, Hall described what he called an "inner fraternity"[4] of physicians, standing at the peak of success in the community, and controlling access by others to that success. If a young physician looks promising (in part by having the right religious and social background, in part by his proper demeanor, in part by the ability perceived in him), he is offered demanding positions at the bottom of the hierarchy. If he is content to work hard for the prestige and intrinsic interest of the position and its promise of better days, he is gradually doled out better positions and patients, his movement to the top slowly and carefully nourished by his superiors. If he persists he receives more and more recommendations, referrals, consultations, and other kinds of invitations to interact with the men at the top. If he becomes impatient, he is dropped from the system and sustains no such interaction.[5]

What mechanism is dominant in this system? To quote Hall, "The inner fraternity . . . has one dominant method of functioning. Its basic activity is referred to here as 'sponsorship.' By sponsorship is meant simply that established members of the inner fraternity actively intervene in the career lines of newcomers to the profession. By so doing they influence the careers of those selected. . . . Sponsorship has a dual purpose. It facilitates the careers of those selected and relegates those not so selected to a position where they compete under decidedly disadvantageous terms."[6] And what is sponsorship? It is the precise opposite of avoidance and the personal boycott.

Hall's emphasis on the positive side of avoidance is useful because it allows us to perceive how stable or established colleague groups and their powers are maintained and how new individuals are brought into them. But his emphasis neglects the consequences of the negative aspects of patronage. What happens to those who do *not* get the approval of the inner fraternity, to whom patronage is not given, or from whom it is withdrawn? The inner fraternity

[3] Oswald Hall, "Types of Medical Career," *American Journal of Sociology*, LV (1949), 243–253.

[4] See Chapter 5.

[5] Oswald Hall, "The Stages of a Medical Career," *American Journal of Sociology*, LIII (1948), 327–336.

[6] Oswald Hall, "The Informal Organization of the Medical Profession," *Canadian Journal of Economics and Political Science*, XII (1946), 32–33.

controls access only to the brand of success it represents, not to work as such or to other kinds of success. Furthermore, it is difficult to imagine in reality the structure that Hall implies—that of a single inner fraternity and, outside it, rogue males or isolated, individualistic practitioners. With some exceptions it is very difficult to practice without referral and consultative relations among colleagues, and it is very difficult to practice without a hospital affiliation. Assuming that these requirements are commonly met, then it follows that even outside the inner fraternity there must be fairly stable, organized colleague groups. In other words, as my discussion of types of medical practice indicated, there can be numerous "fraternities" in a single community, and there are certainly numerous "fraternities" in the profession as a whole. As my discussion of types of medical practice did *not* indicate, however, these colleague groups are built up by the mechanisms of patronage and boycott; and, by the very consequences of the mechanisms themselves, they must be fairly well segregated from each other.

Characteristics of Informal Organization

Let us try to visualize logically the structural consequences of the mechanism of boycott by hypothesizing a heuristic free-market situation in which individual practitioners are free to select the work they will undertake and to choose the colleagues with whom they will divide their labor. On this level, the control of professional standards is exercised largely by willingness to work with one man and unwillingness to work with another. In the latter case avoidance occurs. But avoiding a man does not mean that he cannot work at all. Indeed, one may assume that a man excluded from one circle will eventually find another circle of colleagues whose standards are compatible with his and who will cooperate with him in the course of his work. Assuming that these fraternities, circles, or networks are created on the basis of common standards within permissive limits, deviants may be excluded from one but will find another that will accept them. Many differences in standards are likely to exist *between* networks by virtue of the nature of the process that differentiated them in the first place. Furthermore, given the role of boycott in creating such networks, there is not likely to be very much interaction between them. Insofar as working networks of practitioners require such institutions as hospitals for their continuance, and insofar as there are several such institutions in the same community, different networks are likely to be associated with different institutions.

In a structure of this nature there is comparatively little opportunity for those in one network to be very much aware of the existence of others with other standards, and even when awareness may exist there is little leverage by which one could influence the other because each has severed connections with the other and is independent of the other. Since it is a segregating process that leads to and maintains such networks, and since the individual's behavior is less controlled by such a process than classified and assigned to a collectivity of like people, we can see how within a single profession, even one quite free of lay interference, organized variations in professional performance can develop and stabilize.

The picture I have presented is fairly abstract and logically idealized, emphasizing what is probably never completely the case in reality—a prompt and rapid process of sorting individuals. Several aspects of reality must certainly qualify its operation. First, since entrance into practice by individuals is continuous over time, there are always individuals in the process of being sorted, which reduces the homogeneity of any colleague group at any point in time. Second, however, homogeneity is increased by the fact that some of this sorting takes place without waiting for avoidance to operate: in the face of the modesty of their own aspirations or the discouragement of teachers in medical school, some sort themselves so accurately or humbly that they never have to be excluded by others. Third, the existence of stable organizations of practice precludes the unfettered operation of purely individual choice and selection. There are, for example, senior people with a historical right to membership even though they have relaxed their standards. Colleagues may not expel them; instead they are merely sealed off, encapsulated, and perhaps neutralized within the group or organization. These men violate homogeneity but remain members nonetheless. Fourth, some circumstances allow more rapid evaluation and sorting than others: a colleague group formed around a division of labor, in which each man can see and evaluate the other's work, is likely to sort itself out more quickly than a group that barely goes beyond cooperative social and economic relations. Indeed, one might suspect that the former will be more likely to be homogeneous in its *technical* standards than the latter, the latter more homogeneous in its *social standards*. Finally, it is necessary to remember that the personal boycott is not invoked promiscuously. Given the reluctance to criticize I have discussed in detail, we should expect sorting by boycott to be slow and erratic. However loose and halting the process, though, I believe that enough of it goes on to be emphasized usefully by my sketch of informal organization.

There are no adequate data available to test the truth of my suggestions, but there are certainly some that confirm the existence of an informal structure in the community that sorts medical people into definable networks of consultation and cooperation.[7] Like some critics of community stratification studies, Winick did not find that colleague integration was closely related to the prescription of drugs to the same degree as did the Coleman, Katz, and Menzel study of the adoption of a new drug. Winick suggested that in the larger cities, such as the one he studied, of about 750,000, the professional's experience is more individual and diffuse, lacking the tendency to an integrated organization that may be found in smaller communities.[8] This is probably true to a degree, but what evidence there is argues that such a structure of networks as I have suggested exists everywhere. Though the studies of drug adoption by Coleman, Katz, and Menzel, as well as that by Winick, suggest some of the sifting process of choice as I have hypothesized, the structure is best discovered by studying the everyday process of referral and by determining the existence of differences in orientation and practice that mark off, for example, the academician from the practitioner,[9] and the elite from the lowly.[10] Certainly in a city as large as Chicago, Solomon's study presents very persuasive evidence of a

[7] James S. Coleman, Elihu Katz, and Herbert Menzel, *Medical Innovation, A Diffusion Study* (Indianapolis: Bobbs-Merrill Co., 1966).

[8] Charles Winick, "Diffusion of an Innovation Among Physicians in a Large City," *Sociometry*, XXIV (1961), 384–396.

[9] Cf. Patricia Kendall, "The Relationship Between Medical Educators and Medical Practitioners," *Journal of Medical Education*, XL (1965), Part II, pp. 137–245.

[10] Jerome Carlin, *Lawyers' Ethics* (New York: Russell Sage Foundation, 1966).

system of stratification in the differences he found in the personal characteristics, training, and practice of staff members of various hospitals in the city.[11] While much evidence remains to be gathered, it does seem plausible that the informal organization I have described is characteristic of American medicine.[12]

The Paradox of Professional Controls

Given this informal organization, what is its implication for professional controls? It follows from the very type of process which "controls" behavior that while those who are engaged in any single fraternity are likely to be socially motivated to maintain its current standards, those who are boycotted are put into a position where none of these motivational controls can work to support the standards of the group from which they were excluded. Indeed, they are ejected and segregated beyond visibility to the others. While there are probably social links between adjacent fraternities in the form of individuals with connections in both, it does not seem to require a very large city to find individuals who know nothing about each other.[13] I would in fact suggest that in large communities there are whole circles of practitioners who do not know others and who are not aware of others' standards and practices except in the most abstract way. In such a system as this, furthermore, even if men in one network knew how the men in other networks performed, and deplored it, the suspension of cooperative relations between individuals in separate networks has destroyed whatever leverage might have existed to influence each other's performance.

The mechanism of personal boycott, therefore, paradoxically

[11] David N. Solomon, "Ethnic and Class Differences Among Hospitals as Contingencies in Medical Careers," *American Journal of Sociology*, LXVI (1961), 463–471.

[12] The method I have used—tracing the pattern of relationships by referrals, other communications and the exchange of resources, and by boycotts and other limitations on both communication and the exchange of resources—is relevant to determining the informal organization of both consulting and scientific professions. For law, see the discussion of stratification in Carlin, *op. cit.* For science, see, for example, Diana Crane, "Social Structure in a Group of Scientists: A Test of the 'Invisible College' Hypothesis," *American Sociological Review*, XXXIV (1969), 335–352. Here, as elsewhere in my analysis, concepts relevant to the study of medicine prove equally relevant to the study of education, law and science.

[13] See the sociograms in Coleman *et al.*, *op. cit.*

operates to place offenders beyond further professionally acceptable controls, and the informal organization of internally homogeneous networks segregated from interaction with each other sustains if not reinforces the differences in standards among networks. Apart from civil suit, which is a *nonprofessional* source of leverage over practice, such nationally imposed devices as hospital accreditation requirements, which have little influence on the ambulatory care that constitutes the bulk of medical practice, and the local county professional society, whose influence is largely political and economic, what is left to concerned leaders of the profession is exhortation and, hopefully, instruction of anonymous practitioners by means of articles in professional journals which may not be read.

Insofar as writers in journals have prestige and manage to attract the attention of members of the profession, they may influence some aspects of the technical and ethical standards of a man's practice irrespective of the network to which he belongs. But much research on methods of educating and persuading people points to the conclusion that such influence, when unsupported by everyday work settings or personal contact, is likely to be slight.[14] In fact, the most severe handicaps to effective influence are likely to be posed by the fact that while these "leaders" are prominent and therefore visible to those in less prestigious networks, those in the latter are neither visible to nor in interaction with the leaders. Attempted communication from the top is therefore based on inadequate understanding of the point of view and everyday problems of work faced by obscure practitioners.[15] What is more, the latter sustain each other's views of what must be done to cope with their problems. Perhaps this is why the huge volume of medical sermons seems to have little impact on the everyday clinical practitioner.

What I have suggested is that the disjunctive process of social control characterizing the concrete, everyday practice of American physicians creates a structure of relatively segregated small circles of practitioners, some of which are so isolated from others that the

[14] See Joseph Klapper, *The Effects of Mass Communication* (New York: The Free Press of Glencoe, 1960); and Everett Rogers, *Diffusion of Innovations* (New York: The Free Press, 1962).

[15] See Kendall, *op. cit.*, and Carlin, *op. cit.*

conditions necessary for influencing behavior across the various circles are missing. Furthermore, I have argued that the mechanism of control is particularly compatible with the practitioner's experience rather than being an oversight or an aberration. The consequence is that a "single" inclusive profession can contain within it and even encourage markedly different ethical and technical practices, limited in a very superficial way by the common core of training required for licensing and by the writings of the leaders of the profession. Insofar as the local practitioner population is large enough, the segregated networks are at least partly ordered by prestige, and only the higher levels are linked in with (and contribute to) the national and international associations representing various formal aspects of the profession. But since individuals in those high-prestige inner fraternities have been segregated and have segregated themselves from those on the less prestigious levels, their conception of the reality of medical work and their public presentation of professional norms cannot fail to be built around their own very special citadels of practice and teaching.[16]

This split and fragmented structure underlying the serene façade of the "profession as a whole" is, I suggest, characteristic of many other if not all occupations which I would define as consulting professions. It is a function of the formal autonomy of professions and the ideology stemming from consultative, or clinical, work. The characteristic mechanism of control flows from the ideology and is allowed to be the prime mechanism by the protected autonomy of the profession. The mechanism of avoidance is neither peculiar to medicine nor to professions in general. It is, after all, one of the most common in our lives. It is important in the present context because the profession is so free of the direct control of clients, lay employers, and the state that it is under little compulsion to use any other form of control. *Within* the profession the use of other forms of control is discouraged by the claim that they are destructive of the professional's work and motives to work. Given the mechanism, *the resultant structure* confirms itself in that by its nature it cuts off information about performance which, if it were better known to the elite of the profession, might motivate them to consider the use of other types of control. As it is, leadership and

[16] Carlin, *op. cit.*

rank and file is each prevented from seeing the world of medical work from any but the special perspective of each.

Profession as Organization

In the first two parts of this book I have been treating a profession as an organization of workers first and as a set of ideas and knowledge only second. In this I adopt more the approach of Karl Mannheim than of Max Weber, taking social organization as the central fact for analysis. Emphasizing the position of an occupation in a political economy and the nature of the settings in which it works, I have argued that the Ethic called professionalism does not distinguish professions from other occupations and is not useful for explaining the character of the crucial professional activity of self-regulation. Furthermore, the Ethic I did find useful and necessary for explaining that portion of self-regulation which organization could not was one that was derived from the "situated actions" of consultative, practical work itself and from the social origins of its performers, not from the more general Ethic. The general Ethic seems to reflect primarily the occupation's task of attempting to persuade society to grant and sustain its professional status.

Organization was found on a number of levels of both abstraction and reality. I tried to trace it out as far as seemed necessary for a rudimentary analysis of a profession. I specified first of all the organization established by the relatively persistent relationships among various occupations into which the profession is fitted—the division of labor. Here, organization is found in the way the legal and working relations of the various occupations are ordered by the technical interdependence or overlap of their work, and by the authority some have over others. This is not a customary approach, but a formal table of organization for the medical division of labor could be drawn which is quite comparable to those conventionally drawn for corporate enterprises or other obvious "organizations." Second, there is that organization of official spokesmen which has legal identity and which by its negotiation with the sovereign state is engaged in establishing, maintaining, defending, and expanding the legal or otherwise political advantages of the occupation. This is the formal organization of the profession, where the Professional Ethic serves an important function in persuading the state and the public to support the profession. Third, there is the variety of settings in which the members of the profession work, all of which, even the private office of a solitary medical entrepreneur, develop stable patterns of relationships in which we may find social organization. Each practice itself constitutes an organization, even if some are not formally or legally specified. And individual practices or work settings which develop stable exchange or referral relations with others may also be treated as organized systems. Such work settings, resting on the legal and political advantages maintained by the formal organization of the profession, represent the reality in which abstractions about "the profession" as such, about the division of labor within the profession, and between the profession and other occupations, are illustrated and tested empirically. These settings, I have insisted, are the proving grounds for the formal profession's professions of ethicality and competence. Finally, there is the organization which I have called informal. Here, while the sorting and sifting of cooperative colleague relations which creates the organization is deliberate and conscious enough, its organized outcome is largely neither acknowledged nor recognized *as organization* by its participants, and, unlike all other forms of organization I have discussed, has no official standing. In fact, being the organization of men with various qualities and standards of performance into self-sustaining and self-segregated groups, it explicitly contradicts the official fictions that all licensed men are qualified to work and that all formally qualified men work equally competently and ethically. The orientation toward work I have characterized as "clinical" stems from the consultative character of the work itself and serves the important function of justifying the mechanisms which create the informal organization of professionals.

PART III.

THE SOCIAL CONSTRUCTION OF ILLNESS

"Not merely do the practitioners, by virtue of gaining admission to the charmed circle of colleagues, individually exercise the license to do things others do not do, but collectively they presume to tell society what is good and right for the individual and for society at large in some aspect of life. Indeed, they set the very terms in which people may think about this aspect of life."

—Everett Cherrington Hughes

10.

ILLNESS AS SOCIAL DEVIANCE

IN the first two parts of this book I devoted myself to the analysis of the social organization of the medical profession and its members. In that analysis, my emphasis was on the forms of organization that express the profession's monopoly of practice, its ultimate control of the content of its work. This framework established, it is appropriate now to turn to the work of the profession itself—the diagnosis and treatment of people said to be sick. I wish to explore the implications of the fact that in the course of obtaining a monopoly over its work, medicine has also obtained well-nigh exclusive jurisdiction over determining what illness is and therefore how people must act in order to be treated as ill. In the sense that medicine has the authority to label one person's complaint an illness and another's complaint not, medicine may be said to be engaged in *the creation of illness as a social state which a human being may assume.* To create illness in this fashion—what might be called socially iatrogenic—is generic to medicine, while simply inducing disease, or biological disorder, by mistaken methods of treatment—what is usually called iatrogenics [1]—is but a flaw of technique. Unlike Parsons,[2] I do not argue merely that medicine has the power to legitimize one's acting sick by conceding that he really is sick. My argument goes further

[1] See Robert H. Moser, ed., *Diseases of Medical Progress* (Springfield: Charles C Thomas, 1964); David M. Spain, *The Complications of Modern Medical Practices* (New York: Grune and Stratton, 1963).

[2] Talcott Parsons, *The Social System* (New York: The Free Press of Glencoe, 1951), pp. 428–447.

than that. I argue here that by virtue of being the authority on what illness "really" is, *medicine creates the social possibilities for acting sick.* In this sense, medicine's monopoly includes the right to create illness as an *official social role.* It is true that the layman may have his own "unscientific" view of illness diverging from that of medicine, but in the modern world it is medicine's view of illness that is officially sanctioned and, on occasion, administratively imposed on the layman. It is part of being a profession to be given the official power to define and therefore create the shape of problematic segments of social behavior: the judge determines what is legal and who is guilty, the priest what is holy and who is profane, the physician what is normal and who is sick.[3]

It may be argued that medicine is inappropriately placed in the same category as law and religion because law is man-made and therefore varies from one society to another and religion is based on supernatural revelation which is not amenable to the usual scientific methods of verification, whereas medicine addresses itself to an unchanging biological reality that is as independent of man as the realities of physics and chemistry. The "laws" of medicine are therefore invariant unlike those of law, and they are empirically verifiable unlike those of religion. A broken leg is everywhere the same and so can hardly be "created" by medicine in the same way that lawyers and legislators create law. Such an argument, however, fails to distinguish physical from social reality. I must insist that, just like law and religion, the profession of medicine uses normative criteria to pick out what it is interested in, and that its work constitutes a social reality that is distinct from (and on occasion virtually independent of) physical reality.

In the tradition of the sociology of knowledge recently expounded by Berger and Luckmann,[4] I wish to devote the next few chapters to illness as a social rather than biological state, how it differs from other social states, and what types of illness-as-social-state there are. Further, I shall ask what role the profession has

[3] In Holzner's terms, professions are "epistemic communities." Burkart Holzner, *Reality Construction in Society* (Cambridge: Schenkman Publishing Co., 1968), p. 68.

[4] Peter L. Berger and Thomas Luckmann, *The Social Construction of Reality, A Treatise in the Sociology of Knowledge* (Garden City: Doubleday and Co., 1966), and Holzner, *op. cit.*

had in delineating illness, what characteristics of the profession and its institutions are responsible for some of the peculiarities of contemporary conceptions of illness, and, finally, how professional institutions, in interaction with lay institutions, organize the process of being ill and of receiving medical treatment. I shall discuss how medicine creates the social role of illness.

Throughout the discussion it is necessary to bear in mind that I am not attempting to deal with the "causes" of the set of measurable and empirically verifiable signs which the physician sometimes calls disease. That is an essentially medical question. Instead, I shall attempt to deal with the "causes" of labeling one set of attributes illness and not another and the "causes" of the experience and behavior of people who have been diagnosed in a particular way. That is a generically sociological question. The behavior of the "sick" varies from one culture to another, very often independently of disease, and constitutes a reality in itself. So does the behavior of the healer vary from culture to culture. It is the analysis of what Mechanic calls the "illness behavior" of the patient [5] along with the analysis of the "diagnosis behavior" and "treatment behavior" of the physician, not the analysis of physical signs, that I wish to present. What is their relation to physical signs?

Biological and Social Deviance

A great deal has been written on the problem of defining what illness "is." [6] But whatever else it may be, illness is a type of deviation, or *deviance*, from a set of norms representing health or normality.[7] Considerable debate has revolved around what the norms are from which illness deviates—whether, for example, illness is devia-

[5] David Mechanic, *Medical Sociology* (New York: The Free Press, 1968), pp. 115–157.

[6] For a general discussion of conceptions of disease, see W. Riese, *The Conception of Disease: Its History, Its Versions and Its Nature* (New York: Philosophical Library, 1953).

[7] See Daniel Offer and Melvin Sabshin, *Normality, Theoretical and Clinical Concepts of Mental Health* (New York: Basic Books, 1966); Marie Jahoda, *Current Concepts of Positive Mental Health* (New York: Basic Books, 1958); F. C. Redlich, "The Concept of Health in Psychiatry," in A. Leighton *et al.*, eds., *Explorations in Social Psychiatry* (New York: Basic Books, 1957), pp. 138–158. See also the discussion in David Mechanic, *Medical Sociology* (New York: The Free Press, 1968), pp. 33–44.

tion from the statistically average state of a population or deviation from the positive and active norm of optimal health. In all cases, however, the idea of deviation from some standard is present. Human, and therefore social, *evaluation of what is normal, proper, or desirable is as inherent in the notion of illness as it is in notions of morality.* Quite unlike neutral scientific concepts like that of "virus" or "molecule," then, the concept of illness is inherently evaluational. Medicine is a moral enterprise like law and religion, seeking to uncover and control things that it considers undesirable.

But as I have already noted, medicine is kept apart from religion and law because, unlike them, it is believed to rest on an objective scientific foundation that eschews moral evaluation. Illness is thought to involve viruses and molecules and thus to constitute a physical reality independent of time, space, and changeable moral evaluation. Thus, from the bones of men long dead, who spoke long forgotten tongues and practiced now wholly obscure customs, we can independently of their culture draw evidence of fractures, arthritis, rickets, and the like.[8] It is because it is believed to be independent of human culture (though human culture may influence its prevalence and treatment) that illness is felt to be different, more "objective" and stable than such clearly social forms of deviance as crime. In this view illness is biological rather than social deviance, subject to the same biophysical law in man as in mouse, rabbit, or monkey. Whether we evaluate it or not, it is always "there," independent of us. In the same sense it is independent of medicine, hardly created by it.

However, the view of illness as biological deviance is essentially abstract and programmatic. While we may subscribe to it as a measure of faith, we cannot rely upon it as our sole guide for analysis without wholly ignoring the interpretive character of social reality. Only among human animals is there language and meaning. In human society, naming something an illness has consequences *independent* of the biological state of the organism. Consider two men in different societies, both with the same debilitating infection: in one case, the man is said to be ill, put to bed, and taken care of by others; in the other case, he is said to be lazy, and he is

[8] See Ellis R. Kerley and William A. Bass, "Paleopathology: Meeting Ground for Many Disciplines," *Science*, CLVII (1967), 638–644.

abused by others. The course and outcome of the disease may be the same biologically in both cases, but the social interplay between the sick man and others is significantly different. And consider the social consequences of diagnosis behavior: one diagnosis may lead to "cure," another diagnosis may lead to death. While disease may be "there," it is what we, as social beings, think and do about it that determines the content of our lives. As Berger and Luckmann put it,

> On the one hand, man *is* a body, in the same way that this may be said of every other animal organism. On the other hand, man *has* a body. That is, man experiences himself as an entity that is not identical with his body that, on the contrary, has that body at its disposal. In other words, man's experience of himself always hovers in a balance between being and having a body, a balance that must be redressed again and again.[9]

Diagnosis and treatment are not biological acts common to mice, monkeys, and men, but social acts peculiar to men. Illness as such may be biological disease, but the idea of illness is not, and neither is the way human beings respond to it. Thus, biological deviance or disease is defined socially and is surrounded by social acts that condition it.

Nonetheless, while the idea of illness and the acts of diagnosis and treatment are social in that they flow from human knowledge, medical knowledge is thought to be "scientific," which is to say more reliable, "objective," and less variable than other forms of knowledge or belief. Therefore, it may seem reasonable to use medical conceptions of illness as a relatively stable and authoritative definition of what is "really" or "basically" wrong with a person, proceeding from there to investigate—as have many anthropologists and sociologists—the way social custom, psychological need, ignorance, and the like complicate the course of illness and treatment. The sociologist would therefore study the social circumstances surrounding medically diagnosed illness. He selects his questions for research and classifies his cases on the basis of stable scientifically and medically defined illnesses. This, I suggest, is an important and

[9] Berger and Luckmann, *op. cit.*, p. 48.

valuable approach, but it is not the only one, and it is not necessarily the most useful.

There are several reasons why the sociologist should not restrict himself to the adoption of medical conceptions of illness and its treatment. First, it may be unwise in the light of history. Even the most cursory reading of the history of medicine leads to the knowledge that many of today's modern medical conceptions of illness are not the same as they were in the "modern" medicine of yesterday and that at least some of tomorrow's "modern" medicine will contradict today's. Modern medicine is not absolute: it is a social institution dominant in our time and place but not in others. Merely a glimpse of the pitiful arrogance of the "science" of modern times past should encourage us to be somewhat reluctant to rush into the arrogance of a present time that will one day be past. Today's unwitting, unstated assumptions will not all survive. Thus, while modern medicine is the best scientific knowledge we have, it is not final.

Second, it must be remembered that, judged by scientific standards of verifiability or reliability, the corpus of modern medicine constitutes an extremely heterogeneous collection of illnesses, from stable signs and complaints directly connected to an infectious microorganism at one extreme, to such vague things as "mental illness" on the other.[10] Indeed, medicine seems to be in a fairly confused state of transition in which the old "hard" variables seem increasingly unsatisfactory and subjective factors created by social life become themselves "causes." The more sophisticated contemporary medical scientists have been led into theories of stress and psychosomatic illness to explain the curiously variable response of the human body to the ostensibly objective world of physical and chemical stimuli. As we shall see in Chapter 12, over the past few decades the steady accumulation of findings under fully controlled circumstances has thrown doubt on the scientific foundation of medical usages that, while efficacious, may not be so for the reasons heretofore assumed. In short, the unambiguously scientific status of a compound fracture is not to be found in many or even most other

[10] Brian MacMahon and Thomas F. Pugh, "Causes and Entities of Disease," in Duncan W. Clark and Brian MacMahon, eds., *Preventive Medicine* (Boston: Little, Brown and Co., 1967), pp. 11–18.

attributes that are called illness and managed by medicine: while one may be on secure grounds taking the medical conceptions of the fracture as given, one is on unsteady, shifting ground working with other medical conceptions of "illness."

Third, and most important, there is no *substantive* necessity for a sociology of medicine to adopt the ontology of medicine unless it is desired to perform the same task as the medical practitioner or investigator—to test and refine medical conceptions of illness and its treatment. If there is anything unique about sociology, it is its preoccupation with the social reality of human life which, while never wholly independent of other levels of reality, can be treated usefully as a reality in itself. Black magic may not be an appropriate explanation of the physical signs manifested by a patient for a physician who seeks the "real" cause of the "actual" sickness so as to be able to treat it effectively, but it is a perfectly appropriate explanation for the content of the individual's social behavior should he believe in black magic. Indeed, while the physician can use biophysical science to explain the *signs* he labels as illness, he himself cannot explain the behavior of the sufferer by reference to that science. For the task of explaining the "illness behavior" of the sufferer, and for the task of explaining the "diagnosis behavior" of the man who treats him, "scientific medicine" is simply irrelevant. Whether or not the illness diagnosed by the physician "really" exists, what its biophysical etiology may be, what its proper therapy is—these are questions of very limited relevance to the sociologist's concern with the explanation of social behavior. They become relevant to the sociologist only when he decides to join with the physician in investigating and treating medically defined illness.

Thus, two kinds of imputed deviance figure in the notion of illness: biological and social. Insofar as the idea of deviance itself implies singling out something to be bad or undesirable, it is generically moral and therefore social. But, once granting the moral designation of deviance, illness can be analyzed as both biological and social deviance. In the case of the analysis of biological deviance, the armamentarium of medicine is appropriately (though not always efficaciously) used. In the analysis of social deviance, sociology is appropriate. In the case of illness as biological deviance, the assumption is that the deviant signs that the doctor sees are independent of the vagaries of human culture and are successfully manageable by the same scientific medical techniques everywhere, no matter how human culture varies. Illness takes on the appearance of solid objectivity and universality, the task for medicine being to explain its cause and discover its proper treatment. The label of illness itself is not problematic.

From the sociological point of view, however, the task is somewhat different. The problem to manage is the idea of illness itself—how signs or symptoms get to be labeled or diagnosed as an illness in the first place, how an individual gets to be labeled sick, and how social behavior is molded by the process of diagnosis and treatment. The validity of the imputation is beside the point, for the illness that is of interest to the sociologist may or may not have a foundation in biological reality, but it *always* has a foundation in social reality in that it is recognized and labeled by people, whatever their scientific competence, and is taken into account by their behavior. Adopting the view that illness is biological deviance from the normal or the desirable is therefore inappropriate for the sociologist. Instead, it seems proper for a sociology of medicine to analyze illness as a form of social deviance which is *thought* to have a biophysical cause and to require biophysical treatment. Perhaps more precisely and inclusively, we might define illness as a form of social deviance the treatment of which is the licensed domain of the medical profession. Sociology's generic concern is with the scientific study of the behavior surrounding that which is called illness—what is social about being and becoming sick and about diagnosing illness. In any particular empirical case, the "sickness" may or may not be biologically "real," but the sick role is always socially "real." Therefore, while it is reasonable for the physician to use the notion that illness is biological deviance, it is no less reasonable for the sociologist to use the notion that illness is social deviance.

Sociological Approaches to Deviance

Even though it is so obvious as to be self-evident that the designation of illness is a social act that picks out some human attribute, evaluates it as undesirable, and leads to efforts to control or eradicate it, there is virtually no sociological theory of deviance that includes within it a clear and unambiguous place for illness. In what is perhaps the most sophisticated and well-developed sociological theory of deviance—that of Talcott Parsons [11]—only illnesses which the individual is himself motivated to adopt are emphasized. In general treatises on deviance,[12] crime is the major area for analysis, with some reference to such things as drug addiction, alcoholism, and mental illness, but there is virtually never any reference to heart disease, pneumonia, and cancer. This is very odd indeed. If it is so self-evident that illness is a form of social deviance, why has it not been dealt with by sociologists interested in social deviance?

The answer, I believe, is both interesting and instructive. Until recently, sociologists of deviance have recognized only one of the two tasks for analysis that I discussed above. They have followed the model of medicine in setting as their task the determination of some stable, objective quality or state of deviance (e.g., criminal behavior) and have sought to determine its etiology. They have failed to recognize the other task of studying the way conceptions of deviance are developed and the consequences of the application of such conceptions to human affairs.[13] In other words, they have failed to recognize that their own "scientific" stance is itself a stance located in time and space and as such is a problematic object of study. They have, furthermore, failed to recognize that consequential human behavior stems from the meanings that actors impute to their experience, not from the meanings that an "objective" observer may impute. Just as they have reified "profession" so they have reified "deviance."

Given this medicine-like stance, it is quite understandable why sociological approaches to deviance have excluded unambiguously medical disease from their purview. Insofar as the task is to make objective, scientific determination of the essential nature of deviance,

[11] See Talcott Parsons, *op. cit.*, pp. 249–325.

[12] See, for example, Albert K. Cohen, *Deviance and Control* (Englewood Cliffs: Prentice-Hall, Inc., 1966).

[13] A somewhat similar distinction is made between the approach of an objective observer who can detect and define norm violation without concern for the views of the participants, and that of studying deviance as a product of the participants of a society rather than as an absolute, by Stanton Wheeler, "Deviant Behavior," in Neil J. Smelser, ed., *Sociology: An Introduction* (New York: John Wiley & Sons, 1967), p. 607.

and insofar as the discipline involved claims for itself only those areas it is competent to deal with, it follows that the sociologist would naturally exclude from his domain any form of deviance which is believed to have a nonsocial "cause." So it is that ordinary disease, which is thought to have biophysical causes, is excluded. Such things as mental illness are included because socially influenced motivation is thought to be one prime element in etiology. Indeed, in most conventional sociological theories of deviance, the thrust of the analysis is to explain how an individual or a group is *motivated* to perform a deviant act or take on a deviant attribute. The central explanation of etiology in traditional medicine is a physical event like exposure to a microorganism. The central explanation in the social and psychological sciences is some kind of motivation. Cancer is excluded not only because it is thought to have a physical cause but also because, unlike mental illness, socially induced motivation is thought to play no important role in its etiology. Cancer is helped along, it is true, by such elements of social life as the custom that encourages people to inhale tobacco smoke, but it is certainly not caused by the symbolic qualities of social life as such. What is overlooked is that the way people respond toward the disease *is* caused by the symbolic qualities of social life.

Furthermore, I suspect that the exclusion of medicine and illness from conventional sociological theories of deviance stems in part from the belief that the approach of medicine to illness is so authoritative that one has no choice other than to adopt it. Even so sophisticated a critic as Becker, who provides us with the foundation for a quite different approach to deviance, implies that there is some special sanctity to biological conceptions of illness that rules them out of sociology's purview.[14] But that sanctity is not necessarily given by the scientifically "hard" qualities of medical knowledge and treatment. Rather, it represents human agreement or consensus. Disease is put into a special category by sociologists because they mistake extensive social consensus for facts independent of consensus; yet a fact is established as a fact only by human consensus. Consensus among humans about what physical signs and symptoms are un-

[14] Howard S. Becker, *Outsiders, Studies in the Sociology of Deviance* (New York: The Free Press of Glencoe, 1963), p. 5.

desirable (and therefore deviant) is high for a great number of the cases labeled "illness"—they do not seem very arbitrary. But that the consensus is high does not make it any the less a social construction. In the case of physical illness, consensus is so extensive and taken for granted that we are inclined to impute to it a reality independent of our agreement. Indeed, as I shall note in Chapter 12, it is this remarkable core of unquestioned consensus that has facilitated the steady expansion of medicine's jurisdiction, drawing more and more types of social deviance into the class, "illness," quite independently of demonstrably accurate conceptions of etiology or of efficacious methods of treatment.

No matter what the reasons for sociology's peculiar avoidance of illness as a major form of deviance, it seems clear that there are two distinct tasks connected with the sociological analysis of deviance as such. One is modeled after the task of medicine: determining the cause (and hopefully the cure) of a given set of signs, symptoms, behaviors, or attributes that are authoritatively labeled as deviance. The label itself—of illness, crime, sin, or whatever—is taken for granted, even though, as values, beliefs, and knowledge change, so will the signs, behaviors, or attributes that will be labeled and so will the label itself. Patently, this approach is deeply rooted in its own time and place, serving or even representing the dominant control institutions of that time and place. In the case of what is labeled illness, the dominant institution in our day is medicine. If the sociologist wishes to undertake the task of determining etiology and treatment in the case of illness, he must obviously use medical conceptions of disease as his foundation, building upon it his own findings about the contribution of social variables to the etiology and management of disease. In other areas of deviance, such as in criminology, the sociologist may create out of concrete laws his own conceptions of crime and may himself create theories of etiology and management.

The other task is one that is essentially defined by the sociology of knowledge. It is created by the recognition that deviance is not a state as such, so much as an evaluation of the meaning of a state. Its problem for analysis then becomes not the etiology of some state so much as the etiology of the *meaning* of a state. Thus, it asks questions like: How does a state come to be considered deviant?

How does it come to be considered one kind of deviance rather than another? Is there patterning in the way deviance tends to be imputed? What does the imputation of a particular kind of deviance do to the organization of the interaction between interested parties? While the first approach focuses on the physical behaviors, attributes, or signs themselves, this task in contrast focuses on the source and consequences of the meaning attached to the behaviors. This task does not require explanation of the cause of the behavior so much as it requires explanation of the cause of the meaning attached to behavior. It therefore requires studying those who impute deviance fully as much as it requires studying the deviants (who may impute deviance to themselves). Like the sociologist of knowledge, it attempts to stand outside the society it studies.[15] In the present case of illness, it requires standing outside medicine and its conceptions. This is the approach I shall adopt here.

The Situational Orientation to Deviance

The germ of such a systematic perspective on deviance is provided by what might be called a situational theory of deviance, one consonant with the way I have already treated professional performance. Characteristically, the approach assumes little about the motivation or the etiology of the behavior declared deviant. It implies that peoples' behavior may be usefully studied as a direct response to the immediate environment or social situation in which they find themselves, quite apart from their prior motives or values.[16] It focuses on the etiology and effects of the *declaration* that behavior is deviant and on the way the status of being deviant is organized by the pressures of the immediate social life in which the individual finds himself. By and large, there is as yet no truly well-elaborated or self-conscious situational "theory" of deviance, but enough has been written during the past decade or so to allow me to outline it here.

The clearest statement is to be found in the work of Howard S.

[15] In his criticism of the "outsider's" task, Gibbs fails to recognize the problematic relationship between the two tasks. See Jack P. Gibbs, "Conceptions of Deviant Behavior: The Old and the New," *Pacific Sociological Review*, IX (1966), 9–14.

[16] See the discussion of "situational adjustment" in Howard S. Becker, "Personal Changes in Adult Life," *Sociometry*, XXVII (1964), 40–53.

Becker.[17] He points out that what is called deviance in human society is something that breaks a social rule or norm. It may exist as an act or attribute independently of social rules or norms—as breaking a window exists independently of laws and breaking a leg exists independently of medicine—but it cannot exist *as social deviance* independently of the social rules or norms that assign the *meaning* of deviance to the act or attribute. In this sense, deviance is created by social rules and cannot exist independently of social life. "Whether an act is deviant, then, depends on how other people react to it." [18] It follows that the *perception and designation* of deviance is at least as important as the actual *act or behavior* in determining whether the social role of deviance will be assumed or not. Indeed, in that accusations of deviance can occur when the act or behavior did not actually take place—as in a false charge—it can be said that the social role of deviance can exist in the *absence* of any "objective" act or attribute and is therefore not created by such acts or attributes. The problem is not to explain given acts or attributes but to explain the attribution of deviance. The etiology of deviance as a social role does not thus lie in the individual "deviant" so much as in the social process of creating rules that make acts or attributes deviant, of labeling people as deviants or offenders, and of managing those labeled as deviants. By distinguishing between the physical act or attribute and the social meaning assigned to it, by emphasizing the extent to which the shape of social deviance is created by those who make the rules and enforce them rather than by the physical act or attribute that may be involved, and by leaving open the question of the "real" etiology of the act or attribute said to be deviant, Becker provides a framework within which illness can easily be fitted. In the writing of Edwin Lemert we have a diffuse and unsystematic but nonetheless useful set of ideas to aid in developing such a framework.

Lemert's work emphasizes the difference between forms of deviance that are (1) merely idiosyncratic characteristics of a person that distinguish him from others (sometimes invidiously) but that may be dealt with as merely part of the way he performs a socially acceptable "normal" role, and (2) forms of deviance that them-

[17] See Becker, *Outsiders, op. cit.*
[18] *Ibid.*, p. 11.

selves become roles, part of the social structure. Much of what physicians and psychiatrists deal with are of the former character. A businessman may perform his role in an especially obnoxious way, but even though he may be unpopular he remains nonetheless a businessman; if he has a cold and comes to work, his performance of his role as businessman may be altered, but the attributes of having a cold are not organized into a new role. This Lemert calls "primary deviance" and claims is of little importance for the individual, either psychologically or sociologically, because it does not involve "symbolic reorganization at the level of self-regarding attitudes and social roles." [19] Primary deviance is merely symptomatic: it is, let us say, mere difference rather than deviance. To be different is "not significant until [the differences] are organized subjectively and transformed into active roles and become the social criteria for assigning status. The deviant individuals must react symbolically to their own behavior aberrations and fix them in their sociopsychological patterns. The deviations remain primary deviations. . . . as long as they are rationalized or otherwise dealt with as functions of a socially acceptable role." [20]

Significant deviance is *secondary*—that is, it becomes socially organized as *deviance* rather than as mere difference. Deviance becomes organized into a specifically deviant role that helps one defend oneself, attack, or adapt to the problems posed by the reactions of others to one's primary deviation. In actually adopting such a role, an individual must reorganize his view of himself, others, and his relation to them, and often find a specific deviant subculture and social organization that can facilitate his adaptation.

In *Social Pathology*, Lemert suggests a process of "interaction" in the course of which secondary deviation develops that is similar in many ways to what Parsons suggested as the source of motivation to deviance.[21] Some primary deviations are singled out by others as undesirable, so they penalize the deviant. This leads to more deviation and still stronger penalties, in the course of which the

[19] Edwin Lemert, "Social Structure, Social Control and Deviation," in Marshall Clinard, ed., *Anomie and Deviant Behavior* (New York: The Free Press of Glencoe, 1964), p. 82.

[20] Edwin Lemert, *Social Pathology* (New York: McGraw-Hill Book Co., 1951), p. 75.

[21] See Talcott Parsons, *op. cit.*, pp. 252–256.

individual comes to resent those penalizing him. The deviant is stigmatized, social distance solidifies, and he turns to a deviant role. Lemert goes on to note that when a deviant role is adopted, an integrational process may come into play and other roles may be segregated from or subordinated to it. New claims and loyalties result from the attempt to minimize tensions, from the dangers of visibility, and from the penalties in general. But a deviant role need not assume primacy and so may be practiced covertly, segregated from normal roles. The severest problems occur when no traditional or well-defined role for the deviant behavior exists, no deviant social organization and special culture, no special skills and techniques. Where they do exist, however, the adjusted deviant accepts his new role, the status it involves, and the rewards obtained from it: he becomes in essence a "professional" deviant.

The basic point of the distinction between primary and secondary deviation is that significant deviance is a function of others' responses to an individual's characteristics or an individual's response to himself. The characteristics themselves are of *less* importance to producing and forming that deviance than are the social responses to them, the labeling that gives them meaning. In this sense, "social control [itself] must be taken as an independent variable, rather than as a constant, or merely reciprocal societal reaction to deviation. Thus conceived, social control becomes a 'cause' rather than an effect of the magnitude and variable forms of [primary] deviation."[22] Once this is understood, it should be clear that *secondary deviation can be produced when an individual is not himself motivated to adopt it, and when no "objective" or "real" primary deviation existed in the first place.* What is important is the *imputation* of deviance to one individual by significant others (including himself) and the attending process whereby a conventional deviant role is created for or by him. Whether or not he is "really" deviant or has personal qualities motivating him to be deviant is quite beside the point. What is to the point is the character of the system of social control—its typical labels for deviance, its power to organize it into stable roles—and the character of the available system of deviant roles and groups. These motivate him to regard himself as a deviant.

The "societal reaction," then, is seen to cause significant types of

[22] Lemert, "Social Structure," *op. cit.*, p. 83.

deviance, and mere individual differences in role performance are ruled out of significance. Focus on the societal reaction requires us to scrutinize the interrelations between groups and associations in modern social life. The societal reaction is particularly important when we remember that comparatively few norms in modern society may be said to be shared by all within it. Modern society may be visualized as a number of groups and groupings, many of which have different norms than the others. Lemert postulates a "value pluralism" that is by no means restricted to modern society. Such pluralism is significant because it provides a foundation for contingent deviance. For example, "when dominant values of a culturally distinct group are extended to become a basis for normative regulation of . . . populations having divergent values . . . by definition or fiat, certain cultural practices of the minority cultural groups become crimes, subject to sanctions and penalties imposed by the dominant group or elite." [23]

Apart from that "ethnic pluralism," there is also "neo-technic pluralism," in which "the individual leaves the arena of primary groups and enters into numerous associations and unstructured situations with . . . members representing disparate values." [24] In such associations, "the values which emerge as dominant therein may vary greatly from those of individuals considered distributively. When the association becomes part of an alignment with other associations, the values made dominant in society through the activities of such alignments are even further removed from those of individuals in the various constituent associations. By the same token, the norms set up or legislated to insure the dominance of these remote values may be greatly discrepant or in direct conflict with those held to be appropriate by individuals." [25] These associations "succeed in having their special values advanced, protected or entrenched through enactment of legal norms. . . . In many instances the legal norms represent no values of individuals or groups but rather the results of compromises reached through group interaction in legislatures." [26]

[23] *Ibid.*, pp. 64–65.
[24] *Ibid.*, p. 67.
[25] *Ibid.*, p. 68.
[26] *Ibid.*, p. 69.

Thus, many norms of our society are constructions of special groups, and if they are recognized by law they are at least partially the norms of groups with political privilege (e.g., professionals) if not power (e.g., labor and capital). They are by no means to be considered the norms of individuals or of primary groups throughout the society: they are in essence outside individuals and primary groups, and the simple contingency of having the bad luck to run afoul of them can make deviants of those individuals or groups. In this sense, many of those norms are *imposed* on people irrespective of their own beliefs.

But because those norms by their nature tend to be artificial and do not actually represent those of any living group, they are difficult to be applied mechanically, across the board. Instead, regulatory agents must in some sense constantly be interpreting the intent of the norms and the meaning of possibly offending behavior: the control process itself represents a series of arbitrary decisions bearing as much if not more on the circumstances in which the agent of social control finds himself, and on the character of the agent himself, as on the actual behavior of a potentially defined offender. In this sense, *the norms themselves, and the agents who deal with them, are as problematic as the individual deviants.* Analysis must focus less on "the essential definitions like mental disorder and alcoholism than on the processes by which organizations recognize or do not recognize them as moral defects or disease, make them a basis for excusing other deviant acts, or choose to assign or not assign benefits to those to whom the deviations are attached. . . . *Valuation* [on the part of control agents] *becomes a central concept in the explanation of deviation.*" [27] Thus, the private and public agencies which are organized to deal with the deviant serve to *create* the deviant social role, and by studying the "societal control culture," [28] we will learn why some people are labeled deviants and not others. By studying the social biases in the way cases are identified and norms are applied we will understand why the known or believed universe of deviance is what it is. By studying the social control processes trained upon the deviant once he is singled out,

[27] *Ibid.*, p. 96.
[28] Lemert, *Social Pathology, op. cit.*, pp. 68–71.

we can learn why his deviation disappears or persists and how it is organized into secondary deviation. This is essentially the view suggested by Becker when he defines deviant behavior as that which people label such, and when he insists on the greater need to explain enforcement than the behavior that comes to be labeled deviant.

Implications of the Situational Orientation

What are the implications of these considerations for a theory of deviance? First, they urge us to avoid assigning stable individual attributes to deviants, for their deviance is socially defined and assigned to a person, not necessarily inhering in anything actually connected to them. Social deviance, then, is ultimately *imputed,* not merely "there." Thus, if we wish to develop a useful picture of deviance, the wisest course does not lie in using the attribute imputed to the deviant, for we run the risk of believing that it is actually there. Second, what is defined as deviance may be quite outside the control or desires of the individual involved and so need not necessarily be motivated. The individual's motivation may, however, figure in the way the imputed deviance becomes organized, that is, how he responds to the other's imputation of deviance to him. Hence, a useful and inclusive view of deviance will not use notions of motivation, though it must of course deal with the problem. Third, insofar as a critical element in deviation is whether or not it gets organized socially, and insofar as this seems to be a function of the way others respond to, manage, or otherwise treat it, a strategic picture must take into account significantly different modes of managing or responding to imputed deviance.

These considerations emphasize that because, like beauty, deviance is in the eye of the beholder (even though it be conceded that the eye does see something to which we may ascribe a reality), study of the definer or beholder is as important as study of the deviant. Consequently, insofar as possible, I assume that deviance is a social construct and ask what kinds of conceptions and assumptions agents of control use in formulating its character, what criteria they use to gather evidence supporting it, what are their typical biases, and how their management in effect molds its character.

The Place of Illness

Using the situational view of deviance to analyze illness, one is immediately obliged to distinguish between illness as a purely biophysical state and illness as a human, social state. Illness as a biophysical state involves changes in bone, tissue, vital fluids, or the like in living organisms, human or not. Illness as a social state involves changes in behavior that occur only among humans and that vary with culture and other organized sources of symbolic meaning. While illness as a biophysical state exists independently of human knowledge and evaluation, illness as a social state is *created and shaped by* human knowledge and evaluation. Thus, when a veterinarian diagnoses a cow's condition as an illness, he does not merely by diagnosis change the cow's behavior: to the cow, illness remains an experienced biophysical state, no more. But when a physician diagnoses a human's condition as illness, he changes the man's behavior by diagnosis: a social state is added to a biophysical state by assigning the meaning of illness to disease. It is in this sense that the physician creates illness just as the lawmaker creates crime, and that illness is a kind of social deviance analytically and empirically distinct from mere disease. As a kind of social deviance, the etiology of illness is not biological but social, stemming from current social conceptions of what disease is, limited perhaps by whatever few biological facts are universally recognized, and ordered by organizations and occupations devoted to defining, uncovering, and managing illness. As social deviance, illness may be expected to vary in its content and organization fairly independently of biophysical reality. It may be a primary deviation, qualifying the way one performs his everyday roles, or it may be a secondary deviation, constituting an organized role in itself that displaces others. And, finally, one may expect that it can be distinguished from other kinds of social deviance by the meanings imputed to it. It is the task of classifying those meanings so as to be able to discern sociological types of illness that I turn to now.

11.

SOCIOLOGICAL TYPES OF ILLNESS

IN the last chapter I distinguished between what is biophysical about illness and what is social. I argued that what is social about illness is analytically independent of what is biophysical. In its social form, illness is a meaning assigned to behavior by the actor or by those around him, and illness behavior is ordered by that meaning. Part of the meaning assigned to illness as such is that of deviance. But since many things are considered deviant we cannot understand the social character of illness until we are able to distinguish the meaning of illness from that of other forms of deviance. To make such distinction requires the development of a taxonomy which systematically differentiates logical and empirical types of deviance and, within the general category of illness, types of illness. In this chapter I shall attempt to create such a taxonomy.

Criteria for a Taxonomy of Deviance

The purpose of classifying types of deviance here is practical as well as theoretical. I plan to use my classification in later chapters both to illuminate the relationships among the three established professions and to predict the behavior of those classified. Aside from the ordinary criterion of logical exclusiveness, other criteria will guide the classification. First, given the fact that I am concerned with the social nature of deviance, the scheme will not be based on the biophysical attributes of individuals or on the acts to which meaning is attributed. Thus, it will not be based on the physical signs by which a physician diagnoses a disease or on the proven offenses by which a judge or jury determines crime. Instead, the classification will be based on the meanings that people impute to physical attributes or concrete acts whether or not the imputation is, in the professional view of doctors and judges, "correct." By such a tactic we liberate ourselves from the imperfect medicine and law of our and others' time without precluding the possibility of using their meanings should we choose to adopt their perspective.

Second, the proper system of classification will not be based on present or past ideas about the etiology or cause of the attributes or acts to which deviance is imputed unless those ideas be treated as meanings rather than facts, for I have adopted the sociology-of-knowledge approach to deviance. This specification applies even to the notion of motivation, which, if used, will be used as an imputation rather than a truth. Indeed, motivation is one important meaning connected with the label of deviance. As Brim has noted, "Our society is more willing to tolerate (i.e., sanction mildly or not at all) deviance stemming from ignorance or lack of ability if only a person means well, has his heart in the right place, has good intentions."[1] In this sense, the kind or quality of motivation imputed to a person who is labeled deviant has a great deal of influence on how a physician, priest, judge, spouse, witch, or medicine man behaves toward him. The "real" cause of the behavior, the person's "real" motivation, is less important than belief in its correctness: the complaints of a person with a "real" but undiagnosed or unlabeled illness lead his examiners to treat him as a malingerer or a hypochondriac, not as a sick man. One might therefore classify deviance on the basis of etiology, as Brim suggests,[2] but one must take care to devote oneself to etiology as an imputation rather than as a fact.

Third, since what are being classified are meanings, and since meanings vary from time to time, place to place, perspective to perspective, independently of a great many human attributes and behaviors, it follows that a sound system of classification must specify the time, place, or perspective in which a meaning is im-

[1] See Orville G. Brim, Jr., "Socialization Through the Life Cycle," in Orville G. Brim, Jr., and Stanton Wheeler, *Socialization after Childhood* (New York: John Wiley & Sons, 1966), p. 42.

[2] *Ibid.*, pp. 40–41.

puted before it can connect meaning with behavior. That is to say, the act of haranguing a street crowd can, in one time and place, be imputed the meaning (and motivation) of divine possession, in another the meaning of lunacy, and in still another of an enemy of the state. To understand how people respond to such an act, one must specify their time, place, and perspective: one cannot predict their responses by the act itself. Finally it seems most useful to develop a scheme for classifying types of social deviance in such a way as to be able to predict how people will behave toward the person who has been labeled deviant. This is to say, it seems desirable to select meanings which lead to definite ways of managing or responding to the individuals to whom they apply. The more strategic the meanings used for the taxonomy, the more important the responses to the meanings will be in human interaction.

The Social Meanings of Illness

The requirements for classification stated, the problem now becomes to pick out the strategic meanings used in the process of imputing deviance. Let us begin with the meaning of illness. As Parsons has pointed out,[3] in our time the term "illness," when used to give meaning to perceived deviance, implies that what is thought to be deviant does not arise through the deliberate, knowing choice of the actor and that it is essentially beyond his own control—that is, it is unmotivated. Furthermore, it implies that what is wrong with him is determinable by rational knowledge, and is likely to be known to and manageable by a special class of practitioners holding such knowledge. One does not therefore "judge" a sick person, for he is not to be held responsible for himself. Rather, he should put himself, or be put, into the hands of one of a number of specialists who have the knowledge and skill to help him return to as normal a state as possible. The help of those specialists usually takes the form of education and training or treatment and manipulation: economic or physical punishment is not considered to be an effective or moral method of management.

In his discussion of the social meaning of illness, Parsons goes

[3] The following discussion is based on Talcott Parsons, *The Social System* (New York: The Free Press of Glencoe, 1951), pp. 428–447.

on to delineate "the sick role." Four particular aspects of the role of the sick person are specified as follows: (1) the individual's incapacity is thought to be beyond the exercise of his own choice, and so he is *not held responsible* for it. Some curative process apart from his own motivation is necessary for recovery. (2) His incapacity is grounds for his *exemption from normal obligations.* (3) Being ill is thus to be able to *deviate legitimately*, but legitimation is conditional on the sufferer's recognition that to be ill is undesirable, something one assumes the obligation to overcome. (4) Insofar as he cannot get well by himself, the sufferer is therefore expected to *seek competent help* for his illness and to *cooperate* with attempts to get him well.

It is clear that as Parsons has defined it, the sick role requires that the incumbent seek competent help and therefore that he adopt the *patient* role. The sick role functions to put the deviant into the doctor's hands. It is composed of a set of conditions that move the sick person into the doctor's care: it thus enables the doctor to bring his competence to bear on the sick person. The physician's role in turn makes acceptable to the patient the things the physician must do in order to perform his function.

The sick role is analytically significant because it constitutes a form of deviance that is caught up in a process of social control that at once seals the deviant off from nondeviants and prevents him from becoming permanently alienated. It insulates the sick person from the well, depriving the former of unconditional legitimacy and reinforcing the latter's motivation *not* to fall ill, while at the same time pushing the former into professional institutions where he becomes dependent on those who are not sick. "The sick role is . . . a mechanism which . . . channels deviance so that the two most dangerous potentialities, namely, group formation and successful establishment of the claim to legitimacy, are avoided. The sick are tied up, not with other deviants to form a 'subculture' of the sick, but each with a group of non-sick, his personal circle and, above all, physicians. The sick thus become a statistical status class and are deprived of the possibility of forming a solidary collectivity. Furthermore, to be sick is by definition to be in an undesirable state, so that it simply does not 'make sense' to assert a claim that the way to deal with the frustrating aspects of the social system is 'for everybody to get sick.'"[4]

Imputing Responsibility and Seriousness

Parsons' notion of the sick role has stimulated a number of people in the field.[5] And with good reason, for it is a penetrating and apt analysis of sickness from a distinctly sociological point of view. However, a number of problems are raised by Parsons' formulation which must be resolved if the notion of the sick role is to have some useful relation to social reality. Let me take up the problems one by one.

First, one must note that Parsons' discussion of the patient-doctor roles is intended to be relevant mainly to modern industrial society, not to all human societies. In this sense, much of what he says about such roles has no necessary relationship to his characterization of the sick role as such except in the context of Western societies.[6] Nonetheless, we may expect to find attributes of the sick role even where modern scientific medicine does not exist. What is *generically* critical to the sick role is a series of social imputations and expectations, *a specific societal reaction,* not modern medicine as such. There is no logical reason why absolution from blame need rest on a medical foundation, for it can also rest on a supernatural foundation or even a foundation of chance or luck. The point is that there is absolution from blame, no matter what the rationale for it, and that where such absolution exists, the deviant is managed permissively rather than punitively. The first characteristic of the sick role—not holding the deviant responsible[7] for his deviance—thus speci-

[4] *Ibid.,* p. 477.

[5] See, for example, Gerald Gordon, *Role Theory and Illness* (New Haven, Connecticut: College and University Press, 1966).

[6] Cf. Parsons, *op. cit.,* pp. 475–476.

[7] The idea of personal responsibility is a critical foundation for Western society, if not all societies. Its importance may not be overemphasized even though I cannot dwell on it at any length here. For some important distinctions among types of responsibility in a medical setting, see Thomas S. Szasz, *Law, Liberty and Psychiatry* (New York: The Macmillan Co., 1963), pp. 124–125. For an empirical study of its importance, see C. Richard Fletcher, "Attributing Responsibility to the Deviant: A Factor in Psychiatric Referrals by the General Public," *Journal of Health and Social Behavior,* VIII (1967), 185–196.

fies a meaning assigned to deviance that has significant implications for the way others respond to the deviant whether or not the premises of modern Western medicine are adopted.

The second aspect of the sick role—exemption from normal obligations—cannot be accepted at general, face value because variation in the degree and quality of exemption is closely related to whether or not the sufferer will be encouraged to seek treatment and even to whether exemption will be conditional or not. The degree of exemption defines whether one can adopt a specific sick role or not. In instances of what is considered minor illness, exemption is only from some of the obligations connected with an everyday role, allowing one to perform it in a somewhat variant way "because" of indisposition. In what is considered major illness, one is exempted from everyday role obligations entirely and is allowed to adopt a specific sick role instead.[8] In extreme cases—as in the "magical fright," whereby a person who believes that powerful black magic has been invoked against him obliges the magician by dying,[9] and in the self-confirming Siriono response to an individual's inability to eat by assuming he is a hopeless case and abandoning him on the trail to starve and be eaten [10]—"exemption" from ordinary obligations is so thoroughgoing that death is the consequence. Underlying and explaining the degree of exemption, then, is an imputation of a degree of seriousness to the deviance. Exemption is a *consequence* of the seriousness imputed to the deviance. By the same token, the conditional legitimation given to the behavior of the person thought to be sick, as well as the requirement that he seek competent help for the alleviation of his incapacity, are consequences of the core meanings of illness. The assignment of nonresponsibility to the person labeled deviant legitimizes his behavior so that it is conditionally acceptable to others, who "manage" or "control" him by

[8] For an empirical exploration, see Andrew C. Twaddle, "Health Decisions and Sick Role Variations: An Exploration," *Journal of Health and Social Behavior*, X (1969), 105–115.

[9] See W. B. Cannon, "Voodoo Death," *American Anthropologist*, XLIV (1942), 169–181; John Gillin, "Magical Fright," *Psychiatry*, I (1948), 387–400; W. Lloyd Warner, *A Black Civilization* (New York: Harper, 1936), pp. 240–243.

[10] Alan Holmberg, "Nomads of the Long Bow: The Siriono of Eastern Bolivia," *Smithsonian Institution Publication* No. 10 (1950), pp. 86–87.

exempting him from ordinary obligations but nonetheless requiring him to cooperate with treatment.

I believe that it is possible to use the variables stated or implied by Parsons' analysis of the sick role to serve as the foundation for a system of classifying not only illness but also other forms of deviance. The two prime variables suggested by my discussion are (1) the imputation of responsibility to the person being labeled (with all that responsibility implies for imputed motivation) and (2) the degree of seriousness imputed to his offense (with all that it implies for adopting a new role). These may be treated as independent variables from which flow variations in what is expected of the deviant, how people will behave toward him, and therefore how he will act. Whether or not a person is believed to be responsible for his perceived offenses bears closely on his moral identity and on the obligations others may feel toward him, for when a man is believed to be responsible for his misbehavior, punishment is likely to be involved in its management and moral condemnation is attached to him.[11] When he is not held responsible for it, even though the behavior itself is not what people expect of him and therefore requires some sort of control, management is likely to involve instruction, treatment, or at most permissive constraint.

The imputation of responsibility as a "ground" for behavior [12] is important precisely because it allows us to predict some of the more critical ways in which the deviant will be responded to—the content of the societal reaction. The imputation of seriousness predicts the quantity and quality of management. For example, the medical distinction between a mild upper respiratory infection and a life-threatening cardiac arrest, like the legal distinction between the offenses of jaywalking and of murder, distinguishes differences of intensity that reflect differences in quality of response. Beyond a certain point, the strength of the societal reaction in itself forces primary deviation to become secondary. Even if the societal reaction does not contain within it prescriptions for the degradation ceremony that may formally create secondary deviation,[13] we should

[11] See the extensive and sophisticated discussion of Vilhelm Aubert and Sheldon Messinger, "The Criminal and the Sick," *Inquiry*, I (1958), 137–160.

[12] See Harold Garfinkel, "Conditions of Successful Degradation Ceremonies," *American Journal of Sociology*, LXI (1956), 420–424.

[13] *Ibid.*

expect that, when responded to strongly enough by others, the individual will himself organize a specifically defensive or offensive role. Thus, not mere degree or quantity of response in and of itself is what is important here. What is analytically of prime importance is the assumption that at a certain point the strength of the imputation of deviance leads to the assignment by self or others of a special deviant role to the individual. It is the strength of the societal reaction, measured by the seriousness it imputes to deviance, that may be used to predict whether primary or secondary deviation will result.

A Trial Classification of Deviance

Let us use these two dimensions to create a trial classification of deviance so that we can perceive better how it might work and what it may lack. Table 1 represents such a tentative trial with, as illustration in each cell, a label appropriate to the societal reaction of the contemporary middle class. As I have already noted re-

TABLE 1. TYPES OF DEVIANCE, BY QUALITY AND QUANTITY OF THE SOCIETAL REACTION

(Contemporary American Middle-Class Reaction)

Imputation of Seriousness	*Imputation of Responsibility*	
	Individual Held Responsible	*Individual Not Held Responsible*
Minor Deviation	"Parking violation" Slight addition to normal obligations; minor suspension of a few ordinary privileges.	"A Cold" Partial suspension of a few ordinary obligations; slight enhancement of ordinary privileges. Obligation to get well.
Serious Deviation	"Murder" Replacement of ordinary obligations by new ones; loss of ordinary privileges.	"Heart Attack" Release from most ordinary obligations; addition to ordinary privileges. Obligation to seek help and cooperate with treatment.

peatedly, the use of such labels (and the attributes and behaviors to which they are attached) varies by time, place, and perspective, so that any particular label may be placed in one specific cell only by adopting a given historical, cultural, professional, or other social viewpoint. What I hypothesize to be stable and independent of time, place, and perspective is not the label but the way the deviance is managed once responsibility or its lack is assigned—the obligations and privileges allowed deviants by those labeling them. So far as the deviant's own behavior goes, in both cases of the imputation of seriousness to his deviance secondary deviation is produced, the deviant organizing his behavior into a new role, with a sharp change in obligations and privileges.

The first thing to note about the table's representation of societal reactions which distinguish between the individual's responsibility and lack of responsibility is that it reflects two of the major social control institutions of our time—law and medicine. It does not reflect directly the professional point of view of those institutions—a task I shall undertake for medicine in the next chapter—but rather the way those institutions are embodied selectively in American middle-class reactions to deviation. Superficially, and accurately in only the most qualifiedly general way, "crimes" are those deviant acts or attributes for which people are held responsible or accountable, and "illnesses" are those for which they are not. The reactive consequence of imputing the former is punishment, whether by fine or imprisonment; the consequence of the latter is permissiveness conditional on treatment.

The other axis of classification—imputed seriousness—distinguishes the magnitude of the societal reaction, the consequences of which are either to leave the offender in his "normal" role, somewhat tempered and qualified by now-deviant attributes (that is, primary deviation, in Lemert's terms) or to push him into a new, specifically deviant role (i.e., secondary deviation). This is to say, one does not become a criminal upon being convicted of a petty offense any more than one is rushed to the hospital and put on the critical list upon being thought to have a cold.

In the case of illness the table makes a prime distinction between illness or impairment that is not organized into a special role and that which is. In the former case, exemplified by "a cold," a great many recognized illnesses and impairments fall as temporary or permanent, acute or chronic attributes of the individual that can be accommodated to while performing the roles of everyday life. No single biological "cause" or "system" joins them all together, for among them will be found what a physician may diagnose as virus or bacterial infections, trauma, and malformations, all of most diverse apparent origin, related to diverse organs, members, and systems. Furthermore, we will find there what physicians might call very serious or even inevitably fatal illness: they will fall there before they are so diagnosed and can remain there indefinitely so long as they do not impose severe material limits on performance. By and large, it is the societal reaction that establishes the homogeneity of the items falling into the category, nothing else. The same, of course, can be said for illnesses which become organized into a special role, exemplified by "heart attack": what joins them together is their identification as serious or severe and their being stripped of ordinary obligations. Such identification places the person in a new role. The biological qualities of the illness are tangential except in the context of a specific social situation involving a specific set of agents with a given diagnostic bias.

Furthermore, I might point out that some of what are *medically* labeled as illness fall into the column in which the individual is held responsible for the deviance imputed to him—that is, they become like crimes. In our present-day society, for example, lay and professional reactions toward venereal diseases tend to reflect preoccupation with the way the infection was obtained—a way for which they hold the sufferer responsible.[14] Such preoccupation is not found in the case of infections more innocently arrived at (as from the legendary toilet seat). In another context, it was observed that medical personnel withheld respect, and even care from people who attempted suicide, or were victims of brawls, or of accidents thought to occur by reason of drunkenness or carelessness.[15] While these reactions may not be prominent in the modern middle-class world, they are probably more common than we think, particularly

[14] See, for example, the description in Howard S. Becker *et al.*, *Boys in White* (Chicago: University of Chicago Press, 1961), pp. 323–327.

[15] Barney G. Glaser and Anselm L. Strauss, *Awareness of Dying* (Chicago: Aldine Publishing Co., 1965), p. 83.

where the sufferer has already been warned and so was expected to know better than to become sick. In any event, it must be emphasized that what might be an illness medically, sometimes in our culture and often in others, *can* fall into the left-hand column of my table as a "crime" and will be managed accordingly by those who impute to the individual responsibility for it. This *social* taxonomy is independent of a *biophysical* or medical taxonomy, though it can accommodate its content.

Legitimacy, Stigma, and Permanence

The trial scheme seems to distinguish some major differences in societal reaction, yielding a typology of deviance that contains within itself both important social meanings involved in labeling and the outcomes of labeling in the form of obligations and privileges allowed to or required from the deviant. But it is nonetheless too simple a scheme to differentiate empirically significant variations in the form that socially organized illness behavior may take. It must be expanded enough to encompass those variations, but not so much as to lose the esthetic and practical virtues of simplicity.

In order to discern some of the inadequacies of the trial scheme, let us reconsider the third aspect of Parson's sick role: the conditional legitimacy assigned to the deviance.[16] To the degree that recovery is believed possible, the sick person's exemption is temporary and its legitimacy conditional on trying to get well, as Parsons indicates. But this temporary exemption is proper only for what are considered acute illnesses. It is quite inappropriate for many kinds of aberrations, including those called chronic disease and disability or impairment.[17] In such cases, legitimacy is not conditional on try-

[16] For an empirical exploration, see Frank A. Petroni, "The Influence of Age, Sex and Chronicity in Perceived Legitimacy to the Sick Role," *Sociology and Social Research,* LIII (1969), 180–193.

[17] For a review of a great deal of material bearing on impairment and disabling illness, see Roger Barker *et al.,* "Adjustment to Physical Handicap and Illness: A Survey of the Social Psychology of Physique and Disability," *Social Science Research Council Bulletin,* 55 (revised 1953); and Beatrice A. Wright, *Physical Disability, a Psychological Approach* (New York: Harper and Row, 1960). For an attempt to make sense of these problems sociologically see Eliot Freidson, "Disability as Social Deviance," in M. B. Sussman, ed., *Sociology and Rehabilitation* (Washington, D.C.: American Sociological Association, 1966), pp. 71–99.

ing to get well, for it is believed impossible to do so. The legitimacy of the exemption is in fact absolute and invariant so long as "incurability" is imputed to the aberration. It is true that *acceptance* by others hinges on maintaining properly undisturbed social relations with them [18] and that, in our society, legitimacy is, in the case of impairment, conditional on improving oneself even though one is incurable in an absolute sense. A chronically ill or permanently impaired person who "expects too much" or "makes too many demands" is likely to be rejected by others. In that case, legitimacy is not conditional on seeking help as it is for illness believed to be acute and curable. Rather, legitimacy is conditional on limiting demands for privileges to what others consider appropriate (to what others believe one cannot be held responsible for).[19] In such an instance, then, the legitimacy of deviant behavior is *unconditional,* the variable being the limits on the amount and type of deviant behavior. I suspect that in our time more varied types of behavior and a greater amount of deviant behavior are likely to be considered legitimate, even if conditionally, for the person believed to have an acute, curable illness, than for one believed to have a chronic, "incurable" impairment.

Another special situation in which the concept of legitimacy seems to be involved is that occurring when stigma is attached to an attribute or act. If we follow Goffman's discussion of stigma, we see it as a societal reaction that "spoils" normal identity. It is a reaction that, if it does not require the performance of a normal role, at least requires that the normal role be performed incompletely, be itself deformed, and that everyday interaction be in some sense strained. What is analytically peculiar about the assignment of stigma is the fact that while a stigmatized person need not be held responsible for what is imputed to him, nonetheless, somewhat like those to whom responsibility is imputed, he is denied the ordinary privileges of social life. As the term itself implies, the societal reaction, although ambiguously, attributes moral deficiency to the

[18] See Erving Goffman, *Stigma: Notes on the Management of Spoiled Identity* (Englewood Cliffs, New Jersey: Spectrum Books, 1963).

[19] See the discussion in Edwin J. Thomas, "Problems of Disability from the Perspective of Role Theory," *Journal of Health and Human Behavior,* VII (1966), 2–13.

stigmatized. Furthermore, unlike other imputed qualities, stigma is by definition ineradicable and irreversible: it is so closely connected with identity that even after the cause of the imputation of stigma has been removed and the societal reaction has been ostensibly redirected, identity is formed by the fact of *having* been in a stigmatized role: the cured mental patient is not just another person, but an ex-mental patient; the rehabilitated criminal gone straight is an ex-convict. One's identity is permanently spoiled. We do not similarly label people ex-traffic offenders, or ex-asthmatics—cases in which stigma is not attached to the deviation.[20]

Essentially, I believe it can be said that while many of those stigmatized by others are not held responsible for their deviance, the assignment of stigma in essence withholds legitimacy from the privileges they seek and imposes special obligations on them. In this it resembles crime more than illness. As I have already noted in referring to Goffman's analysis, the stigmatized person's *identity*, if not health, is incurably spoiled, in that having been a stigmatized deviant remains a part of his identity even though the physically visible or institutional stigmata have been removed. A stigma, furthermore, interferes with normal interaction, for while people need not hold the deviant responsible for his stigma, they are nonetheless embarrassed, upset, or even revolted by it. The "good" stigmatized deviant is therefore expected to take special pains to organize his behavior and his life in such a way as to save others from embarrassment. For "normal" illness, many normal obligations are suspended; only the obligation to seek help is incurred. But in the case of the stigmatized, a complex variety of new obligations is incurred. Whereas in the former instance the burden of adjustment (through permissiveness and support) lies on the "normals" around the sick person, the burden in the latter lies on the stigmatized person when he is around "normals."

Finally, and obviously, in the light of what has already been said, I may note that Parsons' fourth component of the sick role—the obligations to seek competent help and to cooperate in treatment—is relevant to acute curable illness, but relevant to others only in a quite variable way. Some attributes defined as illness, impairment,

[20] See the discussion of Thomas J. Scheff, *Being Mentally Ill: A Sociological Theory* (Chicago: Aldine Publishing Co., 1966), pp. 55–101.

or deficiency remain merely that—an idiosyncrasy of the person, adjusted to by others without any special problem or expectation that he seek treatment. The slightly hard-of-hearing person, the "sickly" woman, and those with "rose fever" and "lumbago" all establish the legitimacy of their foibles without incurring the obligation to seek help, perhaps because, or as long as, their claim to privilege is rather modest. Even if their "illnesses" are "curable" or "improvable," so long as they are the basis for only minor claims, others seem to apply little pressure to them to seek treatment. At the other extreme are those which have been explicitly defined as chronic, hopeless, or incurable. These two do not maintain legitimacy by seeking competent help: they gain legitimacy by having been defined as chronic.

An Expanded Classification of Illness

Close examination of the four elements of the sick role postulated by Parsons leads inevitably to the conclusion that we cannot rest content with the trial classification, which merely distinguishes "crime" from "illness," and minor crime or illness from crime or illness organized into a criminal or sick role. Foregoing concern with "crime," which is not the focus of interest here, it is patent that "illness" as a form of deviance must be classified in a more complicated way to mirror the implications of words like "chronicity" and "stigma." This is the task I shall undertake now.

The key to ordering the classifying of the societal reaction elicited by such labels as "acute," "chronic," and "stigma" is, I believe, the notion of legitimacy. In Parsons' analysis one may remember that the notion of legitimacy is important in distinguishing the criminal from the sick. In the case of the sick role in particular, however, it is a special kind of legitimacy that is operative—conditional and temporary legitimacy. In Parsons' analysis, it is precisely the conditional character of the legitimacy that motivates the sick to seek care and/or return to normal. But where imputed illness is thought to be incurable or chronic, its legitimacy can no longer be conditional; the legitimacy of being considered deviant is in effect unconditional. And when a stigmatized illness is imputed, one may say that the illness is actually illegitimate; it is not an acceptable kind of deviance even though it may be thought to be an illness. In sum, one may distinguish three kinds of legitimacy: (1) *conditional legitimacy,* the deviant being temporarily exempted from normal obligations and gaining some extra privileges on the condition that he seek the help necessary to rid himself of his deviance; (2) *unconditional legitimacy,* the deviant being exempted permanently from normal obligations and obtaining additional privileges in view of the hopeless character imputed to his deviance; and (3) *illegitimacy,* the deviant being exempted from some normal obligations by virtue of deviance for which he is not held technically responsible, but gaining few if any privileges and taking on some especially handicapping new obligations.

This third dimension of classification is present in Table 2, along with examples of the "illnesses" likely to be assigned to each of the categories by the middle class of our time. In evaluating the examples, one must remember that other social groups or cultures in this and other times and places would assign deviance differently and use different labels. Most important to remember is that the ideology (if not the actual behavior) of contemporary professionals in the health field asserts that to the professional all is legitimate, that there is no illegitimate illness. There may be illegitimate ways of *acting* sick, but not of *being* sick. Should we create a table for the professional societal reaction, and should we choose to mirror the professional ideology, we would have to leave the "illegitimate" column empty. We would, however, have to think carefully about the social nature of such medical labels as "hypochondriasis" and "malingering." [21]

The first distinction to be noted in the table is that between the rows, "minor" and "serious." These differences in reaction to and imputation of deviance are significant here because they recognize the empirical fact of the strength of response to an attribute. They are also important because they imply the analytical distinction between deviance that is allowed to remain an individual attribute (an idiosyncratic mode of performing everyday roles), and deviance that becomes organized into a special role (distinct from one's other roles and even on occasion central to one's identity, dominating all other roles). It is only in the latter case, along the second

[21] See Thomas S. Szasz, "Malingering: 'Diagnosis' or Social Condemnation," *AMA Archives of Neurology and Psychiatry,* LXXVI (1956), 438–440.

TABLE 2. TYPES OF DEVIANCE FOR WHICH THE INDIVIDUAL IS NOT HELD RESPONSIBLE, BY IMPUTED LEGITIMACY AND SERIOUSNESS

(*Contemporary American Middle Class Societal Reaction*)

Imputed Seriousness	*Illegitimate (Stigmatized)*	*Conditionally Legitimate*	*Unconditionally Legitimate*
Minor Deviation	Cell 1. "Stammer" Partial suspension of some ordinary obligations; few or no new privileges; adoption of a few new obligations.	Cell 2. "A Cold" Temporary suspension of few ordinary obligations; temporary enhancement of ordinary privileges. Obligation to get well.	Cell 3. "Pockmarks" No special change in obligations or privileges.
Serious Deviation	Cell 4. "Epilepsy" Suspension of some ordinary obligations; adoption of new obligations; few or no new privileges.	Cell 5. "Pneumonia" Temporary release from ordinary obligations; addition to ordinary privileges. Obligation to cooperate and seek help in treatment.	Cell 6. "Cancer" Permanent suspension of many ordinary obligations; marked addition to privileges.

row, that special deviant roles may be said to exist. In cell 1, stigma somewhat spoils one's regular identity, but does not replace it. In cells 2 and 3, "illness" or "impairment" qualifies but does not replace regular roles, the qualification being temporary in cell 2 and permanent in cell 3. The *sick role,* as Parsons defines it, is only to be found in cell 5 of the table. *Stigmatized roles* are to be found in cell 4, and, insofar as nothing more can be done for them by experts, *chronic sick or dying roles* are to be found in cell 6.[22]

By means of my classification I have identified six analytically distinct varieties of deviance that might all ordinarily have been

[22] See Aaron Lipman and Richard S. Sterne, "Aging in the United States: Ascription of a Terminal Sick Role," *Sociology and Social Research,* LIII (1969), 194–203.

called "illness." Each implies quite different consequences for the individual and for the social system in which he is to be found, consequences for personal identity on the one hand, and for the formation of deviant strata in society on the other. Each is managed or treated differently by those around the deviant. The deviant must therefore behave differently in turn.

Illness as Process

The analytical categories to be found in Table 2 are, naturally, static and fixed by the nature of the taxonomic method. However, neither the physician's view of disease nor the sociologist's view of deviance can afford to confuse static taxonomic categories with reality. Organically, diseases have onsets, climaxes, and outcomes that, during any single course, pass through identifiable stages marked by stable configurations of signs and symptoms. This movement is also to be observed in human efforts at finding meaning in experience. In medicine, the physician's diagnostic (or labeling) behavior may also be seen to have a course, moving from one diagnosis (or imputation of deviance) to another in the process of trying to find a consequential method of management: some diagnoses are imputed only after all others have yielded negative results. And so it is with the lay middle-class societal reaction of our time—that the first response to perceived illness is likely to be found in cell 2, and end there. If, however, the perception of deviance persists and responses to it intensify, responses may move to any one of the other cells, though they are most likely to move to cell 5—the sick role—first, and only then move to other possibilities.[23]

One way to see these sequential relationships is to take the set of possibilities commonly surrounding poliomyelitis a decade ago in the United States and arrange them according to my classification.[24] This is tentatively done in Table 3. The first perception tends to be of a cold (Cell 2), but then the individual is moved into a sick role

[23] We must not forget that people also anticipate the occurrence of deviance. Some seek to prevent it by special precautions. Others, like those descending from the unhappy Long Island couple from whom Huntington's chorea is traced, may anticipate only death at an early middle age. I am indebted to Paul J. Sanazaro for this reminder.

[24] Here I rely on Fred Davis, *Passage Through Crisis, Polio Victims and Their Families* (Indianapolis: Bobbs-Merrill Co., 1963).

TABLE 3. SYMPTOMS AND SEQUELAE OF POLIOMYELITIC BY TYPE OF DEVIANCE

(Lower-Middle Class Americans, 1955) *

Imputation of Seriousness	*Illegitimate*	*Conditionally Legitimate*	*Unconditionally Legitimate*
Minor	"Limp" Cell 1	"Cold" Cell 2	"Weak" Cell 3
Serious	"Cripple" Cell 4 ←	"Polio victim" Cell 5	→ Cell 6 "Iron lung case"

* Cf. Fred Davis, *Passage Through Crisis, Polio Victims and Their Families* (Indianapolis: The Bobbs-Merrill Co., 1963).

and diagnosed as having poliomyelitis (Cell 5). If no ill effect is thought to follow, recovery is said to occur and the person is returned to normal, for it is in the nature of the sick role to be temporary.[25] But following illness a number of other things can and do happen. Matters may progress to the point where recovery, even survival is thought to be impossible, leading into a chronic sick or dying role (Cell 6). Or as a consequence of infection, severe paralysis may follow such that the individual needs braces and supports to move about and must learn to play the stigmatized role of the cripple (Cell 4). Or he may recover sufficiently to be left with only a slight, visible limp, which is a mildly stigmatized part of his normal roles (Cell 1). Or finally, he may be left with some relatively easily concealed, minimal muscular impairment that merely marks his personal manner of performing everyday roles—labeled scholarly or unathletic, without stigmatizing him (Cell 3). Generally, I suspect that most movements through these categories are irreversible in any single course of illness, though miraculous recoveries have been known to occur, as have remissions.

25 The cyclical character of the movement from normal to sick and back to normal is stressed in Bernard Goldstein and Paul Dommermuth, "The Sick Role Cycle: An Approach to Medical Sociology," *Sociology and Social Research*, XLVII (1961), 1–12.

This course of movement through the various categories of deviance is not unusual. Rather, it is normal and everyday procedure for one to assume that he has a cold that will go away by itself before he assumes he has pneumonia, to assume a sprain before a fracture, eyestrain before glaucoma, nervousness before psychosis. It is also obvious that seeking help and cooperating in treatment do not always end the matter: it may lead to assignment to a stigmatized form of deviance, or it may have after-effects in the form of impairment. Since movement or reassignment is quite common, and since the points of movement can be labeled and therefore conventionalized, their meaning common for all engaged in the movement, it is appropriate to call the movement a career—a conventionally patterned sequence of social events through which people pass. And thus we may impose form on change, pointing to the orderly social processes experienced by the deviant by the use of the concept of career.[26] We can define the points of the sequence by the roles or imputations that the individual experiences in the course of his movement through various agencies of social control, medical or otherwise.

The concept of career does more than merely arrange the various types of deviance like beads on a string of time. It also provides a conceptual mechanism that links individuals and their experience to the community, lay and professional, for in his movement from one position to another, the individual typically has experience with different agents and agencies of social control.[27] On the most ordinary level of primary deviation he is largely in contact with his intimates, familial or otherwise. But, by Parsons' definition, when he moves into the sick role in the United States, he is obliged to move into the purview of a professional, usually the physician. Similarly, when he moves across to one of the other roles connected with illness and disability, he is likely to move into the purview of other agents—a medical specialist, to take the most common contingency. Thus, the shape of his career of illness can be constructed out of

[26] See the remarks on the use of the idea of career for understanding the etiology of social deviance in Howard S. Becker, *Outsiders, Studies in the Sociology of Deviance* (New York: The Free Press of Glencoe, 1963), pp. 19–39.

[27] See Elaine Cumming, *Systems of Social Regulation* (New York: Atherton Press, 1968).

the sequence of agents and agencies he passes through, much as the shape of an occupational career is often constructed out of the sequence of jobs and employers a man holds during his working life.

By and large, I would argue that constructing the career of the deviant on the basis of the agents and agencies (that is, the segments of the social structure) he moves through is more useful analytically than constructing it directly out of the changes in the deviance imputed to him or out of his own changes in self. Social structure is more concrete and so more objective and easier to identify without question. Changes in both deviance and identity can be reasonably (though not wholly) predicted from position in the social structure. Furthermore, focus on the agents and agencies rather than on their subjects has the virtue of continuously reminding us that the process of "treatment" is a process of control that *always* rests upon a societal reaction—*always* on the imputation or diagnosis of deviance and only sometimes on "actual" deviance. Defining the career by such agents requires us to examine the characteristic imputational biases of these agents in order to understand why the fate of individuals confronting them varies less than the attributes of those individuals themselves. Indeed, the character of the system of professional concepts and services constitutes a critical analytical factor in the sociological study of illness and other forms of social deviance. While I have already addressed myself to the organization of such professional services in earlier chapters, I have not addressed myself to the character of the medical concepts of deviance that permeate the organization. This is the task of the next chapter.

12.

THE PROFESSIONAL CONSTRUCTION OF CONCEPTS OF ILLNESS

IN the last two chapters I attempted to sketch a generically sociological conception of deviance in general and a classification of illness as deviance in particular—a conception based on the social meanings assigned to behavior rather than on the physical properties of the behavior itself. By the nature of the case the sketch had to be quite abstract, for variation in time, place, and perspective involves variations in the behaviors to which social meaning is assigned, as well as variations in social meaning itself. Thus, while in our day people are not likely to be held responsible for manifesting the symptoms of "influenza," in another day their complaints might have been taken to be symptomatic of supernatural punishment for their moral transgressions. Indeed, the relative prominence of such a particular social meaning as illness in a time is an important reflection of the quality of human experience in that time. It is, furthermore, the most important foundation upon which the strength of a profession rests, a foundation which establishes and supports the profession's claim to honor, income, and power. Where illness is the ubiquitous label for deviance in an age, the profession that is custodian of the label is ascendant.

In this chapter I wish to examine, first, the social sources of the strength of medical labels in the United States and, second, the consequences of our emphasis on health for the social meanings that are attached to deviant behavior in our time. I then wish to discuss the character of medicine's role in defining illness—in creating illness as a social meaning. Finally, I wish to discuss the varied factors that influence the way the medical practitioner perceives and defines the behavior he labels illness. Thus, in this chapter I wish to deal with *medicine as one kind of societal reaction to deviance* and to suggest some of the determinants of the content and organization of that societal reaction.

The American Emphasis on Health

In his paper, "Definitions of Health and Illness in the Light of American Values and Social Structure," Talcott Parsons has argued that notions of health and illness are especially emphasized by American values.[1] This is not an original observation, since a number of analysts have commented on such an emphasis, but it is elaborated into a usefully organized discussion. Parsons points out that societies can vary a great deal in the degree to which various types of deviance are differentiated. In the past the most common tendency has been to characterize deviance in religious terms, but gradually over time other characterizations arose and became differentiated. Where differentiation in the meanings of deviance has taken place, however, there has been a tendency to emphasize one meaning over another. In India, for example, Parsons claims that major emphasis in the recent past was on the requirements for ritual purity. In the Soviet Union primary emphasis is said to be on the commitment of the citizen to doing his work well for the benefit of the state. In England, primary emphasis is said to be on commitment to law. The United States, however, emphasizes the value of health over such other values as ritual purity or law. According to Parsons, the American value system emphasizes activism, worldliness, and instrumentalism. Activism refers to an orientation to mastering the environment rather than adjusting to it; worldliness, to the valua-

[1] Talcott Parsons, "Definitions of Health and Illness in the Light of American Values and Social Structure," in Talcott Parsons, *Social Structure and Personality* (New York: The Free Press of Glencoe, 1964), pp. 258–291.

tion of practical secular pursuits rather than esthetic or mystical gratification; instrumentalism, to the absence of a definite ideal goal for the system, so that movement in the right direction substitutes for the attainment of such a goal. For the individual, this value pattern is focused on universalistically judged achievement. Health becomes valued greatly because it is an essential condition for such achievement, involving as it does the imputed capacity to perform tasks and roles adequately.

Parsons goes on to note that in the United States an individual's deviance is more likely to be seen as a disturbance of capacity—that is, as illness—than is likely in other societies. Furthermore, consonant with its emphasis on activity and achievement, the aspect of sickness likely to be encouraged most in the United States is "the obligation to cooperate fully with the therapeutic agency, that is, to *work* to achieve his own recovery." [2] Demonstration of the motivation to cooperate in treatment (and therefore to return to normal) is thus a prime element of the legitimate performance of the sick role. In the Soviet Union, in contrast, where the attainment of a collective goal is emphasized more heavily than individual capacity for personal achievement, the problem of responsibility for deviance is said by Parsons to be more pressing than the problem of cooperation in treatment; that is, there is suspicion of malingering. Once it is clear that the individual is "really sick" through no fault of his own, however, treatment is considerably more supportive than in the United States and considerably less preoccupied with making the patient work at getting better or getting him back to normal as soon as possible.[3] Indeed, Parsons argues that while illness is the primary type of deviance in the United States, it is not in the Soviet Union, where, he claims, ritual and therefore unproductive conformity to the goals of the regime is primary.

[2] *Ibid.*, p. 284.

[3] There is in fact some evidence that hospital care in the Soviet Union is more permissive and kindly than is the case for the United States, though this may be a function of the greater ratio of staff to patients than found here. One might on the other hand note that in the Soviet Union there seems to be a tendency to label political dissenters "mentally ill," thereby using medical definitions for political purposes as was done in the United States for Ezra Pound and General James Walker.

The Institutional Division of Labor for Deviance

Deviance, then, is more likely to be considered a problem of health in the United States than a problem of law, ritual purity, or political commitment. This does not mean, of course, that other social meanings will not be attached to some forms of deviance but rather that illness will be a more common label than others. It also means that the profession which is officially designated as the one competent to diagnose and treat illness will have within its jurisdiction considerably more deviant behavior to deal with than other professions preoccupied with social control. What is involved is a division of labor among professions—an institutional matter as well as a matter of social norms. Indeed, it is possible to represent the classification of types of deviance presented in the last chapter as a classification of professional jurisdiction. We can say with rough security that law deals with acts of imputed deviance for which the actor is held to be accountable and made to pay, while medicine deals with imputed deviance for which the actor is not believed responsible and which is "treated" rather than "punished." Paralleling Table 1 of the last chapter, Table 4 represents the professional division of labor in defining and dealing with deviance.

This representation of the major control institutions is obviously incomplete, for another major institution, religion, is missing. The absence of religion in a representation of the *official* control institutions of American society is accurate, however, in that the Constitutional separation of church and state prevents the official adoption

TABLE 4. DOMAINS OF LAW AND MEDICINE, BY IMPUTED SERIOUSNESS AND MANAGEMENT

Imputed Seriousness	*Labels of Law, Imputing Responsibility*	*Labels of Medicine, Not Imputing Responsibility*
Minor	"Petty Offense"	"Minor Illness"
(Management)	(Fine, Probation)	(Ambulatory care)
Serious	"Felony"	"Life-Threatening Illness"
(Management)	(Imprisonment)	(Hospitalization)

by the state of religious labels of deviance. It must use legal or medical labels. Of course, definitions of deviance that have a specifically religious source—for example, disapproval of divorce, of violation of the Sabbath, or of deliberate termination of pregnancy—are on occasion reflected in the law. Nonetheless, religious institutions may merely contribute to the formation and maintenance of official control institutions in the United States rather than themselves be official. Unlike law and medicine, religion leaves its mark on official institutions only through its influence on the public opinion that molds public policy.

Quite apart from the special legal position of religion in the United States, however, I would insist that over the past century it has, quite independently of its legal position, suffered significant decline in virtually all industrial countries as a source for viable definitions of deviance. So, too, though to lesser degree, has law. Like Rieff, I believe that "the hospital is succeeding the church and the parliament as the archetypal institution of Western culture." [4] The hospital is becoming such an archetypal institution largely through a process whereby human behavior is being reinterpreted. Disapproved behavior is more and more coming to be given the meaning of illness requiring treatment rather than of crime requiring punishment, victimization requiring compensation, or sin requiring patience and grace.

As late as the nineteenth century, medicine was a relatively unimportant institution, humble before the majesty of religion and law. But with the growth of medical science, more and more human behavior began to seem to stem from specific "causes" over which prayer, human choice, and will had little control. And medical discoveries allowed the successful treatment of such problems. From this core of scientific discovery grew a vague halo of authority that encouraged the wholesale extension of medical definitions of deviance into areas of behavior previously managed by religion and law. As Szasz put it,

> Starting with such things as syphilis, tuberculosis, typhoid fever, and carcinomas and fractures we have created the class, "ill-

[4] Philip Rieff, *Freud: The Mind of the Moralist* (Garden City: Doubleday and Co., 1961), p. 390.

> ness." At first, this class was composed of only a few items all of which shared the common feature of reference to a state of disordered structure or function of the human body as a physical-chemical machine. As time went on, additional items were added to this class. They were not added, however, because they were newly discovered bodily disorders. The physician's attention has been deflected from this criterion and has become focussed instead on disability and suffering as new criteria for selection. Thus, at first slowly, such things as hysteria, hypochondriasis, obsessive-compulsive neurosis, and depression were added to the category of illness. Then, with increasing zeal, physicians and especially psychiatrists began to call "illness" . . . anything and everything in which they could detect any sign of malfunctioning, based on no matter what norm. Hence, agoraphobia is illness because one should not be afraid of open spaces. Homosexuality is an illness because heterosexuality is the social norm. Divorce is illness because it signals failure of marriage.[5]

The increasing emphasis on the label of illness, then, has been at the expense of the labels of both crime and sin and has been narrowing the limits if not weakening the jurisdiction of the traditional control institutions of religion and law. Indeed, my own suspicion is that the jurisdiction of the other institutions has been weakened absolutely because the thrust of the expansion of the application of medical labels has been toward addressing (and controlling) the *serious* forms of deviance, leaving to the other institutions a residue of essentially trivial or narrowly technical offenses.

The medical mode of response to deviance is thus being applied to more and more behavior in our society, much of which has been responded to in quite different ways in the past. In our day, what has been called crime, lunacy, degeneracy, sin, and even poverty in the past is now being called illness, and social policy has been moving toward adopting a perspective appropriate to the imputation of illness. Chains have been struck off and everywhere health

[5] Thomas S. Szasz, *The Myth of Mental Illness* (New York: Harper and Row, 1964), pp. 44–45.

professionalism has been raised to legitimate the claim that the proper management of deviance is "treatment" in the hands of a responsible and skilled profession. The labels of sin and crime being removed, what is done to the deviant is likely to be said to be done for his own good, done to help him rather than punish him, even though the treatment itself may constitute a deprivation under ordinary circumstances. His own opinions about his treatment are discounted because he is said to be a layman who lacks the special knowledge and detachment that would qualify him to have his voice heard.

This movement to reinterpret human deviance as illness has its roots in humanitarianism. As Wooton noted,

> Without question, therefore, in the contemporary attitud towards antisocial behavior, psychiatry and humanitarianism have marched hand in hand. Just because it is so much in keeping with the mental atmosphere of a scientifically-minded age, the medical treatment of social deviants has been a most powerful, perhaps even the most powerful, reinforcement of humanitarian impulses; for today the prestige of humane proposals is immensely enhanced if these are expressed in the idiom of medical science.[6]

The consequence of the movement, however, is the strengthening of a professionalized control institution that, in the name of the individual's good and of technical expertise, can remove from laymen the right to evaluate their own behavior and the behavior of their fellows—a fundamental right that is evidenced in a hard-won fight to interpret the Scriptures oneself, without regard to dogmatic authority, in religion and, the right to be judged by one's peers, in law.[7] The work of Thomas S. Szasz may be cited as a major effort to dissect the character of this newly emergent problem of the

[6] Barbara Wootton, *Social Science and Social Pathology* (London: George Allen and Unwin, 1959), p. 206.

[7] "Thus the medicalization of deviance results in the political castration of the deviant." Jesse R. Pitts, "Social Control: The Concept," *International Encyclopedia of the Social Sciences* (New York: The Macmillan Company and The Free Press, 1968), Vol. XIV, p. 391.

relationship of institutionalized expertise to the individual right of equality and self-determination.[8]

In evaluating the character of these developments, it is very important to separate demonstrable scientific achievement from the status of the occupation involved and the success it has had in establishing its jurisdiction. The jurisdiction that medicine has established extends far wider than its demonstrable capacity to "cure." Nonetheless, success at gaining general acceptance of the use of "illness" to label a disapproved form of behavior carries with it the assumption that the behavior is properly managed only by physicians. Similarly, the fact that physicians are willing to manage or deal with a problematic form of behavior leads to the illogical conclusion that the behavior must be an illness. For example, the "drunkard" is relabeled an "alcoholic," and "alcoholism" becomes a disease that should be treated by a physician rather than by the courts or the church. Such jurisdiction is established even though knowledge of etiology and a predictably successful method of treatment is as absent in medicine as it is in religion or law.[9] Thus, the medical profession has first claim to jurisdiction over the label of illness and anything to which it may be attached, irrespective of its capacity to deal with it effectively. In such a fashion do we see that the rise to social prominence of a social value such as health is inseparable from the rise of a vehicle for the value—an organized body of workers who claim jurisdiction over the value. Once official jurisdiction is gained, the profession is then prone to create its own specialized notions of what it is that shall be called illness. While medicine is hardly independent of the society in which it exists, by becoming a vehicle for society's values it comes to play a major

[8] Thomas S. Szasz, *Law, Liberty and Psychiatry* (New York: The Macmillan Co., 1963).

[9] The desire to do away with the punitive treatment of alcoholics leads even so sophisticated a student as Jellinek to the curious tactic of noting that while no one has untangled the facts sufficiently to know the cause or cure of "alcoholism" (if it is a single entity rather than many separate ones, each with a different "cause"), nonetheless it is a disease. What is a disease? "*A disease is what the medical profession recognizes as such.*" That is, we do not know what the causes are, but because physicians call it a disease, it must therefore be something caused by natural forces over which the deviant has no control! See E. M. Jellinek, *The Disease Concept of Alcoholism* (New Haven: Hillhouse Press, 1960), p. 12. And see Thomas S. Szasz, "Alcoholism: A Socio-Ethical Perspective," *Washburn Law Journal,* VI (1967), 255–268.

role in the forming and shaping of the social meanings imbued with such value. What is the thrust of that role?

The Physician as a Moral Entrepreneur

Clearly, neither medicine nor the physician may be characterized as passive. As a consulting rather than scholarly or scientific profession, medicine is committed to treating rather than merely defining and studying man's ills. It has a mission of active intervention guided by what, in whatever time and place it exists, it believes to be ill in the world. Furthermore, it is active in seeking out illness. The profession does treat the illnesses layman take to it, but it also seeks to discover illness of which laymen may not even be aware. One of the greatest ambitions of the physician is to discover and describe a "new" disease or syndrome and to be immortalized by having his name used to identify the disease. Medicine, then, is oriented to seeking out and finding illness, which is to say that it seeks to create social meanings of illness where that meaning or interpretation was lacking before. And insofar as illness is defined as something bad—to be eradicated or contained—medicine plays the role of what Becker called the "moral entrepreneur." [10] Medical activity leads to the creation of new rules defining deviance; medical practice seeks to enforce those rules by attracting and treating the newly defined deviant sick.

At first thought it may seem peculiar to include the medical man with bluenoses, reformers, and others who are more obviously moral entrepreneurs. The physician's job is not generally seen to be moral; he is supposed to treat illness without judging. There is, however, an irreducible moral judgment in the designation of illness as such, a judgment the character of which is frequently overlooked because of the virtually universal consensus that exists about the undesirability of much of what is labeled illness. Cancer is so obviously undesirable to everyone that its status as an illness seems objective and self-evident rather than what it is—a social valuation on which most people happen to agree. Even recognizing this, however, it must be observed that the word "illness" is often used explicitly for the purpose of avoiding moral condemnation, for the

[10] See Howard S. Becker, *Outsiders* (New York: The Free Press of Glencoe, 1963), pp. 147–163.

humanitarian seeks to have it adopted in order that people will not be inclined to punish a deviant. By labeling something like alcoholism an "illness" and declaring an appallingly filthy derelict to be sick, the intention is to avoid moral condemnation.

However, while the label of illness does seem to function to discourage punitive reactions, it does not discourage condemnatory reactions. The "illness" is condemned rather than the person, but it is condemned nonetheless. The person is treated with sympathy rather than punishment, but he is expected to rid himself of the condemned attribute or behavior. Thus, while (ideally) the person may not be judged, his "disease" certainly is judged and his "disease" is part of him. Moral neutrality exists only when a person is *allowed* to be or do what he will, without remark or question. Positive moral approval, of course, exists where a person is *urged* to be what he may not wish to be. Clearly, the physician neither approves of disease nor is neutral to it. When he claims alcoholism is a disease, he is as much a moral entrepreneur as a fundamentalist who claims it is a sin. His mission is to impute social and therefore moral meaning to physical and other signs that are, but for such meaning, fit only for the licking and biting by which animals treat themselves.

However, there is a division of labor in such moral entrepreneurship in medicine. The everyday practitioner's task is to assign a medical label to symptoms that laymen have already singled out as undesirable. Clearly, on occasion the practitioner is a true entrepreneur when he finds illness of which the layman is unaware, but essentially his task is modest and unassuming. The major moral entrepreneurs in medicine are those seeking to influence public opinion and political policy, and of these there seem to be three kinds. There are, first, the public spokesmen for the organized profession or its specialties. They seek to alert the public to the important dangers of a given disease or of the virtues of a given kind of health—dental, mental, or otherwise. Their activities tend to be fairly sober and technical appeals for the public to undertake preventive health practices, including seeing their physicians. Second, there are the major moral entrepreneurs of medicine itself, some of whom may be individual practitioners whose avocation is crusading in health matters, but most of whom are not full-time practitioners at all; instead, they are associated with organized community health institutions like hospitals, clinics, medical schools, and health departments. These are the technical advisers who are interviewed most commonly by the public press on issues of health policy and who are called to give testimony before legislative bodies. The thrust of their activity is toward political power to implement measures designed to improve what they see to be the public health. In association with representatives of organized medical interests, and reinforced by interested lay bodies, they have also been responsible for most of the legislation that has, in the name of humanitarianism, attempted to remove such ills as alcoholism, drug addiction, mental illness, and mental deficiency from the jurisdiction of the courts and to place them under the jurisdiction of the health professions.

Finally may be mentioned the special lay interest groups, sometimes led by physicians but always including at least one prominent physician, which crusades each against the menace of its own specially chosen disease, impairment, or presumably disease-inducing agent.[11] Here, untrammeled by professional dignity, are the most flamboyant moral entrepreneurs in health, each concerned with arousing the public to give it the attention and resources that can only be gained at the expense of the other, each trying to create in the public mind profound pity and horror at its own specially chosen human failing. Some groups are concerned with establishing the application of the label of illness to conditions not considered illness before (as in the case of alcoholism), others with removing the stigma of some diseases (like leprosy) by changing their labels (to Hansen's disease), and others with redefining an illness (like epilepsy) so that it moves in the public mind from the category of chronic, serious, or incurable to minor or at least curable or controllable.

With the possible exception of the everyday practitioner, who spends most of his working time on routine and minor ailments and who has occasion to relieve his patients of worry (and relieve himself of patients worrying at him) by deprecating their symptoms

[11] See the provocative discussion in Joseph R. Gusfield, *Symbolic Crusade, Status Politics and the American Temperance Movement* (Urbana: University of Illinois Press, 1966). And see Joseph R. Gusfield, "Moral Passage: The Symbolic Process in Public Designations of Deviance," *Social Problems*, XV (1967), 175–188.

and stressing their health, most of the activities of the active moral entrepreneurs of health are permeated by the tendency to see more illness everywhere around and to see the environment as being more dangerous to health than does the layman.[12] Impatient of available statistics based on the number of cases actually diagnosed and reported by everyday practitioners, they are prone to emphasize the seriousness of the health problem preoccupying them by estimating the cases presently undiagnosed and therefore untreated. Their estimates, furthermore, are likely to be based on a broader definition of the illness or impairment than the public uses—seeing "blindness" where the layman sees extremely bad vision,[13] "mental illness" where the layman sees "nervousness" or "problems," and "alcoholism" where the layman sees "heavy drinking." In short, the moral entrepreneur in medical affairs is likely to see illness where the layman sees something other than illness, or sees merely individual variation within broad boundaries of the normal. And he is likely to see a serious problem where the layman sees a minor one. They are biased toward illness as such and toward creating secondary deviance—sick roles—where before there was but primary deviance.

The Bias Toward Illness in Everyday Practice

This characteristic bias toward illness is manifested not only by the active moral entrepreneur of health but also by the everyday practitioner. Indeed, Scheff calls it a medical decision-rule.[14] Scheff points out that since he believes that the work he does is all for the good of the client, the health professional typically assumes that it is better to impute disease than to deny it and risk overlooking or missing it. This posture is in contrast with the legal sector, in which it is assumed that it is better to allow a guilty man to go free than to mistakenly convict an innocent man. In short, the decision-

[12] It is in the light of these comments that it may be profitable to evaluate the finding that "underreporting of symptoms [by laymen] is a more prevalent problem than overreporting," in S. V. Kasl and Sidney Cobb, "Health Behavior, Illness Behavior and Sick Role Behavior," *Archives of Environmental Health,* XII (1966), 256.

[13] For an enlightening analysis of blindness see Robert A. Scott, *The Making of Blind Men* (New York: Russell Sage Foundation, 1969).

[14] See Thomas J. Scheff, *Being Mentally Ill: A Sociological Theory* (Chicago: Aldine Publishing Co., 1966), pp. 105–127.

rule guiding the medical activity of practitioners is to be safe by diagnosing illness rather than health.

There is some interesting evidence supporting Scheff's specification of medicine's characteristic "decision-rule." In one study of X-ray readings for tuberculosis cited by Scheff, for example, out of 14,867 films, 1,216 were interpreted as providing positive indication of tuberculosis that were subsequently interpreted as negative (this being defined as a "false positive"), while only 24 of those interpreted as negative were later declared positive (defined as "false negatives").[15] Clearly, what tendency there was, was toward imputing illness rather than health. A fair amount has been written about variations in diagnosing pathology from such ambiguous evidence as chest films and electrocardiograms, only some of which indicates a greater proportion of diagnoses of illness over those of health.[16] The problem of evaluating such evidence lies in the lack of direct evidence on the accuracy of the diagnosis, independent of opinion. As Peterson and others have pointed out, given the ambiguity of the evidence, in which definitive postmortem findings are lacking, one is never sure whether an inclination to diagnose pathology is due to objective signs perceptible to one observer but not another,[17] or due, as Scheff suggests, to use of a decision-rule that when in doubt it is wiser to diagnose illness than not.

Rather better evidence supporting Scheff's notion lies in his citation of a 1934 survey by the American Child Health Association of doctors' judgments of the advisability of tonsillectomy for 1,000 school children. It was described by Bakwin as follows: Of the

[15] L. H. Garland, "Studies on the Accuracy of Diagnostic Procedures," *American Journal of Roentgenology, Radium Therapy, and Nuclear Medicine,* LXXXII (1959), 25–38, cited in Scheff, *op. cit.,* p. 112.

[16] See the following examples: A. L. Cochrane *et al.,* "Observers' Errors in Taking Medical Histories," *Lancet,* CCLX (1951), 1007–1009; A. L. Cochrane and L. H. Garland, "Observer Error in the Interpretation of Chest Films: An International Comparison," *Lancet,* CCLXIII (1952), 505–509; L. G. Davies, "Observer Variation in Reports on Electrocardiograms," *British Heart Journal,* XVIII (1956), 568; G. S. Kilpatrick, "Observer Error in Medicine," *Journal of Medical Education,* XXXVIII (1963), 38–43; Barkev S. Sanders, "Completeness and Reliability of Diagnoses in Therapeutic Practice," *Journal of Health and Human Behavior,* V (1964), 84–94.

[17] See Osler L. Peterson *et al.,* "A Study of Diagnostic Performance: A Preliminary Report," *Journal of Medical Education,* XLI (1966), 797–803.

1,000 children, "some 611 had [already] had their tonsils removed. The remaining 389 were then examined by other physicians, and 174 were selected for tonsillectomy. This left 215 children whose tonsils were apparently normal. Another group of doctors was put to work examining these 215 children, and 99 of them were adjudged in need of tonsillectomy. Still another group of doctors was then employed to examine the remaining children, and nearly one-half were recommended for operation."[18] Since it is very unlikely that each group of physicians would overlook the severity of signs in fully one-fourth of the cases it saw, it seems more plausible to conclude that each used a sliding scale of severity rather than an absolute criterion. Like the teacher who gives a certain proportion of failing grades no matter what the over-all quality of his class, so the physicians studied were inclined to remove a certain proportion of tonsils no matter what the range of signs observed. Some proportion of primary deviations (inflamed throats or swollen glands) must be defined as secondary deviations.

From Bakwin's example it should be clear that the notion of the medical decision-rule refers to procedures as well as diagnoses—that it points to what are sometimes called "unnecessary surgery" and "overprescribing" as natural consequences of the decision-rule, not, as is charged by critics within the profession, as a consequence of carelessness or ignorance.[19] However, more than the decision-rule alone seems to be implicated in such practices. First, it may be noted that even though Bakwin claims that the motive of financial gain could not have been involved in the tonsillectomy study because almost all the children had their tonsils removed in free clinics, it is difficult to deny that financial motives have on occasion encouraged diagnosis and treatment that might not otherwise have occurred. Furthermore, the desires of patients themselves cannot be discounted. As Fry pointed out,[20] tonsillectomies were at the

18 Harry Bakwin, "Pseudodoxia Pediatrica," *New England Journal of Medicine*, CCXXXII (1945), 691–697.

19 For a collection of many such criticisms, though lacking in a sense of proportion, see Martin L. Gross, *The Doctors* (New York: Dell Publishing Co., 1968).

20 See John Fry, "Are All 'T's and A's' Really Necessary?" *British Medical Journal*, I (1957), 124–129.

peak of their popularity in the early 1930's, a popularity shared among children's parents and physicians. Finally, I might mention the thrust toward active intervention that is inherent in clinical practice as such.[21] While the physician's job is to make decisions, including the decision not to do anything, the fact seems to be that the everyday practitioner feels impelled to do something, if only to satisfy patients who urge him to do something when they are in distress. In this context may be mentioned the report by Peterson, Barsamian, and Eden[22] that when the Stein-Leventhal syndrome is diagnosed, *it is almost always in error*. That mistaken diagnosis is so popular because the syndrome refers to the only type of infertility that can be benefited by surgery. By making the diagnosis the doctor can do something and encourage the patient to feel that everything is being done in order to help.

Thus, it would seem plausible to predict that "overdiagnosis" and "overprescribing" are most likely to be found in conditions (a) where the physician is most likely to gain some benefit from it, (b) where the patient is in distress but the signs and symptoms are ambiguous, and (c) where some conventional and popular diagnosis and treatment are available which are not absolutely contradicted by what signs and symptoms there are. All three conditions do not have to exist together for such behavior, since we find the tendency to "overdiagnose" acute appendicitis[23] even under the English National Health Service where financial gain is apparently not seriously at issue.[24] Similarly in the United States, where the physician does not stand to gain by increasing the sale of drugs, venality cannot explain adequately the notoriously voluminous and

[21] See the report of a survey finding that a prime reason why physicians prescribe is the reported fear of not doing anything, in Harry F. Dowling, "How Do Practicing Physicians Use New Drugs?" *Journal of the American Medical Association*, CLXXXV (1963), 233–236. The "bias toward active intervention" supported by an optimism about the outcome is discussed sensibly in Talcott Parsons, *The Social System* (New York: The Free Press, 1951), pp. 466–469. These two aspects of the clinical mentality certainly support the medical decision-rule.

[22] Peterson, *op. cit.*

[23] See the odd data in H. B. M. Murphy, "Personality and the Vermiform Appendix," *Journal of Health and Human Behavior*, VII (1966), 153–162.

[24] J. A. Campbell and D. C. McPhail, "Acute Appendicitis," *British Medical Journal*, I (1958), 852–855.

sometimes iatrogenic prescribing habits of American physicians.[25] Furthermore, it should be apparent that the medical decision-rule is not always operative. Indeed, it is sometimes reversed to create "underdiagnosis." Under the conditions of practice during the post-war Stalinist era in the Soviet Union,[26] as under the conditions of the practice of psychiatry (if not medicine in general) in the military,[27] the systematic pressure of the situation is to discourage the diagnosis of at least some illness, mental or otherwise. Similarly, among general practitioners and other first-line consultants in no position to alienate their clients, we should expect underdiagnosis of such a stigmatized illness as "psychosis." These exceptions to the medical decision-rule should not be deprecated—if only because they may be taken to illustrate again how work settings overrule general value orientations and decision-rules—but they are exceptions to the general rule, likely to be deplored more than over-diagnosis by leaders of the profession.

In the course of discussing the evidence supporting the notion that there is on the part of the medical profession an inclination to impute (or diagnose) illness rather than health, I have suggested some of the factors that may underlie what the profession itself calls overdiagnosis and overtreatment. Such factors may be seen as variables encouraging or conditioning the profession's decision-rule. The question still remains: So what? What are the consequences?

Consequences of the Bias Toward Illness

The diagnostic bias of medicine flows unchecked from its special mission of the discovery and treatment of a form of deviance whose objectivity is unquestioned. Because the biophysical status of medical signs is confused with the moral and social status of the meaning of illness, no serious question is raised about medicine, as it is routinely raised about the courts, concerning the social and moral

25 See Bernard Barber, *Drugs and Society* (New York: Russell Sage Foundation, 1967), p. 128. And see Leighton E. Cluff *et al.*, "Studies in the Epidemiology of Adverse Drug Reactions," *Journal of the American Medical Association,* CLXXXVIII (1964), 976–983.

26 See Mark G. Field, *Doctor and Patient in Soviet Russia* (Cambridge: Harvard University Press, 1957).

27 See Roger W. Little, "The 'Sick' Soldier and the Medical Ward Officer," *Human Organization,* XV (1956), 22–24; and especially the forthcoming material on the military psychiatrist by Arlene K. Daniels.

danger of labeling (or diagnosing) mistakenly. Medicine's concern is largely (though not without exceptions) with the *biophysical* consequences of diagnosis and treatment—whether they are accurate or efficacious. Its concern is not with the social consequences. Secondarily, there is some concern with the financial cost to the patient or his agent. The social consequences to the *identity* of the person being labeled are rarely considered. However, these consequences can be important.

In an only semiserious analysis, Meador discourses on the notion of "nondisease," which is a diagnostic label that is established after a man is incorrectly diagnosed as ill of a particular disease and then, after closer investigation, ruled not to have that disease.[28] For example, a man with heavy pigmentation and low blood pressure (in and of themselves, primary deviations) could be suspected of having Addison's disease (a secondary deviation). Upon discovering that his skin color stems from a Cherokee grandfather and that his adrenal function is within normal limits, however, his doctor may declare that, like a number of people at the lower limit of normal blood pressure, he does not have Addison's disease—he has non-Addison's disease. He is specifically healthy in the sense that Addison's disease is one specific thing he surely does not have. All false positives that have been investigated and subsequently found to be false therefore become nondiseases. And a number of syndromes—among them the mimicking syndrome, the normal-variation syndrome, the laboratory-error syndrome, and the roentgenologic-overinterpretation syndrome—are common sources for false positives and the creation of nondiseases.

Superficially, it would seem that having a nondisease is hardly more serious than the cost, the temporary worry, and the annoyance incurred in the space of time between the initial (false positive) diagnosis and the final outcome. Medicine argues conventionally that it is more serious to miss a disease by carelessness, ignorance, or accident, than to temporarily diagnose one. What is forgotten, however, is that illness is a social meaning, not all of which is supplied or controlled by the physician. Some illnesses may not be undone and may never become nondiseases in the world of the

[28] C. K. Meador, "The Art and Science of Nondisease," *New England Journal of Medicine*, CCLXXII (1965), 92–95.

patient. In the case of mental illness, for example, merely having been mentally ill marks the normal status of the ex-patient. If one is diagnosed as having a *stigmatized* illness, being cleared of it is not possible: simply having been suspected of it is stigmatizing. Such a consequence should certainly give pause to the employment of medicine's usual decision-rule, humanitarian though the motivation for its use may be.

Medical Variation in Labeling and Management

I have pointed out that the task—indeed the mission—of the medical man is to find illness. This is to say, the task is to authoritatively label as illness what a complainant suspects to be illness, and also to label as illness what was not previously labeled at all, or what was labeled in some other fashion, under some other institution's jurisdiction. While it is true that some of the medical task is to minimize the societal reaction to some forms of deviance—deprecating the seriousness of lay responses to some and tempering the ferocity of responses to others—on balance it seems accurate to say that the prime consequence of medical activity is to increase the total number of illnesses by which deviance may be characterized, and, in the course of so doing, to attempt to increase the intensity of the societal reaction to such illnesses by stressing their seriousness to individual or public health. It is therefore engaged in creating, indeed pressing for the proliferation of situations that create deviant illness roles.

In order to evaluate this important social consequence of medical activity it is necessary to understand the foundation of knowledge and practice upon which it rests. First of all, one may note the perfectly obvious fact that for a great many cases, agreement in labeling (diagnosing) and in management does not exist throughout the health professions. There are varied schools and opinions in medicine such that the label (diagnosis) applied to a problematic individual and the methods used in managing him or his complaint will to a measurable degree vary independently of his complaints and behavior. Medicine is not a completely homogeneous institution, for diagnostic and therapeutic prejudices are organized into loose "schools" that cut across the health sector. Another way of pointing this out is to refer to the recognition of varying medical "opinions" about the interpretation and management of signs and symptoms, all more or less legitimate.

In the fields of allergy and dermatology there are biochemical and psychologistic schools of thought, the differences among which are similar to the organic-functional schism in psychiatry. In general surgery, as in the surgical specialties, there are "conservative" schools that avoid removing tissue wherever possible or that wait a long time before deciding to do so, and "radical" schools that "go in on it" as soon as possible or that seek out new techniques of safely removing what was never removed safely before. And in internal medicine, as in the medical specialties, there is the chemotherapy school, akin to the heroic therapists of the nineteenth century, which uses drugs liberally, and there is the "conservative" school, akin to the Hippocratics, which is loath to use drugs at all except where absolutely necessary. The most marked and complex divisions are at present to be found in the general area of mental health. As Strauss and his associates have shown,[29] although the general somatic-psychological dichotomy can organize mental health roughly, there is a significant differentiation into a number of "ideologies." These opinions are organized into loose schools by virtue of the understandable desire of one man to work with and send his clients to others who share his own opinions about illness and its management. They thus tend to be organized into networks of like-minded practitioners, perhaps differently located in the division of labor among the specialists, but joined by a referral habit.

It follows from the existence of such schools that, in more cases than may be at first apparent, whether or not one will be diagnosed or treated in a certain way depends in part on what is "actually" wrong and in part on the bias of the professional agent one chooses and the referral system in which one is located. I mean this in a quite ordinary and everyday way—in the removal or nonremoval of tonsils, of an appendix, or of a lung; in the prescription of aspirin or of massive doses of antibiotics; in the use of verbal psychotherapy or electroconvulsive therapy; in the use of radiation in lieu

[29] See the programmatic statement by Leonard Schatzman and Anselm Strauss, "A Sociology of Psychiatry: A Perspective and Some Organizing Foci," *Social Problems*, XIV (1966), 3–16; and see Anselm Strauss *et al.*, *Psychiatric Ideologies and Institutions* (New York: The Free Press of Glencoe, 1964).

of surgery; in the use of anesthetics in childbirth. Patently, if a patient does not (as do some of the better educated) deliberately select a "school"; and if, once among the proponents of such a school, he adopts no active, aggressive voice in his treatment, the opinions of the medical men into whose hands he has fallen determine much of what will happen to him.

While the existence of such variant opinion is an obvious fact to anyone who knows much about medicine, it is not an insignificant fact. It is important in that it points to systematically organized, self-sustaining sources of differences in the labeling and management of deviance in medicine that, by their very existence, call into question the stability and objectivity of the corpus of medical knowledge. Such differences are not to be found solely at the fringes of medicine but also on occasion at its established and routine core. Shared by all medical men is the tendency to impute disease: dividing them in some cases is the disease to be imputed or, if not the disease, the approach to be adopted toward the disease. Excluding from our attention the growing number of diseases on which there is unanimity in diagnosis and treatment which, by virtue of such consensus, we may take to be objective and scientific for our time, there is still the problem of understanding the evidential foundation of labels and modes of management for which there is not general consensus. How can the practitioner cultivate a given diagnosis and method of management for which there is insufficient supporting evidence to force profession-wide unanimity? How are varying concepts of illness (and labels) for the same complaint sustained? How are varying philosophies of treatment supported? How are the different sick roles established and maintained? The answers to these questions, I believe, lie in the subjective character of the personal clinical experience of the medical practitioner.

The Interpretation of Personal Clinical Experience

The primary characteristic of the situation we find when a patient seeking help interacts with a physician trying to give help is mutual hope. The patient would not be likely to seek help if he did not believe a physician could help him, and the practicing physician would not undertake help if he did not feel he could do something effective. Each expects improvement or cure, and each interprets his personal experience on the basis of that expectation. And, more often than not, each is self-motivated to believe, on the basis of personal experience strained through interpretation, that something effective has been done. In consequence, the patient feels better and the physician feels that his ministrations are responsible for the patient's improvement. This accomplishment occurs far more independently of the chemical or physical agents used in treatment than the patient or the physician believes. The practicing physician's philosophy of treatment is thus supported by the evidence of his wish-ridden senses, which tell him that his patient has improved. And another physician's quite different philosophy of treatment is similarly supported by the perception of patient improvement. The patients who stay oblige in both cases by feeling and reporting improvement. The others leave without, it is believed, "giving the treatment a chance."

Apparent improvement independent of the "objective" agent used in treatment can be explained by several facts. First, as I have argued earlier, human experience is interpretive in character, not a passive function of "natural" physical agents. This has more and more been discovered to be an assumption without which one cannot understand the outcome of many controlled experimental studies of the therapeutic value of drugs. In his conclusions to his now-classic survey of a century of experimental work on pain, for example, Beecher emphasizes the inseparability of sensation from perception, the overriding importance of what he calls "the reaction component." Indeed, in the case of analgesic (pain-reducing) agents, he concludes that their principal effect is not on "dulling" the original sensation so much as on the reaction to the sensation.[30]

The obvious implication of Beecher's work is that the *patient* or subject is unreliably subjective and introspective in his response. However, because of the work of such men as Beecher, more and more attention is being paid to two facts less obvious to the profession: the degree to which the *physician* or experimenter contributes to the patient's response, and the degree to which the *physician* or experimenter is an objective or neutral rather than subjective and biased recorder of results. Until quite recently, evaluation of healing

[30] Henry K. Beecher, *Measurement of Subjective Responses* (New York: Oxford University Press, 1959), pp. 188–189.

practice has been guided by what Neil Friedman called, "the dogma of immaculate perception, the belief that the data collector is a non-person, the general avoidance of the social psychology of . . . research . . . all part and parcel of that governing ideology, that unattainable image of cleanliness."[31] However, increasing recognition of the powerful role of subjective responses in medical treatment has led to the development of double-blind experimental designs[32] that try to control not only (1) the patient's subjective "reaction component" but also what is not so commonly recognized, (2) the clinician's contribution to the patient's interpretation of his experience, and (3) the subjective reaction component of the clinician himself in evaluating the results of his treatment.

All three variables, I suggest, must figure in an adequate explanation of how the profession can sustain successfully "schools" of diagnostic and therapeutic opinion and behavior that contradict each other and practices that will some day be recognized as worthless. This is particularly apparent when we examine the past, toward which, unlike the present, we can more easily sustain a certain tolerant detachment. Let us take an Egyptian physician of 1500 B.C., using remedies recorded in the Ebers papyrus. Why would he prescribe crocodile dung cynically, without believing in its value? And how can his eyes fail to record its valuelessness? The answer is simple. The physician is likely to have faith in his remedy, and his faith will be communicated to his patient, who will become helpful and interpret his symptoms hopefully after receiving his medicine. Such patient variation in response, answering to the physician's faith in his remedy, has been shown to operate with chloropromazine, LSD, and many other modern drugs today;[33] we have no reason to believe patients were less subject to such influence yesterday. Thus, the clinician himself influences the patient to interpret his symptoms hopefully or hopelessly, depending on the clinician's own views. Furthermore, the physician's *observations* are likely to be biased by his own attitudes. His faith in his own

[31] Neil Friedman, *The Social Nature of Psychological Research* (New York: Basic Books, 1967), p. 142.

[32] For methods of clinical trials, see L. J. Witts, ed., *Medical Surveys and Clinical Trials* (London: Oxford University Press, 1959).

[33] See Arthur K. Shapiro, "A Contribution to a History of the Placebo Effect," *Behavioral Science*, V (1960), 109–135.

remedies is likely to lead him to "observe" improvement or cure: why else would he continue to employ crocodile dung time after time? Medical treatment and its everyday clinical (firsthand and personal) evaluation is a matter of complicity between doctor and patient, with the physician, even though his perspective is inevitably different from that of the patient, nonetheless tending, like the patient, to interpret his experience self-supportively.[34]

The notion of placebo is of course central to these observations. The word is commonly used to refer solely to that circumstance in which a physician uses a method of treatment not because he believes in its therapeutic value but because he believes it to be a harmless method of humoring a demanding patient. This definition assumes that the physician is a detached scientist who knows what "really" has therapeutic value and who sometimes uses other things just to please his patients. However, it is patently impossible to imagine that the physician of yesterday did not believe in most of his remedies, including those we now consider valueless. And it is just as impossible to believe that the physician of today believes solely in clearly efficacious remedies. Even today we must assume that physicians use many valueless drugs and procedures unwittingly and that they use them because their personal experience tells them wrongly that they are "getting results." To take such circumstances into account, Shapiro's definition of placebo would seem more useful than the traditional one: "any therapy (or that component of any therapy) that is deliberately used for its presumed effect on a patient, symptom or illness, but which, unknown to patient and therapist, is without specific activity for the condition being treated." [35]

As Shapiro put it, "a salient characteristic of medicine has always been the presence of the doctor's deep intellectual and emotional investment in a theory and practice. The treatments were frequently elaborate, detailed, expensive, time-consuming, fashionable, esoteric,

[34] See the comments on the apostolic function of the physician in Michael Balint, *The Doctor, His Patient and the Illness* (London: Pitman Medical Publishing Co., 1960). And see the discussion of the clinical approach in David Mechanic, *Medical Sociology* (New York: The Free Press, 1968), pp. 196–208.

[35] Arthur K. Shapiro, "The Curative Waters and Warm Poultices of Psychotherapy," *Psychosomatics*, VII (1966), 21–23.

and at times dangerous. A majority were later judged to be ineffective. The greater a physician's interest in a theory of therapy, particularly if it is of his own innovation or if he is a recent convert, the more effective that therapy will appear to be. . . . A greater intellectual and emotional investment is inherent in a physician using a new drug or treatment. This may explain, in part, the reports of almost universal effectiveness accompanying the introduction of new therapies."[36] As he noted elsewhere, with documentation, "The efficaciousness of a drug may increase 30 per cent or from 0 to 100 per cent when the *doctor* is told that the agent is active and not a placebo. Placebo effectiveness may decrease from 70 to 25 per cent when [staff] attitudes toward [the] treatment change from positive to negative."[37] Such variation does not occur solely when drugs are used. Beecher, for example, estimates the placebo effect of surgical procedures to be about 35 per cent.[38] Indeed, Shapiro's review of the literature to 1960 leaves little doubt of the importance of social and psychological variables in creating and interpreting the practitioner's clinical experience, medical or surgical.[39]

It is worth pointing out here that the medical literature on error in diagnosis and on placebo reaction has a curious limitation of approach which reflects the peculiar mentality of the profession. The underlying assumption of most such medical research seems to be that while the doctor may err because of ignorance or lack of skill (both of which could be remedied by better recruitment, better education, and better supervision) or because of the unscientific character of a diagnostic concept or procedure (which more research will remedy), he could not possibly have a bias of approach, a subjective bias. But in the light of several decades of extramedical research on human perception and judgment,[40] it seems clear that no human being can avoid some such bias. The

[36] Arthur K. Shapiro, "Etiological Factors in Placebo Effect," *Journal of the American Medical Association,* CLXXXVII (1964), 713.

[37] Arthur K. Shapiro, "Factors Contributing to the Placebo Effect," *American Journal of Psychotherapy,* XVIII (1964), 78, italics added.

[38] Henry K. Beecher, "Surgery as Placebo, a Quantitative Study of Bias," *Journal of the American Medical Association,* CLXXVI (1961), 1102–1107.

[39] Shapiro, "Contribution," *op. cit.*

[40] Much of this literature is reviewed in M. Sherif and C. V. Hovland, *Social Judgment* (New Haven: Yale University Press, 1961).

prime question posed by medical research—whether or not bias exists at all—is therefore either very naïve or very arrogant. Being human, physicians are bound to manifest a subjective bias. The research question should not be merely to determine the existence of such bias but rather, at the same time that bias is measured, to collect information about the physician and the social setting in which he works in order to explain the sources of his bias. The question may be addressed on a number of levels. A recent study of the sentences given convicted criminals by judges, for example, asks how the sentence given to one case influences the sentence given to succeeding cases.[41] Analogies between legal and medical judgment are not so farfetched as to prevent an exploration of the same mechanisms in medicine. On another level of analysis one must certainly ask how the social characteristics of the physician himself—his religious background, ethnicity, sex, social class—enter into the prejudices he is likely to have in favor of certain diagnoses and modes of management. And on still another level one may ask how the characteristics of the setting in which he works—the type of patients he most often sees, the patient load, his contact with colleagues, and the like—influence the content and direction of the choices and responses he makes. Such questions have hardly been raised about the physician's approach to his work, let alone explored systematically.

Sources of the Clinical Construction of Illness

Whatever else, it should be apparent from the material I have reviewed that at least one of the variables contributing to the maintenance of varied diagnostic and therapeutic practices in contemporary medicine lies in the dependence of clinical practice on the practitioner's optimistic, pessimistic, or other personal bias in his approach to his patient, and in his interpretation of the signs and symptoms presented to him. The practicing physician is likely to believe in the therapy he uses; in believing, he influences the patient to respond favorably and influences himself to see improvement if

41 Edward Green, "The Effect of Stimulus Arrangements on Normative Judgment in the Award of Penal Sanctions," *Sociometry*, XXXI (1968), 125–137.

not cure. Facilitating this bias is the tendency of all practices to select "appropriate" cases out of the total number of cases available. This selectivity has been manifested throughout history. Of course, at least since the Hippocratics, "hopeless" cases have been refused. In the case of "Royal Touch" therapy in later times, whereby a member of royalty cured by touching the patient afflicted with what was called the King's Evil, we are informed that there was frequently careful screening of patients, "and only one treatment per person was allowed (thus decreasing the possibility of failure)." [42] And in our own day, the selectivity of psychiatric practice [43] and family service agencies [44] has been notorious. Recently, attention has turned to the tendencies of other treatment agencies to select cases on rather limited groups—as examples may be cited Krause's observations on the practices of a rehabilitation center [45] and Scott's on the selection of cases by agencies for the blind.[46]

These examples of selectivity are not solely instances of social injustice. For my present purposes they are better seen as examples of how consulting practices may create for themselves conditions that systematically bias their case experience so that their *conception of illness* is inapplicable to the world outside their practice. Such bias may stem from the deliberate selectivity of the practitioner, or it may stem from the way cases select themselves—that is, according to the kind of people who are inclined to perceive a symptom to be serious and to seek medical consultation.[47] In both cases, the outcome is the same: the creation of an illness (or diagnostic con-

[42] Shapiro, "Contribution," *op. cit.*, p. 111.

[43] A. B. Hollingshead and F. C. Redlich, *Social Class and Mental Illness* (New York: John Wiley & Sons, 1958).

[44] See Richard A. Cloward and Irwin Epstein, "Private Social Welfare's Disengagement from the Poor: The Case of Family Adjustment Agencies," in Mayer N. Zald, ed., *Social Welfare Institutions* (New York: John Wiley & Sons, 1965), pp. 623–644.

[45] Elliott A. Krause, "After the Rehabilitation Center," *Social Problems*, XIV (1966), 197–206.

[46] Robert A. Scott, "The Selection of Clients by Social Welfare Agencies: The Case of the Blind," *Social Problems*, XIV (1967), 248–257. And see Scott, *op. cit.*

[47] See David Mechanic, "Response Factors in Illness: The Study of Illness Behavior," *Social Psychiatry*, I (1966), 11–20; Irving K. Zola, "Culture and Symptoms—An Analysis of Patients' Presenting Complaints," *American Sociological Review*, XXXI (1966), 615–630.

cept) that, while intended to be universal, instead applies to at best a special segment of the population.

Diagnostic categories, prognoses, and courses of treatment, insofar as they are empirically developed, are all built up on the basis of clinical experience with cases that happen to present themselves (or be presented) within the purview of the professional sector. The tendency of the practitioner is to assume that what he personally perceives in cases with whom he comes to deal also exists in the people in the everyday world outside his purview. (Indeed, he *imposes* this view on the world outside.) He is prone to overlook the fact that a social process organizes the bringing in of certain cases to him; he is likely instead, as Mechanic has observed, to assume that the cases he sees are no different from those he does not.[48] And so he develops conceptions of illness that may have an inaccurate and artificial relationship to the world.

A number of examples may be cited. Schmideberg notes that for a long time it was thought that Buerger's disease was prevalent among East European Jewish males, mostly because Buerger's contacts with patients were restricted largely to Mount Sinai Hospital in New York City, which served predominantly Jewish patients.[49] In the case of "high blood pressure," it was discovered with some surprise that a fair proportion of the general population outside the consulting room manifests the signs without any apparent complaint or ill effects.[50] The great physician Sydenham obtained the impression that scarlet fever was a mild disease, without serious complications—an impression stemming apparently from his contact with primarily well-off rather than poor patients.[51] Until the late 1940's "histoplasmosis was thought to be a rare tropical disease, with a uniform, fatal outcome. Recently, however, it was discovered that it is widely prevalent, and with fatal outcome

[48] David Mechanic, "Some Implications of Illness Behavior for Medical Sampling," *New England Journal of Medicine,* CCLXIX (1963), 244–247.

[49] Melitta Schmideberg, "Social Factors Affecting Diagnostic Concepts," *International Journal of Social Psychiatry,* VII (1961), p. 322.

[50] Scheff, *op. cit.,* p. 115. See also Zola, *op. cit.*

[51] George Rosen, "People, Disease and Emotion: Some Newer Problems for Research in Medical History," *Bulletin of the History of Medicine,* XLI (1967), 9–10. See also L. G. Stevenson, " 'New Diseases' in the Seventeenth Century," *Bulletin of the History of Medicine,* XXXIX (1965), 1–21.

or impairment extremely rare." [52] Similarly, the limited and biased experience of the consulting room has been projected into the population at large in the case of heart disease, only to be brought up short by the discovery of so-called hidden cardiacs, apparently functioning as normal people in spite of the presence of the signs of illness. Indeed, I suspect that the picture of general "unfitness," both physical and psychological, that emerged from the mass medical examinations of World War II and the subsequent continuing of Selective Service was a function of a conception of illness and unfitness built up by collating the signs presented in the consulting room into a label, and then applying the label to signs found elsewhere, forgetting that those who get into consultation with given signs do not all necessarily function the same way as those who have the same signs but who do not seek consultation. It may be inappropriate to label as "diseases" or "serious conditions" those signs and symptoms which incapacitate or worry only those seeking consultation and not others.

Comparing the reporting of illness to the reporting of crime [53] can serve as an instructive aid to exploring the factors that, by underlying the act of seeking professional help, shape the character of the cases the clinical practitioner will see and therefore the image of illness he will obtain. At first thought it would seem that medical case experience poses somewhat different problems to analysis than police case experience, in part because when people believe themselves to be sick, they are far more likely to "turn themselves in" than people who believe themselves to have committed a crime. But this is an inaccurate parallel. Directly analogous to the sick person is not the criminal but the victim. The analogy is particularly interesting in that the victim, like the sick person, does not always report the crime to the police—he does not always seek redress. The most obvious case is the crime of petty theft. Like the victims of such crimes, those ill with what they regard as minor

[52] J. Schwartz and G. L. Baum, "The History of Histoplasmosis," *New England Journal of Medicine,* CCLVI (1957), 253–258, cited in Scheff, *op. cit.,* p. 117.

[53] See the discussion in John I. Kitsuse and Aaron V. Cicourel, "A Note on the Uses of Official Statistics," *Social Problems,* XI (1963), 131–139. And, for suicide, see Jack D. Douglas, *The Social Meaning of Suicide* (Princeton, N.J.: Princeton University Press, 1967).

difficulties are unlikely to seek professional help. White and others estimated that two out of three people who feel sick do not seek out medical care and that in any given month only one per cent of those who report illness in a household survey will be hospitalized.[54] Zola reviews similar and even more striking estimates and also reviews materials from other cultures. He points out that people will not seek care for "aberrations" they do not consider unusual or serious; as examples he mentions such aberrations ordinary in other cultures as diarrhea, sweating, skin diseases, coughing, trachoma, low back pain, fatigue, hallucinations, and dysmenorrhea.[55] The list could obviously be extended to include examples I have already mentioned elsewhere, such as the "milder" symptoms of histoplasmosis, but the point is clear that institutions of medical practice lack any systematic or representative contact with and knowledge of the symptoms (and signs connected with them) that people consider to be everyday and minor.

Underreporting of crimes by victims also includes another variable of importance, however, as exemplified by the crime of rape, statutory or otherwise. To be raped is, theoretically, not the fault of the victim, but it is stigmatized nonetheless, so that the victim is not likely to report it as a crime. Similarly, if one is engaged in an illegal or stigmatized activity—homosexual behavior, for example—at the time of being a victim of assault or extortion, one is unlikely to report the crime. Direct parallels exists for illness, as exemplified by venereal disease, which is not only less likely to be taken to a physician than nonstigmatized illnesses, but which is also underreported by physicians themselves, as a study by Gelman in New York recently found.[56] Similarly, the habitual practice of illegal or stigmatized or "shameful" acts frequently thought to be symptomatic of illness by psychiatrists—for example, homosexual acts, imaginative heterosexual acts, onanistic acts, illegal abortions, or

[54] Kerr L. White, "Patterns of Medical Practice," in Duncan W. Clark and Brian MacMahon, eds., *Preventive Medicine* (Boston: Little, Brown and Co., 1967), p. 854.

[55] Zola, *op. cit.*

[56] Anna C. Gelman *et al.*, "Current Status of Venereal Disease in New York City: A Survey of 6,649 Physicians in Solo Practice," *American Journal of Public Health,* LIII (1963), 1912.

the illegal use of drugs like marijuana [57]—these too are unlikely to be reported to physicians unless the patient believes them to be connected with the illness for which he wants help. Even in psychiatric practice these are the activities which patients are likely to conceal, or about which they are likely to lie.[58]

I have suggested two of the variables likely to lead to the underreporting of illness by prospective patients and consequently to restrictions on the accuracy of the information that the practitioner and his profession will have about the signs and symptoms involved. Should the profession define an illness by signs and symptoms that the general population considers to be trivial and unimportant, or shameful and stigmatized, the profession's conception of that disease is likely to be distorted and partial, resting on highly limited knowledge of and experience with its attributes, and on inadequate statistics of incidence, prevalence, and significance. In such cases, the practitioner is less informed and less qualified to evaluate the "illness" than are those who are able to go into the community and study the relevant behaviors and responses that actually take place. Limited clinical experience is *certain* to lead to inaccurate (usually underrepresentative) conceptions of its prevalence. It is also likely to lead to a conception of the illness which is hardly objective or self-evident.

From my discussion I think it becomes possible to suggest the circumstances under which professional conceptions of the disease itself, and its incidence, are likely to be both accurate and appro-

[57] Cf. Edwin M. Schur, *Crimes Without Victims, Deviant Behavior and Public Policy* (Englewood Cliffs, New Jersey: Prentice-Hall, 1965), who writes largely from a legal point of view in evaluating the punishment of such crimes as homosexuality. What he overlooks is that while as a crime homosexuality has no victim, as an illness the homosexual is a victim of a disease and must be treated as such. Substituting medical for legal definitions does not, as I have noted earlier, substitute moral approval for moral repugnance or freedom from constraint.

[58] See the discussion of Szasz, *Myth of Mental Illness, op. cit.*, p. 272. I would suspect that physicians, including psychiatrists, consistently underestimate the amount of lying or concealment their patients subject them to. That this can be done successfully in spite of extensive questioning by psychiatrist, psychologist, and sociologist over several months, even in the face of suspicion, is demonstrated by the case of Agnes. See Harold Garfinkel, *Studies in Ethnomethodology* (Englewood Cliffs, New Jersey: Prentice-Hall, 1967), pp. 116–185, 285–288.

priate. Clearly, in those circumstances where the layman's conception of illness corresponds to that of the profession, the illness being thought to be acute and serious, to require immediate professional attention, to imply no moral stigma or illegality, and, finally, hampered by no significant barrier to the utilization of services, members of the profession will see most instances of morbidity and will have a fairly precise conception of the range of variation of signs and symptoms and a comparatively true picture of its incidence. Under such circumstances, one may not raise serious questions about its use of the label of illness and its conceptions of that illness. The same precision may be gained without meeting any of the requirements specified should mandatory, standardized examination and testing be instituted—as it is in the case of newborn infants in American hospitals, and in some educational, industrial, and military settings—though insofar as laymen do not themselves recognize an "illness," the professional conception remains problematic.

Finally, I might mention what should, for purposes of symmetry if not logic, be called the "overreporting" of illness—the creation of a picture of illness by the profession as more prevalent in the community than in fact it is or as a more serious problem than subsequent events seem to show, whether because of its imputed prevalence or because of serious consequences or correlates imputed to it. In considering this question, the first thing to recall is the profession's tendency to impute illness rather than health, and its tendency to take illness more seriously than the layman. These tendencies by themselves should lead one to expect at least the moral entrepreneurs of the profession to be more alarmed by what they come into contact with than their actual selective case-finding would imply. Thus, underrepresentative case experience is likely to be overemphasized by the profession: just as law-enforcement officials and other moral entrepreneurs are likely to report "crime waves" on the basis of underrepresentative and biased statistics, so are physicians likely to report "epidemics." Such reporting behavior is especially likely to occur when some new and rather dramatic practice or behavior excites the public morality. As Becker has pointed out, when marijuana first attracted public attention in the 1920's and early 1930's, physicians began reporting psychoses associated with its use, reports which disappeared by the 1940's but which seem to have been renewed in the late 1960's when marijuana became prominent in the public eye again.[59] Becker's analysis emphasizes the patient as the source of such reports, but it is just as possible that it is the physician's aroused moral interest.[60] Similarly, the quantitative weight of medical opinion (advanced in spite of the fact that the physician is in a very poor position to come into knowing contact with a fair cross-section of users) seems, in the face of the evidence available, to bend over backward to be conservative and to overestimate the potential dangers of use.

These comments have been designed more to point out than to actually grapple with the problem of the nature of the evidence available to the practitioner that in turn is responsible for shaping his concepts of illness. Furthermore, they have been restricted almost entirely to the experience of the everyday clinical practitioner, who, I believe, has been and is still the prime source of information about illness available to medicine. Recent developments have led to the increasing use of evaluational techniques designed to control the practitioner's own wishful thinking in evaluating the correctness of his diagnosis and the effectiveness of his therapy.[61] But it will be a long time before double-blind experiments and thoroughly controlled demonstrations have sifted through most of the established practices of contemporary medicine.

Other developments have led to the initiation of ambitious attempts to determine the signs and symptoms prevalent in whole communities, independently of the case-finding (and limited reporting) of practitioners.[62] But the problem I perceive is not solved by field studies of the true incidence of a disease in a given population.

[59] Howard S. Becker, "History, Culture and Subjective Experience: An Exploration of the Social Bases of Drug-Induced Experiences," *Journal of Health and Social Behavior,* VII (1967), 163–176.

[60] For an argument that a profound normative difference underlies varying interpretations of the evidence surrounding the consequences of marijuana use, see Erich Goode, "Marijuana and the Politics of Reality," *Journal of Health and Social Behavior,* X (1969), 83–94.

[61] See Edgar F. Borgatta, "Research Problems in Evaluation of Health Service Demonstrations," *Milbank Memorial Fund Quarterly,* XLIV (October, 1966, Part II), 182–201, and Avedis Donabedian, "Evaluating the Quality of Medical Care," *Milbank Memorial Fund Quarterly,* XLIV (July, 1966, Part II), 166–206.

[62] For present sources of data see Forrest E. Linder, "Sources of Data on Health in the United States," in Clark and MacMahon, *op. cit.,* pp. 55–66.

All such studies will do is to collect precise information about the distribution of signs and symptoms *that have already been labeled* diseases on the basis of consulting-room experience and professional evaluation. The problem is whether or not it is fitting and proper to label such signs and symptoms diseases in the first place and serious diseases in the second place. This problem can be settled (or at least debated intelligently) by determining *how people function* in the community even though they manifest such signs and symptoms that have heretofore been labeled illness. Given the bias of the profession toward imputing illness and toward urging the seeking of professional treatment, and given the specially structured source of its experience with patients seeking help, its *concepts of illness are themselves problematic.* In the case of psychiatry, Szasz claims that situations of contact between psychiatrist and layman vary so much in the content of what occurs in them that a system of "psychiatric nosology" which is developed on the basis of private office practice is neither meaningful nor serviceable in such other situations of practice as the mental hospital or the military.[63] His claim is not answered by studies that try to determine the proportion of people in a community who may be labeled mentally ill on the basis of criteria developed in a private psychiatric practice that comes into contact with but a tiny proportion of the population in the first place.

The Sociology of Medical Knowledge and Procedure

In this chapter I have devoted myself as best I could to a sketch of what is certainly a task of such magnitude that no single man could ever accomplish it by his own efforts alone—a sociological analysis of the medical profession's conceptions of deviance. It was noted how the use of the label of illness, identified with and officially controlled by the profession of medicine, has grown at the expense of legal, but more particularly religious labels. The growth in such use is ultimately supported by our contemporary society's emphasis on the value of health but, since the medical profession has an official mandate to define and treat illness, it is necessary to analyze those characteristics of the profession that contribute to the exact form in which the meaning of illness is constructed.

[63] Szasz, *Law, Liberty and Psychiatry, op. cit.*, pp. 24–36.

The profession is first of all prone to see illness and the need for treatment more than it is prone to see health or normality. Within the profession, however, variations in orientation to illness and treatment are organized into schools. Those different approaches are sustained by self-confirming and self-sustaining selectivity in the cases accepted, as well as by the tendency for the physician and the patient to demonstrate placebo reactions. And where there is free choice to visit or not to visit the physician, the patient's conceptions of illness place limits on the number and kind of cases the doctor will see, thereby influencing his conception of the components of the illness he sees, in addition to its seriousness and its prevalence and, in fact, whether or not an illness "exists."

In my discussion I have not referred to the superb clinical discoveries that give such grandeur to the history of medicine, nor have I referred to the increasing sophistication of medical investigation and procedures, which begin to remove some of the practice of subjectivity from the frailly human hands of the physicians. These accomplishments have been described and rightly applauded in many accessible books. My intent is not to deny or deprecate them. Far from it. My goal in this chapter has merely been to demonstrate, sometimes securely and sometime speculatively, how medical concepts of illness and its management are at least in part shaped by the social institutions in which they arise, and by the relation of those institutions to the society of which they are a part. Put another way, I have been attempting to show how medical knowledge and procedures are themselves a function of the social character of medicine as an organized professional enterprise, politically sustained and practiced in a given way, with given self-deceptions and institutionally limited experience. The content of this enterprise is at once drawn from and imposed on the experience of the layman of the society in which the professional practices. In the next chapter, I propose to address myself to the societal response of the layman himself to the deviance he perceives, and to show how he is led into the use of medical services.

13.

THE LAY CONSTRUCTION OF ILLNESS

THE point of my discussion in the last chapter was merely a variant of the central point I am trying to make about the notion of illness—namely, that it is a social creation, and that the values and the organized limits on the experience of its professional creators influence how and when it will be created, as well as some of its content. For these notions of illness to be put into practice, however, it is imperative for the consulting profession that the layman become aware that he is ill and thus put himself into its hands. This is a difficult problem, for although the individual may be aware that he has some difficulty, he may not believe that it is an illness; or if he does, he may not think that it is serious enough for him to seek professional help or that it is so amenable to professional ministrations as to be worth seeking help. In a simple society the healer has no such problem, for folk practitioners merely specialize in what everyone knows: with no significant difference in conceptions of illness and treatment separating them from their patients, they are likely to treat all whom they think they should be treating. But difficulty in reaching patients is intrinsic to modern medicine, for where there is a profession there is by definition a lay population ignorant of at least some of its esoteric body of knowledge and practice, and therefore always in some way responding differently to its ills than would the profession.

The problem for analysis that confronts us now is to understand better how the medical system comes to be brought to bear on the layman, the degree to which it shapes the meaning of his illness, and the degree to which it, in turn, is shaped by the responses of the layman. As I have already noted, what medicine comes to define as an illness is in part a function of the way its experience is limited by the characteristics of the laymen who happen to enter the consulting room: the laymen who do enter the consulting room are not a representative sample of the total population. Entrance into the consulting room follows an organized social process that is highly selective. The grounds for selection are not the profession's conceptions of illness, and the organization of the process is in important ways independent of the organization of the profession. Rather, the critical variables are to be found in lay conceptions of deviance from "health," only some of which may be of professional origin, and in the structure of lay social life, only some of which may be in contact with professional institutions. In this chapter I wish to devote myself to the analysis of the way those variables enter into the process by which the layman is led to believe that he may be ill and to seek out the physician.

The Social Meanings of Pain

Patently, the first step in the process of deciding that one is ill lies in the experience of distress, difficulty, or some other deviation from expectations. Perhaps the most rudimentary and universal experience connected with what is called illness is sensing the form of distress called "pain." Certainly, the foundation for the experience is biological; it is, furthermore, a foundation which men share with other animals. Nonetheless, even this clearly biological experience is not responded to in a merely biological fashion. As I have already noted in discussing Beecher's works,[1] responses to pain have a tendency to vary more than the variation in the objective stimulus that is supposed to be creating the pain. Individuals, of course, differ among themselves in the way they respond to pain, as Petrie,[2] among others, has shown, but as a sociologist I am more

[1] Henry K. Beecher, *Measurement of Subjective Responses* (New York: Oxford University Press, 1959).

[2] See Asenath Petrie, *Individuality in Pain and Suffering* (Chicago: University of Chicago Press, 1967).

interested in the evidence that responses to pain are predictable on the basis of group membership and that the social meanings ascribed to pain are shared by members of groups.

In a now classic study, Zborowski [3] and his staff interviewed eighty-seven male patients, most of whom suffered from such neurological ailments as herniated discs and spinal lesions, and most of whom were of Italian, Jewish, and "Old American" backgrounds. Assuming that, since their disorders were all similar, the actual physical pain suffered by the patients would vary within fairly narrow limits, the problem of investigation thus became the determination of variations in response to pain. The hospital staff itself seemed to feel there were ethnic differences in such response. The staff believed that Jews and Italians were similar in being more sensitive to pain, and more prone to "exaggerate" the experience of pain than were "Old Americans" and people of north European origins. The investigators explored such differences.

They found that Jews and Italians were quite similar in that, in responding to pain in the hospital, they gave free expression to their emotions and wanted to avoid being alone when suffering. However, the social context in which each expressed his pain differed. The Italian husband was more likely to be stoical at home, where he plays a masculine and authoritarian role prescribing stoicism; in the hospital, however, he tended to be rather emotional about his pain. In contrast, the Jewish husband tended to be quite emotional at home. Jewish culture does not seem to include stoicism among the attributes required of the patriarch—a fact supported by recalling the complaints of Job when he was covered with boils. Thus, the Jewish husband tended to be quite emotional both at home and in the hospital. However, he tended to use his expression of suffering as a device for manipulating others, including the hospital staff. Once in hospital, and once satisfied that adequate care was given to him, he became more restrained in his responses to pain.

In contrast to Jews and Italians, "Old Americans" seemed to try to conform to the medical notion of the ideal patient, seeking to

[3] M. Zborowski, "Cultural Components in Response to Pain," in E. G. Jaco, ed., *Patients, Physicians and Illness* (New York: The Free Press of Glencoe, 1958), pp. 256–268.

cooperate with hospital personnel and to avoid being a nuisance. They tried to avoid expressing in public any emotional reaction to their pain. When being examined by the doctor they seemed to be trying to "assume the detached role of an unemotional observer who gives the most efficient description of his state for a correct diagnosis and treatment."[4] They would admit they were in pain, but when they could not repress moans and the like, they tended to withdraw in order to express them in private.

The patients also differed in their *attitudes* to pain. The Italians seemed to be more concerned with the discomfort of the pain itself, while the Jews were rather more concerned with the significance of the pain for the state of their health, the former complaining and the latter worrying. Consistent with this observation was another—that the Italians sought drugs for the relief of pain and stopped complaining upon feeling none. The Jews, however, were reluctant to take such drugs, concerned not only with the dangers of addiction, but also with the fact that the drug merely overcame the pain rather than cured them of the cause. Even after the pain had been masked by drugs, the Jews continued to worry. The Italians developed great confidence in the doctors who could relieve their pain, but the Jews maintained a degree of skepticism because the doctors had not yet actually cured them. The "Old Americans" were similar to the Jews in that they were anxious primarily about what the pain signified about the state of their health. They were different from the Jews in that they were optimistic about the powers of medicine and about the outcome.

A number of subsequent studies seem to confirm the accuracy of Zborowski's observations.[5] A laboratory study by Sternbach and Tursky administered electric shocks to housewives and, in Mechanic's words, found that

> Italian women showed significantly lower tolerance for shock, and fewer of them would accept the full range of shock stimulation used in the experiment. The investigators believe that

[4] *Ibid.*, p. 264.

[5] Such was reported without detail in Andrew C. Twaddle, "Health Decisions and Sick Role Variations: An Exploration," *Journal of Health and Social Behavior*, X (1969), 108.

> this response is consistent with the Italian tendency to focus on the immediacy of the pain itself, as compared with the future orientation of the Jewish concern. Similarly, they believe that their finding that "Yankee" housewives had faster and more complete adaptation of the diphasic palmar skin potential has an attitudinal correlate to their "matter of fact" orientation to pain. As they note: "This is illustrated by our Yankee subjects'" modal attitude toward traumata, as they verbalized it in the interviews: "You take things in your stride." No such action-oriented, adapting phrase was used by the members of the other groups. The similarly undemonstrative Irish subjects may "keep a tight upper lip" but "fear the worst," a noxious stimulus being a burden to be endured and suffered in silence.[6]

Zola's work, contrasting the behavior of Italian with Irish, noted that the Italians were comparatively more preoccupied with and disturbed by pain, and with the "diffuse physical and social effects of being sick." [7] Furthermore, the Italians reported a greater average number of symptoms connected with the illness, emphasizing the diffuseness of their response to illness.[8] Perhaps it was this "exaggeration" of responses to the illness that led the staff to label many more of the Italians as "psychiatric problems" than available evidence supported and, in the case of a group of women with no organic evidence for symptoms, to label many more Italian than Irish or Yankee.[9]

[6] David Mechanic, *Medical Sociology* (New York: The Free Press, 1968), pp. 125–126, citing R. A. Sternbach and B. Tursky, "Ethnic Differences among Housewives in Psychophysical and Skin Potential Responses to Electric Shock," *Psychophysiology*, I (1965), 241–246.

[7] J. D. Stoeckle, I. K. Zola, and G. E. Davidson, "On Going to See the Doctor, The Contributions of the Patient to the Decision to seek Medical Aid," *Journal of Chronic Disease*, XVI (1963), 987. For a more elaborate report see Irving K. Zola, "Culture and Symptoms—An Analysis of Patients' Presenting Complaints," *American Sociological Review*, XXXI (1966), 615–630.

[8] One might also note Croog's study of Army inductees, finding that Italian and Jewish respondents reported the greater number of symptoms of illness. Sidney H. Croog, "Ethnic Origins and Responses to Health Questionnaires," *Human Organization*, XX (1961), 65–69.

[9] Irving K. Zola, "Problems of Communication, Diagnosis and Patient Care: The Interplay of Patient, Physician and Clinic Organization," *The Journal of Medical Education*, XXXVIII (1963), 829–830.

Symptoms and the Lay Definition of Illness

Clearly, pain is not a variable that may be treated as a biological constant in the process leading to the definition of illness. Nor is it a variable that can be explained solely by reference to individual psychological differences. Responses to pain also vary by the ethnic or cultural experience of the group from which the individual has learned what meanings to find in his experience and which provides the individual with continual reinforcement for such meanings. Furthermore, since it is not the pain itself so much as the *meaning* of pain that is the critical variable, it follows that in order to understand how it is that people come to consider themselves ill when they feel pain we must isolate some of the critical meanings revolving around the perception of pain. However, pain is not the only experience that people come to consider a symptom of possible illness. Even if we restrict ourselves to our own medically oriented culture, we must recognize that a wide variety of attributes or experiences in which pain does not figure may come to be considered symptoms of illness. One may feel tired or irritable; one may feel he does not see or hear properly; or one may be preoccupied with the presence of painless and nonincapacitating attributes like a skin lesion, a swelling, a discharge, or a cough. Pain is not involved in all or even most things felt to be symptoms. Many things believed to be symptoms do not incapacitate the "sufferer" in any significant way. Thc only element common to all the examples is the imputation of deviation from what is considered desirable, or normal.

In the course of specifying some of the important criteria by which people determine whether or not deviation exists, it seems useful to review a few studies that sought to explore the way people distinguish between health and illness. Among one group of laymen studied by Apple,[10] the belief that an attribute represented a symptom of illness seemed to hinge upon two criteria: (1) the recency or novelty of the experience, behavior, or attribute; and (2) the degree to which it interferes with ordinary activities. Clearly these two criteria are closely related, for what is considered an "ordinary activity" is a function of what has been routine over

[10] Dorrian Apple, "How Laymen Define Illness," *Journal of Health and Human Behavior,* I (1960), 219–225.

time. Therefore, a behavior, attribute, or experience "of recent onset" constitutes by definition a potential interference or interruption or change in routine activities and the expectations connected with them. Other studies have also found the layman to emphasize the significance of "symptoms" that interfere with ordinary activities. For example, Baumann found that laymen distinguish among three criteria: health as (1) a feeling of well-being, (2) an absence of symptoms, and (3) a state of being able to perform those activities that a person in good health should be able to do.[11] And in a study of the meaning of health and illness to a group of Frenchmen, Herzlich also found an emphasis on the importance of the capacity to carry on daily activities rather than on "organic reality which is itself ambiguous." [12]

Clearly, if one is inclined to begin to think of himself as possibly ill only when he perceives himself to be unable by virtue of some new difficulty to carry on his ordinary daily activities, what he picks out as a symptom of illness is contingent on what his routine capacities and experiences are in the light of his ordinary daily activities. If, for example, one has had poliomyelitis as a child, with slight paralysis of one leg which has since been compensated for by the greater muscular development of the other leg, one's subsequent daily activities will have been adjusted to one's capacity, and a routine capacity and experience will have been established. Once the routine is established, one's slight limp would not, then, constitute a symptom of illness. The limp is, in Lemert's terms, a primary deviation to which one accommodates by developing a routine. But when one has *not* had such a limp, and suddenly finds he cannot walk in the fashion to which he is accustomed, he will discern a symptom of what may be "illness," particularly if the symptom is unexpected in everyday experience. Thus, if one's life is composed routinely of such experiences as coughing, or if one has very slowly and "routinely" over the years come to develop more and more of a cough, one is hardly likely to pick coughing out as a symptom

[11] Barbara Baumann, "Diversities in Conceptions of Health and Physical Fitness," *Journal of Health and Human Behavior,* II (1961), 39–46. And see the discussion of how American males in their sixties came to decide they were "well" or "not well" in Twaddle, *op. cit.,* pp. 107–108.

[12] Claudine Herzlich, "Quelques Aspects de la Représentation Sociale de la Santé et de la Maladie," *Revue Psychologie Française,* IX (1964), 1–14.

worth seeking help for or worth reporting at a medical examination.[13]

It seems, then, that people who live in a society where medically defined illness and impairment are extraordinarily common will, because they are accustomed to them, report markedly fewer symptoms of illness than would a medical examiner. Furthermore, they are likely to believe they have fewer illnesses than would the examiner. Indeed, like the physicians who evaluated the necessity for tonsillectomy (discussed in the last chapter), I would suggest that laymen everywhere are likely to report spontaneously about the same number of symptoms, irrespective of the number of illnesses discernible to medical men. It is almost as if the human being is able to define only a fixed proportion of his experience as miserable; thus, the disease-ridden Oriental peasant may recognize and report no more symptoms than the healthier American bourgeois. Conversely, it is almost as if the human being must be dissatisfied with some proportion of his life and experience, for even if the American has many fewer of the symptoms and diseases than the Oriental, he may find as many symptoms to report.

Thus, what the layman recognizes as a symptom or illness is in part a function of deviation from the culturally and historically variable standard of normality established by everyday experience. However, as I noted in an earlier chapter, not all deviance is picked up and attended to. In Lemert's terms, much remains primary in character, unorganized into a special role or identity. The imputation of seriousness is critical in distinguishing between those that are merely noted and those that become organized into a career of illness. Obviously, it is involved in the processes of reporting and attending to symptoms and, by definition, it is a social variable rather than a constant biological fact.

One might suspect that the finding that there is a general tendency for laymen to report fewer symptoms and illnesses than physicians [14] is as much a function of attention as it is of differential knowledge and perception: the layman may be aware of the signs

[13] See Julius Roth, *Timetables* (Indianapolis: Bobbs-Merrill Co., 1963), for the problem of the cough in diagnosing tuberculosis.

[14] Stanislav V. Kasl and Sidney Cobb, "Health Behavior, Illness Behavior, and Sick Role Behavior," *Archives of Environmental Health*, XII (1966), 256.

and symptoms that a physician would label a symptom of an illness, but he may not ascribe the same importance to them. Thus, in rural Greece the childhood diseases of measles, mumps, chicken pox, and whooping cough are certainly perceived by the peasant, but they do not arouse concern, any more than do such "routine" illnesses as meningitis, scrofula, trachoma, malaria, salmonella, or amoebiasis.[15] He underreports such "illness," not because he is unaware of it, but because he differs with the medical world's conception of what is serious. Similarly, in Koos's study of rural America, it was found that the lower the social class, the less the tendency to consider a list of symptoms to be important enough to need medical attention.[16] And in a recent study of New Yorkers, while the majority did recognize a large proportion of a list of twenty-two descriptions of behaviors to involve "mental" or "emotional trouble," only two of the twenty-two were felt by a majority to need psychiatric treatment.[17]

Culture and the Use of Medical Services

Lay definitions of symptoms and illness are important for our understanding of whether or not laymen will believe themselves to be ill. They are also important for our understanding of the next step of our analysis: whether laymen, after coming to believe they might be ill, then consult a physician. Believing oneself to be ill does not in itself lead to the use of medical services. Some people dose themselves rather than see a practitioner; others do not seek consultation from a physician for a variety of reasons. If the layman believes he has an illness which medical men do not believe in—for example, among Latin Americans, the "mal ojo," or evil eye—he has good reason for treating himself or for seeking a nonmedical practitioner who knows how to deal with it. Similarly, if he feels that his illness is best managed by physical manipulation, it follows that he will use a chiropractor rather than a physician.

Implicit in a conception of illness is participation in a given cul-

15 See Richard and Eva Blum, *Health and Healing in Rural Greece* (Stanford: Stanford University Press, 1965), p. 53.

16 Earl L. Koos, *The Health of Regionville* (New York: Columbia University Press, 1954), pp. 32–33.

17 Jack Elinson *et al.*, *Public Image of Mental Health Services* (New York: Mental Health Materials Center, 1967), p. 24.

ture or system of knowledge and meaning. There are, of course, wide variations in the content of the cultures of human groups, but for the purpose of my analysis here, the essential characteristic of any of those widely varying human cultures is their compatibility with that of modern medicine. Naturally, the lay cultures of modern Western industrial societies are more likely to include ideas of illness and treatment similar to modern medicine than are the cultures of the simpler or non-Western societies of the world. Furthermore, *within* modern Western societies, those members of the population who are most like the members of the medical profession in attitude and knowledge manifest a culture or subculture that is more likely to lead them to demonstrate medically approved conceptions of illness than are those least like the profession. Within modern societies, the empirical variables of socioeconomic status—most particularly formal education—seem to be the most useful indicators of such compatibility.

Using the community studies of such people as Koos [18] and the results of national surveys reported by such people as Gurin and his associates [19] and Feldman,[20] it seems useful at this point to sketch out some of the substantive differences in orientation toward illness and medical care to be found among the middle and the lower or working class in the United States.[21] First, there is the matter of "knowledge"—"scientific" or medically approved knowledge. Lower-class individuals are comparatively ignorant of the nature of the extent and character of bodily functions. They are prone to think of and describe their experience with illness in the now-antiquated notions still exploited by patent-medicine advertisements—notions of qualities of the blood, of the necessity to "purge the system," of the importance of the state of the liver and kidneys to health, and the like. Consonant with these now medically unfashionable ideas, the lower-class person is more prone to use, if not folk remedies, then at least traditional patent remedies for

18 Koos, *op. cit.*

19 G. Gurin *et al., Americans View Their Mental Health* (New York: Basic Books, 1960).

20 Jacob J. Feldman, *The Dissemination of Health Information* (Chicago: Aldine Publishing Co., 1966).

21 And see the graphic descriptive material in Raymond S. Duff and August B. Hollingshead, *Sickness and Society* (New York: Harper and Row, 1968).

many of his ailments. It follows that the lower class is less likely to use medical services than the middle class.

Aside from his antiquated notions of bodily functions, the working-class person also has a very concrete and literal approach to his health, which is based on how he feels. This approach is quite different from the detached, abstract objectivity that the well-educated person is likely to use in looking at himself. In the case of the working class, the definition of symptoms and of possible illness tends to arise directly from sensations of pain, discomfort, or incapacity. In contrast, the middle-class person more often defines significant symptoms independently of discomfort or even incapacity; he is inclined to use intellectual criteria of "danger signals" that involve at best the anticipation of discomfort. Furthermore, the middle-class individual is more likely to adopt preventive measures.

In all, these differences in culture lead to differences in the likelihood that the perception of symptoms or illness will lead to entrance into medical consultation. The lower-class person is not, like the middle-class person, committed deeply to the knowledge of medicine. Indeed, he shows a certain hostility to modern medicine.[22] Virtually everyone doses himself on occasion, but the lower-class person does not seem to be as willing as the middle-class person to seek medical recommendations. Given his basic conceptions of health and illness, and given his understandable inclination to accept his own conclusions about what is wrong with him, he is considerably less likely than the middle-class man to enter into medical consultation.

The Organization of the Entrance to Care

In the process of imputing meaning to his experience the individual sufferer does not invent the meanings himself but rather uses the meanings and interpretations that his social life has provided him. Thus, one can predict the behavior of a collection of individuals without reference to their individual characteristics, by refer-

[22] Cf. William A. Gamson and Howard Schuman, "Some Undercurrents in the Prestige of Physicians," *American Journal of Sociology*, LXVIII (1963), 463–470 and Zena Smith Blau, "Exposure to Child-Rearing Experts: A Structural Interpretation of Class-Color Differences," *American Journal of Sociology*, LXIX (1964), 596–608.

ring solely to the content of the social life in which they participate. Social life, however, does not consist only of a content. It also consists of a structure—an organization of people's relations each to the other. It is the organization of social life that sustains, enforces, and reinforces conformity to the cultural content of social life. We can see this clearly when we examine anew the process of perceiving symptoms, suspecting illness, and seeking to act ill. It may be the individual himself who becomes aware that something may be wrong with him. But at the next step of the process he cannot act as an individual: when he actually attempts to act as if he were ill by seeking privileges and release from ordinary obligations, he requires both the approval of those around him and their agreement that his complaints "really" represent sickness. If those around him do not agree with his interpretation of his difficulty they demand that he fulfill his obligations. He is likely to obtain their agreement and aid only if he shows evidence of symptoms the others believe to be illness and if he interprets them the way others find plausible.[23] The organization of people into families and other kin groups, neighborhoods, work groups, cliques, and the like thus operates to enforce particular views of illness and its treatment irrespective of the views of isolated individuals within it. Indeed, social structure can force individuals to act sick even though they may not believe themselves to be sick. Usually, however, the individual has internalized the views of his associates, and he is likely to behave "spontaneously" the way he is supposed to.

No small part of the significance of social structure lies in its role in encouraging or discouraging the individual's movement toward medical consultation. This may be seen when we remember that the individual depends on others to grant him the privileges of illness he may seek: they may insist on legitimation of his condition by a physician and move him toward consultation thereby. Or, perhaps more common, when the individual feels discomfort and believes he may be ill, he is likely to seek the advice of those around him to determine whether or not he may be ill and what he should do about it. People often solicit others' advice about what to do and whom to see. Indeed, they even volunteer such advice

[23] See the discussion of this in Judith Lorber, "Deviance as Performance: The Case of Illness," *Social Problems*, XIV (1967), 302–310.

as, "You look terrible, are you sick? Shouldn't you see a doctor?" or, conversely, "That's nothing—what do you want to go to a doctor for?" It is of course quite obvious that some decisions concerning illness may be made privately by the individual, but there is a great deal of data bearing on such topics as polio immunization, choosing a doctor, and seeking psychotherapy that confirms the importance of the social process of seeking advice before, during, and even after one is struggling with a health problem.[24]

Such advice contains an implicit diagnosis of the problem. As important, it tends to constitute a referral to some agent or agency thought competent to deal with the problem, thereby moving the complainant toward care. Even if the advice is solely diagnostic in its content, a diagnosis carries within it a prescription that one seek help from that class of people which deals with the problem specified by the diagnosis. In this sense, we may consider advice-seeking and advice-giving in health affairs among laymen to *organize the direction of behavior by referral* to one or another consultant. And so we can speak of a lay referral system, which is defined by (1) the particular culture or knowledge people have about health and health agents, and by (2) the interrelationships of the laymen from whom advice and referral are sought. There is, then, a cultural content in the system, whether of ethnic or socioeconomic origin, and a network or structure.

Obviously, differences in laymen's relations to professional consultants will make for differences in referrals to professionals and therefore differences in utilization. I have elsewhere used the labels "parochial" and "cosmopolitan"[25] to point to such differences in contact and experience with professionals. The lower-class system in the United States might be called parochial both because of the limitations of its culture and the limitation of its organized connections with medical institutions. Neither lower-class patients nor their lay consultants are very familiar with the range of medical services available. Very often the patient has had no regular contact with an individual physician, and whatever contact he has had

[24] For a review of such literature, see E. Rogers, *Diffusion of Innovations* (New York: The Free Press of Glencoe, 1962).

[25] See Eliot Freidson, *Patients' Views of Medical Practice* (New York: Russell Sage Foundation, 1961), pp. 150–151.

with any source of medical care has been limited. Public or quasi-public clinics being what they are in the United States, the only source of medical care which he is likely to feel he can use freely is the neighborhood practitioner. He and his lay consultants lack both the knowledge and the aggressiveness necessary for the utilization of other alternatives.[26] Furthermore, the influence of the lower-class referral system is intensified by its cohesiveness and by its strongly localized character, kin and friends living together in a local area with little experience outside the area and with a great deal of mutually reinforcing interaction. Dependent for advice on a localized, fairly cohesive group, the lower-class sufferer is unlikely to be encouraged or aided in the seeking of types of professional care that are unfamiliar to that group.[27] With this problem in mind, contemporary union health programs and progressive health programs for the poor in the United States seem to be developing referral agents who have the time to listen to complaints in detail and the knowledge to make specialized referrals.

In contrast to the lower-class, the middle-class patient participates in what I have called a cosmopolitan system. First of all, he needs less help from others. Markedly more prone to make decisions about medical care without the aid of lay consultants outside the household, more familiar with abstract criteria for professional qualifications, better acquainted with a number of professional practices if only by his residential mobility, and more knowledgeable about illness itself, he is likely to feel more secure in his own diagnosis and his own assessment of the virtues of the care he receives. However, if he should ask help from his potential lay consultants, since they are as knowledgeable as he, and since they have had experience in a number of localities, they would likely extend immeasurably his contacts by citing alternative sources of diagnosis and treatment and by the sophistication of their evaluation.[28]

26 See Daniel Rosenblatt and Edward Suchman, "Awareness of Physician's Social Status Within an Urban Community," *Journal of Health and Human Behavior,* VII (1966), 146–153.

27 One must not, however, underestimate the capacity for evaluating physician performance of the lower-class patient. See Arnold I. Kisch and Leo G. Reeder, "Client Evaluation of Physician Performance," *Journal of Health and Social Behavior,* X (1969), 51–58.

28 For a special problem of seeking help, see Nancy Howell Lee, *The Search for an Abortionist* (Chicago: University of Chicago Press, 1969).

Types of Lay Referral Systems

It should be clear that in the course of my discussion I have been condensing the whole set of cultural elements involved in responses to illness—for example, the view of the body, the interpretation of pain and of various symptoms, knowledge of illness, and attitudes toward modern medicine—into the superficially simple and isolated act of utilizing medical services. Utilization is seen as the professionally or officially desired culmination of a social process by which one is brought into contact with medical institutions after one has come to believe he is ill. Indeed, in my analysis I attempt to use utilization as the key dependent variable of the social process of becoming ill. Furthermore, since my independent variables are composed of the content and structure of the lay social life surrounding the initial perception of symptoms, not the characteristics of the individuals showing such symptoms, the dependent variable is composed of *rates of utilization to be found in specific populations.* Insofar as my analysis leads to prediction, then, it does not refer to individuals but to populations.

It should also be clear that in one way or another I have been implying that certain elements of lay experience are critical determinants of utilization. For one thing, I argue that cultural variation from professionally approved notions of illness and treatment will reduce utilization of medical services—an almost ridiculously obvious statement that wants a great deal more systematic and detailed elaboration before it is worth very much serious attention. But I have also been arguing something that should be made much more specific here and that is not half so obvious as the argument about culture. Specifically, I argue that the structure or organization of the lay community is also a factor influencing utilization, in that it organizes the process of becoming ill by pressing the sufferer into or away from the professional consulting room. The organization of lay referrals can enforce a particular orientation toward illness, or it can be so loose as to leave the individual fairly free of others' influence, to make decisions contrary to that of his peers without having to suffer their ridicule or scorn. In sum, I wish to suggest that between them, these two variables—the content and the structure of the system—can be used to create a purely logical typology of lay referral systems that can predict the rates of utilization of professional services.[29]

First, there is a system in which prospective clients participate primarily in an indigenous lay culture that is markedly different from that of professionals and in which there is a highly extended, cohesive lay referral structure. In this indigenous extended system the clientele may be expected to show a high degree of resistance to using health services. If, for example, prospective patients are prone to believe that hereditary gifts such as "touch" are prerequisite to the diagnostic competence of a healer, professional authority is unlikely to be recognized at all, and the illness that emerges is unlikely to be one physicians will impute. The force of such cultural difference is intensified by the extended and cohesive referral structure. Anyone inclined as an individual to try a professional practitioner and unable to do so secretly must first run a gauntlet of antiprofessional advice. Obviously, in this situation the folk or indigenous practitioner will be used by most people, and professional practitioners will be used by few—perhaps by only the socially isolated deviant or the desperate man clutching at straws after all conventional devices have failed.

The second type of lay referral system has the same indigenous culture as the first but varies in having a truncated referral structure which allows the individual to act entirely on his own or at least to consult no one outside of his immediate family. While the culture of the system discourages the individual from seeking a physician, reinforcement by an extended network of interpersonal influence, which leaves the individual more vulnerable to influence by outsiders from the medical system, is missing. All else being equal, the individual may be expected to try professional services sooner and under less desperate circumstances than a person in the indigenous extended system.

The third type is the opposite of the indigenous extended lay referral system. It is found when lay and professional culture are very much alike and when the lay referral structure is truncated. The prospective client is pretty much on his own, guided more or less by his own understandings and experience, with few lay con-

[29] Much of the following, somewhat revised, stems from Freidson, *op. cit.*, pp. 192–207.

sultants to support or discourage his search for help. Since his knowledge and understandings are much like the physician's, he may take a great deal of time trying to treat himself for disorders he feels competent to handle, but nonetheless will go directly from self-treatment to a physician. He is unlikely to use a nonprofessional consultant unless the failure of the medical system makes him desperate.

In the fourth type of lay referral system, the prospective patient is even less likely to use the services of a nonmedical healer. It involves an extended and cohesive referral structure and a culture similar to that of the professional. The acceptance of professional culture is considerably more likely to be reinforced than in the case of a professionally oriented person who participates in a truncated structure, and utilization of professional services is thus likely to be maximal.

In looking at Table 5, one may note that "congruence" defines the *content* of the lay societal reaction to deviance, while "cohesiveness" defines the degree to which that reaction is so organized as to be escapable or inescapable by the individual. Assumed in the idea of cohesiveness is extensive interaction within a relatively homogeneous group of the sort that social psychological studies hold to have great influence on the individual. The disease believed to be involved is one of the things to be held constant in any attempt to predict utilization, for it is obviously a significant variable in that one is unlikely to consult others at all before seeking help for an unambiguously critical illness in circumstances where the accessi-

TABLE 5. PREDICTED RATES OF UTILIZATION OF PROFESSIONAL SERVICES, BY VARIATION IN LAY REFERRAL SYSTEM

Lay Referral Structure	*Lay Culture*	
	Congruent with Professional	*Incongruent with Professional*
Loose, Truncated	Medium to high utilization	Medium to low utilization
Cohesive, Extended	Highest utilization	Lowest utilization

bility of help is high.[30] But I believe that the typology makes sense of utilization both simply and usefully by focusing on the two most generally salient sociological variables involved in the process of seeking medical care. Indeed, its logic seems to have been confirmed generally by several studies that were based on it.

Suchman's study, which was originally planned and formulated with the notion of variations in lay referral systems in mind, sought to determine how such variations were related to ethnic patterns of seeking care in New York City.[31] It was found, for example, that Puerto Ricans had the least positive attitude toward modern medicine, Jews and Protestants the most. Furthermore, the Puerto Rican was found to participate in a parochial organization of homogeneous and closely knit interpersonal relations, which was also associated with poor knowledge about disease, skepticism about medical care, and high dependency in illness. In essence, the findings describe the empirical characteristics of some actual lay referral systems in New York City, including both culture and structure, but without clarifying the logical and consequential relations among them.

The Raphael study[32] used as its dependent variable the utilization of a free child-guidance clinic in Chicago. The essential independent variables were the congruence of community culture with professional notions of mental illness and its treatment (which was roughly measured by the formal educational level of the community) and the degree of social cohesion in the community (which was roughly measured by the proportion of inter- or intra-city migrants). Reasoning that the professional view of mental illness is innovative—that is, not normally to be found in a lay community—Raphael attempted to predict the diffusion and acceptance of that view (measured by clinic utilization) by variations in the level of education of the community and the degree of mobility of its residents.

Classifying her communities by the above typology of lay referral systems, she found that the rates of utilization were lowest in com-

[30] See the review by Irwin M. Rosenstock, "Why People Use Health Services," *Milbank Memorial Fund Quarterly*, XLIV (1966), 94–124.

[31] Edward A. Suchman, "Sociomedical Variations Among Ethnic Groups," *American Journal of Sociology*, LXX (1964), 319–331.

[32] Edna E. Raphael, "Community Structure and Acceptance of Psychiatric Aid," *American Journal of Sociology*, LXIX (1964), 340–358.

munity areas with residents who had comparatively little education and were long-time residents and highest in communities with well-educated, mobile residents. Rates in the other two (mixed) types of community were in between. The structural axis (measured by migration) seemed to be responsible for more variation in rates than was the cultural axis (measured by education), since it was found that the more stable the structure, with less migration, the lower the examined-case rate. Furthermore, Raphael found that in spite of variation in the number of cases examined from the various community areas, there was no statistically significant difference among them in the severity of psychiatric disorder, though there was a tendency for areas with the highest utilization to have sent a greater proportion of children who were not seriously disturbed, and those with the lowest utilization to have sent a greater proportion of severely disturbed children.

Finally, particularly interesting because it points to the linkage of lay with professional systems (to which I shall turn in the next chapter), Raphael examined who had referred the child to the guidance clinic, which is to say, who defined the difficulty as a mental disorder. The definers, or agents of referral, varied by the type of community. The largest proportion of "voluntary referrals" —that is, self-referrals by parents—came from the areas with higher education and from areas with high migration. School and social agency referrals, however, were more likely to come from areas with "incompatible" cultures. In the latter case, then, the child had to become entangled with community agencies in some way before he was likely to be referred, an entanglement that may involve official decisions independent of the child's or the parents' inclinations: the professional system is more likely to have to be imposed on the lay system when the latter deviates from the former.

Raphael's findings raise several important questions about my assumption that the utilization rate of health services can be explained by the type of lay referral system characteristic of a community. First, we must note that the findings do not confirm what was predicted: communities that were classified as "tight-compatible" (cohesive-congruent in the table) did *not* show the highest utilization of services. It was the loosely organized community that showed the highest utilization, which implies that circumstances in which people were free of the influence of others most encouraged utilization. However, Kadushin's study of the undertaking of psychotherapy implies quite the reverse—that a circle of like-minded friends facilitates the decision to seek professional care.[33] And so does the large body of research on personal influence.[34] Consequently, I think it is reasonable to assume that the measures used in Raphael's study are insufficiently precise—that level of education is an inadequate indicator of "culture" which is compatible with professional norms of mental health.

The use of mental-health services tends generally to be stigmatized by the average layman[35] and is likely to be stigmatized also by the Chicago communities studied. The well educated may stigmatize it less, but nonetheless are likely to do so to a significant degree. Such stigmatization is not congruent with the norms of the professionals staffing the mental-health services. Where such stigmatization exists, and where no contact can be made with a special social circle of the sort that Kadushin described,[36] it is plausible that decisions to seek care would be largely individual in character and would be more likely to occur in situations when the person is free to act privately as an individual—in situations in which the referral structure is loose and truncated. And in situations where an individual is not free to act by himself because of participation in a cohesive extended structure, and where his associates stigmatize the use of psychotherapy, the professional sector must intervene to reach out to take what few cases it can get. These are the situations that Raphael's findings seem to represent.

Types of Illness Entering Consultation

Obviously, it is necessary to be rather more specific about the illness involved in utilization and the lay reaction to that illness. The

[33] See Charles Kadushin, "The Friends and Supporters of Psychotherapy: On Social Circles in Urban Life," *American Sociological Review,* XXXI (1966), 786–802, and Charles Kadushin, *Why People Go To Psychiatrists* (New York: Atherton Press, 1968).

[34] Cf. Rogers, *op. cit.*

[35] See Derek L. Phillips, "Rejection, A Possible Consequence of Seeking Help for Mental Disorders," *American Sociological Review,* XXIX (1963), 963–972.

[36] Kadushin, *op. cit.*

medical illness involved in Raphael's study was, for the laymen, stigmatized—more so for the poorly than for the well educated, but stigmatized by all. As I have already noted, stigmatized illnesses are kept secret from others where possible and are underreported to professionals. People inclined to seek treatment for them are likely to do so when they can do so privately and individually, without public knowledge, since, at least in the case of mental illness, the use of the treatment service itself is stigmatized. Therefore, there is likely to be considerable delay in obtaining consultation when individual and private action is difficult. Similarly, if an illness is believed by laymen to be chronic or incurable, we should expect that utilization of professional services will occur less often than when the illness is believed to be curable, and that it will in any case be delayed.[37] That is, late rather than early cases of the illness are likely to enter the consultation room. The illness will not, however, be hidden like a stigmatized illness. Entrance into consultation, then, must be seen in the context of the sociological types of illness the layman defines in contrast to what is defined by the medical world. The notion of the congruence of lay culture with professional definitions must therefore include not only whether or not laymen perceive pain and symptoms but also how they define the illness sociologically. The legitimacy of the illness is not, however, the only dimension defining sociological types of illness. The other is the degree of seriousness imputed to the illness, and on this as well as on the type of legitimacy imputed to the deviance laymen differ from professionals, some of course differing more than others. Types of legitimacy and degree of seriousness each may have consequences for entering consultation.

The kind of legitimacy imputed to the illness seems likely to have the most direct effect on the amount of utilization in that *conditionally legitimate* types of illness frequently (though not always) require legitimation by an authoritative practitioner. Of the corpus of conditionally legitimate illness, we should expect consultation in a large percentage of cases. For the *unconditionally legitimate* illnesses, however, we should expect a lesser proportion to reach con-

[37] See Barbara Blackwell, "The Literature of Delay in Seeking Medical Care for Chronic Illnesses," *Health Education Monographs*, No. 16 (1963), pp. 3–31.

sultation because of their a priori legitimacy and their hopelessness. In what utilization there is, there will be comparatively little preoccupation with obtaining professional legitimation. Instead, improvement or palliation will be sought, or the hope will be pursued that the consultant may be able to redefine the illness as curable. Of the corpus of *illegitimate* illnesses, we should expect the smallest proportion to reach consultation, given the shame and secrecy connected with them, and the ineradicable character of stigma. Some utilization may stem from the hope that by consulting professionals who deny stigma to any illness, a new dignity if not a redefinition of the illness and a new identity may result. Others have simply been driven into professional custody by the rejection of those around them.

Utilization should also vary by the degree of seriousness imputed to the illness. All kinds of illnesses will be less likely to be led into consultation when they are defined as minor than when they are defined as serious. Of the three types of legitimacy, however, those *minor* illnesses defined as *conditionally legitimate* are most likely to reach consultation, for as I have noted, consultation is sometimes required for their legitimation even if they are minor. A lesser proportion of minor cases of *unconditionally legitimate* and *illegitimate* illnesses is likely to enter consultation except in those instances where some hope exists that the lay definitions are mistaken—that a condition is curable or improvable, or that a stigma or stigmatized attribute may be eradicated by professional redefinition or by specific technical procedures.

Entering the Professional Domain

In this chapter my analysis has moved through the entire length of the social course of illness that lies wholly in the domain of the layman, from the ostensibly rudimentary experience of discomfort, through the search for the meaning of the discomfort and for methods of coping with it, to entrance into consultation. Of course, at each point people drop out to go no further: one may decide that the discomfort is "nothing" and the matter be dropped; another may decide that it is only to be suffered and go no further. And one may enter the consultation room of a folk, rather than of a medical, practitioner. But it is the medical consultant who concerns me here, so that my analysis has sought to specify the conditions under which he will be seen.

In the course of my analysis of the conditions leading to the utilization of medical services I emphasized the concept of lay referral system for two reasons. First, it or some such concept seems more useful and appropriate for predicting utilization rates for a community or a similar natural collectivity than does such an individual decision-making model as has been advanced by Rosenstock[38] or an inventory of personal and social variables such as has been listed by Mechanic.[39] Second, and more importantly, I emphasized the concept of lay referral system because implicit in it is the idea of an organized societal reaction to illness, a reaction that is selective in picking out one attribute for attention rather than another, that declares it serious rather than minor, and that exerts potent pressure on the individual to behave accordingly. In short, the lay referral system mobilizes the layman's perception of discomfort and directs it into specific outcomes. In some cases the layman's discomfort remains a primary deviation. In others, however, it is led or pushed down the path toward special management, and it becomes organized into a special role.[40]

When the societal reaction sends the layman into professional consultation, it has moved him into a different domain—that of the profession. Some of the force of the societal reaction must be lost at the door. At the point of entrance into consultation, lay conceptions of illness no longer stand by themselves. They enter into direct and explicit interaction with those of the physician. Furthermore, at the point of entrance into consultation, the layman moves into a new position: he comes to interact as a client with professionals who, by the nature of their status, seek to control the terms and content of their work. Indeed, as professionals, they have succeeded

[38] Rosenstock, *op. cit.*

[39] Mechanic, *op. cit.*, pp. 128–157.

[40] This mode of reasoning also seems applicable to the study of how people come to use legal services, though it has not yet been used in the few studies thus far. For a recent report which reflects the state of the field, see Leon Mayhew and Albert J. Reiss, Jr., "The Social Organization of Legal Contacts," *American Sociological Review*, XXXIV (1969), 309–318.

fairly well in gaining that control. Since the layman is but one object of their work, they see their interaction with him as a problem of management, a problem of controlling as well as curing him. It is that interaction between lay and professional systems, that struggle for control and its outcome, that I turn to in the next chapter.

14.

THE SOCIAL ORGANIZATION OF ILLNESS

IN the last chapter I discussed the variables that seem to be important for predicting the likelihood that members of a population will enter the medical consulting room. Some of the variables are similar to those predicting the likelihood that members of a population will buy a new product or adopt a new innovation.[1] In spite of that similarity, though, there are essential differences between the use of a professionally controlled service or product and the use of a commercial product—differences that stem from the status of the profession. The status of the profession allows it to shape the official recognition of need for service as well as the way that need will be organized by the service it controls. It is in this sense that the social organization of treatment may be seen to create the conditions by which the experience of being ill, the relationships one has with others when ill, and the very life of the sick person become organized. It is these conditions and these consequences that I wish to focus on in this chapter. I wish to show how, once one enters the professional domain, that domain imposes organization on the experience and manifestation of illness.

[1] For a summary of much of this material see Everett Rogers, *Diffusion of Innovation* (New York: The Free Press of Glencoe, 1962).

Medicine as an Official Institution

What is distinct about a complex civilization like ours, compared to a simple society, is the existence of special classes of men who are engaged on a full-time basis in creating knowledge, formulating laws, morals, and procedures, and applying knowledge and moral principles to concrete cases. These men formulate and administer a special corpus of social meanings that is always different in kind from the social meanings of the ordinary citizenry.[2] What these men do contributes to the official *social* order, and although the content of a viable official order is rarely wholly divorced from that of the average citizen, it is different. The official social order is politically and culturally dominant, reflecting the values and knowledge of the dominant classes of the society. It is not necessarily hostile to the values of everyday life, but it is nonetheless imposed on everyday life, and its imposition is supported by organized political, economic and normative forces.

In the modern postindustrial society, the practicing professions compose part of the official order and, as Parsons pointed out, are agents for social control.[3] Supported by the power of the state, they have official mandate to apply their knowledge and values to the world about them. Their mandate is to define whether or not a problem exists and what the "real" character of the problem is and how it should be managed. Given the fact that they have *special* knowledge and values, it cannot fail to be that their conceptions will be different from that of the man on the street: where there are experts, there are laymen by definition. And when experts constitute a profession, their knowledge and values become part of the official order which, however enlightened, liberal, and benevolent, is nonetheless imposed on the everyday world of the layman.

Professionals are said to be schooled in some special skill that is part of civilization. Their job is to apply those skills, and in application they are likely to have some special influence by virtue of their

[2] See the contrast between the "great tradition" and the "little tradition" in Robert Redfield, *Peasant Society and Culture* (Chicago: University of Chicago Press, 1956).

[3] See Talcott Parsons, "Propaganda and Social Control" in his *Essays in Sociological Theory, Pure and Applied* (New York: The Free Press of Glencoe, 1949), pp. 275–309.

relations with organized political power in the community and by virtue of their prestige among laymen. They are not merely experts but rather incumbents in official positions.[4] As the state assumes more responsibility for the welfare of the layman, professionals become members of the class of caretakers, and the possibilities increase for differences between their perspective and that of laymen. Given the official status of the profession, what happens to the layman—that is, whether or not he will be recognized as "really" sick, what the sickness will be called, what treatment will be given him, how he will be required to act while ill, and what will happen to him after treatment—becomes a function of professional rather than lay decision. As functionaries who, by virtue of their professional qualifications, are granted the license to make everyday decisions related to the welfare of their clientele, they certify sick leave, sign workmen's compensation and insurance forms, commitment forms, and eligibility forms of many kinds. Furthermore, on an everyday basis they serve as gatekeepers to special resources (the most obvious of which are hospital beds and "ethical" drugs) that cannot be used without their permission. Thus, the behavior of the physician and others in the field of health constitutes the objectification, the empirical embodiment, of certain dominant values in a society.

It is important to understand the consequences of medicine's official status for the freedom of the patient to follow his own notions of illness and illness behavior. While the layman does exercise choice in seeking professional care, it is a considerably less free choice than in the nonprofessional marketplace. The range of choice is limited by the licensing of healers. Given that limited range, the choice tends to be more among institutions than among products or services. To quote an economist's characterization of the medical marketplace,

> The physician, not the patient, combines the components of care into a treatment. In other markets the consumer, with varying degrees of knowledge, selects the goods and services he desires from the available alternatives. In medical care,

[4] See Eliot Freidson, *Professional Dominance* (New York: Atherton Press, forthcoming), Chapter 4.

> however, the patient does not usually make his choice directly. . . . He selects a physician who then makes . . . choices for him.[5]

It is as if the housewife could choose the store she wished to patronize but not which of the articles in the store she could buy. The choice is made for her by those who run the store on the basis of their conception of what she "really" needs, which may be no articles at all, articles she does not want, or, if she is lucky, just what she wants.

Types of Practice and the Marketplace

There is, however, more leeway open to the medical consumer in the early stages of his illness than I have implied. Such leeway is available by virtue of the fact that there are various kinds of stores in the medical marketplace, some having different stock than others, and some having a different relationship to the consumer than others. Some are analogous to the small neighborhood groceries, carrying a variety of wares, open at all hours to get what business they can, and otherwise obliging to their customers; others are analogous to shops with an exclusive franchise over scarce and desirable goods. Some are embedded in the local customs and the round of life of the neighborhood; others are separate from the neighborhood, physically and culturally. When the prospective patient enters the former he is relatively free to choose the services he will get; when he chooses the latter he is likely to have to settle for what will be given him.

Let us recall where the analysis is at this point. Those who have chosen to use no practitioner have dropped out of my concern, as have those who have chosen a nonmedical practitioner. We are confronted with those who believe themselves to have an illness requiring medical consultation. Now, we may ask, what consultant do they choose, and with what consequences for the social definition of their illness and for the organization of their illness behavior? On the whole, given the inclination of lay as well as medical men to impute common and minor illness first, before deciding on an unusual and serious illness, the initial choice of medical consultants

[5] Paul J. Feldstein, "Research on the Demand for Health Services," *Milbank Memorial Fund Quarterly*, XLIV (1966), Part II, p. 138.

by laymen is likely to be of some kind of generalist—the consultant who handles the common and minor ills of everyday life. In nations where practice is still carried on in individual, neighborhood offices, the consultant most likely to be chosen first is the general practitioner, the internist, or the pediatrician.[6]

Those everyday consultants have practices which depend for their clientele upon the individual's own choice of their services or upon other laymen referring the individual. In terms suggested in Chapter 5, they are "client-dependent practices." The very survival of the practices of such consultants tends to depend upon receiving lay referrals. And insofar as lay referrals are inevitably based on lay understandings of illness and its treatment, it follows that survival depends upon the compatibility of the diagnosis and treatment used by the practitioner with those used by laymen. The practitioner must on occasion give in to his patients' prejudices if they are to return to him and to refer other patients to him. Thus, those in such practices are likely to honor lay demands for such popular remedies as vitamin B-12 injections, copious use of antibiotics, and prescription of tranquillizers, sedatives, and stimulants. The content of their diagnostic and treatment practices, like the stock on the neighborhood grocer's shelves, reflects their position between two worlds, at the hinge where the lay system connects with the professional.[7]

The client-dependent practitioner is one who by definition depends upon laymen for the referrals and choices that provide him with his "business." In this, he is similar to the neighborhood shopkeeper. Also like the neighborhood shopkeeper, however, the practitioner always has some relations with the world outside the neighborhood—with pharmaceutical houses, medical societies, hospitals, and specialists. Insofar as the practitioner is a professional, and insofar as he requires the aid of colleagues and medical institutions to carry out his work, he participates in a *professional referral*

[6] Much of the following stems from Eliot Freidson, *Patients' Views of Medical Practice* (New York: Russell Sage Foundation, 1961), pp. 192–207.

[7] See the comments on the way practitioners, due to their fear of losing status and income, were overresponsive to their patients' demands for hospitalization, and for acceptable diagnoses and therapies in Raymond S. Duff and August B. Hollingshead, *Sickness and Society* (New York: Harper and Row, 1968), p. 382.

system that extends outside of the local circle of laymen on whom his practice depends. The professional system is composed of the specialists, clinics, superspecialists, university hospitals, and other institutions standing outside the referring physician's neighborhood. The first-line practitioner in a client-dependent practice refers those cases he cannot deal with effectively to other practices in the professional referral system. Those other practices have much different structural characteristics than his.

Unlike the first-line practitioner, the consultant who receives referrals from other professionals is not dependent on client choice for his professional survival. He is dependent instead on the referrals of colleagues, thus having a *colleague-dependent practice*. As such, he must be sensitive more to the needs and prejudices of professionals than of laymen, and so may be expected to employ medically approved procedures more than those with which the patient has familiarity and sympathy. However, while the patient may choose his own first-line service in the person of the first-line practitioner, once the physician he chooses confesses his failure or incapacity to cure and refers him deeper into the professional system, the patient is often able to do no more than to choose to accept what is offered him or drop out of the system entirely against the weight of medical advice. When he enters a colleague-dependent practice he has little of the influence available to him in client-dependent practice and must accept the services chosen for him. Only in such a practice does the economist's model of the professional marketplace become realized: there, one must take what another says he needs.

These two types of practice imply two gross variations in the shape of interaction in consultation. In client-dependent practice, the patient is likely to be in the position of an equal, or at least of an active participant in the process of diagnosis and management. Being in a relatively early stage of illness and not yet overcome by pain or fear, he always has before him (as the practitioner well knows) the prospect of leaving the office and, instead of coming back, of looking elsewhere for a consultant who uses more familiar notions of illness and treatment. In a colleague-dependent practice, however, the patient is likely to be in the more desperate position of a person whose own conventional remedies and consultants have failed him, with few options open to him. In the former situation the process of treatment is far more likely to be a matter of bargaining and compromise than in the latter, where the weight of professional opinion is heavier than that of the layman. By the same token, in the former situation the choice of illness and of its management is likely to be more variable and flexible than in the latter.

The Professional Task in Consultation

I have spoken of "leverage," of "bargaining," and of "controls" in the consulting room, words which seem more compatible with the economic marketplace and the political arena than with professional consultation. This usage, however, is deliberate, for the thrust of this book is to secularize a phenomenon that has been greatly obscured by a tendency to treat it as something mysteriously apart from normal human affairs, with a mystique other affairs lack. I have emphasized the social, and therefore variable, character of the problem at issue, the ambiguity and arbitrariness of, if not the knowledge, then at least the concepts to which the knowledge is attached, and, particularly in this chapter, the extent to which the work involves a problem of social control.

While the word "control" may seem odd in medical settings where the euphemism "management" is more common, it should be clear that the word is accurate. Obviously, the physician's task is the same as that of any other occupation—to do his work in the ways his knowledge leads him to believe is correct. And, as is the same for some other occupations, his work consists in providing a service to other people. The problem is, how is that service defined and who defines it? As a profession, medicine asserts its autonomy in defining what is "appropriate," "effective," or "good" service. As a profession it claims that its mission is to provide such good service to its clientele. It is not as if the professional, like the obliging shopkeeper, can claim his merit in satisfying the customer by giving him exactly what he wants. Rather, the profession asserts what the customer's "real" wants are by virtue of its special knowledge and, as an "ethical" occupation, attempts to provide services appropriate to those wants it defines. But in order to exercise its mandate the profession must on occasion provide its clients with services they may not want. In doing so, it must in some way manipulate or exercise control over the patient. And while in the exercise of such control the profession may not be motivated by the cynical dishonesty of the legendary salesmen who sell refrigerators to Eskimo, encyclopedias to the illiterate, and oversized suits to undersized men, at least some of the techniques of control the profession uses are likely to be shared with all other occupations that supply services or goods to others. Ethicality is not an issue. It is the demand of work which is critical.

Let us look at consultation more closely. The patient enters consultation with his own tentative definition of what ails him. Put simply, the task of the physician is (1) to determine what is "actually" wrong with the patient, and (2) to get the patient to follow his advice, including the advice that he has nothing "really" wrong with him. These two problematic tasks are usually referred to as the tasks of diagnosis and of treatment. In both cases, what is at issue is performance in a professionally defined manner—that is, the diagnosis of medically approved illnesses on the basis of information considered by medicine to be reliable, and the administration of the properly "scientific" treatment for the illness.[8]

In the case of *diagnosis*, the consultant must obtain information of the sort relevant to medicine rather than to lay cultures. Patently, given the variation in lay culture, the tasks of "taking a history"—collecting information from the patient about past illness and symptoms which may be related to his present complaint—can sometimes be rather difficult. The patient may specify diffuse rather than localized pain, for example, or may express his subjective feelings rather than analyze his symptoms from the point of view of the physician, or may fail to remember anything about the events or experiences leading up to his complaint, or may lack a recollection of whether or not he had any identifiable illnesses, adverse drug reactions, or the like in the past. In the case of *treatment*, the consultant may be confronted with other problems. The patient may disagree with his recommendations, or he may not be accustomed to organizing his life in such a way as to be able to follow instructions about adopting a systematic and self-conscious regimen—even so common a regimen as taking medication regularly, after every

[8] See Milton Davis, "Variations in Patients' Compliance with Doctors' Advice," *American Journal of Public Health*, LVIII (1968), 274–288.

meal (if he takes three meals a day) or every four hours (if he has a watch). How can the physician cope with such problems?

The Organization of Illness in Ambulatory Care

To accomplish his task of diagnosis and treatment the physician may adopt a variety of tactics. First, by restricting himself to a well-educated clientele, he assures himself that his patients will share most of his scientific orientation and so will follow his recommendations. Second, he may devote himself to the long-term "education" or socialization of his clientele by attempting to teach them about his conception of illness and treatment so that they will share his orientation. Third, where his clientele may not be counted on to follow his recommendations outside the consulting room (whether by lack of capacity or motivation), he may attempt to extend his practice into their homes by making home visits or by sending nurses or other paramedical personnel into patients' homes. Or he may try to adjust his practice to their habits by having longer hours, including evenings and weekends, and by locating his practice close to their homes. Fourth, he may try to bypass the patient wherever he can: instead of struggling with a history, the physician may do a thorough physical examination and then order many laboratory screening tests; instead of lecturing about the necessity for regular administration of medication throughout the day, he may administer slow-releasing injections or pills and ask the patient to return regularly for such administration. Finally, I might mention the tactic of co-opting the kin and other laymen around the patient to serve as agents of the practitioner. The patient's social environment thus becomes a therapeutic enterprise guided by professional conceptions of illness and treatment.

All of these devices leave the patient in his community, and most of them are predicated on an ambulatory pattern of care. The patient merely visits a medical setting periodically and briefly, coming from and returning to his kin, friends, and neighbors. In such a situation the physician cannot exercise precise and extensive control. Because of this, ambulatory care, when it includes an attempt to extend medical practices deep into the lay institutions of the community, has been employed primarily for illnesses which are not considered medically serious and for those which are at once chronic and stable enough to require comparatively infrequent professional surveillance. In both cases, illness behavior becomes organized primarily by the life of the lay community.

The social behavior surrounding most cases of illness that are managed on an ambulatory basis is not organized in a very definite fashion. Most frequently, as in the case of the common cold and minor "impairments" in our time, a sick role is not adopted at all and the illness merely tempers the performance of normal roles. Less frequently, but commonly nonetheless, the patient goes through the simple and brief "sick role cycle," [9] involving consultation, a temporary release from some obligations, and a return to "normal." The sufferer's everyday life and his social identity are only touched by such incidents. There is, in fact, in these instances barely enough change in the sufferer's life to allow one to make useful reference to the notion of sick role.

The behavior of the sick person comes to assume a more definite pattern when he is thought to have a chronic illness requiring long-term and sustained contact with a practitioner. Such an organized pattern of behavior emerges when the behavior which is required of him is fairly complex and scheduled, and when by virtue of his belief in the treatment or by virtue of compulsion he may be relied on to conform to professional demands even when ambulatory. Such persons as the patient committed to his daily psychoanalysis, or the juvenile on probation ordered by the court to report daily for counseling in lieu of institutionalization, develop a new organization in their lives, an organization flowing from the professionally defined demands of their treatment. A woman in the later stages of pregnancy, a patient with brittle or labile diabetes, another with a decompensated heart condition, and many others can be seen to develop a round of life tempered by their own view of their illness and organized by the demands of regular professional observation and treatment of their difficulty. It is important to bear in mind that such a round of life is *not* organized by the disease and the biological incapacity it may produce but by pro-

[9] Cf. Bernard Goldstein and Paul Dommermuth, "The Sick Role Cycle: An Approach to Medical Sociology," *Sociology and Social Research*, XLVII (1961), 1–12.

fessional conceptions of the disease and of what is needed to treat it: the disease becomes a professionally organized illness.

However, so long as the patient is ambulatory, the organization of his activities around the demands of professional treatment is never complete. He may backslide, miss an appointment, or be late; the doctor may be called away on an emergency when the patient is due; either may go on vacation, so that the regimen is interrupted. It is only by institutionalization, where a staff is always present to carry out a regimen even when the physician is absent, and where the patient is always present to be treated, that medical management and the organization of the illness become wholly predictable. And since institutionalization separates the patient from the everyday activities he carried out in the community, his behavior must become organized solely by the round imposed by the institution and its treatment of him. Such organization is strengthened greatly by the fact that institutionalization limits the effective societal response to illness to the members of the staff alone, who in turn attempt to organize the experience of and the response to the illness by the way they view the illness and by their view of the proper way to manage it. Institutionalization can effectively neutralize the societal reactions of the patient's community associates.

The Institutional Organization of Responses to Illness

Remembering that for the sociologist, medical treatment constitutes one kind of societal reaction to a type of deviance, the essential fact bearing on the organization of illness in institutions is that the staff, unlike the patient himself or his lay associates, is performing a job. For the job to be performed at all requires some administrative routine, and it requires the reduction of individual patients to administrative and treatment classes, all members in each class to be managed by much the same set of routines. If the job is to be performed to the satisfaction of the staff, procedures that minimize interference with their routine and maximize their convenience are required.

Consequently, we find that there are standard administrative courses through which a patient is likely to travel in spite of variation in his condition from others in the same treatment category.

Rosengren and DeVault[10] observed that in one lying-in hospital the staff attempted to maintain a definite spatial and temporal organization of its work irrespective of individual variations in condition. In the traditional movement from admitting office, to prep room, labor room, delivery room, recovery room, and finally the lying-in room, no step was skipped even when the patient was well past the need of it; instead, she was moved through the step more rapidly than otherwise. By the same token, the staff tolerated the expression of pain by the patient only in the delivery room, where it was considered appropriate to the "illness" and where it could be managed by anesthetic: elsewhere, it was deprecated and ridiculed. And in order to maintain the "routine" tempo of work flow established by the staff, laggard women were helped along (with forceps and other techniques) to get them to deliver on schedule. Another example of the way the staff imposes standardized organization on the course of treatment (and therefore the social course of illness) is to be found in Roth's observations of the way the staff in tuberculosis hospitals has a conception of how long it "should" take to get cured that is imposed on the clinical course of the individual's illness, organizing the progressive steps of managing the illness on the basis of the normative timetable rather than on the results of laboratory tests that may be taken to reflect the biological status of the illness "itself."[11] And I cannot fail to mention, finally, that mordant analysis by Roth of the circumstances in which tuberculosis was and was not treated as infectious.[12]

In the process whereby the treatment institution can impose its own organization on the social behavior connected with illness, two prominent characteristics facilitate staff control. First, the patient may be isolated from the lay community and those of his associates who are concerned with his welfare. Contact with the lay world is carefully rationed where possible. While there may be medical reasons for such isolation, it is frequently a matter of administra-

[10] William R. Rosengren and Spencer DeVault, "The Sociology of Time and Space in an Obstetrical Hospital," in Eliot Freidson, ed., *The Hospital in Modern Society* (New York: The Free Press of Glencoe, 1963), pp. 266–292.

[11] Julius A. Roth, *Timetables, Structuring the Passage of Time in Hospital Treatment and Other Careers* (Indianapolis: Bobbs-Merrill Co., 1963).

[12] Julius A. Roth, "Ritual and Magic in the Control of Contagion," *American Sociological Review*, XXII (1957), 310–314.

tive convenience, minimizing "bother" for the staff more than protecting the patient from disturbance. The social consequences are to isolate the patient from the sources of social leverage that supported him while in ambulatory consultation and that could sustain his resistance to the therapeutic routine in the institution. Second, and more important, is the tendency of the staff of all such institutions to carefully avoid giving the patient or his lay associates much information about the illness and what is supposed to be done for it. Virtually every study of patients in hospital points out how ignorant of condition, prognosis, and the medically prescribed regimen are both the patients and their relatives and how reluctant is the staff to give such information.[13] In Davis' words, describing staff behavior toward parents of children stricken with poliomyelitis, the parents' questions were "hedged, evaded, rechannelled, or left unanswered."[14]

As Davis noted in his analysis, the staff's reluctance to give information is often explained as a desire to avoid an emotional scene with the parents. Sometimes, as Glaser and Strauss note in the case of the dying patient, the staff withholds information in the belief, based on "clinical experience," that it will protect the patient and his family from shock and excessive grief.[15] Sometimes this reluctance to give information is explained by a genuine uncertainty, so that no really reliable information is available. However, as Davis has noted in detail, "in many illnesses . . . 'uncertainty' is to some extent feigned by the doctor for the purpose of gradually getting the patient ultimately to accept or put up with a state-of-being that initially is intolerable to him."[16] Whatever the reason, however, the net effect of the withholding of information is to minimize the possibility that the patient can exercise much control over the way he is treated. If he does not know that he is supposed to have a yellow

[13] See the detailed analysis in Duff and Hollingshead, *op. cit.*, Chapter 13.

[14] Fred Davis, *Passage Through Crisis: Polio Victims and Their Families* (Indianapolis: Bobbs-Merrill Co., 1963), p. 64. For other observations on the extent to which patients are kept ignorant, see Ailon Shiloh, "Equalitarian and Hierarchal Patients," *Medical Care*, III (1965), 87–95.

[15] Barney G. Glaser and Anselm L. Strauss, *Awareness of Dying* (Chicago: Aldine Publishing Co., 1965), pp. 29ff.

[16] Davis, *op. cit.*, p. 67, and see Fred Davis, "Uncertainty in Medical Prognosis, Clinical and Functional," *American Journal of Sociology*, LXVI (1960), 41–47.

pill every four hours, he cannot comment on the fact that it is sometimes overlooked and insist on getting it regularly. And if he does not know that his condition normally responds to a given treatment in a week, he cannot insist on a consultation after several weeks have passed without change in condition or treatment.[17]

A great deal more can be said about the institutional shaping of illness, particularly in qualification of the point I have been trying to make here. Not all treatment institutions are the same, nor are all patients or treatment staffs. For example, the rehabilitation institution studied by Roth and Eddy[18] had a particularly powerful influence on the course of illness behavior because its patients were largely supported by public funds and lacked effective advocates from the community outside. They rarely, therefore, "got well enough" to leave. This helplessness is somewhat tempered by the fact that in rehabilitation, tuberculosis, and other institutions, many patients have similar illnesses and are in a position to socialize and organize each other. When these conditions exist, the patients are able to develop a common conception of the way their illness should be managed and to generate the influence required to impose some of their own conceptions on the staff.[19] Furthermore, institutions can be dominated by a staff ideology which specifies that the patient participate in his treatment. In fact, there are a number of patterns of interaction that reflect the degree of influence and activity allowed the patient in the course of his treatment and that express the meaning of his illness to himself and to those treating him.

Patterns of Interaction in Treatment

I have already suggested that when in treatment in a client-dependent practice, interaction will be fairly free between doctor and patient, the latter initiating and controlling some part of it.

[17] See James K. Skipper, Jr., "Communication and the Hospitalized Patient," in James K. Skipper, Jr., and Robert C. Leonard, eds., *Social Interaction and Patient Care* (Philadelphia: J. B. Lippincott Co., 1965), pp. 75–77.

[18] See Julius Roth and Elizabeth Eddy, *Rehabilitation for the Unwanted* (New York: Atherton Press, 1967).

[19] For a very useful discussion of the implications of such characteristics, see Stanton Wheeler, "The Structure of Formally Organized Socialization Settings," in O. G. Brim, Jr., and Stanton Wheeler, *Socialization After Childhood* (New York: John Wiley & Sons, 1966), pp. 53–116.

Conversely, when in treatment in a colleague-dependent practice, interaction will likely be lesser in quantity and less free, the physician initiating and controlling the greater part of it. By the time the patient reaches the latter practice, which often involves institutionalization, he has been rendered relatively helpless and dependent, perhaps, as Goffman suggests, already demoralized by a sense of having been stripped of some part of his normal identity.[20] In other cases he has been rendered helpless by his failure to find help on his own or by the way his physical illness has incapacitated him.

A second element that seems to be able to predict some part of the quality of the interaction between patient and physician lies in what physicians consider to be the demands of proper treatment for a given illness. This is to say, all that doctors do is not the same and does not require the same type of interaction. Following Szasz and Hollander's typology of doctor-patient relationships[21] but reversing the direction of analysis, we may note that under some circumstances—as in surgery and electroconvulsive therapy—the patient must be thoroughly immobilized and passive, wholly submissive to the activity of the physician. The work itself requires such minimal interaction: attendants, straps, anesthesia, and other forms of restraint are employed to enforce the requirement of submission. This model for interaction Szasz and Hollander call *activity-passivity*. In it, the patient is a passive object.

The second treatment situation, discussed by most writers as *the* doctor-patient relationship, is one in which the patient's consent to accept advice and to follow it is necessary. Here, the patient "is conscious and has feelings and aspirations of his own. Since he suffers . . . he seeks help and is ready and willing to 'cooperate.' When he turns to the physician, he places [him] . . . in a position of power. . . . The more powerful . . . will speak of guidance or leadership, and will expect cooperation of the other."[22] The interaction is

[20] See Erving Goffman, "The Moral Career of the Mental Patient," in his *Asylums* (New York: Anchor Books, 1961), pp. 125–161. In the context of the succeeding discussion of interaction, it is also appropriate to cite, in the same book, pp. 321–386, "The Medical Model and Mental Hospitalization."

[21] See Thomas S. Szasz and Mark H. Hollander, "A Contribution to the Philosophy of Medicine," *A.M.A. Archives of Internal Medicine,* XCVII (1956), 585–592.

[22] *Ibid.,* pp. 586–587.

expected to follow the model of *guidance-cooperation,* the physician initiating more of the interaction than the patient. The patient is expected to do what he is told; he assumes a less passive role than if he were anesthetized but a passive role nonetheless, submissive to medical requirements.

Finally, there is the model of *mutual participation,* found where patients are able or are required to take care of themselves—as in the case of the management of some chronic illnesses like diabetes—and therefore where initiation of interaction comes close to being equal between the two. Here, "the physician does not profess to know exactly what is best for the patient. The search for this becomes the essence of the therapeutic interaction." [23] Obviously, some forms of psychotherapy fall here.

Szasz and Hollander's scheme, however, is defective logically and empirically, for their models represent a continuum of the degree to which the *patient* assumes an *active* role in interaction in treatment without being extended to the logical point where the *physician* assumes a *passive* role. Such a defect reflects the characteristically normative stance of the medical thinker: while the existence of situations where the practitioner more or less does what the patient asks him to do may not be denied, such situations are rejected out of hand as intolerably nonprofessional, nontherapeutic, and nondignified to be conceded for mere logic and dignified by the recognition of inclusion.[24] Logic and fact do, however, require recognition, and they dictate the suggestion of two other patterns of interaction—one in which the patient guides and the physician cooperates, and one in which the patient is active and the physician passive. It is difficult to imagine an empirical instance of the latter possibility, which requires that the physician cease being a con-

[23] *Ibid.,* p. 589.

[24] This lack of concern for being logically consistent and systematic is characteristic of virtually all writing about the doctor-patient relationship by medical men. Another interesting analysis of the doctor-patient relationship explores other facets to be found in nature but restricts itself to the "pathological." See F. W. Hanley and F. Grunberg, "Reflections on the Doctor-Patient Relationship," *Canadian Medical Association Journal,* LXXXVI (1962), 1022–1024, where nine "syndromes" are constructed out of three stereotypical patients and three stereotypical physicians. So long as medical writers persist in crippling their logic by normative considerations, they cannot expect serious intellectual consideration.

sultant, so we may label it "merely" a logical construct. For the former instance, however, we may find empirical examples in a fair number of the interactions in client-dependent practices, particularly where the practice is economically unstable and the clientele of high economic, political, and social status.[25]

As I have noted, what distinguishes Szasz and Hollander's models from those I have added is the fact that they represent patterns of relations with patients that medical practitioners *wish* to establish and maintain on various occasions for various illnesses and patients. Assuming one type of interaction pattern is necessary for the therapist's work to proceed successfully, what social circumstances are prerequisite to its existence and how are they established? When the *activity-passivity* model does not automatically exist by virtue of coma or the like, some of the physician's behavior must be devoted to soothing the patient in order to get him to submit to the straps, injections, face-masks or whatever. The basic prerequisite, however, is *power* as such—sustained by the a priori incapacity of the patient, or by *making* the patient incapacitated. Such power is created by the fact that the individual is, let us say, unconscious and in a coma. In other instances, the exercise of power to overcome resistance when the patient is not in a coma is legitimized by the social identity imputed to the patient: he is just an infant, a cat, a retardate, a psychotic, or in some other way not fully human and responsible and so cannot be allowed to exercise his own choice to withdraw from treatment. Aside from circumstances where the patient's identity legitimizes the exercise of force, this pattern of interaction is most likely to be found where cultures diverge a great deal. There, few patients voluntarily enter medical consultation: their participation may be required by political power or may be facilitated by the incapacitating force of the disease itself.

The second pattern of interaction, *guidance-cooperation,* is essentially the one most people have in mind when they speak of the doctor-patient relationship. Obviously, its existence is contingent on a process that will bring people into interaction with the therapist in the first place, the process of seeking help that leads to the choice of utilizing one service rather than another. Here, the patient must

[25] See Freidson, *Patients' Views, op. cit.,* pp. 171–191 for historical and contemporary examples of such relationships.

exercise his own choice. Utilization is not merely something that facilitates establishing the relationship; it constitutes one-half of the battle in interaction: to actively choose to utilize a doctor in the first place requires that one in some degree concede his value and authority in advance[26] and that one in some degree already shares the doctor's perspective on illness and its treatment. The problem of interaction in treatment lies in the details of this acceptance, in the concrete areas in which lay and professional cultures converge. The doctor's tool for gaining acceptance is his "authority," which is not wholly binding by his incumbency in a formal legal position as expert.[27] Here, to the extent that the patient's culture is congruent with that of the professional, the authority of the latter is likely to be conceded in advance and reinforced in treatment by the fact that what the professional diagnoses and prescribes corresponds with what the patient expects and that communication between the two is relatively easy, so that confidence can be established when the professional must make new or unexpected demands on the patient. In this situation, what is problematic most of all is the physician's authority as such: it must be conceded before examination can begin and if treatment is to proceed. It is the *motive* for cooperation. Only secondarily problematic but problematic nonetheless is the capacity of the physician to make his desires for information and cooperation known and the capacity of the patient to understand the physician sufficiently to do as he is told. Essentially, then, faith and confidence on the part of the patient, and authority on the part of the physician, are the critical elements.

Finally, there is the pattern of *mutual participation*. Clearly, the interaction specified by this model requires characteristics on the part of the patient that facilitate communication. Communication is essential in order to determine what is to be done in therapy. Cultural congruence is thus obviously one necessary condition for such free interaction. According to Szasz and Hollander, the relationship "requires a more complex psychological and social organi-

[26] See Theodore Caplow, *The Sociology of Work* (Minneapolis: University of Minnesota Press, 1954), p. 114.

[27] See Eliot Freidson, *Professional Dominance, op. cit.*

zation on the part of both participants. Accordingly, it is rarely appropriate for children, or for those persons who are mentally deficient, very poorly educated, or profoundly immature. On the other hand, the greater the intellectual, educational and general experiential similarity between physician and patient the more appropriate and necessary this model of therapy becomes."[28] However, it is not only educational and experiential similarity but also a collaborative *status* that is required. Here the patient is not to merely accept the authority of the doctor; each must accept the other as an equal in the search for a solution to the problem. Deference on the part of either patient or physician is likely to destroy such mutual participation. Thus, status congruence is necessary to the relationship in order that the interaction of each *can* be fairly equal, and the influence of the doctor on the patient will hinge essentially not on physical power or professional authority but on his capacity to *persuade* the patient of the value of his views.[29]

These characterizations of different patterns of interaction may be used to distinguish (1) the needs of different kinds of medical work, (2) the way different kinds of illness are managed, and (3) the problems of practice that arise when the character of the lay community and particularly the lay referral system varies. (1) Veterinary medicine, pediatrics, and surgery are among those practices obviously prone to require the activity-passivity model, though the families of pets and pediatric patients are prone to interfere more than the model predicts. Internal medicine and general practice are among those prone to require the guidance-cooperation model. And verbal psychotherapy as well as rehabilitation and the treatment of the chronic diseases are all prone to need the mutual-participation model. (2) Stigmatized illnesses that spoil the identities of the sufferers are prone to be managed by the activity-passivity pattern, as are those with severe trauma, coma, and psychosis, and with patients who are extremely variant in culture or capacity: these characteristics prevent the patient *or* the physician from being socially responsive in treatment. In any single community, most "normal"

[28] Szasz and Hollander, *op. cit.*, p. 387.

[29] In this sense the influence of the expert rather than the authority of the professional is indicated.

—which is to say conditionally legitimate—illnesses are prone to be managed by the guidance-cooperation pattern; in those cases not clearly legitimized by lay culture (and so withholding authority from the physician), the mutual participation pattern is likely to be common and the pattern where the patient guides and the physician cooperates is possible. (3) I might note that the activity-passivity pattern of interaction in treatment is most likely to be found where lay culture diverges greatly from professional culture and where the status of the layman is very low compared to the professional. Where these divergences are lesser, the guidance-cooperation pattern is likely to be found, whereas where both the lay culture and status of the patient are very much like that of the professional, the mutual-participation pattern is likely to be used often.

The Conflict Underlying Interaction

In discussing interaction in treatment, I have adopted here, as elsewhere, a situational approach: I have attempted to discern whether some regularities in situations exist such that, by specifying the situation, we can predict the kinds of people likely to be in it, the kinds of illness, and the kinds and amount of interaction likely to take place. This seems to me to be an eminently useful approach, but we should not lose sight of the fact that it is merely an approach specifying regularities across arrays of individuals—statistical regularities. Furthermore, those regularities are defined as *relative*, not absolute. Nonetheless, it is unwise to assume too much regularity in the interaction in treatment settings. While the patient can be more or less excluded from assuming an active role in interaction, he can rarely be wholly excluded. He can at least, as do low-status and poorly educated patients everywhere, practice evasive techniques and act stupid in order to avoid some of what is expected of him. And while the patient can be involved in mutual participation by virtue of his similarity to the therapist, he is never wholly cooperative. Given the viewpoints of two worlds, lay and professional, in interaction, they can never be wholly synonymous. And they are always, if only latently, in conflict. Indeed, I wish to suggest that the most faithful perspective on interaction in treatment is one reflecting such conflict in standpoint, not on assuming an identity of purpose to be discovered by better education or a disposition to cooperate sometimes hidden by misunderstanding or by failure to cooperate.[30]

Hence, interaction in treatment should be seen as a kind of negotiation as well as a kind of conflict. This point is suggested in Balint's psychiatric sense that the patient is using his symptoms to establish a relationship with the physician[31] but more particularly in the sense of negotiation of separate conditions and of separate perspectives and understandings. The patient is likely to want more information than the doctor is willing to give him—more precise prognoses, for example, and more precise instructions. As Roth's study indicated, just as the doctor struggles to find ways of withholding some kinds of information, so will the patient be struggling to find ways of gaining access to, or inferring such information.[32] Similarly, just as the doctor has no alternative but to handle his cases conventionally (which is to say, soundly), so the patient will be struggling to determine whether or not he is the exception to conventional rules. And finally, professional healing being an organized practice, the therapist will be struggling to adjust or fit any single case to the convenience of practice (and other patients), while the patient will be struggling to gain a mode of management more specifically fitted to him as an individual irrespective of the demands of the system as a whole. These conflicts in perspective and interest are built into the interaction and are likely to be present to some degree in every situation. They are at the core of interaction, and they reflect the general structural characteristics of illness and its professional treatment as a function of the relations between two distinct worlds, ordered by professional norms.

The Institutional Organization of Being Ill

Understanding that no social structure organizes human behavior so much as directs it and poses its limits and that the indeterminacy

[30] For a more extended analysis of the conflict see Freidson, *Patients' Views, op. cit.*, pp. 171–191. And see the discussion in Carl Gersuny, "Coercion Theory and Medical Sociology," *Case Western Reserve Journal of Sociology,* II (1968), 14–20.

[31] See Michael Balint, *The Doctor, His Patient and the Illness* (New York: International Universities Press, 1957), *passim.*

[32] See Roth, *Timetables, op. cit.*, and Julius A. Roth, "Information and the Control of Treatment in Tuberculosis Hospitals," in Eliot Freidson, ed., *The Hospital in Modern Society, op. cit.*, pp. 293–318.

introduced by the conflict inherent between perspectives and the struggle for control flowing from it inevitably weaken the direct consequences of social structure for behavior and experience, we can nonetheless make useful and valid generalizations about behavior and experience from social structure alone. In the case of illness, it is necessary to remember that social structure exerts influence on illness in two ways. First, lay social structure organizes the initiation of contact between sick person and therapist: the biophysical course of the illness itself, insofar as spontaneous remission is not involved, is directly influenced by the competence of the therapist with whom the sick person is brought into contact. Second, and more importantly for my concern in this book, both lay and professional social structure organize the social state of being sick: whether or not one is "really" ill and can or must adopt a sick role; whether or not one may assume a new special social identity; whether or not one must assume the status of an object to be worked on by others; and whether or not one can ever again assume a normal identity and status in the everyday community. It is this second sense I refer to when I write of the social organization of illness.

The organization of professional institutions shapes both the status of illness and the organization of the process of assuming that status. As I have noted several times, for most people being ill is an isolated experience, limited in time and in social significance. However, in our day more and more illness becomes long-term. The label of deviance-as-illness has been extended into many new areas of social behavior by health professionals without at the same time being accompanied by effective methods of cure that can dissolve the status of illness quickly and permanently. In addition, the virtual elimination of the acute communicable diseases in our society has left many people alive long enough to experience the traditional chronic diseases, which are also not easily curable. Furthermore, these illnesses, being professional creations in the former case, and a traditional part of the professional domain in the latter, come to be organized by the network of professional institutions engaged in seeking them out, labeling, and managing them. Being ill becomes a long-term experience, frequently of some therapeutic ambiguity, and almost always of an increasingly definite social status as it is led through professional agencies. Its shape and content tend to become a function of the organization of the professional services through which the sufferer passes. Such organization has increasingly come to be extended down into the lay community and, insofar as it is formal organization, comes to impose more and more definite order on the process of being sick.

At an earlier time it may have been that the physician's office and the hospital he uses for acutely ill patients could represent by themselves the essential institutions of healing. At that time, most illness was at best only loosely organized by the scattered entrepreneurial practices of individual physicians. This is no longer true in societies such as ours. As I have pointed out in Chapter 2, there is now an enormous complex of independent, competing, overlapping, and linked institutions devoted to the identification, referral, and management of illness. Their representatives are located throughout the lay community, not only in the person of the first-line physician, but also in such everyday persons as the minister,[33] the school teacher, the personnel manager, and even the policeman.[34] Beyond these immediate representatives of the official order stands the variety of diagnostic and treatment agencies to which tentatively labeled cases of illness or impairment are referred. From the school, for example, come referrals to such practitioners as the dentist, ophthalmologist, otolaryngologist, and the orthopod, and to such institutions as the psychological clinic, the speech clinic, the social agency, and many others.[35] The referral is not of the same informal quality as those of lay associates; it is frequently an official referral, of which records are kept and with which compliance is not necessarily voluntary. Furthermore, it is based on professional and institutional criteria of deviance, not necessarily on those of the

[33] See Elaine Cumming and Charles Harrington, "Clergyman as Counselor," *American Journal of Sociology,* LXIX (1963), 234–243. For an indication of the extent to which the clergyman may serve as a referral agent, see Charles Kadushin, "Social Distance Between Client and Professional," *American Journal of Sociology,* LXVII (1962), 517–531.

[34] See Elaine Cumming *et al.*, "Policeman as Philosopher, Guide and Friend," *Social Problems,* XII (1965), 276–286, and Egon Bittner, "Police Discretion in Apprehending the Mentally Ill," *Social Problems,* XIV (1967), 278–292.

[35] Very little is known about the total system of health, education, and welfare agencies, and, most particularly, about their interrelationships. For a recent (and rare) attempt to characterize it empirically, see Elaine Cumming, *Systems of Social Regulation* (New York: Atherton Press, 1968).

lay community. And it is often independent of the desires of the individual or his lay associates. Such a referral mirrors the fact that the individual's official even if not community identity has been changed from "normal" to "problematic": it is intended to find a more precise label to attach officially to what has been singled out as problematic by the referrers and to prescribe the subsequent course of its official management.

While they may be specialized, initial referrals from official community institutions tend to be to fairly open diagnostic units. They are open in that they function to catch, attract, or receive a variety of tentatively labeled deviants; and they are diagnostic in that they begin to discriminate among them, setting them on different management routes. Here is where the discrimination between the malingerer and the "really" sick occurs; where a troublesome child is set on the road to being delinquent, feeble-minded, emotionally disturbed, brain-damaged, or whatever; where the "hard-of-hearing" become "really" deaf, and the "very nearsighted" become legally blind.[36] At such open diagnostic units the clientele is fairly heterogeneous and disorganized, but at the point of official diagnosis it becomes differentiated: some are returned to the community; some are sent to other diagnostic units; and others are kept to be treated or referred deeper into the treatment system connected with the diagnostic unit. In the case of those who are kept, diagnostic label and prescription become solidified and pressure is exerted on the incumbent of the deviant role to accept and cooperate with treatment by behaving "sensibly." If he is left in the community, the treatment agency may work with family, school, employer, and other everyday institutions in order to attempt to carve out a special deviant role in the social space surrounding the individual, a role reflecting the meaning of his illness and the regimen urged on him for his treatment. But if he is institutionalized, he can do no more than play his new deviant role, choosing only to play it badly or well. In concert with those others who have also been sorted into his diagnostic category, whether by all being institutionalized together under the same circumstances or by all seeking each other

[36] For an excellent, detailed picture of the role of agencies in defining and organizing the social role of blindness, see Robert A. Scott, *The Making of Blind Men* (New York: Russell Sage Foundation, 1969).

out for mutual support in a community of which they no longer feel themselves to be a normal part, he comes to take on a new identity, systematically playing an officially created deviant role.

From these comments it would follow that the more formal and rigid the social structure through which the person may be led or pushed, the more definite the social organization of his illness. In ambulatory care the social behavior and experience of the sick person can never be wholly or even mostly controlled by professional notions of illness and treatment. In contrast, when the sick person is institutionalized, the experience of being ill becomes far more amenable to organization by staff demands, for the person tends to lose his social and physical mobility, to be isolated from his lay associates, to be cut off from the information he would need in order to assume an active role in the management of his illness, and to be fitted into administrative routines organized to permit the staff to work in ways they consider effective and convenient. In fact, only when he is institutionalized can the sick person be restricted to performing only one role—that of the patient. In the community he almost always performs other roles along with that of the patient. Those other roles are left at the door on admission to a domiciliary institution and, save for visiting hours, the patient role comes to absorb all the person's efforts, day and night, waking and sleeping, in work and in play.

Since it is the institution that creates and organizes that patient role, we can use the structure of the institution itself to represent the way being sick becomes organized, experienced, and expressed by the individual who is in it. As Sudnow put it, "The categories of hospital life, e.g., 'life,' 'illness,' 'patient,' 'dying,' 'death,' or whatever, are to be seen as *constituted by the practices of hospital personnel* as they engage in their daily routinized interactions within an organization milieu." [37] By the same token we can use the organization of the whole complex of professional agencies leading up to institutionalization to represent the social organization of the career of becoming a sick person. And so it is that a profession and the institutions it dominates may be seen to collaborate with nature in

[37] David Sudnow, *Passing On, The Social Organization of Dying* (Englewood Cliffs, New Jersey: Prentice-Hall, 1967), p. 8.

creating and shaping the character of what its work is designed to manage.

Illness and Knowledge

In this part of my book I made a number of points about the nature of the knowledge and the practice, or the nature of the content of the work, of the profession. I pointed out first that the aim guiding medical work—the alleviation of illness—includes two distinct sets of knowledge. Most obvious is knowledge of the source of the illness and of the likelihood of its alleviation by one set of treatment activities rather than another. This is usually considered to be "the" knowledge of the profession. Less obvious is the knowledge surrounding the identification of illness as a form of social deviance. There, on an evaluative or moral rather than purely neutral, descriptive foundation, the profession picks out some state or characteristic and designates it as the kind of undesirable state which is called illness. I pointed out that the generically sociological task of analyzing illness lies in determining the course of those evaluations, their variety, and their consequences for social life. Addressing myself to that task I indicated that the important consequential meanings connected with contemporary notions of illness are those excusing the individual of any immediate responsibility for becoming ill, those specifying the gravity or seriousness of the illness and, finally, those evaluating the legitimacy of the illness. As those socially diagnostic meanings vary, so do the consequences for the personal life of the individual vary: on the crudest level, he may be punished or indulged in therapy, he may be expected to perform his normal social roles, or instead to adopt a new and special deviant role; more explicitly, he may be expected to take on new obligations while forsaking most normal privileges, or allowed to take on new privileges while forsaking old obligations.

These social meanings delineating how people considered ill are expected to behave are created by lay as well as by professional people, the two frequently differing from each other in the kinds of meaning to be assigned to given symptoms and signs, and therefore in the way each would respond to a deviant. Laymen, for example, are likely to hold an individual responsible for behavior which physicians are likely to consider illness and to manage by punishment where physicians are more likely to manage by treatment. On the other hand, many laymen are likely to ignore and therefore not respond at all to some things which physicians are likely to consider illness and seek to treat. Clearly, unlike medicine with its interest in biological constants, this kind of sociological analysis provided no fixed criteria for evaluating "illness": as a social meaning, illness and its consequences vary as the social characteristics and knowledge of the evaluator vary. Only by adopting one group's perspective can some stability of "diagnosis" be gained. The perspective of the medical profession is of course authoritative in our time, but since most of what is considered illness is managed on a voluntary basis, understanding the perspective of the layman is crucial to understanding how the profession obtains the laymen on whom it works. The work of such a consulting profession cannot be seen accurately from the professional perspective alone: it must be seen as the product of lay and professional perspectives in interaction.

Having explored in Part II the characteristic "mentality" of the practitioner as it bears on autonomy and the organization of his work, in this part I turned to what seemed to me to be the characteristics of the practitioner's relationship to the content of his work, or his knowledge. I pointed out first that the profession of medicine has, over the past century, come to be increasingly influential in defining deviance as illness, even at the expense of legal and religious definitions. And I indicated that medical definitions of deviance have come to be adopted even where there is no reliable evidence that biophysical variables "cause" the deviance and that medical treatment is any more efficacious than any other kind of management. Medicine's expanding jurisdiction over various forms of deviance was seen to be linked with humanitarian movements outside of medicine as well as with the natural tendency of the profession to itself interpret more and more of the world in the light of its own commitment to the idea of disease. Indeed, medicine was seen to be committed to "discovering" illnesses, and was characterized, with some qualification, as following the decision-rule of seeing and diagnosing illness rather than health. In this sense, by virtue of its occupational perspective, medicine always looks for and sees more illness than the lay world. As I pointed out in some detail, what the individual practitioner perceives as illness arises out of the special selection of cases which the particular location and organization of his practice presents to his experience. His commitment to his sense of effectiveness in treating the illness he sees is sustained by the uncontrolled role of his own placebo reactions in clinical practice. Such subjective reactions in clinical practice seem to support and sustain the varied opinions and schools to be found in modern medicine, particularly for those "illnesses" for which present scientific knowledge is insufficiently precise and reliable.

As I noted in my discussion of medical knowledge, a critical determinant of much of what the practitioner *can* know lies in the cases he comes into contact with. Since most cases he sees must bring themselves into the purview of the practitioner, it follows that the layman's inclination to label deviance as illness and therefore to seek medical care is a strategic element in producing medical knowledge, at least so long as the profession is not empowered to examine and treat laymen without their consent. The layman's perception of pain, his interpretation of various sensations and signs, and his faith in medical men as appropriate therapists—all of which are culturally variable—as well as the structure of the lay system in which he participates play a critical role in determining whether or not he will enter consultation and, of course, contribute to the clinical experience of the practitioner. But while lay culture and society may be critical for leading the individual into professional treatment, once the patient is in treatment the professional and his institutions seek, naturally enough, to treat him by professional rather than lay meanings.

In essence, the process of treatment and care may be seen as a process which attempts to lead the patient to behave in the ways considered appropriate to the illness which has been diagnosed, a process often called "management" by professionals. Such management is of course based on the professional's conception of the illness and its treatment and constitutes the professional's notion of the proper way of dealing with the patient so as to best apply his knowledge of treatment. It is also a reflection of the administrative requirement of treatment imposed both by the organization of the institution and by the technological demands of treatment. Professional management generally functions to remove from the patient his identity as an adult, self-determining person, and to press him to serve the moral and social identity implied by the illness which is diagnosed. Within its own institutions, protected by its organized autonomy, the profession has developed knowledge of its own and, by virtue of being a consulting profession, a capacity of its own to shape the behavior and experience of the layman independently of the lay community. In those institutions, the profession does not merely treat a biological state by biochemical or physical techniques: it also organizes the social identity of the layman into being a patient. Thus, in applying its knowledge, the profession cannot avoid making social as well as "purely medical" decisions about the people it deals with.

Illness and the Profession

This conclusion brings my book full circle. I began the book by exploring the circumstances that led to the development of a profession, as well as those that sustain the profession today. I then discussed in some detail how the everyday work of the profession is organized, and some of the ideological and organizational characteristics of the profession which sustain the way by which everyday work is carried on. I turned to the object of the profession's work—illness. Focusing on illness as a social meaning rather than as a biological state, I tried to specify the various social meanings connected with the idea, and the role of the profession in determining which of the various meanings come to be attached to deviance. And finally, I tried to show how the experience of being ill is shaped by lay social life and its relation to professional institutions. In pursuing that problem I was led back to the organization of the profession—its practice and the institutions it dominates. I am led, in fact, to the point of suggesting that when an occupation arises to serve some need or demand on the part of the lay community, and subsequently succeeds in becoming a profession, it gains the autonomy to become at least in part self-sustaining, equipped to turn back and shape, even create that need anew, defining, selecting, and organizing the way it is expressed in social life. This is perhaps the most important consequence for society in granting an occupation professional status. But how desirable is that consequence? Is it in the public interest for society to allow the profession the autonomy to define both need and problem and to control their management? In Part IV, concluding this book, I shall try to suggest answers to that question.

PART IV.

CONSULTING PROFESSIONS IN A FREE SOCIETY

"The organization of professions by means of self-governing institutions places the problem of liberty at a new angle. For now it is the institution which claims liberty and also exercises control."

—Alfred North Whitehead

15.

THE LIMITS OF PROFESSIONAL KNOWLEDGE

IT is often said these days that the world we live in has become so complex that it cannot survive unless it more and more comes to be ordered by the special technical knowledge of the expert or the professional. Indeed, a recent paper celebrating the increasing importance of specialized knowledge in determining social policy refers to the decline of faith and of politics in human affairs.[1] Faith, which all men may possess, and politics, in which all citizens of a democratic society may participate, fade away before knowledge, which only experts possess. Decisions requiring expertise are insulated from the public debate, negotiation, and compromise that is politics; faith in revealed dogma or in a given set of morals is declared out of order.[2] Laymen are excluded from participating in decisions thought to require special expertise, even when those decisions are intended to improve their own well-being.

Clearly, should experts be required to make decisions in areas which previously were managed by the free discussion and exchange of opinions characteristic of a democratic society, and if

[1] Robert E. Lane, "The Decline of Politics and Ideology in a Knowledgeable Society," *American Sociological Review,* XXXI (1966), 649–662.

[2] For a discussion of the relation of dogma, expertise, and opinion to the public opinion process, see Eliot Freidson, "A Prerequisite for Participation in the Public Opinion Process," *Public Opinion Quarterly,* XIX (1955), 105–111.

those areas are increasing in number and scope due to the increased complexity of the technological, economic, and social foundation of our society, we are on the brink of changes in the structure of our society which will have a massive effect on the quality of the lives of the individuals who compose it. The relation of the expert to modern society seems in fact to be one of the central problems of our time, for at its heart lie the issues of democracy and freedom and of the degree to which ordinary men can shape the character of their own lives. The more decisions are made by experts, the less they can be made by laymen.

But even if we accept the premise that expertise has become so important to our time as to be required for our survival, the critical issue of detail still remains: In what areas is expertise absolutely necessary and what not? In those areas where expertise is necessary, does expertise which is demonstrably superior to common opinion actually exist? And where there is expertise, what are its limitations? The nature and limits of expertise as such must obviously be examined carefully and, in the light of its relationship to democracy and freedom, qualified wherever possible. I believe that some very simple but important qualifications can be made. For example, we can all agree that how a road is to be built is a technical question best handled by engineers and other experts. But whether a road *should* be built at all, and *where* it should be located are not wholly esoteric technical questions. There are certainly technical considerations which must be taken into account in *evaluating* whether and where a road should be built, but engineering science contains no special expertise to allow it to decide whether a road is "necessary" and what route "must" be taken. Expertise properly plays a major role in suggesting that already available roads are crowded and determining which routes for a new road would be the easiest or cheapest to construct, but it is social, political, and economic evaluation, not the science of engineering, which, in the light of knowledge, determines whether and where to build a road. Such evaluation is normative in character and is not so esoteric as to justify its restriction to experts. Where laymen are excluded from such evaluation, true expertise is not at issue but rather the social and political power of the expert.

In the above example, I suggest, is to be found the core of a paradigm by which all forms of applied expertise, including medicine, may be analyzed. It is my contention that neither expertise nor the expert who practices it has been examined carefully enough to allow intelligent and self-conscious formulation of the proper role of the expert in a free society. Indeed, I believe that expertise is more and more in danger of being used as a mask for privilege and power rather than, as it claims, as a mode of advancing the public interest. It can be used to conceal more privilege primarily because it is usually treated globally rather than analytically, obscured and mystified by the aura of modern science and the ideology of ethicality. It is my contention that the expert who has become a professional as I have defined it is especially prone to have obtained more influence on public affairs than his actual expertise would suggest. This has occurred primarily because the professional has gained a status which protects him more than other experts from outside scrutiny and criticism and which grants him extraordinary autonomy in controlling both the definition of the problems he works on and the way he performs his work.

Furthermore, I would argue that in medicine, as a virtual prototype of the expert profession, we find the most strategic instance by which we can explore the problem of the relation of expertise and the expert to a free society because it is not, like so many others, protected by the obscurity of performing minutely specialized functions. Conspicuous in the public eye by providing a personal service, medicine has come to dominate an elaborate division of labor, and its jurisdiction is broad and far-ranging, having expanded into areas once dominated by religion and law—i.e., faith and politics. It also has, like the new experts, a firm foundation in science. But like all experts, I believe, it possesses flaws generic to its very status as expert. In these final chapters I shall analyze those flaws of the profession of medicine, hoping to suggest at the same time the flaws which social policy should recognize in all experts. The foundation of my analysis rests on the detailed examination of the profession which constitutes the bulk of this book.

In these concluding chapters I hope to show that *the practice, exercise, or application of expertise is analytically distinct from expertise or knowledge itself*. The distinction raises two serious questions of evaluation. First, there is the question of the reliability of applied expertise, a question which can be evaluated by keeping two assumptions in mind. I assume that we can justify removing decisions from the hands of laymen and placing them in the hands of experts when only the experts have the especially reliable knowledge by which to make correct decisions in the lay interest. Should there be some areas in which experts lack such knowledge, their autonomy to make decisions is not justified and may properly be restricted. Furthermore, I assume that when decisions are at bottom moral or evaluative rather than substantive, laymen have as much if not more to contribute to them than have experts. This assumption reflects the substance of equality in a free society, equality not of ability, knowledge, or means, but moral equality. In this chapter I shall attempt to analyze the degree to which applied knowledge is both reliable and objective. In the next chapter I shall focus on the second problem which flows from the nature of applied knowledge—namely, the capacity of the expert to assure the public that what expertise it does possess will be exercised evenhandedly, with an adequate degree of competence and in the public interest. Through the analysis of these two problems, I hope to be able to conclude my book by suggesting the limits of professional autonomy in controlling both the content and the terms of professional work.

Knowledge and Work

Obviously, the professional is an expert because he is thought to possess some special knowledge unavailable to laymen who have not gone through his special course of professional training. His special professional knowledge may not be demonstrably and consistently efficacious, but it is the best available to the times, and it is taught to all members of the profession in order to prepare them for the proper performance of their work. Being the best available, it follows that its professor—the profession—should be free to use that knowledge for the common good and that the public should allow the profession the autonomy to make decisions for its own good.

But what are the referents of "knowledge" and "expertise"? Obviously, they refer to a body of putative facts ordered by some abstract ideas or theories: we may expect to find them embodied in the treatises and textbooks which provide the formal substance of what experts learn in professional schools and what they presumably know thereafter. However, such knowledge or expertise is extremely limited as a reality: it is locked up in books or heads, and as it is defined it has no link with the activities of consulting, treating, advising, or otherwise working at "being" an expert. A practicing or consulting expert engages in activities, and activity is not, after all, knowledge. The lack of equivalence between knowing and doing requires us to either redefine "knowledge" as that which knowledgeable people do, or to distinguish knowledge as such and to analyze its relationship to what reputedly knowledgeable people do.

Because some kinds of people devote themselves to contributing to the body of knowledge while others devote themselves to applying that body of knowledge to human affairs, it seems appropriate to distinguish the body of knowledge as such from the human activities of either creating that knowledge (research) or applying it (practice). The activities can be judged by their faithfulness to the knowledge and by the degree to which they are founded upon that knowledge. To evaluate the expert and his expertise, then, one does not only evaluate the knowledge of his discipline as such but also the relationship of his activity of being an expert to that knowledge. Thus we must ask, what is the substance of the expert's work as well as of his knowledge? Is systematic and reliable knowledge involved in every facet of his work? Is objective knowledge involved rather than moral or evaluative preference? The answers to such questions allow us to determine the degree to which the work of the expert is justifiably and appropriately protected from the evaluation and influence of laymen.

Analyzing the Content of Work

In Part III of this book my analysis of lay and professional conceptions of illness showed that the content of professional work—the activities presumably embodying special expertise—is neither uniform in its evidential character nor without moral and substantive bias. Even if we assume that the basic knowledge upon which medical practice is founded is objective and reliable, the experiential foundation of practice, being socially organized, is socially biased, and the practice of that knowledge is inevitably social in character. Furthermore, an essential component of what is said to be knowledge is the designation of illness which, I have insisted, is in and of itself evaluative and moral rather than technical in character. My analysis in Part III in fact raised doubts that the content of the profession's work is uniformly of such an esoteric, scientifically reliable character as to justify the profession's claim of autonomy for all of the content of its work. Even if one denies the validity of those doubts, it is clear that the content of the work of the profession may not be treated as if it were qualitatively uniform. In order to understand professional work, it is not enough to delineate it globally as "complex," as requiring a long period of training, and as resting on a body of scientific or theoretical knowledge.[3] Some elements of work are more complex than others; some elements of work are taught self-consciously at school and some are not; some elements of work are evaluative and others neutral. It is intellectually and practically inexcusable to accept a global characterization of professional knowledge and work when uniformity of quality is not present.

At least four distinct elements of the content of professional work may be distinguished and examined for their characteristics. First, it seems well to distinguish basic concepts or theoretical assumptions from empirical knowledge and technique, assumptions which are similar to what Kuhn called "paradigms."[4] In medicine, I would suspect that the most important example of this dimension is the etiological notion of disease, today largely based on the germ theory.[5] Second, there is the selective attention implied by professional notions of pathology which lead to the designation of some human states as "diseases" but not others. If there is a theory or paradigm underlying such selective evaluation, it is not etiological like the germ theory, nor is it a theory of disease so much as a moral theory of health, normality, optimal performance, or some other ideal.[6] Third, given the general theory guiding the activity,

[3] From my discussion and citations in earlier chapters, it should be clear that this is precisely the characterization of virtually all writers on professions.

[4] Thomas Kuhn, *The Structure of Scientific Revolutions* (Chicago: University of Chicago Press, 1964).

[5] Rene Dubos, *Mirage of Health* (Garden City, New York: Anchor Books, 1961).

[6] See Daniel Offer and Melvin Sabshin, *Normality, Theoretical and Clinical Concepts of Mental Health* (New York: Basic Books, 1966).

medicine consists of a large and complex body of knowledge about the empirical chemical, physical, and other characteristics of those states chosen to be illnesses, as well as about empirical techniques by which those states may be arrested, cured, repaired, removed, or improved. Such knowledge, in conjunction with its directing concepts and theories, however, still does not exhaust the dimensions of the content of medical work. A fourth dimension is composed of those occupational usages which are sometimes called techniques of management rather than techniques of treatment. They may also be called the rules determining how knowledge and technique are put into practice or applied. In order to apply "purely" technical knowledge to practical affairs, one must engage in social as well as merely technical activity. The technical activity itself becomes social in that it has social meaning, is embodied in social relationships, and has social consequences for the members of that relationship.

Clearly, the four dimensions of the content of work I have distinguished have rather varied characteristics. How shall we evaluate them? The profession, we must remember, gains special occupational autonomy on the basis of its claim that its work is guided by knowledge too esoteric and complex for the layman to even evaluate, let alone share, that the knowledge guiding its work is as systematic and reliable (scientific) as the age permits, and, finally, that the knowledge is schooled, stemming from a long period of training through which every practitioner goes. The question is, do each of the four dimensions of the content of medical work equally well represent truly esoteric, specially schooled, and scientifically based knowledge? Let us examine them in somewhat more detail.

Looking first at the accepted, general etiological theory of disease, whether humoral, germ, stress, witchcraft, or whatever—is it systematic, schooled, and with a scientific foundation? Such theories always rest on faith to some degree, though some of the available evidence always supports them. As paradigms guiding the organization and direction of professional work activities, they may have their source in a variety of disciplines. Furthermore, they are formulated and elaborated more by members of the profession who are scholars or scientists than by those practicing medicine. While one may not say that the task of formulating and defending such theories can be the prerogative of medicine alone—such "hybrids"[7] as Pasteur having made major contributions to them—the task does seem to be one that requires systematic schooling in science. In this sense, it is a truly esoteric aspect of knowledge in the evaluation of which laymen seem to find no important place, and it is one truly professional element of professional knowledge.

Markedly separate from the theory of disease, however, is the activity of determining what signs or symptoms actually *are* diseases, impairments, and the like. Such determination may stem from etiological theory, in that the presence of a "germ" independently of personal discomfort may be taken to *define* a disease, but this can be done only if one will agree that the presence of a given "germ" is in and of itself undesirable. As I have argued at some length in earlier chapters, to designate something to be a disease is at bottom a moral undertaking, with moral consequences. It involves declaring that some things are undesirable and influencing the life of the person said to possess them by singling him out as bearing an undesirable attribute. Because it is a fundamentally moral task, I suggest, the designation of disease does not rest on a scientific foundation. Just as lawyers are exclusive experts on the technical corpus of the law, but only one of many legitimate voices on whether laws are just, so are physicians exclusive experts on the character of what has already been institutionalized as illness, and only one of many legitimate voices on what is undesirable or deviant, and what deviance is illness. Even assuming that there can be genuine experts in matters of morals in our society, clergymen and philosophers, not physicians and lawyers, come closest to being trained to be such experts. Technically, medicine is equipped to demonstrate that some signs, symptoms, and complaints run a given course or lead to certain consequences. That the consequence is bad or undesirable is for all men to judge, not merely for the physician. Thus, while the medical profession is, as I shall note, more or less exclusively competent to determine the etiology and treatment of many of the signs and complaints which it has isolated, and while it itself can have its own opinion as to the undesirability of some signs, symptoms, and complaints, it does not possess any

[7] Joseph Ben-David, "Roles and Innovations in Medicine," *American Journal of Sociology,* LXV (1960), 557–558.

special competence to justify its being an *exclusive* expert on what is undesirable, what is a disease. It may use its technical knowledge and moral stance to persuade others that something "is" a disease, but in doing so it is acting as moral entrepreneur, which is any man's privilege.

Given general agreement on what is a disease, the core of the profession's technical expertise may be found in its knowledge of the nature of the disease which has been agreed on, and of the methods of treatment which are likely to be efficacious. The profession, after all, represents the best available knowledge and skill of our time for the treatment of disease. This is the science the physician learns. In discussing treatment, however, one must distinguish between the purely technical activities of treatment and the social interaction and manipulation surrounding those acts, between the chemical, radiological, surgical, and other material elements of treatment, and the social organization or administration of such treatment. The former is clearly founded on medical science, that special knowledge of the profession which justifies its autonomy; the latter is not. The latter, the fourth dimension of the content of work, is rather founded on practical, concrete clinical experience which is biased by its own particularistic perspective and by its own normal, self-interested concern with minimizing the inconvenience and unpleasantness of one's work by, for example, hospitalizing a patient so as to restrict his social or physical activity and by keeping him under sedation or otherwise restrained while in hospital. The best part of such management is composed of occupational customs, no more codified and no more put to systematic empirical test than most social customs. This is part of what is called the "art" of medicine. It does not rest on a body of scientific knowledge: at best it rests on common occupational usages rather than individual habits, neither of which is tested on any systematic basis. Aside from the treachery of clinical experience, the profession has no special technical knowledge by which to determine how to manage its treatment.

Clearly, not all the elements of the physician's work rest to the same degree on the training in a body of scientific theory and objective knowledge which is claimed for members of the profession, and which is used to justify the maintenance of professional autonomy. And perhaps not so clearly, I may note that *the questionable elements of the physician's work are precisely the elements involved in the practical application of knowledge to human affairs.* The theoretical, scientific, objective, systematic knowledge of medicine lies in its abstract and "pure" knowledge of the course of illness and in the procedures most likely to cure or alleviate the effects of illness. Such knowledge is abstract and pure in that methods of applying it to practical reality are distinct and separate from it, constituting evaluation, customary usage, personal preference, and even perhaps vested self-interest rather than systematic knowledge guided by some self-conscious theory. Thus, the profession's claim for autonomy in determining the content of its own work is not justified by the character of its knowledge of *how to apply* that knowledge, even though the character of its pure knowledge is acceptable.[8]

Limits of Autonomy over the Content of Work

These distinctions have a direct bearing on social policy in that they suggest some of the guidelines I shall offer to evaluate the question of professional autonomy. Essentially, my position is that there are good reasons for considering it appropriate to place restrictions on the scope of professional autonomy, particularly when the work involved directly affects the public interest. Furthermore, the very claims by which the profession persuades society to grant it autonomy provide the logical and substantive grounds for determining which professional activities may be justifiably influenced by lay society. Those claims have largely been confused with reality by both sociological analysts and by the general public. Such confusion is evident in the way in which professions have been defined. Most writers define a profession by the things it *claims* to be, claims which are so global, diffuse, and unanalyzed that it is impossible to determine empirically what reality they refer to, let alone test the relation of those claims to reality. Here, I have been asking what evidence there is that "knowledge" and "expertise" are used

[8] This is the case, I suspect, for most consulting professions. The reliability of the knowledge which the teacher teaches, for example, is considerably greater than the reliability of the knowledge of how to teach that knowledge.

in the concrete reality of work and how that reality relates to the claims about professional knowledge. The outcome of my analysis suggests that the claim of special expertise is not sustained in the activity of determining the states, processes, or whatever which are to be considered forms of deviance, determining the kind of deviance they are, and determining how knowledge shall be applied to the defined deviance.

Obviously, if my analysis is correct, it follows that in the latter dimensions of the profession's work autonomy is not justified, that those dimensions do not represent a truly esoteric matter which only members of the profession, with their special training, can properly control. It is a question of public, not only professional, policy to determine what diseases should be recognized as illness in the public interest and what not; whether or not a given state or activity is deviant; whether it is illness, crime, or sin, or whatever; whether it is minor or serious, illegitimate, conditionally legitimate, or unconditionally legitimate; and whether medicine or any profession should have jurisdiction over it. In the determination of such moral issues the profession is but one of a number of publics.

In a somewhat more complex and qualified way, my analysis has led me also to the conclusion that it is a question of public, not only professional, policy to determine *how* people said to be ill shall be managed in the course of treatment. It is a moral rather than technical question whether or not civic identity and rights should be sacrificed to the putative demands of a treatment technology. And it is a social rather than medical question to ask what degree of the convenience of the treated should be subordinated to the convenience of the treater, whether or not the treated should be provided with full information about alternative modes of management of treatment and the freedom to choose his mode, whether or not institutionalization should take place, and what the routines of management in institutions should be. For such issues, the profession is a rather special source of advice in that it is expert in what treatment is necessary and therefore what technical limits are imposed on the alternatives for management. But with those limits given, the alternatives remain a matter in which lay choice is quite legitimate and professional autonomy illegitimate.

The Problem of Applied Knowledge

In reviewing the various facets of the content of medical work I have been led to separate the body of scientific knowledge possessed by the profession from the knowledge used in applying knowledge to work situations. The body of knowledge—that is, that which is "known" to the profession at large in a given age in history—includes not merely empirically testable statements about the cause and effective methods of treating disease or impairment, but also general theories about the nature of disease and the selective evaluation of some but not all deviant human attributes as "disease." As I noted, not all of these elements of professional "knowledge" may be said to be inaccessible to or inappropriately evaluated by untrained laymen, so that not all may be said to be fully "professional."

As opposed to the medical knowledge which is medicine as such, there are the practices which grow up in the course of applying that knowledge to concrete patients in concrete social settings. The "pure" medical knowledge is transmuted, even debased in the course of application. Indeed, in the course of application knowledge cannot remain pure but must instead become socially organized as practice. Reorganized as practice by consulting work, general professional knowledge is concretized by customary usage and on occasion suspended by individual judgment. Perhaps most important, because of the practitioner's moral commitment to intervention, action takes place even in the absence of reliable knowledge. This occurs because by definition medicine is a consulting or practicing rather than scientific or scholarly profession. Insofar as it generically involves the practical application of knowledge to human affairs, it involves moral commitments and moral consequences neither justified by nor derived from the esoteric expertise which is supposed to distinguish the profession from other occupations. Medicine is not merely neutral, like theoretical physics. As applied work it is either deliberately amoral—which is to say, guided by someone else's morality—or it is itself actively moral by its selective intervention. As a moral enterprise it is an instrument of social control which should be scrutinized as such without confusing the "objectivity" of its basic knowledge with the subjectivity of its application.

Much of the practical knowledge of the profession is based on personal clinical experience. Indeed, much of the scientific knowledge of medicine stems from individual discoveries by great individual clinicians, and the model of the clinician still so dominates the everyday practice and ideology of medicine as to encourage individual deviation from codified knowledge on the basis of personal, firsthand observation of concrete cases. This deviation is called "judgment" or even "wisdom." In emphasizing the primacy of his personal experience the physician is like all practical men who must act, but his profession and its historians reinforce that primacy by providing him with formal models which idealize the value and authority of such experience. Indeed, the consulting professions in general and medicine in particular encourage the limitation of perspective by its members through ideological emphasis on the importance of firsthand, individual experience and on individual freedom to make choices and to act on the basis of such experience. Such emphasis is directly contrary to the emphasis of science on shared knowledge, collected and tested on the basis of methods meant to overcome the deficiencies of individual experience. And its efficacy and reliability are suspect.

Practical, firsthand knowledge is often called wisdom and is considered a distillate of a lifetime of contemplated experience. Embodied in the memoirs and reflections of elderly men, such wisdom reflects the inevitably limited compass of any single individual's experience and the inevitably biased perspective of his position in a particular social class in a particular society in a particular age. Since it is intimately bound up with the personal life of the knower, its substance coming to form his very identity and to justify his past actions, it is no wonder that it has a dogmatic edge to it, resisting contradiction by embarrassing facts and contorting itself to reconcile contradictions. Such wisdom is usually evaluated by its plausibility—its similarity to the prejudiced experience of others. Given variation in the social location of individuals' perspectives and so the substance of individuals' personal experience, it is unlikely that one man's wisdom is likely to be plausible to many others who are not of the same social class or who do not share much the same perspective. Wherever there is agreement on such wisdom, its source is not application of the rules of logic and evidence so much as the convergence of social perspectives.

Now clearly not all wisdom is false. Many great discoveries in medicine and in other fields were made by men who observed their own personal experience so closely and perceptively as to penetrate into that minute portion which is generally true, made by really wise men who searched themselves and those around them with a certain universalistic purity. But these men are, perhaps literally, one in a million. And furthermore, their wisdom was proven to be true by subsequently collected evidence. As I pointed out in Chapter 1, medical advances were very slow and halting so long as the test of personal clinical experience was the only method by which truth could be determined. The odds of reaching truth by the method being so small, it is rather difficult to see why so much positive imagery surrounds it in professional affairs and why the individual using it is protected from having to demonstrate the validity of his reflections on his experience. It is difficult to see any valid justification for accepting professional knowledge based on custom and personal experience to be so authoritative as to be protected from having to justify itself by logic and, when the latter is lacking, by its compatibility with the customs and personal experience of those outside the profession. If its truth is so fragile as to be unable to survive the clash with others, it does not seem worth protecting. The prerogatives of the profession cannot be formulated as if the average member were as perceptive, honest, precise, and correct in his reflections on his experience as its most wise and creative luminaries, past and present. In areas of professional work where moral evaluation, custom, and personal experience are the guides, the public has every right to insist that it cannot be excluded from participation.

While there is probably no way to avoid relying on personal experience (which may or may not be wisdom) for guidance in the confusion of practical human affairs which have only a sketchy relation to the severe simplicity of scientific knowledge, there are some rules by which personal experience can be assessed before accepting it as a reasonable guide for conduct. All experts, but particularly the established professions of law, medicine, teaching, and psychiatry, are prone to give expert testimony and advice on areas in which they cannot possibly have systematic knowledge—testimony and advice delivered with perfect self-assurance and only rhetorical warnings of uncertainty. Such clinical experience or wisdom can have no credibility whatsoever taken in and of itself. Its foundation being personal, its possessor, no matter how deeply he believes himself, must be required to specify the nature of the experience from which he arrives at his conclusions. In the case of the physician, for example, we must be told in some detail what kind of practice he has had; we must be allowed to know how the social and economic organization of his work has influenced the selection of cases he has seen, as well as the circumstances in which he has seen them. And we must be told in some detail about his personal moral position, so as to evaluate how he selects data out of his universe of experience. Once we know the bias of his personal experience, we can better assess the likelihood that it is indeed wise, and we can better select among the variously conflicting "clinical impressions" experts present to us as truth. Surely such opinions cannot be accepted at face value, nor do they warrant protection by the status of those who present them.

Limiting the Authority of Professional Knowledge

In this chapter I distinguished between the "pure" knowledge and theory of the profession, which is largely confined to codified "science," and the "knowledge" guiding the profession's application of that science to the problems of mankind. As I have noted on more than one occasion earlier in this book, it is the latter which distinguishes the consulting profession from the scientific or scholarly. Such a distinction is hardly original. Price,[9] for example, discussed four "estates," one of which is the scientific, devoted to discovering what is true about the world, and another of which is the professional, devoted to applying available science or systematic knowledge to human problems. In addition to following that conventional distinction I have suggested that the scientific status of the knowledge being applied is not the same as that of application itself.

The consulting profession is called into existence by some need or desire felt by a lay public—a need which laymen define as a

[9] Don K. Price, *The Scientific Estate* (Cambridge: The Belknap Press, 1965), pp. 122–135.

need, a problem to be dealt with. As I pointed out in Chapter 1, medicine did not become a true consulting profession until its ministrations seemed to the public to answer its needs. Since the rise of medicine to the position of a consulting profession, however, we have also seen the rise of the welfare state, which administers, coordinates, and allocates resources to serve the basic and not-so-basic needs of populations running into the millions and which has at its disposal enormous resources of money and power. In determining what the needs of the population are, and what activities are necessary for their service, the state increasingly turns to professionals for guidance. After all, it is precisely in serving those needs that the professional is experienced and one should be guided where possible by experience.

However, what has happened over the past century is that the profession has not merely devoted itself to serving the needs which the public has brought to it. Quite understandably, it has also devoted itself to discovering and delineating new needs by developing its own moral conceptions of what men can or should ideally be. Protected by its prestige and its organized autonomy, it has also come to develop its own institutions for serving public needs, institutions increasingly independent of the public and organized by professional rather than by lay standards. This is to say, after becoming autonomous the profession has less and less come to reflect what the public asks of it and more and more come to assert what the public should get from it. Consulting the profession, the state obtains not only expert opinion on how to serve the needs the public perceives but also partisan opinion about what the public's needs actually are irrespective of lay opinion. Social policy is coming to be formulated on the basis of the profession's conception of need and to be embodied in support for the profession's institutions. But if those conceptions and institutions no longer conform to the public's conception they have lost their justification, for their justification lies not in their objective truth but in their connection with the values and usages of their society and their clientele. Professional "knowledge" cannot therefore properly be a guide for social policy if it is a creation of the profession itself, expressing the commitments and perception of a special occupational class rather than that of the public as a whole.

The basis issue may be put in a rather stark way. The military, we are told by Janowitz, is a profession.[10] But we can only thank the stars for the fact that, by my usage, it is not. If the military were a profession by my usage, it would be free to set its own ends and do to us what it felt was appropriate from its point of view. Our political tradition is that the people control the military, not vice versa. The example of the military, however, might seem unfair, for its aims are surely of a different character than those of medicine, law, teaching, and the ministry. Concerned as they are with Health, Justice, Truth, and Virtue, are not the ends of the established professions so beneficent that they may be given the autonomy to be able to lead us to them? Of course this is true in the abstract, but what, concretely, is health, justice, truth, and virtue? Who is to determine it? Is it a matter for determination by a special class of moralists disguised as experts? Or is it a matter of such importance as to be every man's choice for his own life? I myself do not believe that professions, no matter how beneficent their intent, have either the moral right or the special qualification to make such choices for the individual or for society.

This is a crucial problem involved in the role of professional knowledge in human affairs. Medicine is perhaps the best test of that problem because it is so clearly based on some reliable scientific knowledge and because its good is on the surface the most widely agreed-on of all. But even in medicine there lies at the bottom of its applied efforts a moral rather than objective stance, a stance which, when professionalized, develops its own notions of what is good and its own assertions that the price the client is asked to pay in relinquishing elements of his normal status is at once necessary and worth that good. But unless its moral foundation is that of the community, it will serve not the community but itself. When service to the community is defined by the profession rather than the community, the community is not truly served.

The Role of the Layman in Professional Work

The medical system, like many another professional system, is one predicated on the view that the layman is unable to evaluate

[10] Morris Janowitz, *The Professional Soldier* (New York: The Free Press, 1960).

his own problem and the proper way in which it may be managed: this justifies the imposition by the profession of its own conception of problem and management. The client's rights are specified simply as the right to choose or to refuse professional ministrations. And as in the ballot in totalitarian countries, the client is sometimes not even free to refuse to choose. Once engaged in a service, its terms are largely not a matter of choice, the client's position being similar to that of a child in a juvenile court,[11] considered incapable of managing himself, neither responsible nor competent, protected by none of the rules protecting the rights of adults in the legal system, essentially at the mercy of the good intentions and professional beneficence of court officials. This, I believe, is improper.

Where determination of role and role performance is not based on the necessity dictated by reliable scientific knowledge, there is no justification for excluding the layman from participating in the determination of work. Indeed, since the only justification for a consulting profession's very existence lies in the needs of its clientele, the clientele's own conception of its needs should have a strong influence on its practice. Laymen, therefore, must be able to have something to say about whether or when they wish a service and how that service is to be presented. They must be able to have something to say about what their own good is, and when something really is for their own good. With the decline of the general practitioner and other client-dependent practices, the layman has had less and less chance to gain responsiveness from professionals to his own views. And as the state comes to intervene more and more—a state which has become so large and formal as to be rather distant from the lives of its citizens, and whose notions of public good are guided largely by professions—the individual client has even less opportunity to express and gain his own ends. Some way of redressing the balance must be found.

In suggesting that the profession must become more responsive to its clientele, however, I am clearly raising a danger. I have earlier pointed out that client-dependent practice leads to medical

[11] There is a growing body of literature deploring the ostensibly humanitarian tyranny of the legal treatment of juveniles. A recent study is Aaron V. Cicourel, *The Social Organization of Juvenile Justice* (New York: John Wiley & Sons, 1968).

performance which is not considered to be of high quality. Historically, client dependence has always meant an extremely weak profession. Only when it became autonomous from the community did medicine develop and nourish truly professional research and, after so doing, make the great advances in knowledge of the past four or five decades. By strengthening the role of the client in our own time, is there not the danger that he will interfere with good research and insist on modes of medical treatment which are not materially in his interest?

There is certainly no doubt that in some circumstances the client is likely to be so ignorant of the nature of his problem and of the proper way of solving it as not to be trusted to choose what should be done for his own good. By the same token, he is sometimes likely to be so disturbed by his problem as to be unable to be very rational about its nature and solution. Thus, even if he is intellectually capable of understanding the professional's explanation of what is wrong and what should be done, and of being persuaded by that explanation to do what is asked of him, he is emotionally incapable of using his intellectual faculties. When both ignorance and emotional disturbance are present, the client may simply hurt himself if given the opportunity to judge and participate in the determination of the professional's work. Indeed, the customary professional characterization of the client—virtually part of the professional ideology which, in the case of medicine, goes back at least as far as the Hippocratic corpus [12]—insists on his ignorance and irrationality. Such characterization is the prime justification for the profession's inclination to make the client at best a passive participant in the work—to, in essence, remove from the client his everyday status as an adult citizen, to minimize his essential capacity to reason and his right to dignity. Expertise in general claims its privilege by claiming the client's incapacity.

The question one must answer is, however, how common this ignorant, fearful kind of client is. Surely not all clients are that way, nor are some who are that way in one circumstance the same in others. Here, as elsewhere, an item of professional ideology is accepted uncritically and applied globally, without analytical scru-

[12] *Hippocrates,* tr. W. H. S. Jones, Vol. II, Loeb Classical Library (London: William Heinemann, 1943), pp. 201–203.

tiny or justification. It must be evaluated in light of a number of empirical considerations. Foremost among them is the historical change that has taken place in the nature of the public itself. A century ago the average patient was no doubt illiterate and superstitious, and the difference between the formal education of the average man and the average professional was very great. Since that time, however, universal public education has narrowed that gap markedly, and secular, rational modes of thinking have spread through a continuously enlarging portion of the population. While the average length of formal professional education has increased over the last fifty years, both because of the professionalization of occupations and because of increasing specialization among established professions, the average length of formal education of the public has increased even more. Greater and greater numbers are finishing college and are seeking graduate education. Thus, assuming that formal education means something important (and if we do not make that assumption about laymen we cannot do so for professionals), laymen are far more likely today than yesterday to be able to participate intelligently in the active evaluation and pursuit of the solutions which professionals offer to their problems.

I would go further than that, however, and insist that even when there is a risk to the material well-being of the public in allowing it to participate in the determination of health and other practical professional policies—a risk produced by the possibility that the public would be sufficiently misinformed to reject policies which would improve its well-being, as has apparently occurred in the case of the fluoridation of drinking water—the risk must be balanced against the value of maintaining the civil liberty of the layman. A profession and a society which are so concerned with physical and functional well-being as to sacrifice civil liberty and moral integrity must inevitably press for a "scientific" environment similar to that provided laying hens on progressive chicken farms—hens who produce eggs industriously and have no disease or other cares. The dignity of humanity is not assured by the role the profession is inclined to seek for the layman as a client. Short of *immediate* threats to life itself, the civil dignity of the layman is, I believe, a far more important element of his welfare than much of what the profession, dominated by its own occupational perspective, would call his health.

The Concept of Client Rights

In our courts and in many areas of contemporary life every citizen has certain theoretically inalienable rights sustained by a variety of institutional arrangements designed to protect those rights. On entering the professional domain, however, due process is lost: the citizen is expected to give up all but the most humble rights, to put himself into the hands of the expert and trust his judgment and good intentions. He is expected to take a role which is akin to that of a house pet, or a child, dependent on the benevolence and knowledgeability of the adult caretaker. There is in fact hardly any concept of patient rights in medicine at all, though professional ethical codes and malpractice laws of course specify practitioner obligations.[13] A body of rules specifying such rights should be instituted, and foremost among the rules should be one specifying the right to freely choose whether or not to use professional services and, once using them, the right to participate in determining the way those services will be administered to him. The first right prevents the profession from imposing its own view of what is illness on the layman; the second from destroying the moral identity of a free adult in the course of treatment.

Many more rights might be cited, but these are the most important. They bear directly on the moral position of the consulting professions. If their prime quality stems from their substantive expertise rather than from their status as officials in a political system, then they must get their work done by persuading others of the value of the work rather than by imposing it on involuntary clients.[14] In the case of medicine, this means that officially imposed "treatment," when a person may be declared ill against his will and legally required to be treated in a professional institution, must be limited

[13] The rigidity of occupational "status, rights, and authority" which worries Gilb can only be shaken by the counterbalance of client rights. See Corinne Lathrop Gilb, *Hidden Hierarchies: The Professions and Government* (New York: Harper and Row, 1966).

[14] I have elsewhere analyzed the problem of professional authority, arguing that it more resembles the authority of office than of expertise. See Eliot Freidson, *Professional Dominance* (New York: Atherton Press, forthcoming), Ch. 4.

in the most stringent manner. That is, while the *work* of consulting professions may be protected by law, the *use* of such professions should not be required by law except under the most narrowly restricted circumstances. Such occasions are justified only by evidence that the individual *has actually harmed* or *certainly will harm* others in some *important* way and furthermore that there is in fact a mode of professional treatment or management which will *almost certainly* minimize if not eradicate that harmful state or activity. Someone with cholera, plague, or typhoid clearly meets these criteria, with tuberculosis less clearly, and with alcoholism, other drug habituations, and most mental illnesses hardly at all. The latter are putative illnesses which are not as clearly harmful to others as is infectious disease and which are not amenable to consistent cure by any known method, medical or otherwise.

The issue is not whether or not to control what is believed to be serious deviance, for every society defines and controls deviance. I myself would hope that my society will not choose to control behavior which does not harm others. This is not the issue here, however: the issue is jurisdiction, who has the legal right to define and to manage deviance; it is the official enforcement of the jurisdiction of one rather than another control institution, and the rules by which jurisdiction is established. The primary rule governing jurisdiction should be one which protects the rights of the deviant even if at the expense of what some may claim to be his potential salvation. Without presenting persuasive evidence that it has a unique and efficacious answer which other occupations lack, the medical profession cannot justify legal enforcement of its definition of the deviant and its control of the "services" he shall get. Thus, while I see humanitarian and politically strategic reasons for it, there seems to be little significant scientific or technical reason why alcoholism, drug addiction, homosexuality, mental illness, many impairments, mental deficiency, and many more of the growing mass of ambiguous problems coming to be called "illness" should be "medical" problems and in exclusively medical jurisdiction. Ultimate determination of the ground rules for all types of control, whether based on punishment or treatment, should rest on the law and on principles of due process rather than on some spurious conception of an expertise which is so precise and objective as to be properly insulated from lay influence even when it is lay welfare at issue. Nor, as I shall suggest in the next chapter, is it wise to rely on the indubitably good intentions of professionals.

Limits on the Practice of Knowledge

Toward the beginning of this chapter I used as a preliminary example of the thrust of my analysis the case of the building of roads. The use of such an ostensibly irrelevant example in a book on medicine was quite deliberate, for it is my opinion that my analysis of the expertise of medicine is applicable to the other autonomous occupations whose work involves the application of knowledge to human affairs. Essentially, my point has been that the knowledge of the profession is distinct from the circumstances and conditions in which it is applied, and that while the former may in most cases be said to be the best of our time, and to justify protection against lay interference, the latter is neither codified, systematic, nor objective, reflecting the social position and occupational usages of the profession rather than some special technical expertise deserving of autonomy. In the case of the latter, both the designation of need or problem, and the determination of the arrangements by which knowledge is applied are at issue. These, I argue, are questions on which there is at present no reliable, systematic expertise.

But even if there were a science of administration or teaching, or consulting, or whatever is involved in applying knowledge, the autonomy of practice would still not be justified owing to the fact that, apart from what is purely technical and instrumental about practice, there is embodied in it an ineradicable moral element. It must be decided that a road is *desirable,* that instruction in a given academic subject is *needed,* that a complaint is a symptom of something *bad:* these are not technical decisions alone and cannot be removed from lay debate. And once that decision is debated and agreed on, it must also be decided that given the needed road, homes should or should not be destroyed for its route; given the needed education, it will or will not be taught in such a way as to require students to be sheep; given the definition of a disease, those said to have it should or should not be able to choose whether to have treatment, and should or should not be managed in treatment like objects without dignity or responsibility. These considerations of the moral consequences of the social choices which are inherent in the process of applying knowledge are not merely technical and cannot justifiably be determined by experts alone. Thus, I argue, professional autonomy in determining the content of all of its work is not justified: autonomy in developing the knowledge embodied in the content of work may be appropriate, but autonomy in determining the practical modes of applying that knowledge is not.

16.

THE LIMITS OF PROFESSIONAL AUTONOMY

THE content of the profession's work is not absolutely separable from the social and economic organization—or terms—of its work. For example, as I pointed out in Chapter 12, the medical decision-rule to diagnose illness instead of health may be understood as an ideological commitment to finding illness stemming from the distinctive preoccupation of the profession. But it may also be analyzed as a function of economic self-interest. All else being equal, where the terms of work are such that diagnosing and treating illness will increase income, so also will more illness be found. "Unnecessary" surgery is perhaps the most obvious case in point. Similarly, the way illness is managed in the course of administering treatment is a function of both economic and social factors. The supplicant poor, for example, manage without the "frills" given the demanding rich, and the client-dependent practitioner manages his patients in a different fashion than the colleague-dependent practitioner. In this chapter I wish to analyze professional control of the social and economic organization of work—control over the terms rather than the content of work—and conclude the book with some final remarks about the limits of professional autonomy which my analysis suggests.

Ethicality and Self-Regulation

The profession claims autonomy over the content of work by virtue of the objective and reliable character of its expertise, an expertise which it claims to be so complex and esoteric that only properly trained men can know and evaluate it. In the last chapter I analyzed the evidence supporting that claim. Another claim is also crucial—the claim of service orientation or ethicality. After all, unless the profession's expertise is guided by a concern with the good of humanity, it may not put it to good use. Similarly, without a service orientation, a profession granted control over its work could be expected to take material advantage of its monopoly to serve its own selfish interests. While expertise and ethicality are relevant to both the content and terms of work, it seems to me that in the content of work, expertise is the primary element and, in the analysis of the terms of work, it is ethicality which is central. Special expertise not shared with anyone is the main prerequisite for justifying control over the content of work, while ethicality is prerequisite for being trusted to control the terms of work without taking advantage of such control.

But just as I had to ask in the last chapter, What is expertise or knowledge? so here I must ask, What is ethicality or service orientation? What are its referents? Just as in the case of knowledge most discussions are content to use the word globally, without close scrutiny. Ethicality is treated as a kind of philosophical essence embodied in such formal rituals as codes of ethics or oaths to serve mankind. Or, more often by social scientists, it is treated as a general disposition to behave ethically as measured by verbal expressions that "helping people" is more important than "making money." In both ritual and attitudinal usages, the focus is on good intentions rather than on behavior and practical action. Such good intentions may certainly be prerequisite to good behavior but do not, alas, assure that good behavior will follow after.

I wish to suggest that neither sociological analysis nor public policy is well served by defining ethicality as good intentions, expressed as a formal code or as attitudes. Rather, I wish to suggest that the most useful definition does not lie in codes or in attitudes but in behavior at work. Just as I suggested that expertise assumes empirical status according to what the expert does in his work, so I suggest now that ethicality assumes empirical status of most consequence in the ways that the ethical occupation controls the performance of work. Most particularly pertinent to ethicality as the test of mere claims on trust, I believe, is the way the profession regulates the work of its members. *What professionals do represents their effective knowledge or expertise; how they regulate what they do in the public interest represents their effective service orientation or ethicality.* If the profession organizes itself in such a way as to assure good work in the public interest irrespective of personal or occupational self-interest, we may conclude that it has justified its claims to autonomy over the terms of its work. Let us examine the way the profession's ethical intentions have been realized in self-regulation.

Analyzing the Terms of Work

In analyzing the terms of work it seems useful to distinguish between the economic and the organizational or social terms of work. The former, complicated as they may be, are the simpler of the two, referring to such matters as the income of the profession compared to other occupations, the method of compensation of its members (fee-for-service, salary, capitation, or the like) and the source of compensation (the general public treasury, private philanthropies, specially constituted public or private insurance funds, the sick person himself, or whatever). The economic terms of work may have potentially strong effects on performance. When there has been a plentiful supply of practitioners in relation to demand, for example, competition among practitioners for patients has been very great, leading to severe damage to the quality of both their ethics and their technique. A highly competitive practice setting seems to encourage sharp economic practices, the cutting of technical corners, and other undesirable elements of performance. Furthermore, as spokesmen for the profession have emphasized, the character of the relationship between practitioner and client may be changed when a "third party" is introduced as employer or financial supporter of the practitioner. In such circumstances, the practitioner may put the welfare of his employer or payer before the welfare of the individual client, a tendency which may or may not be desirable for society.[1] Similarly, when left to himself in a fee-for-service market, the practitioner may put his own welfare before that of his client by, for example, urging more medical and surgical services when they are to his advantage and minimizing services when they are not—a tendency which is probably not desirable for anyone but the practitioner.

Apart from the economic framework of work, the terms also include how the work is organized socially. The social organization of work is not completely separate from the economic organization, but it may be analyzed separately and has, as I have shown in Chapters 5 and 6, independent effects on work. The same mode of compensation may have different consequences in different work settings: in the American medical system, which is still dominated by fee-for-service modes of compensation, some variations in performance seem to occur independently of the mode of compensation, varying instead with variation of organization from solo to bureaucratic and from client-dependent to colleague-dependent practice.

In the case of both the economic and the social organization of work, the central question for evaluation is ethicality. Given its organized autonomy, which includes a monopoly to provide services and a legally dominant role in determining the kind of services other occupations provide, does the profession organize itself in such a way as to prevent the practitioner's natural concern with his own economic security and advancement from dominating his ethical concern with the good of his clientele? Does the profession organize itself in such a way as to assure that each of its members works in ways reflecting the highest possible standards? If the profession does regulate itself so as to assure the proper kinds of performance, we may conclude that its claim to the ethicality necessary to guide the practice of its expertise is justified and that its autonomy is in accord with the public interest.

[1] The open nature of this question must be emphasized, for the desirability of putting the individual client's welfare before anything else has been taken as virtually self-evident by liberal writers. There are, however, many circumstances in which it is an entirely moot question whether it is well to sacrifice the good of others for the good of an individual, and, as I noted in Chapter 2, there does not seem to be any compelling reason why it is the physician rather than a third party who should decide when to sacrifice one for the other.

Autonomy and Self-Regulation

Let us examine first the question of autonomy in setting the economic terms of work. In the United States the profession has rather consistently fought against any infringement on what it believes to be its proper freedom. In conjunction with its monopoly over scarce services for which there is a high demand, freedom to set the terms of compensation is, without some form of professional self-regulation in the public interest, obviously subject to abuse. Nonetheless, the profession has not adopted any important method of preventing or even rectifying abuse. Perhaps fearful of infringing on the individual practitioner's freedom, it has failed to institute any systematic method of review to determine whether or not economic freedom, in conjunction with monopoly over services, has been used by practitioners to charge all that the helpless traffic will bear rather than only the decent income to which the practitioner is entitled.

Without an effort at constant review of financial practices, the profession remains rather ignorant of the actual behavior of its members, and is not equipped either to evaluate it or to regulate it. Furthermore, its attempt to encourage methods of adjudicating client complaints about economic practices are hardly efficient enough to be worth remark, for even such as the profession provides to patients in local medical societies are handled so secretively as to keep the layman uninformed of their existence and of his right to a hearing. Virtually the only systematic surveillance of the economic practices of the profession occurs not within the organized profession, but outside, in the organizations, semipublic, and public, which insure the costs of medical and hospital care.[2] And virtually the only effective mechanism of adjudicating disputes also stands outside the profession in the form of the courts.

By and large, I think it fair to say that the profession in the United States has made virtually no effort to insure that its members do not abuse their privileged economic position by seeking more than a "just price." This may be so because the profession's conception of a just price is singularly permissive, though what is a

[2] See, for example, the special issue on utilization review and control mechanisms, *Inquiry*, II (1965), 1–107, published by the Blue Cross Association.

just price for any good or service is a question for which there is no single answer. In some cases, it is generally agreed that it is fair to allow demand in a free market to set the price. In other cases, it is felt that need should take precedence over ability to pay and that the impersonal operation of the market should neither set the price nor by its price limit the demand. Medical care is one example of such a service. The image of a free market in medical care is in any event either vicious or naïve in light of the fact that a monopoly of services is granted the profession through licensing, thereby preventing a free market. Only when physicians have to compete with all other types of would-be healers can the medical care market be said to be truly free.

It is this fact that led Friedman, an ideological supporter of the free market, to suggest that "licensure should be eliminated as a requirement for the practice of medicine." [3] But if we believe that medicine possesses science and integrity markedly superior to competing occupations, we would not be inclined to invite the competition Friedman calls for because of the suffering which could follow upon uninformed consumer choices in a truly free health care market. We do not allow such freedom even to many ordinary consumer products. In this sense, the profession cannot insist on freedom and autonomy in the marketplace at the same time as it insists on having the protection of a monopoly: within the limits of a monopoly, a free market merely means license to the profession without the economic benefits of competition to the consumer. Without regulating its members' economic practices, the profession's autonomy cannot fail to violate the public interest, and its practical ethicality cannot fail to be compromised.

In a recent analysis, somewhat marred by rather crude imputations of conspiracy but useful nonetheless, Rayack [4] has documented at length the various ways in which the profession, or its segments, has failed to regulate its economic policies in the public interest. Given such failure, there seems to be little justification to the pro-

[3] Milton Friedman, *Capitalism and Freedom* (Chicago: University of Chicago Press, 1962), p. 158.

[4] Elton Rayack, *Professional Power and American Medicine* (Cleveland: The World Publishing Co., 1967). And see Seymour Harris, *The Economics of American Medicine* (New York: The Macmillan Co., 1964) for a more neutral analysis.

fession's claim of autonomy over the economic terms of work. This is particularly the case in light of the fact that the profession's economic position has been granted special protection against the operation of normal market mechanisms of control. While the profession has every right to compensation for its services, its specially protected position makes it appropriate and necessary that the public or its representatives dominate in setting the level of compensation. As Rayack put it,

> Wherever there is a need to set standards in the medical market and the possibility of a conflict of interests exists, physicians should not be in policy-making positions.[5]

Apart from the economic terms of professional work there are the terms governing the way work is organized. The question here is whether the profession, left to its own devices by its autonomy, can organize the work of its members in such a way that the public can be assured of a reasonably high standard of performance on the part of every professional—whether, in short, responsible regulation by the profession of the standards of work occurs. My discussion in Part II has examined the question in some detail and need be repeated only briefly here. From the discussion I think it can be said that the profession in the United States regulates the quality of its services primarily by minimal standards for medical education and licensing. There is virtually no other systematic method used to regulate performance throughout the profession, and the laying down of qualifying standards is itself neither an active nor continuing method of regulation. As I have shown, professional performance is rather fragile, subject to modification by client dependence and the isolation of solo practice as well as by the more obvious variables of years since education and the like.

For true regulation of performance continuing into the many years following qualification for licensing, the social setting of practice must be organized to minimize isolation from colleague scrutiny and public accountability so as to encourage humane performance at a high level. In the United States, however, the profession has virtually idealized isolated, solo practice and resisted organizational

[5] *Ibid.*, p. 288.

forms which are more likely to stimulate good performance. Even though the sheer scarcity of physicians has minimized client dependence, no deliberate effort has been made to discourage or prevent isolation in practice or to maximize colleague observation and interaction. In this limited context it can be said that the profession does not organize its work in a way that would allow the regulation of performance by colleagues.

What is even more to the point is the apparent fact that even when work is organized in a way which would allow the regulation of performance, the regulation that does take place is less than one might expect and is not truly regulatory in that its boycott mechanism does not correct or eliminate poor performance. The social background of the practitioner, the nature of consulting or clinical work itself, and the natural solidarity of the occupational class lead to a permissive state of mind which assigns primacy to the evidence of personal experience rather than to the knowledge of which the official expertise of the profession is composed. It also assigns primacy to a sense of responsibility for one's own actions evaluated by one's own personal experience rather than responsibility for those actions of colleagues which do not bear on one's own personal responsibilities. The benefit of the doubt is given to colleague performance which is not given to members of competing occupations, and deficiencies of performance are overlooked in favor of presumed good intentions. "After all," the argument goes, "nobody *wants* to kill a patient." But if one does kill a patient, perhaps good intentions are not enough.

If this is true, then I would suggest that even if the profession were to undertake more systematic efforts to develop organized settings for practice which include within them systematic modes of colleague supervision or review of work performance, its operation of such settings is not likely to be as effective as it can be and, if the profession's claim is taken seriously, as effective as it should be.[6] So long as the profession places heavy reliance on criteria estab-

[6] This is a major point of my argument. William J. Goode, "The Protection of the Inept," *American Sociological Review*, XXXII (1967), 5–19, has pointed out that all groups protect those of their members who are inept. What I describe, therefore, is not unusual permissiveness. However, a group cannot ask for *special* privilege on the basis of a claim that it is extraordinarily skilled and ethical if in fact it does protect its inept members.

lished by personal or clinical experience and judgment, so long as it emphasizes good intentions rather than good performance, and so long as its characteristic disciplinary device is a form of exclusion which operates to segregate levels of performance into relatively homogeneous groups of practitioners, each group with different clinical prejudices, the profession cannot really regulate itself.

Even if these deficiencies are remedied, however, the profession, I believe, cannot be left wholly autonomous in undertaking the task of setting up an organized form of practice which contains a system of self-regulation adequate enough to justify its claim. The technical expertise of the profession of medicine does not include reliable expertise about social organization and its consequences. The profession's habits of organization seem to involve traditional usages modified by practical experience and ideology. Lacking reliable expertise, the profession lacks the resources to make its own decisions intelligently and accurately. And, because the profession's own self-interest is involved in the social as well as the economic organization of practice, there is the danger of bias in the exercise of autonomy in organizing practice, a danger of not being able to recognize and honor the perspective of the layman, whether client or general public.

In setting both the economic and the social terms of work, the material interests of the profession should of course be recognized, represented, and at least partially satisfied, but such interests are little more "professional" than are those of trade unions. Indeed, so far as the terms of work go, professions differ from trade unions only in their sanctimoniousness. And since their preferences for the way the work setting is organized are as often a matter of self-interest as of expertise, the profession's demands do not deserve a status much different than the demands of any organized occupation. As I pointed out in several contexts in earlier chapters, some aspects of the social organization of work may be necessary for the adequate performance of some technical tasks. Aside from participating in the determination of public policy about the economic and social organization of practice as representatives of the profession's legitimate material interests, members of the profession must also participate as experts on the esoteric, technical tasks which must be taken into account in the course of determining how work may best be organized. Thus, only partial influence, not complete control of the terms of work seems justifiable by the criteria of legitimate expertise and of conformity with the public interest. Laymen are at once competent and entitled to have a voice in the way the profession reviews and supervises the performance of its members and to insist on more adequate methods than exist at present. The profession has little basis in either its expertise or its performance for claiming autonomy in regulating itself any way it sees fit. In fact, I would suggest that, paradoxically, it is this very autonomy which is responsible for developing the profession's incapacity to regulate itself in the public interest.

The Flaw of Professional Autonomy

Autonomy is the prize sought by virtually all occupational groups, for it represents freedom from direction from others, freedom to perform one's work the way one desires. In industrial work, the restriction of output represents crudely the efforts of workers to exercise control over their work and thereby gain a degree of autonomy. Similar efforts are found among all who work for others—among waitresses, physicians, students, soldiers, professors, or whatever.[7] However, only those who advance the claim to be professionals assert that their efforts to control the terms and content of work are justified because of the benefit accruing to those clients they work with or on. The freedom they ask for is the same as others: they ask to determine their own working hours, work load, compensation, the kind of work they do, and the way they do it. Unlike lesser workers, however, professionals claim that self-interest is not at issue; they claim to serve humanity before self. But unlike mere amateur humanitarians, they claim that their esoteric expertise is such that only they are able to determine what is wrong with humanity, how it may best be served, and at what price. This claim is what makes professions special, and it is what justifies the autonomy distinguishing them from other occupations. At the heart of most questions of social policy bearing on the professions lies this central question of autonomy, for it bears on who may determine

[7] Perhaps the most pertinent general comments on this phenomenon have been made by Everett C. Hughes, *Men and Their Work* (New York: The Free Press, 1958).

what the problem is, how the problem is to be dealt with, and what price is to be paid for dealing with it.

It is important to understand what professional autonomy is. It is always limited to some degree by the political power which it needs to create and protect it, and those limits vary from time to time and from place to place.[8] Structurally, the autonomy of the consulting profession, when it is great, is an officially created *organized autonomy*, not the autonomy one might gain by evading attention, by being inconspicuous and unimportant. Second, that organized autonomy is not merely freedom from the competition or regulation of other workers, but in the case of such a profession as medicine if not that of less well-established claimants, it is also freedom to regulate other occupations. Where we find one occupation with organized autonomy in a division of labor, it dominates the others. Immune from legitimate regulation or evaluation by other occupations, it can itself legitimately evaluate and order the work of others. By its position in the division of labor we can designate it as a *dominant profession*. Third, insofar as it regulates itself and is not subject to the evaluation and regulation of others, it also *educates itself*. This is to say, its educational or training institutions tend to be self-sufficient and segregated from others—professional schools with their own independent resources and faculties. Those educated for the profession get their training in such schools largely protected from contact with faculties and students from other schools. And finally, when it is a consulting rather than scholarly profession, having the right to regulate its own work also implies that it has been granted the legitimate right to in some way *regulate the clientele* with which it works, rather than having to be finely responsive to the clientele's notions of its needs, like a mere salesman. Thus, the characteristics of professional autonomy are such as to give professions a splendid isolation, indeed, the opportunity to develop a protected insularity without peer among occupations lacking the same privileges.

This is the critical flaw in professional autonomy: by allowing

[8] Corinne Lathrop Gilb, *Hidden Hierarchies: The Professions and Government* (New York: Harper and Row, 1966), has made a major contribution to the political analysis of professions.

and encouraging the development of self-sufficient institutions, it develops and maintains in the profession a self-deceiving view of the objectivity and reliability of its knowledge and of the virtues of its members. Furthermore, it encourages the profession to see itself as the sole possessor of knowledge and virtue, to be somewhat suspicious of the technical and moral capacity of other occupations, and to be at best patronizing and at worst contemptuous of its clientele. Protecting the profession from the demands of interaction on a free and equal basis with those in the world outside, its autonomy leads the profession to so distinguish its own virtues from those outside as to be unable to even perceive the need for, let alone undertake, the self-regulation it promises.

I do not mean to deprecate either the real knowledge or the intent of the profession at large. Both its knowledge and its intent are admirable. The problem is that once given its special status, the profession quite naturally forms a perspective of its own, a perspective all the more distorted and narrow by its source in a status answerable to no one but itself. Once the profession forms such a self-sustaining perspective, protected from others' perspectives, insulated from the necessity of justifying itself to outsiders, it cannot reasonably be expected to see itself and its mission with clear eyes, nor can it be reasonably expected to assume the perspective of its clientele. If it cannot assume the perspective of its clientele, how can it pretend to serve it well? Its very autonomy has led to insularity and a mistaken arrogance about its mission in the world. Consulting professions are not baldly self-interested unions struggling for their resources at the expense of others and of the public interest. Rather, they are well-meaning groups which are protected from the public by their organized autonomy and at the same time protected from their own honest self-scrutiny by their sanctimonious myths of the inherently superior qualities of themselves as professionals—of their knowledge and of their work. Their autonomy has created their narrow perspective and their self-deceiving views of themselves and their work, their conviction that they know best what humanity needs. It is time that their autonomy be tempered.

Historically, the profession's development of a valuable body of knowledge, pure and applied, seems to have required protection from the urgent ignorance of its clientele, the mischief of low-class competitors, and other forces destructive to an infant discipline. The profession had to be protected against the very consequences of its prime reason for being—its dependence upon a clientele which is prejudiced about what it wants and needs at a time when knowledge of how to treat wants and needs had no firm foundation. Freed from trade and competition, supported by the state, institutionalized, it was able to develop its own foundation for knowledge —its own concepts and science—independently of its clientele. So protected, it was also able to develop the capacity to nourish itself, like science and scholarship, pretty much on its own: it developed a body of colleague opinion and colleague-dependent practices. So sustained, it made enormous strides in knowledge and technique. Without its autonomy, medicine may never have made the great discoveries of the past century. But advances in knowledge are one thing, and those in practice are quite another.

No one is nostalgic for the bleeding and purging of nineteenth-century medical treatment: what we have now is patently better. But as the nostalgia for the no doubt mythical GP of the past indicates, the *practice* of medicine has not half so obviously advanced. It is precisely in practice—in the designation of disease, in the management of treatment, in the economic organization of medical care, and in the social organization of medical care—where medicine has not advanced. *While the profession's autonomy seems to have facilitated the improvement of scientific knowledge about disease and its treatment, it seems to have impeded the improvement of the social modes of applying that knowledge.* It is precisely in applying knowledge to human affairs, I submit, where extensive professional autonomy is justified neither morally nor functionally. It is not justified morally because I believe that human beings, even if laymen, have a right to determine what their own problems are and to have a voice in how they are to be managed. It is not justified functionally, I have argued, because it leads the profession to be blind to its own shortcomings and unable to regulate its practices adequately. From these conclusions follows the question of how the application of knowledge to human affairs by professional experts should be organized in the public interest.

Limiting the Autonomy of Professional Practice

In considering how the autonomy of practice must be limited in the public interest, I believe that two principles should be cardinal. First, I believe that in determining what is in the public interest, the prime value which should dominate is the prime value of a free society—the right of men to the dignity of self-determination of ends or goals and to civic equality. This principle bears on the suggestions I shall make about the roles of laymen and experts in the determination of what are official problems and of how they are to be managed. The second cardinal principle bears on the organization of professions—namely, that professional autonomy should not be so great as to cultivate professional control of areas for which its competence does not equip it, areas including the regulation of the profession itself.

From these two principles separately or in concert flow a number of concrete recommendations. Several bear on the internal constitution of the profession itself. First, every effort should be made to recruit professionals from a wide variety of populations. The present tendency to recruit a disproportionate number of entrants from among sons of professionals who are already "socialized" to the professional mystique should be discouraged. Second, the present system of maintaining professional schools as virtually self-sufficient institutions should be discouraged so that the education of the professional of the future will not be wholly dominated by the limited perspective of his own profession. Wherever possible—which is to say in medicine, in courses not requiring contact with patients—professional students should be taught outside the professional school by instructors who are not committed to the profession they are entering, and who will offer them varied perspectives on their future work. Third, once in practice, isolation should be discouraged by every means possible; instead, the individual practitioner should be encouraged to become integrated into regular interaction with other colleagues, guided, as I shall suggest below, by perspectives from outside the profession and answerable to its clientele.

Integration, however, should not be the integration of like-minded practitioners: homogeneous aggregates formed by the colleague boycott should be discouraged. In mixing men the trend toward dominance by academic practitioners should not be pressed too far. The American model of the community-service institution from which no practitioner is wholly excluded should be followed in preference to the growing popularity in the United States of the European model by which academic and institutional practitioners exclude those working in the community. Indeed, I would suggest that the academic professional has as much to learn from the community practitioner about the nonscientific aspects of practice—that is, what is usefully called an illness and how treatment is managed—as the latter has to learn from the former about up-to-date scientific procedures and theories. The present tendency toward greater direction of professional services by guidelines laid down by the academic practitioners (and nonpracticing policy-makers) of the professional school is not without its dangers. The profession should tend more toward a mixing than a sorting of variant perspectives and standards, particularly in those areas where expertise is in fact illusory.

Fourth and finally, the profession must be required to set up mechanisms whereby its members regularly review each other's technical performance and routinely scrutinize each other's economic and social practices in the light of both professional and lay standards, and it must be required to set up procedures whereby persistent deviants are prevented from serving clients improperly.[9] If exclusion must take place, it should be exclusion from work, not interaction. Exclusion may be limited (in the form of losing the privilege of practicing special procedures or working with special kinds of medical problems) or total (in the form of not being able to perform any kind of professional work altogether). Limited exclusion, however, should not be accompanied by boycotting from the circles or institutions in which are men competent to perform that special work, for only by continuous mixing and interaction of various perspectives and competencies can the excluded man be salvaged, and can the informal organization and aggregate of practices of medicine avoid fragmentation into multiple standards of

[9] This recommendation, like many of the others presented here, is meant to apply to university teaching, law, and other consulting professions as much as to medicine. Neither "professional" nor "academic" freedom should be taken to mean freedom to work any way one sees fit.

work quality each standing in different relations to the public seeking help.

Obviously, there are many other modes of preventing the profession from building up a rigid, self-perpetuating mystique about its knowledge, its jurisdiction, its practice, its prerogatives, and its mission. No internal changes in the organization of the profession and of its work are likely to be enough, however. Whatever is done to the professional organization, it is essential that in order to protect the public interest the lay public dominate the formation of policy decisions guiding the planning of services and the determination of the economic and social terms of the performance of work. Lay representation is not satisfied by the present system in which wealthy laymen are honored for their philanthropic donations by being placed on governing boards of private and even public medical, educational, and welfare institutions. Such philanthropists are invited to serve on boards because they are supporters of the professional perspective. They should represent the perspective of the public, however, which may be quite independent of that of the profession. While they should certainly be honored for their donations and support, they should not serve in a position which their very support disqualifies them from performing adequately. In planning and other policy decisions, laymen who clearly represent the perspectives of specific segments of the public, including competing occupations, should participate.[10] To guard against their conversion to the professional mystique, they should have terms of office not so short as to prevent them from learning enough about the issues to be able to cope with the real and pretended expertise they must evaluate, nor so long as to have become identified with the perspective of the experts. And since only the elderly and the economically comfortable classes can afford to donate time to planning, policy, and governing boards, its members should be paid a fee to make it possible for less affluent individuals to serve.

In discussing the layman's participation in forming professional policy, I have emphasized more the constitution of the policy groups

[10] In this context I would join with those deploring the predominance of wealthy philanthropists on college governing boards but would deplore almost as much the predominance of professors and students, who have their own vested interests and limited perspectives.

than the substance of policy itself. This is not the place for details, but some critical issues may be mentioned briefly here. First and foremost, to my mind, is the issue of creating legal categories of professionally designated problems and making it mandatory that those said to fall in the categories make use of professional services and become the wards of professionals, without free choice or due process. Compulsory education and compulsory inoculation are obvious examples which we are inclined to consider justified: other examples are to be found in the commitment of narcotics addicts, tuberculars, and those said to be mentally ill. This process of defining deviance legislatively, independently of those said to suffer it, is one which should be subject to the most stringent limitations. The only justification for the legislative definition of deviance and the legal requirement that it be controlled irrespective of the individual's own choice is the protection of the well-being or rights of those whom the putative deviant may threaten. The rights of the deviant himself must be protected by the legal processes of a free society rather than by reliance on the good intentions of professionals which are, as I have shown, not always so well practiced as to assure protection. Similarly, in matters of jurisdiction over human problems neither the good intentions nor the prestige of an established profession should be allowed to substitute for careful evaluation of its actual expertise: a very large proportion of the accelerating increase in health care costs may be ascribed to the exclusion or restriction of competing occupations which have as much claim to expertise in a number of important areas (including mental illness, rehabilitation, geriatrics, retardation, alcohol and other addictions, and preventive services) as has medicine. And finally, policy-making boards should carefully distinguish between the substance of expertise and the modes of applying or practicing expertise as well as the terms which underlie the practice of expertise. They should feel obliged to scrutinize the latter closely without fear that a "purely professional matter" is at issue.

By attempting to minimize the rigidity and insularity of the profession itself, to insure that other perspectives are strongly represented as checks and balances in determining professional policies of interest to the public, much can be accomplished both to improve the profession's integrity and to adjust its mission to the needs of society. These, however, are devices for general community policy and need not influence markedly the day-to-day services which the client uses. For the latter, some clear concept of client rights is necessary, a concept dominated by the premise that the good of the individual is a matter which the individual himself has the ultimate right to determine, a matter which cannot be determined by expertise, professional or otherwise. Medicalization of deviance must not de-politicize deviance. Similarly, when the good of society or the public is at issue, that good is to be determined by the members of society through the courts rather than by some special class morality masked as expertise and institutionalized by legislative or bureaucratic fiat. Given that premise, it follows that the right of the individual to refuse services must in most instances be honored, and that having chosen to use a species of service does not entail giving up the right to be informed of the concrete alternatives of diagnosis and treatment available to him, including the alternative of withdrawing from the service after trying it.

In spite of recent federal requirements that clients participating as "subjects" in research give "informed consent," and in spite of the legal releases required for such procedures as surgery, it is my impression that clients are more often bullied than informed into consent, their resistance weakened in part by their desire for the general service if not the specific procedure, in part by the oppressive setting they find themselves in, and in part by the calculated intimidation, restriction of information, and covert threats of rejection by the professional staff itself.[11] Such bullying, even if it does stem from a well-intentioned belief that the client's own good is at issue, must be replaced by greater attempt at instruction and persuasion and, if that should fail, by the humility of being willing to allow the client the greater value of the dignity of his own choice. I assert this to identify unequivocally my own moral posture in these recommendations: I do not believe that it is anyone's prerogative, professional or whatever, to impose his own notion of good on another; I believe that the greatest good is each man's freedom to

[11] For some descriptions of the way postmortem autopsy permission is obtained by physicians from next-of-kin, see Raymond S. Duff and August B. Hollingshead, *Sickness and Society* (New York: Harper and Row, 1968), pp. 320–329.

choose his own good even if in so doing the result is one that others may regard as harmful to him; and I believe that in imposing one's own notion of good on others one always does the harm of reducing their humanity.

Finally, it is necessary to note the degree to which destructive ignorance and irrationality may be released by reducing professional autonomy—the risk that what is good and useful about professions may be damaged. This very real problem is, however, characteristically evaluated only from the professional point of view which stresses the ignorance and irrationality of laymen without concern for their counterpart in the ignorance and irrationality of professionals. There is no doubt that my recommendations, if followed, would make it less comfortable to be a professional than it has been these fifty years. However, I believe that the danger of reducing the professional to a hack in these times of extreme reliance on professionals is very slight. The situation of consultation itself, after all, favors the professional, for it is he who is the one with something to give. Furthermore, the professional should also be protected by statute and by the courts. That he needs and deserves protection is not denied: that he must be protected by lack of accountability to the public is the assumption I have been denying.

The Illusions of Expertise and Ethicality

In these two concluding chapters I have been carrying on both a practical and, somewhat less emphatically, a theoretical argument. My practical argument has revolved around evaluating the degree to which consulting professions justify their claim to autonomous control over their own affairs and, in the light of my evaluation, suggesting how professional autonomy must be limited in the public interest. My theoretical argument stems from the central point of this book, that professions are best characterized as a type of occupation which has attained a special form of occupational organization, in part by virtue of making a persuasive claim that it possesses special knowledge and ethicality. Knowledge and ethicality are not treated as facts but as claims which may or may not be true. I have attempted to evaluate those claims.

In contrast to my own position, most sociological conceptions of the nature of professions emphasize as elements of definition the centrality of knowledge or expertise and of service orientation or ethicality. But they never clearly indicate what is meant by those terms. Both expertise and ethicality have been used in a rather global fashion, never having definite referents connected with the concrete state of being a professional or doing professional work. Expertise has been used to refer to an abstract body of knowledge, and ethicality has been used to refer either to formal documents or oaths or to a set of attitudes held by individuals. In neither case is there clear reference to behavior or to the activity of work which constitutes the reality of being a professional. Without such clear reference, there is no sensible criterion available for distinguishing between a claim and a fact, intent and behavior, promise and fulfillment.

I suggested that the nature of professional knowledge or expertise is best evaluated by examining professional work and that the nature of professional ethicality is best evaluated by examining professional modes of regulating work in the public interest. In the case of professional work I pointed out that only a segment of it consists of reliable and objective knowledge—that is, something deserving of the name "expertise"—and that the rest of it consists of moral judgments and occupational custom or usage. In the case of professional modes of regulating work I pointed out that whatever the code of ethics, whatever the intent of the individuals composing the profession, the profession does not in fact practice forms of regulation which assure the public that care of a uniformly high quality is available to all men irrespective of their economic or social status. In neither its expertise nor its ethicality, therefore, is the profession's claim to autonomous control over the terms and content of its work justified. Whether or not it therefore *constitutes* a profession by the usual definitions is a question I shall not attempt to answer.

In this conclusion I do not mean to single out as a special butt the profession of medicine. I believe that once one insists on relating them to men doing particular kinds of work organized in particular ways, the expertise and ethicality claimed by and imputed to *all* professions become, if not illusions, then at least more frail and flawed than one might expect. Used uncritically, the words, "disinterested expert" or "professional" serve as cachet to privilege and authority. The words taken at face value, however, are illusory, for what they refer to even after one separates the sheep with "real" knowledge and service orientation from the goats in sheep's clothing is essentially only knowledge and intent in the abstract. But knowledge must be practiced to be used, and intent must be proved by action. Granting this knowledge and intent, the question is how they are realized. I have argued that by the very fact of having to practice knowledge, work must be done for which there is in effect no expertise. But by virtue of its organized autonomy, the consulting profession is able to believe itself to be expert in any case. Its autonomy, which insulates it from having to take seriously the world outside, encourages a sense of omniscient mission in the profession which prevents it from being thoroughly honest with itself or the world outside. We may grant it both professional knowledge and professional intent—that is not the issue. Rather, it is the work setting in which its autonomy places it, and its product—the perspective by which it sees itself and the world—which is at issue. These, which are a function of the very position of organized autonomy and of dominance in a division of labor, are what limit the profession. And these are what need correction.

Setting and perspective declare the matter of this book. In it, I have been stimulated by Berger and Luckmann, who declare that "reality is socially defined. But the definitions are always *embodied*, that is, concrete individuals and groups of individuals serve as definers of reality. To understand the state of the socially constructed universe at any given time, or its change over time, one must understand the social organization that permits the definers to do their defining." [12] The consulting profession's position of organized autonomy, which includes its monopoly over special work, and its special place in the social order, permits the profession to create an important segment of the socially constructed universe. What it creates is composed of its relatively reliable knowledge, its sense of mission, and its practical institutions. The substance of those creations arises from the experience of the creators. The experience of the creators is a function of the perspective they have gained by virtue of being in an especially protected, autonomous position in the social struc-

[12] Peter L. Berger and Thomas Luckmann, *The Social Construction of Reality* (Garden City, New York: Doubleday and Co., 1966), p. 107.

ture, a position which systematically discounts the experience and evaluation of the laymen outside.

All more or less sustained by the prestige of the professional status, insulated from the force of other occupational perspectives, buoyed up by the helplessness of the client, segregated even from the judgment of peers by the sanctified privacy of the consulting room, the classroom, the confessional, and the office, lulled by their indubitably ethical intent, all consulting professions are able to forget that they are composed of men, that in the practice of knowledge there is often so much uncertainty as to preclude the pretense of expertise. Indeed, they have not only come to create their own knowledge independently of their clients and impose it on their clients. They have also come to create their own conception of themselves as professions and see their conception adopted by outsiders, including sociologists, to represent what professionals actually are rather than what professionals think they are or claim to be. Confusing their knowledge with their practice, and their moral commitments with their knowledge, they claim all they do to be their exclusive prerogative; confusing their intent with their practice, they claim ethicality as their specially redeeming quality. Sustaining this confusion of claim and wish with the reality of action is the protection from external scrutiny provided by their official monopoly and the protection from self-scrutiny provided by their view of themselves and their occupational customs.

I must again say that I do not single out medicine as an especially villainous profession. When I think of what I have learned from studying physicians, I test this against what I see of myself as a teacher and as a consultant—in short, as a practicing professional. In such work I am not much different from physicians. I too am a moral entrepreneur in my classroom and in this book. I too must rely here and in consultative settings on my "clinical judgment." And I would rather not have to review the teaching of my colleagues, be reviewed by them, and work with those whose work offends me. In general, when I test what I have learned about medicine against my experiences with my colleagues teaching in universities, it seems to me that whatever difference exists is in favor of physicians. As a profession medicine is better regulated and provides a more honest product than does university teaching. But that superiority is only relative. As the archetypal profession, it is not honest enough. Dishonesty is not, however, its intent. The profession is, like the others, now blinded by the glitter of its own status, then made myopic by the way its work encourages specially curious practices which merely put out of sight that which offends. With the best of intentions it cannot see itself clearly, and since its status protects it from others, it cannot be seen clearly by them either. It is the special status which is the villain. If the profession is to be made more honest its status must be modified. And since medicine possesses jurisdiction over an area to which more and more basic human values and activities are being assigned, it is essential for society that the status of medicine be modified.

At the time of writing this book it has been popular for some to press for community participation in many public decisions which have heretofore been made solely by elected officials, their advisers, and civil servants who claim expertise and professional autonomy. While this interest may lead to some permanent changes in the way by which public decisions are made, attention to the issue will almost certainly decline in the future. It will decline because of the institutionalization attending reform, because of the professionalization of the community participants, because of the attrition of enthusiasm by the tedious pace of peaceful change, because of the rise of other issues to attention, and because of the irreducible fact that expertise does exist and is needed for the public good in so many areas as to make it virtually impossible to explain and debate every one.

But even if interest fades, the problem will remain and will become greater in the future. Insofar as the outcome of my analysis questions the capacity of professions to be what they claim to be, it poses a serious question to the wisdom of supporting the trend of granting more and more occupations the autonomy of professions, and trusting them to serve rather than determine the public interest. There is a real danger of a new tyranny which sincerely expresses itself in the language of humanitarianism and which imposes its own values on others for what it sees to be their own good. Insofar as my analysis has been successful in delineating the question of what is expertise and what concealed class morality, and what is actual performance rather than unrealizable ethical intent,

I hope it can clarify the problem of determining how far professions may be given the authority to determine their own work. It is my own opinion that the professions' role in a free society should be limited to contributing the technical information men need to make their own decisions on the basis of their own values. When he preempts the authority to direct, even constrain men's decisions on the basis of his own values, the professional is no longer an expert but rather a member of a new privileged class disguised as expert.

INDEX OF NAMES

INDEX OF SUBJECTS